Fodor's

U.S. & BRITISH
VIRGIN ISLANDS

23rd Edition

JUN 2 8 2012

Fodor's Travel Publications   New York, Toronto, London, Sydney, Auckland
www.fodors.com

Eugene Fodor:
The Spy Who Loved Travel

As Fodor's celebrates our 75th anniversary, we are honoring the colorful and adventurous life of Eugene Fodor, who revolutionized guidebook publishing in 1936 with his first book, *On the Continent, The Entertaining Travel Annual.*

Eugene Fodor's life seemed to leap off the pages of a great spy novel. Born in Hungary, he spoke six languages and graduated from the Sorbonne and the London School of Economics. During World War II he joined the Office of Strategic Services, the budding spy agency for the United States. He commanded the team that went behind enemy lines to liberate Prague, and recommended to Generals Eisenhower, Bradley, and Patton that Allied troops move to the capital city. After the war, Fodor worked as a spy in Austria, posing as a U.S. diplomat.

In 1949 Eugene Fodor—with the help of the CIA—established Fodor's Modern Guides. He was passionate about travel and wanted to bring his insider's knowledge of Europe to a new generation of sophisticated Americans who wanted to explore and seek out experiences beyond their borders. Among his innovations were annual updates, consulting local experts, and including cultural and historical perspectives and an emphasis on people—not just sites. As Fodor described it, "The main interest and enjoyment of foreign travel lies not only in 'the sites,'... but in contact with people whose customs, habits, and general outlook are different from your own."

Eugene Fodor died in 1991, but his legacy, Fodor's Travel, continues. It is now one of the world's largest and most trusted brands in travel information, covering more than 600 destinations worldwide in guidebooks, on Fodors.com, and in ebooks and iPhone apps. Technology and the accessibility of travel may be changing, but Eugene Fodor's unique storytelling skills and reporting style are behind every word of today's Fodor's guides.

Our editors and writers continue to embrace Eugene Fodor's vision of building personal relationships through travel. We invite you to join the Fodor's community at fodors.com/community and share your experiences with like-minded travelers. Tell us when we're right. Tell us when we're wrong. And share fantastic travel secrets that aren't yet in Fodor's. Together, we will continue to deepen our understanding of our world.

Happy 75th Anniversary, Fodor's! Here's to many more.

Tim Jarrell, Publisher

FODOR'S U.S. & BRITISH VIRGIN ISLANDS
Editor: Douglas Stallings

Writers: Carol M. Bareuther, Lynda Lohr

Production Editors: Evangelos Vasilakis, Emily Cogburn
Maps & Illustrations: David Lindroth, *cartographer;* Bob Blake, Rebecca Baer, *map editors;* William Wu, *information graphics*
Design: Fabrizio La Rocca, *creative director;* Guido Caroti, Siobhan O'Hare, *art directors;* Tina Malaney, Nora Rosansky, Chie Ushio, *designers;* Melanie Marin, *senior picture editor*
Cover Photo: (Virgin Gorda, British Virgin Islands): FB-Fischer/imagebroker/age fotostock
Production Manager: Angela L. McLean

23rd Edition

ISBN 978-0-679-00963-4

ISSN 1070–6380

SPECIAL SALES
This book is available at special discounts for bulk purchases for sales promotions or premiums. Special editions, including personalized covers, excerpts of existing books, and corporate imprints, can be created in large quantities for special needs. For more information, write to Special Markets/Premium Sales, 1745 Broadway, MD 3-1, New York, NY 10019, or e-mail specialmarkets@randomhouse.com.

AN IMPORTANT TIP & AN INVITATION
Although all prices, opening times, and other details in this book are based on information supplied to us at press time, changes occur all the time in the travel world, and Fodor's cannot accept responsibility for facts that become outdated or for inadvertent errors or omissions. So **always confirm information when it matters,** especially if you're making a detour to visit a specific place. Your experiences—positive and negative—matter to us. If we have missed or misstated something, **please write to us.** Share your opinion instantly through our online feedback center at fodors.com/contact-us.

PRINTED IN CHINA

10 9 8 7 6 5 4 3 2 1

CONTENTS

Fodor's Features

CONTENTS

ABOUT
THIS BOOK

Our Ratings

At Fodor's, we spend considerable time choosing the best places in a destination so you don't have to. By default, anything we recommend in this book is worth visiting. But some sights, properties, and experiences are so great that we've recognized them with additional accolades. Orange **Fodor's Choice** stars indicate our top recommendations; black stars highlight places we deem **Highly Recommended**; and **Best Bets** call attention to top properties in various categories. Disagree with any of our choices? Care to nominate a new place? Visit our feedback center at www.fodors.com/feedback.

Hotels

Hotels have private bath, phone, TV, and air-conditioning, and do not offer meals unless we specify that in the review. We always list facilities but not whether you'll be charged an extra fee to use them.

> For expanded hotel reviews,
> visit **Fodors.com**

Restaurants

Unless we state otherwise, restaurants are open for lunch and dinner daily. We mention dress only when there's a specific requirement and reservations only when they're essential or not accepted—it's always best to book ahead.

Credit Cards

We assume that restaurants and hotels accept credit cards. If not, we'll note it in the review.

Budget Well

Hotel and restaurant price categories from ¢ to $$$$ are defined in the opening pages of the respective chapters. For attractions, we always give standard adult admission fees; reductions are usually available for children, students, and senior citizens.

Listings
- ★ Fodor's Choice
- ★ Highly recommended
- ⊠ Physical address
- ✛ Directions or Map coordinates
- ⌂ Mailing address
- ☎ Telephone
- 🖷 Fax
- ⊕ On the Web
- ✍ E-mail
- 🎫 Admission fee
- ☉ Open/closed times
- Ⓜ Metro stations
- ⊟ No credit cards

Hotels & Restaurants
- 🏨 Hotel
- ⇱ Number of rooms
- ⌂ Facilities
- ⑩ Meal plans
- ✕ Restaurant
- ✍ Reservations
- 🏛 Dress code
- ✎ Smoking

Outdoors
- 🏌 Golf
- ⚠ Camping

Other
- ☾ Family-friendly
- ⇨ See also
- ⊠ Branch address
- ☞ Take note

Experience the U.S. & British Virgin Islands

WHAT'S WHERE

1 St. Thomas. The familiar and foreign mingle perfectly here. Resorts run the gamut from plain and simple to luxurious. Go for the shopping, sights, and water sports. But tranquil it isn't.

2 St. John. St. John is the least developed of the USVI, two-thirds of which is a U.S. national park. With its excellent snorkeling, good restaurants, and comfortable villas and resorts, many find this the perfect island.

3 St. Croix. The largest of the U.S. Virgin Islands is 40 mi south of St. Thomas. Choose St. Croix if you like history, good restaurants, decent shopping, and good (but not great) beaches.

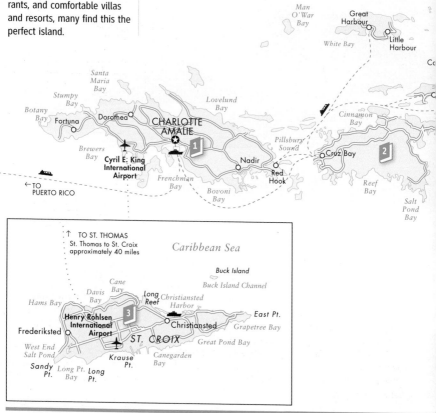

Man O'War Bay

Great Harbour

White Bay

Little Harbour

Santa Maria Bay

Stumpy Bay

Botany Bay

Fortuna

Dorothea

Lovelund Bay

CHARLOTTE AMALIE

Cinnamon Bay

Pillsbury Sound

Cruz Bay

Brewers Bay

Cyril E. King International Airport

Nadir

Red Hook

Reef Bay

← TO PUERTO RICO

Frenchman Bay

Bovoni Bay

Salt Pond Bay

↑ TO ST. THOMAS
St. Thomas to St. Croix approximately 40 miles

Caribbean Sea

Buck Island

Buck Island Channel

Cane Bay

Davis Bay

Long Reef

Christiansted Harbor

Hams Bay

Henry Rohlsen International Airport

Christiansted

East Pt.

Grapetree Bay

Frederiksted

ST. CROIX

Great Pond Bay

West End Salt Pond

Krause Pt.

Canegarden Bay

Sandy Pt.

Long Pt. Bay

Long Pt.

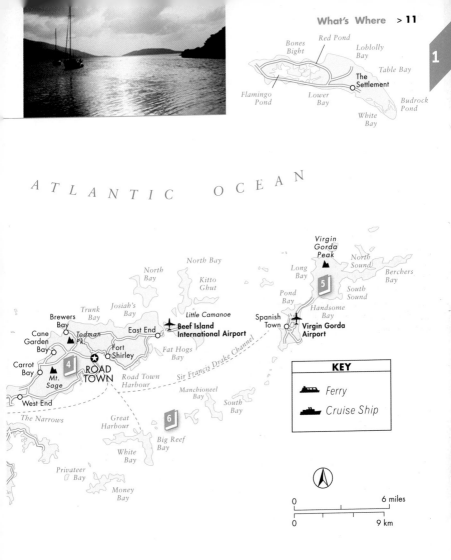

Bones Bight

Red Pond

Loblolly Bay

Table Bay

The Settlement

Flamingo Pond

Lower Bay

Budrock Pond

White Bay

A T L A N T I C O C E A N

Virgin Gorda Peak

North Sound

Berchers Bay

North Bay

Long Bay

North Bay

Kitto Ghut

Pond Bay

South Sound

Josiah's Bay

Little Camanoe

Spanish Town

Handsome Bay

Trunk Bay

Brewers Bay

East End

Beef Island International Airport

Virgin Gorda Airport

Cane Garden Bay

Todman Pk.

Fort Shirley

Fat Hogs Bay

Sir Francis Drake Channel

Carrot Bay

Mt. Sage

ROAD TOWN

Road Town Harbour

Manchioneel Bay

South Bay

West End

The Narrows

Great Harbour

Big Reef Bay

White Bay

KEY

Ferry

Cruise Ship

Privateer Bay

Money Bay

0   6 miles

0   9 km

4 **Tortola.** A day might not be enough to tour this island because you're meant to relax while you're here. Go to Tortola if you want to do some shopping and enjoy a larger choice of good restaurants than you can find on the other British Virgins.

5 **Virgin Gorda.** Progressing from laid-back to more laid-back, mountainous and arid Virgin Gorda offers beautiful beaches but fewer restaurants and many fewer shopping opportunities than Tortola.

6 **Other British Virgin Islands.** There are actually about 50 islands in the British Virgin chain, many of them completely uninhabited, but others have a single hotel or at least a beach that is popular with sailors.

VIRGIN ISLANDS PLANNER

Ferries in the Virgin Islands

There is frequent and regular daily ferry service connecting St. Thomas, St. John, and Tortola. In most cases, you can leave your St. John or Tortola hotel early in the morning and still make a flight back home from St. Thomas if you are leaving in mid-morning.

There's also service several times a week to Virgin Gorda from St. Thomas and St. John, but since this trip takes longer, you must sometimes spend a night in St. Thomas or Tortola before your return flight. There's daily ferry service between Tortola and Virgin Gorda, but you have to make a connection if you are coming over from St. Thomas or St. John, so it's important to take a ferry to Road Town and not West End if you need to make this change.

There's also service several times a week between St. Thomas and St. Croix; otherwise, you can take a Seaplane, which has frequent daily departures.

For more information on USVI ferry schedules, check out the Web site ⊕ www.vinow.com. For BVI ferry schedules, check out the Web site ⊕ www. bviwelcome.com.

Flying to the Virgin Islands

It's fairly easy to get to St. Thomas by air from the U.S., with many nonstop flights as well as connecting flights from San Juan. There's no air service to St. John; you must take a ferry from St. Thomas. For St. Croix, you must usually connect in either Miami or San Juan. The only direct air service to the British Virgin Islands is through Tortola (always a connecting flight on a smaller plane). You can get a charter flight to Virgin Gorda or Anegada, or ferries connect Tortola to the rest of the Virgin Islands.

Getting Around

Once in the Virgin Islands, you can use ferries to hop from one island to another, though not all services are daily, and some ferries don't run frequently (or reliably). There are also small planes, but they aren't really cost-effective if you plan on visiting several islands unless you have a large transportation budget.

Many visitors rent cars, especially in the USVI and on Tortola and Virgin Gorda, but taxis will suffice if you don't plan on doing a lot of independent exploring or eating too much outside your resort. You can also rent a jeep on Anegada, though some people opt for taxis there, too. Jost Van Dyke is small enough that most visitors walk or use an island-based taxi service. On the smaller private islands, there may be no cars at all.

The major chains are represented in the USVI and on Tortola, but only local companies operate in Virgin Gorda and the smaller islands. It's a good idea to reserve a car in advance since companies can run out, particularly during the high season.

Be aware that, while cars will be standard U.S. vehicles, you drive on the *left* in the Virgin Islands—even in the U.S. Virgin Islands. Roads are often not well marked regardless of which island you are on, so it's a good idea to pick up a detailed road map once you land.

For more travel info, see the Travel Smart chapter.

Restaurant Basics

Everything from fast food to fine cuisine in elegant settings is available in the Virgin Islands. Prices run about the same as you might expect to pay in New York City. Don't be afraid to sample more local fare at roadside stands throughout the islands. One popular island-style fast food basic is the paté, a fried pastry filled with conch, salt fish, or hamburger, which islanders call, simply, "meat." Most restaurants, except the simplest roadside stands, take major credit cards. Dress is generally casual, though there are a few upscale places that still require men to wear a jacket, though never a tie. Virgin Islanders, however, would never wear swim attire in town, and most upscale restaurants will expect men to wear long pants at dinner. Mealtimes are similar to what you'll find at home.

Hotel Basics

There are many types of lodgings in the Virgin Islands, from luxury resorts to moderately priced hotels to small inns. Many visitors opt to rent a private villa, which might range from a sumptuous retreat on the beach to a simpler house in the hills. Many of these have private pools. The high season generally runs from mid-December through mid-April. After that, rates may drop by a third or more, with the lowest rates reserved for the period in the late fall, when hurricanes are most common. Rates during the Christmas holidays may be double those during the rest of the year.

Calling Home

If you have a GSM mobile phone, then regular phone calls in the USVI may be included in your wireless plan; however, you may have to pay extra to send or receive text messages or to use data features. Most companies charge hefty roaming fees for the BVI, but from some points on the west end of Tortola, you can pick up a signal from St. John.

Checking E-mail

Most hotels now offer some kind of Internet service, sometimes even Wi-Fi. This service is not always free, so check with your resort regarding any charges. There are also Internet cafés on all the U.S. Virgin Islands and on Tortola. There are no Internet cafés elsewhere in the BVI.

Smoking

You can still smoke almost everywhere in the USVI, including bars and restaurants. However, smoking is not allowed in any public places in the BVI, including bars and restaurants.

FERRY ROUTES
AND TRAVEL TIMES

A T L A N T I C   O C E A N

Great Harbour

JOST VAN DYKE
Inter Island Boat Service
New Horizon

45 min.

35 min.

ST. THOMAS

**CHARLOTTE AMALIE–
CRUZ BAY**
Transportation Services STT
Varlack Ventures

Cyril E. King
International
Airport

CHARLOTTE
AMALIE

50 min.

ST. JOHN

Crown Bay

MARRIOTT
Reefer

10 min.

Phillips' landing

Marriott
12 min.

Red Hook
15 min.

Cruz Bay

RED HOOK–CRUZ BAY
PASSENGER ONLY
Transportation
Services
Varlack Ventures
CAR BARGE
Boyson Inc.
Global Marine
Love City

WATER ISLAND
Water Island
Ferry

45 min.

120 min.

← **PUERTO RICO**
Transportation
Services STT

C a r i b b e a n   S e a

90 min.

0		6 miles
0		9 km

*ST. CROIX
V.I. Sea Trans

Christiansted

*St. Croix Island is made to fit for this diagram. It is not true to scale.

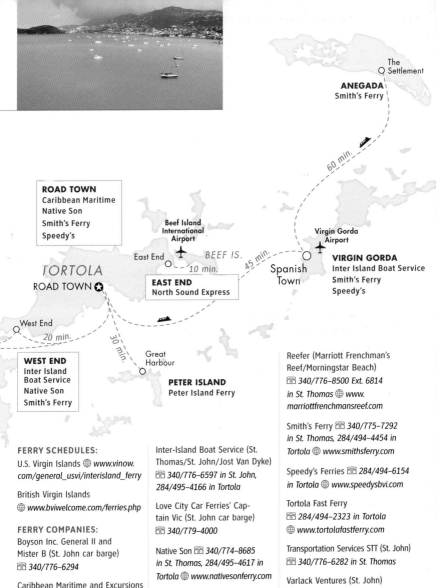

ROAD TOWN
Caribbean Maritime
Native Son
Smith's Ferry
Speedy's

ANEGADA
Smith's Ferry

The
Settlement

Beef Island
International
Airport

BEEF IS.

East End
10 min.

45 min.

60 min.

Virgin Gorda
Airport

TORTOLA
ROAD TOWN ⊙

Spanish
Town

VIRGIN GORDA
Inter Island Boat Service
Smith's Ferry
Speedy's

EAST END
North Sound Express

West End
20 min.

30 min.

Great
Harbour

PETER ISLAND
Peter Island Ferry

WEST END
Inter Island
Boat Service
Native Son
Smith's Ferry

Reefer (Marriott Frenchman's
Reef/Morningstar Beach)
☎ 340/776-8500 Ext. 6814
in St. Thomas ⊕ www.
marriottfrenchmansreef.com

Smith's Ferry ☎ 340/775-7292
in St. Thomas, 284/494-4454 in
Tortola ⊕ www.smithsferry.com

Speedy's Ferries ☎ 284/494-6154
in Tortola ⊕ www.speedysbvi.com

Tortola Fast Ferry
☎ 284/494-2323 in Tortola
⊕ www.tortolafastferry.com

Transportation Services STT (St. John)
☎ 340/776-6282 in St. Thomas

Varlack Ventures (St. John)
☎ 340/776-6412 in St. John
⊕ www.varlack-ventures.com

V.I. SeaTrans (St. Thomas and
St. Croix) ☎ 340/776-5494 in St.
Thomas ⊕ www.goviseatrans.com

Water Island Ferry (Water Island)
☎ 340/690-4159

FERRY SCHEDULES:
U.S. Virgin Islands ⊕ www.vinow.
com/general_usvi/interisland_ferry

British Virgin Islands
⊕ www.bviwelcome.com/ferries.php

FERRY COMPANIES:
Boyson Inc. General II and
Mister B (St. John car barge)
☎ 340/776-6294

Caribbean Maritime and Excursions
Road Town Fast Ferry ☎ 340/777-
2800 or 866/903-3779

Global Marine's Tug Life aka
Roanoke (St. John car barge)
☎ 340/779-1739

Inter-Island Boat Service (St.
Thomas/St. John/Jost Van Dyke)
☎ 340/776-6597 in St. John,
284/495-4166 in Tortola

Love City Car Ferries' Captain Vic (St. John car barge)
☎ 340/779-4000

Native Son ☎ 340/774-8685
in St. Thomas, 284/495-4617 in
Tortola ⊕ www.nativesonferry.com

New Horizon Ferry Service
☎ 284/495-9278 in Tortola

North Sound Express
☎ 284/495-2138 in Tortola

Peter Island Ferry (Peter Island
Resort) ☎ 284/495-2000 in
Tortola ⊕ www.peterisland.com

U.S. & BRITISH VIRGIN ISLANDS TOP ATTRACTIONS

Tossing Back a Painkiller, Jost Van Dyke

(A) Whether you go for the original at the Soggy Dollar Bar or the unique rum punch at Foxy's Tamarind, no trip to the Virgin Islands would be complete without a stop for nightlife and a few swigs of something at Jost Van Dyke. As if the beautiful beach at White Bay weren't enough.

Visiting the Baths, Virgin Gorda

(B) The unique boulder formations at The Baths make this beach one of the most unique in the Caribbean and create unique tidepools and grottoes. The swimming and snorkeling here is absolutely amazing, despite the crowds that can gather, especially on cruise-ship days; however, similar, less crowded beaches are nearby.

Staying at Maho Bay Camps, St. John

(C) Back in 1976, when ecoresorts were not as wildly popular an idea as they are now, Maho Bay Camps started with 18 permanent canvas tents on wooden platforms above beautiful Maho Bay. The unique set-up allows you to "camp" but still sleep in a real bed with a roof over your head.

Diving in Anegada

(D) Whether you are into reef or wreck diving, the clear, bright blue waters here make visibility tremendous, and the protected reef system is still alive and teeming with fish.

Snorkeling at Coki Beach, St. Thomas

(E) The best beach on St. Thomas for snorkeling is right next to the island's popular aquarium attraction, Coral World. You can buy food from the huts and have a thoroughly fun beach day. It's not a quiet beach, but the amenities make an extended stay a lot easier.

Taking in the View at Sky World, Tortola

(F) The views from this vantage point high above the island are stunning. On a very clear day, you can see both St. Croix (some 40 miles away) and Anegada (a mere 20 miles away).

Visiting the Caves, Norman Island

(G) It is believed that uninhabited Norman Island was the inspiration for Robert Louis Stevenson's *Treasure Island*. Boaters are drawn to three sea-level caves at Treasure Point, which are a popular sight for snorkelers since they are deep enough that they resemble a night dive.

Hiking the Reef Bay Trail, St. John

(H) St. John's best hike is led by rangers from the national park service. Along the way, you'll see island flora and fauna, the ruins of the Reef Bay planation, and petroglyphs. Best of all, a safari bus will take you to the trailhead, and a boat will bring you back to park service headquarters for a reasonable price.

Chartering a Yacht, Tortola

(I) The charter yacht capital of the Caribbean is one of the best places to go for either a bareboat or crewed yacht charter. Boaters can easily reach more than 50 different islands and dozens of anchorages and snorkeling spots, including many deserted beaches that are not reachable any other way than by boat.

Sampling Cruzan Rum at its Factory, St. Croix

(J) After a tour of the distillery and processing facilities here, you can sit down in the pub and taste some samples of the many different kinds of rum that are still produced here. Connoisseurs can even buy bargain-priced vintages, though the fruity varieties will satisfy most rum-soaked palates.

WEDDINGS AND HONEYMOONS

There's no question that the Virgin Islands are a popular destination for a honeymoon. Romance is in the air here, and the white, sandy beaches, turquoise water, swaying palm trees, balmy tropical breezes, and perpetual summer sunshine put people in the mood for love. It's easy to understand why the Virgin Islands are fast becoming a popular wedding destination as well. They are easy to reach from the U.S. and offer a broad array of hotels and resorts. A destination wedding is no longer exclusive to celebrities and the superrich. You can plan a simple ceremony right on the beach or use your resort's chapel. Every large resort has a wedding planner, and there are independent wedding planners as well. Although the procedures in the British Virgin Islands are a little different, planning your wedding is relatively simple regardless of where you are.

Getting Married in the USVI

You must first apply for a marriage license at the Superior Court (in either St. Thomas or St. Croix; St. John has no court office). The fee is $50 for the application and $50 for the license. You have to wait eight days after the clerk receives the application to get married, and licenses must be picked up in person on a weekday, though you can apply by mail. To make the process easier, most couples hire a wedding planner to help them with this process. If you plan to get married at a large resort, most have planners on staff to help you with the paperwork and all the details, but if you're staying in a villa, at a small hotel or inn, or are arriving on a cruise ship, you'll have to hire your own.

The wedding planner will help you organize your marriage-license application as well as arrange for a location, flowers,

music, refreshments, and whatever else you want to make your day special. The wedding planner will also hire a clergyman if you'd like a religious service or a nondenominational officiant if you prefer. Indeed, many wedding planners are licensed by the territory as nondenominational officiants and will preside at your wedding.

Superior Court Offices: St. Croix Superior Court (⌂ *Box 929, Christiansted 00820* ☎ *340/778–9750*). **St. Thomas Superior Court** (⌂ *Box 70, St. Thomas 00804* ☎ *340/774–6680*).

Wedding Planners: Anne Marie Weddings (✉ *5000 Enighed PMB 7, St. John P340/693–5153 or 888/676–5701* ⊕ *www.stjohnweddings.com*). **Weddings the Island Way** (⌂ *Box 11694, St. Thomas 00801* ☎ *340/777–6505 or 800/582–4784* ⊕ *www.weddingstheislandway.com*).

Getting Married in the BVI

Getting married in the BVI is a breeze, but you must make advance plans. To make things go more smoothly, hire a wedding planner to guide you through the ins and outs of the BVI system. Many hotels also have wedding planners on staff to help organize your event. Hotels often offer packages that include the ceremony; accommodations for you, your wedding party and your guests; and extras like massages, sailboat trips, and champagne dinners.

You must apply in person for your license ($110) weekdays at the attorney general's office in Road Town, Tortola, and wait three days to pick it up at the registrar's office there. If you plan to be married in a church, announcements (called *banns* locally) must be published for three consecutive Sundays in the church bulletin. Only the registrar or clergy can perform ceremonies. The registrar charges $35 at the office and $100 at another location. No blood test is required.

Contacts BVI Wedding Planners and Consultants (☎ *284/494–5306* ⊕ *www.bviweddings.com*).

How to Dress

In the Virgin Islands, basically anything goes, from long, formal dresses with trains to white bikinis. Floral sundresses are fine, too. For the men, tuxedos are not the norm; a pair of solid-colored slacks with a nice shirt is. If you're planning a wedding on the beach, barefoot is the way to go.

If you decide to marry in a formal dress and tuxedo, you're better off making your selections at home and hand-carrying them aboard the plane. Yes, it can be a pain, but ask your wedding-gown retailer to provide a special carrying bag. After all, you don't want to chance losing your wedding dress in a wayward piece of luggage. And when it comes to fittings, again, that's something to take care of before you arrive in the Virgin Islands.

Your Honeymoon

Do you want champagne and strawberries delivered to your room each morning? A breathtaking swimming pool in which to float? A five-star restaurant in which to dine? Then a resort is the way to go. If you're on a tight budget or don't plan to spend much time in your room, there are also plenty of cheaper small inns and hotels throughout the USBVI to choose from. On the other hand, maybe you want your own private home in which to romp naked—or just laze around recovering from the wedding planning. Maybe you want your own kitchen in which to whip up a gourmet meal for your loved one. In that case, a private villa rental is the answer. That's another beautiful thing about the Virgin Islands: the lodging accommodations are almost as plentiful as the beaches, and there's one to match your tastes and your budget.

Popular Honeymoon Resorts

If you are looking for some serious time together with few distractions, you can always head to one of the private-island resorts in the BVI. **Guana Island** and **Peter Island** are luxurious, but **Cooper Island Beach Club** offers both privacy and moderate prices.

Many honeymooners choose the laid-back luxury of **Caneel Bay** on St. John or the **Rosewood Little Dix Bay** or **Biras Creek** on Virgin Gorda. Those looking for more creature comforts might consider the **Ritz-Carlton** on St. Thomas or the **Renaissance Carambola Beach Resort** on St. Croix (which has a good golf course). The **Sugar Mill Hotel** on Tortola is simple and small but still gracious, while the **Surfsong Villa Resort** on Beef Island, Tortola, offers the privacy advantages of a villa with some hotel amenities. St. Thomas's **Wyndham Sugar Bay Resort and Spa,** though also popular with families, has an on-site wedding coordinator and is the island's only true all-inclusive resort.

IF YOU LIKE

A private villa on any of the islands will afford the most privacy, and there are choices in all sizes and prices ranges.

The Beach

Even if you're not a connoisseur, a day or two on the sand is central to a complete vacation here. Your hotel may border a beach or provide transportation to one nearby, but don't limit yourself.

You could spend one day at a lively, touristy beach that has plenty of watersports facilities and is backed by a bar, and another at an isolated cove that offers nothing but seclusion. Here are our favorites:

The Baths, Virgin Gorda, BVI. Swimming among the giant boulders here is a highlight of any trip despite the crowds.

Buck Island, St. Croix, USVI. The softest sandy beach in St. Croix isn't exactly *on* St. Croix.

Cane Garden Bay, Tortola, BVI. This silky beach is often Tortola's busiest.

Coki Beach, St. Thomas, USVI. Come here for St. Thomas's best off-the-beach snorkeling.

Long Bay West, Tortola, BVI. Although the water is not calm, this is one of Tortola's finest beaches and still quite swimmable.

Magens Bay, St. Thomas, USVI. St. Thomas's busiest beach is one of the most beautiful in the Caribbean, if not the world.

Trunk Bay, St. John, USVI. This national park beach is picture-perfect, and has an underwater snorkeling trail.

West End Beaches, St. Croix, USVI. Find a spot near Sunset Grill and relax.

White Bay, Jost Van Dyke, BVI. You won't have to travel far to find a bar on this long stretch of sand.

Diving and Snorkeling

Clear water and numerous reefs afford wonderful opportunities for both diving and snorkeling in the Virgin Islands. Serious divers usually head to the BVI, but don't neglect St. Croix, which is also a good dive destination.

Anegada, BVI. The reefs surrounding this flat coral-and-limestone atoll are a sailor's nightmare but a snorkeler's dream.

The Baths, Virgin Gorda, BVI. Snorkelers in the BVI need not worry that they'll miss out because they can't reach the deeper reefs and wrecks. Virgin Gorda's most popular beach is dotted with giant boulders that create numerous tide pools, making it a great place to explore underwater. It's especially good for kids.

Buck Island, St. Croix, USVI. Buck Island Reef National Monument is St. Croix's best-known snorkeling spot, where there's a marked trail among the coral formations. Take a catamaran for a more relaxing trip.

The Reefs of St. Croix, USVI. Cane Bay Wall is the most popular dive site in St. Croix, and that's where you can find the high concentration of dive operators.

Snorkeling Tours, St. John, USVI. If you want to do a day-sail-and-snorkeling trip, then St. John is a good place to leave from. You'll have easy access to a wide variety of islets and cays, so the boat can drop anchor in several places during a full-day sailing trip.

The Wreck of the Rhone, off Tortola, BVI. This exceptionally well-preserved royal mail steamer, which sank in 1867, is one of the most famous wreck dives in the Caribbean. But snorkelers won't feel left out in these clear waters.

History

Columbus, pirates, European colonizers, and plantation farmers and their slaves are among the people who have left their marks on these islands, all of which are benefiting the tourism industry, a relatively recent development.

The U.S. National Park Service maintains several sites in the U.S. Virgin Islands, so keep your annual America the Beautiful Pass handy for free or discount admissions.

Annaberg Plantation, St. John, USVI. You can sometimes see living-history demonstrations at the most popular plantation ruins on St. John.

Christiansted, St. Croix, USVI. With several historic buildings, including Fort Christiansvaern, the island's main town is a place to do more than just shop and dine.

Copper Mine Point, Virgin Gorda, BVI. The remains of a 16th-century copper mine are a popular tourist site here.

Old Government House Museum, Tortola, BVI. The former seat of the island's government is now a museum. It can be found right in the heart of Road Town.

Seven Arches Museum, St. Thomas, USVI. A trip to this museum, in a restored 18th-century home, will give you a sense of how St. Thomas residents lived in the colonial heyday.

Whim Plantation Museum, St. Croix, USVI. A lovingly restored plantation house is St. Croix's best-preserved historical treasure. It's also an island cultural center.

Sleeping in Style

The Virgin Islands have some fine resorts, though not all the best places are necessarily the most luxurious. St. Croix in particular is known more for its small inns than for big, splashy resorts. In the British Virgin Islands (and even St. John), the best options are usually much more laid-back. You're paying for a sense of exclusivity and personal attention, not lavish luxury. You won't be disappointed by these choices.

Caneel Bay, St. John, USVI. Caneel has been a standard-bearer since it opened in the 1950s, but the sense of luxury here is decidedly laid-back. Still, we can't resist those seven gorgeous beaches.

Carringtons, St. Croix, USVI. We have loved Claudia and Roger Carrington's small, friendly B&B in the hills outside Christiansted from the beginning, and see no reason to change our minds now.

Cooper Island Beach Club, BVI. Our favorite private-island retreat in the BVI is not the most luxurious—not by a long shot. But we can think of no better place to get away from it all without having to raid the kids' college fund.

Ritz-Carlton, St. Thomas, USVI. Built like a palatial Italian villa, this is the best Ritz-Carlton in the Caribbean; there's elegance everywhere.

Sugar Mill Hotel, Tortola, BVI. We love this small hotel's romantic, tropical ambience, and the restaurant is one of our favorites on Tortola.

Villa Greenleaf, St. Croix, USVI. This B&B comes with the frills, but it's hardly a resortlike experience. Think of a visit to a well-heeled aunt in the Caribbean. We like that thought.

ISLAND FINDER

	ST. THOMAS	ST. JOHN	ST. CROIX	TORTOLA	VIRGIN GORDA	JOST VAN DYKE	ANEGADA
APPEAL							
Crowds	●	◑	◑	◑	○	◑	○
Urban Development	●	◑	●	◑	○	○	○
Family-friendly	●	●	◑	●	◑	○	◑
BEACHES							
Beautiful	◑	●	◑	◑	◑	●	●
Deserted	○	●	◑	◑	●	◑	●
ENTERTAINMENT							
Cultural and Historic Sights	●	◑	◑	◑	○	○	○
Fine Dining	●	◑	◑	◑	◑	○	○
Nightlife	◑	◑	◑	◑	○	●	○
Shopping	●	◑	◑	◑	○	○	○
Casinos	●	◑	○	○	○	◑	○
LODGING							
Luxury Resorts	●	◑	◑	◑	●	○	○
Moderately Priced Resorts	●	○	●	◑	◑	◑	◑
Small Inns	●	◑	●	◑	○	○	◑
NATURE							
Wildlife	◑	●	◑	◑	●	◑	◑
Eco-tourism	◑	●	◑	◑	●	○	○
SPORTS							
Golf	●	○	◑	○	○	○	○
Scuba Diving	●	◑	●	●	●	◑	●
Snorkeling	●	●	◑	●	●	●	●
Fishing	●	◑	●	◑	●	○	◑

●: noteworthy; ◑: some; ○: Nothing: little or none

FREQUENTLY ASKED QUESTIONS

Is it safe to travel to the Virgin Islands? Crime certainly happens in the Virgin Islands, and there are sections of Charlotte Amalie, St. Thomas, and Christiansted, St. Croix, that you would not want to walk through even during the day, but for the most part, crime in the USVI and BVI is much lower than in most large U.S. cities. Petty theft of belongings from your car or on the beach can be a problem in many islands, but in general the crime in the BVI is somewhat less than in the USVI.

Are there any all-inclusive resorts in the Virgin Islands? Just one. The Wyndham Sugar Bay Resort on St. Thomas is the only true all-inclusive resort in the Virgin Islands. Some of the private-island resorts in the BVI do offer full-meal or all-inclusive plans, but they are as far from the typical all-inclusive resort experience as you could possibly imagine. Few resorts (even those that do offer meal plans) include alcoholic drinks, as you'd find at an all-inclusive resort in the Dominican Republic or Jamaica.

How expensive is food in the Virgin Islands? You should expect to pay at least 30% more for groceries in the Virgin Islands than you would at home, and on some of the smaller islands, you'll pay an even larger premium. But there are good, U.S.-style supermarkets on St. Thomas and St. Croix, and decent markets on St. John and Tortola.

Can I bring a cooler of food with me? Many people pack a few staples in their checked luggage (especially if there is a particular brand you might not find in the supermarkets in the Virgin Islands). It's best not to bring fresh fruits and vegetables since they might be confiscated. And you can certainly pack a cooler of frozen or refrigerated food to bring with you to the U.S. Virgin Islands, but you'll have to check it

in. Airlines no longer allow cold-packs in carry-on luggage (because they exceed the 3-ounce rule for liquids). And be extra-careful about bringing frozen meat into the British Virgin Islands; you must file a $25 importation permit.

How much should I tip at a restaurant? Sometimes you'll see a service charge of about 10% on your restaurant bill (especially in the BVI); when this is the case, tip a little extra (about 5%). Otherwise, tip as you would at home, about 15%.

How much should I tip at my hotel or resort? Many hotels and resorts in the Virgin Islands add a hefty service charge of 10% to 15%, but that money doesn't always find its way to the staff. It's not inappropriate to leave $2 or $3 per day for the maid or $1 per bag to the bellhop. Tip taxi drivers in the USVI about 15% of the fare.

Do I need a passport to visit the U.S. Virgin Islands? No, you do not need a passport to visit the U.S. Virgin Islands; however, you will pass through customs, and you will also undergo an agricultural inspection. And you must also provide proof of citizenship (an original birth certificate with raised seal *plus* a government-issued photo ID) on your return.

What about entry into the British Virgin Islands? You do need a passport if you fly into the British Virgin Islands. If you travel to the BVI by *ferry* from the USVI, you can use one of the new, less expensive Passport Cards issued by the U.S. government, or you can use your regular valid passport. But a birth certificate and driver's license are no longer enough.

⇨ *For more help on trip planning, see the Travel Smart chapter.*

WHEN TO GO

The high season in the USBVI is traditionally winter—from December 15 to the week after the St. Thomas Carnival, usually the last week in April—when northern weather is at its worst. During this season you're guaranteed the most entertainment at resorts and the most people with whom to enjoy it. It's also the most fashionable, the most expensive, and the most popular time to visit—and most hotels are heavily booked. You must make reservations at least two or three months in advance for the very best places (sometimes a year in advance for the most exclusive spots). Hotel prices drop 20% to 50% after April 15; airfares and cruise prices also fall. Saving money isn't the only reason to visit the USBVI during the off-season. Summer is usually one of the prettiest times of the year; the sea is even calmer, and things move at a slower pace (except for the first two weeks of August on Tortola, when the BVI celebrate Carnival). The water is clearer for snorkeling and smoother for sailing in the Virgin Islands in May, June, and July.

Climate

Weather in the USBVI is a year-round wonder. The average daily temperature is about 80°F, and there isn't much variation from the coolest months. Rainfall averages 40 to 44 inches per year. But in the tropics rainstorms tend to be sudden and brief, often erupting early in the morning and at dusk.

In May and June what's known as the Sahara Dust sometimes moves through, making for hazy spring days and spectacular sunsets.

Toward the end of summer hurricane season begins in earnest, with the first tropical wave passing by in June. Islanders pay close attention to the tropical waves as they form and travel across the Atlantic from Africa. In an odd paradox, tropical storms passing by leave behind the sunniest and clearest days you'll ever see. (And that's saying something in the land of zero air pollution.)

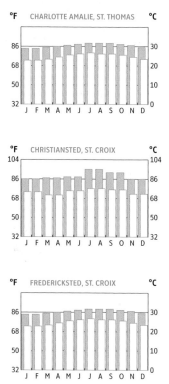

ON THE CALENDAR

The USBVI's top seasonal events are listed below, and any one of them could provide the stuff of lasting memories. Contact local tourism authorities for exact dates and for more information.

October–April

Ongoing The **Candlelight Concert Series** at Whim Plantation is an ongoing classical music program—the only such program of its kind on St. Croix—that presents concerts on Friday and Saturday evenings throughout the year on the grounds of the historic plantation.

November

On Thanksgiving weekend, the **Annual Coral Bay Thanksgiving Regatta** brings together boat owners for a two-day race event sponsored by the Coral Bay Yacht Club.

December

Winter For the best in local *fungi* bands (bands that make music using household items as instruments), stop by the **Scratch-Fungi Band Fiesta** during the last two weeks of December.

December–January St. Croix celebrates Carnival with its **Crucian Christmas Festival,** which starts in late December. After weeks of beauty pageants, food fairs, and concerts, the festival wraps up with a parade in early January.

February

Every February, St. Croix celebrates its natural bounty with the **St. Croix Agriculture and Food Fair,** also called "AgriFest."

In mid-February, the **Water Island Classical Music Festival** takes place at Paradise Point on Water Island. The free concerts are served by special ferry service from Crown Bay Marina.

On Valentine's Day, St. John always hosts at **Celebration of Love** at Trunk Bay, a free vow-renewal ceremony right on the beach.

March

Spring Locals and yachties gather at Foxy's bar on Jost Van Dyke in the British Virgin Islands for the annual **St. Patrick's Day** celebration.

The annual **St. John Blues Festival** brings musicians from all over to play for five nights in Coral Bay and Cruz Bay.

March–April

During Easter weekend St. Thomas Yacht Club hosts the **Rolex Cup Regatta,** which is part of the three-race Caribbean Ocean Racing Triangle (CORT) that pulls in yachties and their pals from all over.

The internationally known **BVI Spring Regatta & Sailing Festival,** which includes the competition for the Nation's Challenge Cup, begins during the last week in March and continues into the first weekend in April, with parties and sailing competitions on Tortola and Virgin Gorda.

Join the fun at the **Virgin Gorda Festival,** which culminates with a parade on Easter Sunday.

April

In April, foodies will prosper when local restaurateurs get together to celebrate the **St. Croix Food and Wine Experience,** a four-day celebration of all things food-related. One of the highlights is "A Taste of St. Croix," a special one-night event when the top restaurants on the island serve up their soup dishes; the event often sells out the same day the highly coveted tickets become available.

The **VI Carnival St. Thomas** takes place at the end of April for two weeks of fun and festivities featuring both cultural events and entertainment.

May

Every May hordes of people head to Tortola for the three-day **BVI Music Festival** to listen to reggae, gospel, blues, and salsa music by musicians from around the Caribbean and the U.S. mainland.

The **St. Croix Half Ironman Triathlon** attracts international-class athletes as well as amateurs every May for a 1-mi (2-km) swim, a 7-mi (12-km) run, and a 34-mi (55-km) bike ride; it includes a climb up the Beast on Route 69.

Late May means that it's time for **Foxy's Wood Boat Regatta** on Jost Van Dyke, which has been sponsored by Foxy's and Tortola's West End Yacht Club for well over 30 years. The race brings together myriad older wooden boats for two days of racing excitement.

June–July

Summer Events of the **St. John Festival** celebrating the island's heritage and history continue throughout the month of June—including beauty pageants and a food fair—culminating with the annual parade on Independence Day.

July

The St. Thomas Gamefishing Club hosts its **July Open Tournament** over July 4 weekend. There are categories for serious marlin anglers, just-for-fun fishermen, and even kids who want to try their luck from docks and rocks.

All three of the USVI celebrate Independence Day on **July 4** with fireworks, though the biggest celebration is on St. John.

August

Try your hand at sportfishing, as anglers compete to land the largest catch at the **BVI Sportfishing Tournament.**

August sees two weeks of joyful revelry during Tortola's **BVI Emancipation Festival** celebrations.

St. Thomas

WORD OF MOUTH

"Get a taxi and head to Bolongo [Bay] Beach Resort if you want an active beach scene or Secret Harbour beach resort for a quiet spot. Both have a restaurant and beach bar/food. Secret Harbour has very good snorkeling off the right side of the beach. Take towels."

—Virginia

WELCOME TO ST. THOMAS

TOP REASONS TO GO

★ **Shop till you drop:** Find great deals on duty-free jewelry, timepieces, and electronics along Charlotte Amalie's Main Street—but don't forget to pick up some locally made crafts as well.

★ **Tell Fish Stories:** Go in search of magnificent blue marlins and other trophy-worthy fish in the waters around St. Thomas from June through October.

★ **Get Your Sea Legs:** Charter a yacht (or just take a regularly scheduled day sail) to cruise between the islands any time of year, or join the International Rolex Regatta in March. It's also a short hop over to the British Virgin Islands from St. Thomas.

★ **Hit the Links:** Play through the "Devil's Triangle," an intimidating cliff-side trio of holes at Mahogany Run Golf Course.

★ **Take a Dip:** Swim at Magens Bay, considered by many to be one of the most beautiful beaches in the world.

1 Charlotte Amalie. The capital of the USVI has the lion's share of the island's historic sights, not to mention good restaurants, excellent shopping, and some recommendable inns and hotels. Many ferries leave from the dock here, as does seaplane service. The island's main cruise terminal is also here.

2 East End. Most of the island's large beach resorts (not to mention some of the best beaches) are on the East End, about a 30-minute drive from Charlotte Amalie. Red Hook, the main ferry hub for St. Thomas, is also here.

2

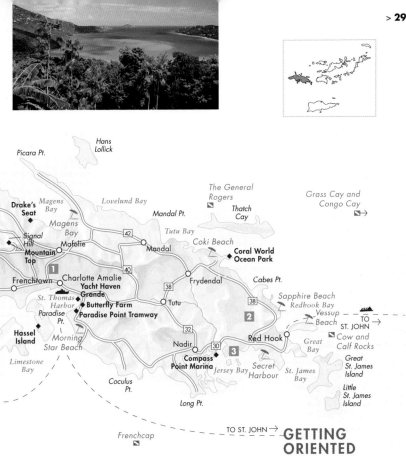

Picara Pt.

Hans Lollick

Lovelund Bay

The General
Rogers

Grass Cay and
Congo Cay

Mandal Pt.

Thatch
Cay

Drake's Seat
Magens
Bay

Magens
Bay

Tutu Bay

42

Coki Beach

**Coral World
Ocean Park**

Signal
Hill

**Mountain
Top**

Mofolie

Mandal

40

Frenchtown

Charlotte Amalie
**Yacht Haven
Grande**

Frydendal

Cabes Pt.

St. Thomas
Harbor

Butterfly Farm

38

Sapphire Beach
Redhook Bay

Paradise
Pt.

Paradise Point Tramway

Tutu

38

Vessup
Beach

**TO
ST. JOHN**

**Hassel
Island**

Morning
Star Beach

32

2

Cow and
Calf Rocks

Limestone
Bay

Nadir

30

Red Hook

Great
Bay

Great
St. James
Island

Coculus
Pt.

**Compass
Point Marina**

3

Jersey Bay

Secret
Harbour

St. James
Bay

Little
St. James
Island

Long Pt.

Frenchcap

TO ST. JOHN →

GETTING ORIENTED

3 South Shore. There are a few beach resorts along the South Shore, as well as some restaurants. Compass Point Marina is a popular destination for charter yachts.

4 West End. Aside from Frenchtown and Magens Bay, most of West End is residential, though the main airport is just west of Frenchtown. There are some less-visited beaches beyond Magens Bay, such as Hull Bay, as well as a few restaurants in the hills around Mafolie.

St. Thomas is 13 mi (21 km) long and less than 4 mi (6½ km) wide, but it's extremely hilly, and even an 8- or 10-mi (13- or 16-km) trip could take well over an hour. Don't let that discourage you, though; the mountain ridge that runs east to west through the middle and separates the island's Caribbean and Atlantic sides has spectacular vistas.

ST. THOMAS PLANNER

Do You Need a Car?

You will want to rent a car if you are staying in a private villa, but if you are staying in a hotel on the beach, you can usually get by with taxis, though getting a taxi every day can be expensive. If you are a family or group of four, then a car can be a more cost-effective solution since taxi rates are per person.

CAR RENTALS

Major car-rental companies, including Avis, Budget, and Hertz have locations at the airport; Avis and Budget also have branch offices. Local rental companies include Dependable Car Rental, Discount Car Rental, and E-Z Car Rental.

Contacts **Avis** (☎ 340/774–1468). **Budget** (☎ 340/776–5774). **Dependable Car Rental** (☎ 340/774–2253 or 800/522–3076 ⊕ www.dependablecar.com). **Discount Car Rental** (☎ 340/776–4858 ⊕ www.discountcar.vi). **E-Z Car Rental** (☎ 340/775–6255 or 800/524–2027). **Hertz** (☎ 340/774–1879).

Getting Here and Around

By Air: American, Continental, Delta, Spirit, United, and US Airways fly to St. Thomas from the U.S. Cape Air flies from San Juan.

By Ferry: There's frequent service between St. Thomas and St. John, and Tortola, and less frequent service to Virgin Gorda and Jost Van Dyke. Virgin Islands ferry schedules are published on the Web site of the Virgin Islands Vacation Guide & Community. There's also a ferry from Charlotte Amalie's waterfront to the Marriott Frenchman's Reef Hotel. Finally, VI Sea Trans offers service several times a week to St. Croix. In St. Thomas, ferries leave from both Charlotte Amalie and Red Hook. Remember that a passport is now required to travel between the USVI and BVI by ferry. The actual schedules change, so you should check with the ferry companies to determine the current schedules.

Contacts **Virgin Islands Vacation Guide & Community** (⊕ www.vinow.com). **VI SeaTrans** (☎ 340/776–5494 ⊕ www.goviseatrans.com).

Bus Travel: On St. Thomas the island's large buses make public transportation a very comfortable—though slow—way to get from east and west to Charlotte Amalie and back (service to the north is limited). Buses run about every 30 minutes from stops that are clearly marked with Vitran signs. Fares are $1 between outlying areas and town and 75¢ in town. Some open-air safari vans also follow the bus route, and these drivers charge the same fares as Vitran—hence the nickname "dollar busses."

Taxi Travel: USVI taxis charge per person and have a set schedule of fares. Drivers usually take multiple fares, especially from the airport, ferry docks, and the cruise-ship terminal. Most taxis are either safari-style or enclosed, air-conditioned vans. They can be hailed on the street (especially in town and near major shopping malls and attractions) and can also be called. There are taxi stands in Charlotte Amalie across from Emancipation Garden (in front of Little Switzerland, behind the post office) and along the waterfront.

Contacts **East End Taxi** (☎ 340/775–6974). **Islander Taxi** (☎ 340/774–4077). **V.I. Taxi Association** (☎ 340/774–4550).

Where to Stay

You can let yourself be pampered at a luxurious resort, or if your means are more modest, there are cheaper hotels in lovely settings throughout the island. There are also guesthouses and inns with great views (if not a beach at your door) and great service at about half the cost of what you'll pay at the beachfront pleasure palaces. Many of these are west and north of Charlotte Amalie or overlooking hills—ideal if you plan to get out and mingle with the locals. There are also inexpensive lodgings (most right in town) that are perfect if you just want a clean room to return to after a day of exploring or beach-bumming. East End condominium complexes are popular with families. Although condos are pricey, they have full kitchens, and you can definitely save money by cooking for yourself—especially if you bring some of your own nonperishable foodstuffs. Though you may spend some time laboring in the kitchen, many condos ease your burden with daily maid service and on-site restaurants; a few also have resort amenities, including pools and tennis courts.

Where to Eat

The beauty of St. Thomas and its sister islands has attracted a cadre of professionally trained chefs who know their way around fresh fish and local fruits. You can dine on everything from terrific cheap local dishes such as goat water (a spicy stew) and *fungi* (a cornmeal polentalike side dish) to imports such as hot pastrami sandwiches and raspberries in crème fraîche.

HOTEL AND RESTAURANT PRICES

Restaurant prices are for a main course at dinner and include any taxes or service charges. Hotel prices are per night for a double room in high season, excluding taxes and service charges which can add an additional 18%, and meal plans (except at all-inclusives).

WHAT IT COSTS IN U.S. DOLLARS

	¢	$	$$	$$$	$$$$
Restaurants	under $8	$8–$12	$13–$20	$21–$30	over $30
Hotels	under $150	$150–$275	$276–$375	$376–$475	over $475

Essentials

Banks The major banks on St. Thomas are First Bank, Banco Popular, and Scotia Bank, each of which has several branches in convenient locations.

Safety To be safe, keep your hotel or vacation villa door locked at all times, stick to well-lighted streets at night, and use the same kind of street sense that you would in any unfamiliar territory. Don't wander the streets of Charlotte Amalie alone at night. If you plan to carry things around, rent a car—not an open-air vehicle—and lock possessions in the trunk. Keep your rental car locked wherever you park. Don't leave cameras, purses, and other valuables lying on the beach while you snorkel for an hour (or even for a minute), no matter how many people are nearby.

Tour Options V.I. Taxi Association (☎ *340/774–4550* ⊕ *www. vitaxi.com*) offers a $25 per person, two-hour tour, but there are many other tour options. For $60 for two people, you can also hire a taxi for a customized three-hour drive around the island.

Visitor Information USVI Division of Tourism (☎ *340/774– 8784 or 800/372-8784* ⊕ *www. usvitourism.vi*). **Virgin Islands Hotel and Tourism Association** (☎ *340/774-6835* ⊕ *www. virgin-islands-hotels.com*).

EATING AND DRINKING WELL IN THE VIRGIN ISLANDS

Take a mix of indigenous and imported ingredients—everything from papaya to salt cod. Blend this with the cooking styles of people like the ancient Amerindians, Africans, Europeans, East Indians, and Asians, and you have the melting pot that is traditional Virgin Islands cuisine.

Despite its American flag status and the abundant fast-food and Continental-style restaurants that dominate the islands, the traditional cuisine of Virgin Islands cuisine still maintains a foothold here. The best places to sample the authentic flavors of the islands are at local restaurants, bakeries, and mobile food vans, as well as the many food fairs and fish fries that tak`e place throughout the year. When you order an entrée—a "plate of food" as a meal is called—it will often be accompanied by a green salad, and a choice of three starchy side dishes. It's no wonder that a favorite saying is: "Better belly bus' than good food waste."—Carol Bareuther

SNACKS

Be sure to try the popular **Caribbean pate** *(pah-teh)*, a triangular-shaped fried pastry stuffed with spicy ground beef, conch, or salted fish. And nothing beats **mango-ade, passion fruit punch,** or **soursop juice** to tame the heat (pates often boast a touch of fiery scotch bonnet peppers among their ingredients). For a tamer snack, look for **johnny-cakes** (fried cornmeal cakes) or hush puppy-like **conch fritters.** Another tasty refresher is **coconut water,** the nectar of freshly cracked coconuts. **Dundersloe,** the Virgin Islands version of peanut brittle, is often sold by vendors outside of shopping centers.

2

FRUIT

Tropical fruits are abundant throughout the islands. Make sure to sample juicy, sweet mangoes, floral-scented papaya (great with a squeeze of lime), tart star fruit (bite into it or slice it up), and finger-long fig bananas, which are sweeter than stateside varieties. Other fruits, like soursop and passion fruit are messy to eat by hand, but try them in juices and ice creams. Fruit also plays a starring role in desserts like tarts, which are filled with sweetened coconut, guava, pineapple, or mango.

VEGETABLES

Common vegetables include okra, spinach and other greens, sweet potatoes, eggplants, green plantains, and gnarly root vegetables like tannia, cassava, and boniato. Kallaloo is a popular soupy vegetable stew made with spinach and okra, seasoned with fresh herbs, and further flavored with crab, fish, or ham.

SEAFOOD

Popular fish varieties include snapper, grouper, yellowtail, mahi mahi, and wahoo, which are often fried or grilled and served whole. Lobster and conch also are prevalent, the latter appearing in everything from ceviche salads to soups. The unofficial national dish for the Virgin Islands is "Fish and fungi," simmered fish with okra-studded cornmeal mush.

MEAT

Meat plays a prominent role in soups on the islands. Goat water (mutton stew) and

souse (pig foot stew) make hearty meals, and typically are served with dumplings or bread. Curried goat is a classic dish worth a taste. For something less spicy, try simply prepared chicken and rice.

STARCHES

Don't be thrown off by unexpected naming conventions. For example, "peas and rice" may be made with red beans, kidney beans, or black beans (no peas). Potato stuffing, a mix of mashed white potatoes, tomato sauce, and seasonings, isn't used to stuff anything. And "fungi" (fun-gee) is not mushroom but a polenta-like dish of African origin made from cornmeal studded with chopped okra. More straightforward are the fried plantains, and boiled sweet potatoes, yams, and tannia that are sliced and served with fish and poultry.

DRINKS

Rum, a spirit made from sugarcane, has a significant history in the Virgin Islands, dating back to the rise of sugarcane plantations in the mid-1700s. Rum is still produced here, and available in numerous styles (and flavors). For a lower-proof sipper, try mauby, a somewhat bitter, root beer-like drink traditionally used as folk medicine. Mauby is made from the bark of the mauby tree, which is steeped with sugar and spices and served ice-cold. For a morning eye-opener, some islanders recommend "bush tea," an herbal infusion of native plants.

By Carol M.
Bareuther

Because it's the transportation hub of the Virgin Islands, most visitors land on hilly St. Thomas even if they don't linger. Visitors who stay longer may be drawn by the legendary shopping and the wide variety of water sports, activities, beaches, and accommodations. The bustling port of Charlotte Amalie is the main town, while Red Hook sits on the eastern tip. The west end of the island is relatively wild, and hotels and resorts rim the southern and eastern shores.

If you fly to the 32-square-mi (83-square-km) island of St. Thomas, you land at its western end; if you arrive by cruise ship, you come into one of the world's most beautiful harbors. Either way, one of your first sights is the town of Charlotte Amalie. From the harbor you see an idyllic-looking village that spreads into the lower hills. If you were expecting a quiet hamlet with its inhabitants hanging out under palm trees, you've missed that era by about 300 years. Although other islands in the USVI developed plantation economies, St. Thomas cultivated its harbor, and it became a thriving seaport soon after it was settled by the Danish in the 1600s.

The success of the naturally perfect harbor was enhanced by the fact that the Danes—who ruled St. Thomas with only a couple of short interruptions from 1666 to 1917—avoided involvement in some 100 years' worth of European wars. Denmark was the only European country with colonies in the Caribbean to stay neutral during the War of the Spanish Succession in the early 1700s. Accordingly, products of the Dutch, English, and French islands—sugar, cotton, and indigo—were traded through Charlotte Amalie, along with the regular shipments of slaves. When the Spanish wars ended, trade fell off, but by the end of the 1700s Europe was at war again, Denmark again remained neutral, and St. Thomas continued to prosper. Even into the 1800s, while the economies of St. Croix and St. John foundered with the market for sugarcane, St. Thomas's economy remained vigorous. This prosperity led to the development of shipyards, a well-organized banking system, and a large merchant class. In 1845 Charlotte Amalie had 101 large importing houses owned by the English, French, Germans, Haitians, Spaniards, Americans, Sephardim, and Danes.

Charlotte Amalie is still one of the world's most active cruise-ship ports. On almost any day at least one and sometimes as many as eight cruise ships are tied to the docks or anchored outside the harbor. Gently rocking in the shadows of these giant floating hotels are just about every other kind of vessel imaginable: sleek sailing mono- and multihulls that will take you on a sunset cruise complete with rum punch and a Jimmy Buffett soundtrack, private megayachts that spirit busy executives away, and barnacle-bottom sloops—with laundry draped over the lifelines—that are home to world-cruising gypsies. Huge container ships pull up in Sub Base, west of the harbor, bringing in everything from breakfast cereals to tires. Anchored right along the waterfront are down-island barges that ply the waters between the Greater Antilles and the Leeward Islands, transporting goods like refrigerators, VCRs, and disposable diapers.

The waterfront road through Charlotte Amalie was once part of the harbor. Before it was filled in to build the highway, the beach came right up to the back door of the warehouses that now line the thoroughfare. Two hundred years ago those warehouses were filled with indigo, tobacco, and cotton. Today the stone buildings house silk, crystal, linens, and leather. Exotic fragrances are still traded, but by island beauty queens in air-conditioned perfume palaces instead of through open market stalls. The pirates of old used St. Thomas as a base from which to raid merchant ships of every nation, though they were particularly fond of the gold- and silver-laden treasure ships heading to Spain. Pirates are still around, but today's versions use St. Thomas as a drop-off for their contraband: illegal immigrants and drugs.

DRIVING IN ST. THOMAS

Traffic can be bad, especially in Charlotte Amalie at rush hour (7 to 9 and 4:30 to 6). If you need to get from an East End resort to the airport during these times, find the alternate route (starting from the East End, Route 38 to 42 to 40 to 33) that goes up the mountain and then drops you back onto Veterans Highway. All drivers should get a copy of *Road Map St. Thomas–St. John,* available on the island anywhere you find maps and guidebooks.

EXPLORING ST. THOMAS

To explore outside Charlotte Amalie, rent a car or hire a taxi. Your rental car should come with a good map; if not, pick up the pocket-size "St. Thomas–St. John Road Map" at a tourist information center. Roads are marked with route numbers, but they're confusing and seem to switch numbers suddenly. Roads are also identified by signs bearing the St. Thomas–St. John Hotel and Tourism Association's mascot, Tommy the Starfish. More than 100 of these color-coded signs line the island's main routes. Orange signs trace the route from the airport to

DID YOU KNOW?

Charlotte Amalie is the busiest cruise port in the Caribbean and one of the busiest in the world. As many as eight cruise ships may call in a single day.

Red Hook, green signs identify the road from town to Magens Bay, Tommy's face on a yellow background points from Mafolie to Crown Bay through the north side, red signs lead from Smith Bay to Four Corners via Skyline Drive, and blue signs mark the route from the cruise-ship dock at Havensight to Red Hook. These color-coded routes are not marked on most visitor maps, however. Allow yourself a day to explore, especially if you want to stop to take pictures or to enjoy a light bite or refreshing swim. Most gas stations are on the island's more populated eastern end, so fill up before heading to the north side. And remember to drive on the left!

CHARLOTTE AMALIE

Look beyond the pricey shops, T-shirt vendors, and bustling crowds for a glimpse of the island's history. The city served as the capital of Denmark's outpost in the Caribbean until 1917, an aspect of the island often lost in the glitz of the shopping district.

Emancipation Gardens, right next to the fort, is a good place to start a walking tour. Tackle the hilly part of town first: head north up Government Hill to the historic buildings that house government offices and have incredible views. Several regal churches line the route that runs west back to the town proper and the old-time market. Virtually all the alleyways that intersect Main Street lead to eateries that serve frosty drinks, sandwiches, and West Indian fare. There are public restrooms in this area, too. Allow an hour for a quick view of the sights.

A note about the street names: in deference to the island's heritage, the streets downtown are labeled by their Danish names. Locals will use both the Danish name and the English name (such as Dronningens Gade and Norre Gade for Main Street), but most people refer to things by their location ("a block toward the Waterfront off Main Street" or "next to the Little Switzerland Shop"). You may find it more useful if you ask for directions by shop names or landmarks.

Numbers in the margin correspond to points of interest on the Charlotte Amalie map.

WHAT TO SEE

All Saints Anglican Church. Built in 1848 from stone quarried on the island, the church has thick, arched window frames lined with the yellow brick that came to the islands as ballast aboard ships. Merchants left the brick on the waterfront when they filled their boats with molasses, sugar, mahogany, and rum for the return voyage. The church was built in celebration of the end of slavery in the USVI. ⊠ *Domini Gade* ☏ *340/774–0217* ☉ *Mon.–Sat. 9–3.*

Cathedral of St. Peter & St. Paul. This building was consecrated as a parish church in 1848, and serves as the seat of the territory's Roman Catholic diocese. The ceiling and walls are covered with a dozen murals painted in 1899 by two Belgian artists, Father Leo Servais and Brother Ildephonsus, and depict scenes from both the Old and New Testaments. The San Juan–marble altar and walls were added in the 1960s. ⊠ *Lower Main St.* ☏ *340/774–0201* ☉ *Mon.–Sat. 8–5.*

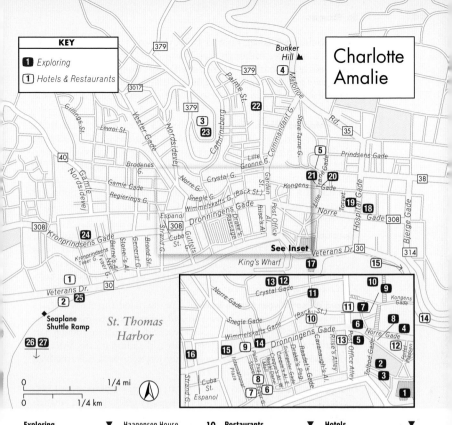

Charlotte Amalie

Danish Consulate Building. Built in 1830, this structure once housed the Danish Consulate. Although the Danish consul general, Søren Blak, has an office in Charlotte Amalie, the Danish Consulate is now in the Scandinavian Center in Havensight Mall. This building is not open to the public. ⊠ *Take stairs north at corner of Bjerge Gade and Crystal Gade to Denmark Hill.*

Dutch Reformed Church. This church has an austere loveliness that's amazing considering all it's been through. Founded in 1744, it's been rebuilt twice after fires and hurricanes. The unembellished cream-color hall gives you a sense of peace—albeit monochromatically. The only other color is the forest green of the shutters and the carpet. Call ahead if you wish to visit at a particular time, as the doors are sometimes locked. ⊠ *Nye Gade and Crystal Gade* ☎ *340/776–8255* ✆ *Weekdays 9–5.*

Educators Park. A peaceful place amid the town's hustle and bustle, the park has memorials to three famous Virgin Islanders: educator Edith Williams, J. Antonio Jarvis (a founder of the *Daily News*), and educator and author Rothschild Francis. The last gave many speeches here. ⊠ *Main St., across from post office.*

Edward Wilmoth Blyden Marine Terminal. Locally called Tortola Wharf, it's where you can catch the *Native Son* and other ferries to the BVI. The restaurant upstairs is a good place to watch the Charlotte Amalie harbor traffic and sip an iced tea. Next door is the ramp for the *Seaborne Airlines* seaplane, which offers commuter service to St. Croix, the BVI, and Puerto Rico. ⊠ *Waterfront Hwy.*

☙ **Emancipation Garden.** Built to commemorate the freeing of slaves in 1848, the garden was the site of a 150th anniversary celebration of emancipation. A bronze bust of a freed slave blowing a symbolic conch shell commemorates this anniversary. The gazebo here is used for official ceremonies. Two other monuments show the island's Danish-American connection—a bust of Denmark's King Christian and a scaled-down model of the U.S. Liberty Bell. ⊠ *Between Tolbod Gade and Ft. Christian.*

☙ **Enid M. Baa Public Library.** Like so many other structures on the north side of Main Street, this large yellow building is a typical 18th-century town house. The library was once the home of merchant and landowner Baron von Bretton. He and other merchants built their houses (stores downstairs, living quarters above) across from the brick warehouses on the south side of the street. This is the island's first recorded fireproof building, meaning it was built of ballast brick instead of wood. Its interior of high ceilings and cool stone floors is the perfect refuge from the afternoon sun. You can browse through historic papers or just sit in the breeze by an open window reading the paper. ⊠ *Main St.* ☎ *340/774–0630* ✆ *Weekdays 9–6, Sat. 10–4.*

☙ **Ft. Christian.** St. Thomas's oldest standing structure, this monument was built between 1672 and 1680 and now has U.S. National Landmark status. This remarkable building has, over time, been used as a jail, governor's residence, town hall, courthouse, and church. A multimillion-dollar renovation project was started in 2005 to stabilize the structure and halt centuries of deterioration. Delays have plagued the project, including the

Fort Christian (1672–80), the oldest surviving structure in St. Thomas.

discovery of human skeletal remains buried in the walls from when the structure was used as a Lutheran church. You can see from the outside the four renovated faces of the famous 19th-century clock tower. ⊠ *Waterfront Hwy. east of shopping district* ☎ *340/776–8605.*

Frederick Lutheran Church. This historic church has a massive mahogany altar, and its pews—each with its own door—were once rented to families of the congregation. Lutheranism is the state religion of Denmark, and when the territory was without a minister, the governor—who had his own elevated pew—filled in. ⊠ *Norre Gade* ☎ *340/776–1315* ⏱ *Mon.–Sat. 9–4.*

Government House. Built in 1867, this neoclassical white brick-and-wood structure houses the offices of the governor of the Virgin Islands. Inside, the staircases are of native mahogany, as are the plaques hand-lettered in gold with the names of the governors appointed and, since 1970, elected. Brochures detailing the history of the building are available, but you may have to ask for them. ⊠ *Government Hill* ☎ *340/774–0294* 🎫 *Free* ⏱ *Weekdays 8–5.*

Grand Hotel. This imposing building stands at the head of Main Street. Once the island's premier hotel, it has been converted into offices and shops. ⊠ *Tolbod Gade at Norre Gade* ☎ *340/774–7282* ⏱ *Weekdays 8–5, Sat. 9–noon.*

Haagensen House. Behind Hotel 1829, this lovingly restored home was built in the early 1800s by Danish entrepreneur Hans Haagensen and is surrounded by an equally impressive cookhouse, outbuildings, and terraced gardens. A lower-level banquet hall showcases antique prints and photographs. Guided tours begin at Hotel 1829, then continue to Haagensen House. The tour includes stops at two other restored 19th-century homes, a rum factory, amber museum, and finally the lookout tour at Blackbeard's Castle. Tours are given between 9 am and 3 pm on days a cruise ship is in port. ⊠ *Government Hill* 🕾 *340/776–1234 or 340/776–1829* 🖭 *Tours $20 guided, $12 self-guided* ⊘ *Oct.–May, daily 9–3; June–Sept., by appointment only.*

Hassel Island. East of Water Island in Charlotte Amalie harbor, Hassel Island is part of the Virgin Islands National Park, as it has the ruins of a British military garrison (built during a brief British occupation of the USVI during the 1800s) and the remains of a marine railway (where ships were hoisted into dry dock for repairs). The island is accessible via daily guided kayak tours.

Hotel 1829. As its name implies, the hotel was built in 1829, albeit as the private residence of a prominent merchant named Alexander Lavalette. The building's coral-color facade is accented with fancy wrought-iron railings, and the interior is paneled in dark wood, which makes it feel delightfully cool. From the terrace there's an exquisite view of the harbor framed by brilliant orange bougainvillea. You can combine a visit to this hotel with a walking tour of Haagensen House, Villa Notman, Britannia House, rum factory, amber museum, and the lookout tower at Blackbeard's Castle just above the hotel. ⊠ *Government Hill* 🕾 *340/776–1829 or 340/776–1234* ⊕ *www.hotel1829.com* 🖭 *Tour $20 guided, $12 self-guided* ⊘ *Oct.–May, daily 9–3; June–Sept., by appointment only.*

Legislature Building. Its pastoral-looking lime-green exterior conceals the vociferous political wrangling of the Virgin Islands Senate. Constructed originally by the Danish as a police barracks, the building was later used to billet U.S. Marines, and much later it housed a public school. You're welcome to sit in on sessions in the upstairs chambers. ⊠ *Waterfront Hwy. across from Ft. Christian* 🕾 *340/774–0880* ⊘ *Daily 8–5.*

Market Square. A cadre of old-timers gathers daily—especially early Saturday mornings—at this 18th-century slave market to sell local fruits such as mangoes and papayas, strange-looking root vegetables, and bunches of fresh herbs. Sidewalk vendors offer brightly colored fabrics, tie-dyed clothing, and handicrafts at good prices. ⊠ *North side of Main St., at Strand Gade* 🕾 *340/774–0450* ⊘ *Mon.–Fri. 9–5, Sat 5–5.*

Memorial Moravian Church. Built in 1884, this church was named to commemorate the 150th anniversary of the Moravian Church in the Virgin Islands. ⊠ *17 Norre Gade* 🕾 *340/776–0066* ⊘ *Weekdays 8–5.*

☾ **99 Steps.** This staircase "street," built by the Danes in the 1700s, leads to the residential area above Charlotte Amalie and to Blackbeard's

Castle, a U.S. national historic landmark. The castle's tower, built in 1679, was once used by the notorious pirate Edward Teach. Today, it's home to the largest collection of life-size pirates crafted out of bronze and copper in the world. If you count the stairs as you go up, you'll discover, as have thousands before you, that there are more than the name implies. ⊠ *Look for steps heading north from Government Hill.*

Pissarro Building. Housing several shops and an art gallery, this was the birthplace and childhood home of Camille Pissarro, who later moved to France and became an acclaimed 19th-century impressionist painter. The art gallery contains three original pages from Pissarro's sketchbook and two pastels by Pissarro's grandson, Claude. ⊠ *Main St. between Raadets Gade and Trompeter Gade.*

Roosevelt Park. First called Coconut Park, this park was renamed in honor of Franklin D. Roosevelt in 1945. It's a great place to put your feet up and people-watch. A renovation in 2007 added five granite pedestals representing the five branches of the military, bronze urns that can be lighted to commemorate special events, and bronze plaques inscribed with the names of the territory's veterans who died defending the United States. There's also a children's playground. ⊠ *Norre Gade.*

★ **Seven Arches Museum and Gallery.** This restored 18th-century home is a striking example of classic Danish–West Indian architecture. There seem to be arches everywhere—seven to be exact—all supporting a "welcoming arms" staircase that leads to the second floor and the flower-framed front doorway. The Danish kitchen is a highlight: it's housed in a separate building away from the main house, as were all cooking facilities in the early days (for fire prevention). Inside the house you can see mahogany furnishings and gas lamps and brightly-colored abstract canvases painted by the museum's curator, a local artist. ⊠ *Government Hill, 3 buildings east of Government House* ☎ *340/774–9295* ⊕ *www.sevenarchesmuseum.com* ✒ *$5 donation* ⊗ *By appointment only.*

Synagogue of Beracha Veshalom Vegmiluth Hasidim. The synagogue's Hebrew name translates as the Congregation of Blessing, Peace, and Loving Deeds. The small building's white pillars contrast with rough stone walls, as does the rich mahogany of the pews and altar. The sand on the floor symbolizes the exodus from Egypt. Since the synagogue first opened its doors in 1833, it has held a weekly service, making it the oldest synagogue building in continuous use under the American flag and the second-oldest (after the one on Curaçao) in the Western Hemisphere. Guided tours can be arranged. Brochures detailing the key structures and history are also available. Next door the Weibel Museum showcases Jewish history on St. Thomas. ⊠ *15 Crystal Gade* ☎ *340/774–4312* ⊕ *www.onepaper.com/synagogue* ⊗ *Weekdays 9–4.*

U.S. Post Office. While you buy stamps, contemplate the murals of waterfront scenes by *Saturday Evening Post* artist Stephen Dohanos. His art was commissioned as part of the Works Project Administration in the 1930s. ⊠ *Tolbod Gade and Main St.*

☺ **Vendors Plaza.** Here merchants sell everything from T-shirts to African attire to leather goods. Look for local art among the ever-changing selections at this busy market. ⊠ *Waterfront, west of Ft. Christian* ⊙ *Weekdays 8–6, weekends 9–1.*

☺ **Water Island.** This island, the fourth-largest of the U.S. Virgin Islands, floats about ¼ mi (½ km) out in Charlotte Amalie harbor. A ferry between Crown Bay Marina and the island operates several times daily from 6:30 am to 6 pm Monday through Saturday, and from 8 am to 5 pm on Sunday and holidays at a cost of $10 round-trip. (On cruise-ship days, a ferry goes direct from the West India Company dock, but only for those passengers on the bike trip.) From the ferry dock, it's a hike of less than a half-mile to Honeymoon Beach (though you have to go up a big hill), where Brad Pitt and Cate Blanchett filmed a scene of the movie *The Curious Case of Benjamin Button.* Get lunch from a mobile food van that pulls up on weekends. ⊠ *Ferry at Crown Bay Marina, Rte. 304, Estate Contant* ☎ *340/690–4159 for ferry information.*

Weibel Museum. In this museum next to the synagogue, 300 years of Jewish history on St. Thomas are showcased. The small gift shop sells a commemorative silver coin celebrating the anniversary of the Hebrew congregation's establishment on the island in 1796. There are also tropically inspired items, such as menorahs painted to resemble palm trees. ⊠ *15 Crystal Gade* ☎ *340/774–4312* 🖻 *Free* ⊙ *Weekdays 9–4.*

EAST END

Although the eastern end has many major resorts and spectacular beaches, don't be surprised if a cow or a herd of goats crosses your path as you drive through the relatively flat, dry terrain. You can pick up sandwiches from a deli in the Red Hook area if you want a picnic lunch.

☺ **Coral World Ocean Park.** This interactive aquarium and water-sports cen-
Fodor's Choice ★ ter lets you experience a variety of sea life and other animals up close and personal. Coral World has an offshore underwater observatory, an 80,000-gallon coral reef exhibit, and 21 jewel aquariums displaying the Virgin Islands' coral reef habitats and unusual marine life. The park also has several outdoor pools where you can pet baby sharks, feed stingrays, touch starfish, and view endangered sea turtles. Daily feedings take place at most exhibits.

In addition, the park operates several activities, both above and below the water. The Sea Trek Helmet Dive allows you to walk along an underwater trail with a high-tech helmet that provides a continuous supply of air (and which keeps your head dry). Snuba, a cross between Scuba and snorkeling, allows you to snorkel deeper underwater connected to the top by an air hose rather than carrying your air on your back as you would when diving. Shark and Turtle Encounter programs let you observe these fascinating animals as they swim around you. Get a big, wet, whiskered kiss while taking a swim in the sea lion pool, or choose to have a personal encounter with a sea lion on dry land. Buy a cup of nectar and let the friendly, rainbow-colored lorikeets perch on your hand and drink. Finally, the Nautilus semi-submersible allows

CLOSE UP

In Search of Pirates

The line between fact and fiction is often fluid, and it ebbs and flows according to who is telling the tale. So it is with the swashbuckling seafarers of St. Thomas such as Bluebeard, Blackbeard, and Sir Francis Drake. But you'll find the story—we don't promise that it's completely true—if you follow the pirate trail.

Start atop Bluebeard's Hill to the east of Charlotte Amalie. Today this is the site of Bluebeard's Castle hotel. According to legend, it was Bluebeard—in reality Eduard de Barbe-Bleue—who picked this prime location to build a stone watchtower from which he could keep an eye on approaching enemies. Bluebeard kept his most prized booty, the lovely Señorita Mercedes, prisoner in the tower. That is, of course, until Mercedes broke free and discovered his gold-filled treasure chests along with gushing love letters to several other young ladies. Just as mean as her mate, Mercedes invited all of Bluebeard's paramours to the tower to pillage his plunder. Today you can walk the hotel grounds, gaze up at the still-standing watchtower, and enjoy an incredible view of the harbor. From this outlook you can spot yet another pirate-named tower.

High atop Blackbeard's Hill, rising north of Fort Christian and Government House, is Blackbeard's Castle.

No one knows if Blackbeard—better known as Edward Teach—ever visited this site, but historians agree that this infamous pirate did indeed sail the Caribbean Sea in the early 18th century. Learn all about Teach and his treacherous band via guided tours that take place between 9 and 3 when a cruise ship is in port. The cost is $20 per person for a guided tour, $12 for a self-guided tour. Life-size—and lifelike—statues of pirates dot the route and look ready to issue an "Argh," "Aye," and "Ahoy, matey!"

Drive over the hill to Drake's Seat. Named for the English privateer Sir Francis Drake, this popular scenic overlook is supposedly where Drake spied ships approaching from what are now the British Virgin Islands. Don't let anyone tell you that the wooden bench is where Drake sat, however. Scholars have a hard enough time trying to prove that Drake really stood on this spot.

Finally, head back into downtown Charlotte Amalie and to Royal Dane Mall. This winding trio of brick-and-stone-paved alleyways is home to a couple of bronze plaques inscribed with historical facts about the island. One of them tells about buried pirate treasure. Some doubt it's really here. Others never stop dreaming of the day they'll find it.

---

you to look at the abundant sea life and coral reefs around Coki Point from a depth of 8 feet in air-conditioned comfort without ever leaving the vessel, which has underwater observation windows but stays on the surface. ⊠ *Coki Point north of Rte. 38, Estate Frydendal* ☎ *340/775–1555* ⊕ *www.coralworldvi.com* 🎫 *$19, Sea Lion Swim $105, Sea Lion Encounter $65, Sea Trek $58, Snuba $52, Shark and Turtle Encounters $32, Nautilus $20* ☉ *Daily 9–4. Off-season (May–Oct.) hours may vary so call to confirm.*

Coral World Ocean Park offers interactive sea life encounters.

Red Hook. In this nautical center there are fishing and sailing charter boats, dive shops, and powerboat-rental agencies at the American Yacht Harbor marina. There are also several bars and restaurants, including Molly Molone's, Duffy's Love Shack, and the Caribbean Saloon. One grocery store and a deli offer picnic fixings—from sliced meats and cheeses to rotisserie-roasted chickens, prepared salads, burritos, and freshly baked breads. Ferries depart from Red Hook en route to St. John and the British Virgin Islands.

SOUTH SHORE

Butterfly Garden. Coral World has reopened the former Butterfly Farm at Havensight, which had closed for the second half of 2010 for a renovation between owners. Take a guided tour through this tropical garden wonderland where hundreds of beautiful butterflies from around the world fly freely all around you. Discover the fascinating life cycle of the butterfly—from meandering caterpillar to fluttering, winged insect. Marvel at the beauty of their colorful winged markings and the uniqueness of their various shapes and sizes. A bird show is included in admission. The gift shop sells unique butterfly jewelry and souvenirs. ⊠ *Havensight Mall, adjacent to the West Indian Company cruise ship dock, Havensight* ☎ *340/715–3366* ✉ *$15* ☉ *Daily 8:30–4. Off-season (May–Oct.) hours may vary so call to confirm.*

Compass Point Marina. It's fun to park your car and walk around this marina. The boaters—many of whom have sailed here from points around the globe—are easy to engage in conversation. Turn south off

Route 32 at the well-marked entrance road just east of Independent Boat Yard. ⊠ *Estate Frydenhoj.*

Frenchtown. Popular for its bars and restaurants, Frenchtown is also the home of descendants of immigrants from St. Barthélemy (St. Barths). You can watch them pull up their brightly painted boats and display their equally colorful catch of the day along the waterfront. If you chat with them, you can hear speech patterns slightly different from those of other St. Thomians. Get a feel for the residential district of Frenchtown by walking west to some of the town's winding streets, where tiny wooden houses have been passed down from generation to generation. ✛ *Turn south off Waterfront Hwy. at post office.*

French Heritage Museum. Next to Joseph Aubain Ballpark, the museum houses artifacts such as fishing nets, accordions, tambourines, mahogany furniture, and historic photographs that illustrate the lives of the French descendants during the 18th through 20th centuries. Admission is free, but donations are accepted. ⊠ *Intersection of rue de St. Anne and rue de St. Barthélemy* ☎ *340/774–2320* ✉ *Free* ⊗ *Mon.–Sat. 9–6.*

☺ ★ **St. Thomas Skyride.** Fly skyward in a gondola to Paradise Point, an overlook with breathtaking views of Charlotte Amalie and the harbor. There are several shops, a bar, a restaurant, and a wedding gazebo; kids enjoy the tropical bird show held daily at 10:30 am and 1:30 pm. A ¼-mi (½-km) hiking trail leads to spectacular views of St. Croix. Wear sturdy shoes, as the trail is steep and rocky. ⊠ *Rte. 30, across from Havensight Mall, Havensight* ☎ *340/774–9809* ✉ *$21; Sky Jump $30* ⊗ *Thurs.–Tues. 9–5, Wed. 9–9.*

WEST END

The west end of the island is lusher and quieter—fewer houses and less traffic. Here there are roller-coaster routes (made all the scarier because the roads have no shoulders) but also incredible vistas. Leave time in the afternoon for a swim. Enjoy a slice of pizza at Magens Bay. A day in the country will reveal the tropical pleasures that have enticed more than one visitor to become a resident.

☺ **Drake's Seat.** Sir Francis Drake was supposed to have kept watch over his fleet and looked for enemy ships from this vantage point. The panorama is especially breathtaking (and romantic) at dusk, and if you arrive late in the day, you can miss the hordes of day-trippers on taxi tours who stop here to take a picture and buy a T-shirt from one of the many vendors. ⊠ *Rte. 40, Estate Zufriedenheit.*

Estate St. Peter Greathouse and Botanical Gardens. This unusual spot is perched on a mountainside 1,000 feet above sea level, with views of more than 20 islands and islets. You can wander through a gallery displaying local art, sip a complimentary rum punch while looking out at the view, or follow a nature trail that leads you past nearly 70 varieties of tropical plants, including 17 varieties of orchids. ⊠ *Rte. 40, Estate St. Peter* ☎ *340/774–4999* ⊕ *www.greathousevi.com* ✉ *$5* ⊗ *Mon.–Sat. 8–4.*

☺ **Mountain Top.** Rebuilt and reopened in January 2011 after a devas-
★ tating fire that destroyed the structure in May 2009, St. Thomas's
famous viewpoint is once again a good place to sip a banana daiquiri
and see spectacular views. Head out to the observation deck—more
than 1,500 feet above sea level—to get a bird's-eye view that stretches
from Puerto Rico's out-island of Culebra in the west all the way to
the British Virgin Islands in the east. There's also a restaurant, restrooms, and shops that sell everything from Caribbean art to nautical
antiques, ship models, and touristy T-shirts. Kids will like talking to
the parrots—and hearing them answer back. ⚓ *Head north off Rte.
33, look for signs, Mountain Top* ⊕ *www.greathouse-mountaintop.
com* ☒ *Free* ☺ *Daily 8–5.*

BEACHES

All 44 St. Thomas beaches are open to the public, although you can
reach some of them only by walking through a resort. Hotel guests
frequently have access to lounge chairs and floats that are off-limits to
nonguests; for this reason, you may feel more comfortable at one of
the beaches not associated with a resort, such as Magens Bay (which
charges an entrance fee to cover beach maintenance) or Coki Beach.
Whichever one you choose, remember to remove your valuables from
the car and keep them out of sight when you go swimming.

☺ **Coki Beach.** Funky beach huts selling local foods such as meat pate
Fodor's Choice (fried turnovers with a spicy ground-beef filling), picnic tables topped
★ with umbrellas sporting beverage logos, and a brigade of hair braiders
and taxi men give this beach overlooking picturesque Thatch Cay a
Coney Island feel. But this is the best place on the island to snorkel
and scuba dive. Fish, including grunts, snappers, and wrasses, are like
an effervescent cloud you can wave your hand through. Ashore you
can find conveniences such as restrooms and changing facilities, both
of which received a much-needed renovation in 2010. There are also
beefed up security and regular police patrols in the area after a shoot-
ing incident in 2010. ☒ *Rte. 388, next to Coral World Ocean Park.*

Lindquist Beach. The newest of the Virgin Islands' public beaches has a
serene sense of wilderness that isn't found on the more crowded beaches.
A lifeguard is on duty between 8 am and 5 pm. Picnic tables and restrooms are available. Try snorkeling over the offshore reef. There's a $2
per person entrance fee. ☒ *Rte. 38, at end of a bumpy dirt road.*

★ **Sapphire Beach.** A steady breeze makes this beach a boardsailor's paradise. The swimming is great, as is the snorkeling, especially at the reef
near Pettyklip Point. Beach volley-
ball is big on the weekends. Sapphire Beach Resort and Marina has
a snack shop, bar, and water-sports
rentals. ☒ *Rte. 38, Sapphire Bay.*

Secret Harbour. Placid waters make
it easy to stroke your way out to
a swim platform offshore from the

DID YOU KNOW?

While driving on the left side is
the rule on St. Thomas, steering
wheels are not on the right. That's
because most cars are imported
from the United States.

Secret Harbour Beach Resort & Villas. Nearby reefs give snorkelers a natural show. There's a bar and restaurant, as well as a dive shop. ⊠ *Rte. 32, Red Hook.*

Vessup Beach. This wild, undeveloped beach is lined with sea grape trees and century plants. It's close to Red Hook harbor, so you can watch the ferries depart. Calm

waters are excellent for swimming. West Indies Windsurfing is here, so you can rent Windsurfers, kayaks, and other water toys. There are no restrooms or changing facilities. It's popular with locals on weekends. ⊠ *Off Rte. 322, Vessup Bay.*

Brewer's Beach. Watch jets land at the Cyril E. King Airport as you dip into the usually calm seas. Rocks at either end of the shoreline, patches of grass poking randomly through the sand, and shady tamarind trees 30 feet from the water give this beach a wild, natural feel. Civilization has arrived, as one or two mobile food vans park on the nearby road. Buy a fried-chicken leg and johnnycake or burgers and chips to munch on at the picnic tables. ⊠ *Rte. 30, west of University of the Virgin Islands.*

Morningstar Beach. Nature and nurture combine at this ¼-mi-long (½-km-long) beach between Marriott Frenchman's Reef and Morning Star Beach Resorts, where amenities range from water-sports rentals to beachside bar service. A concession rents floating mats, snorkeling equipment, sailboards, and Jet Skis. Swimming is excellent; there are good-size rolling waves year-round, but do watch the undertow. If you're feeling lazy, rent a lounge chair with umbrella and order a libation from one of two full-service beach bars. At 7 am and again at 5 pm, watch the cruise ships glide majestically out to sea from the Charlotte Amalie harbor. ⊠ *Rte. 315, 2 mi (3 km) southeast of Charlotte Amalie, past Havensight Mall and cruise-ship dock.*

Hull Bay. Watch surfers ride the waves here from December to March, when huge swells roll in from north Atlantic storms. The rest of the year, tranquillity prevails at this picturesque neighborhood beach. Enjoy hot pizza, barbecue ribs, and a game of darts at the Hull Bay Hideaway Bar & Restaurant, home of the annual Bastille Day Kingfish Tournament held each July. ⊠ *Rte. 37, at end of road on north side.*

☺
Fodor'sChoice
★
Magens Bay. Deeded to the island as a public park, this heart-shaped stretch of white sand is considered one of the most beautiful in the world. The bottom of the bay is flat and sandy, so this is a place for sunning and swimming rather than snorkeling. On weekends and holidays the sounds of music from groups partying under the sheds fill the air. There's a bar, snack shack, and beachwear boutique; bathhouses with restrooms, changing rooms, and saltwater showers are close by. Sunfish and paddleboats are the most popular rentals at the water-sports kiosk. East of the beach is Udder Delight, a one-room shop that serves a Virgin Islands tradition—a milk shake with a splash of Cruzan

rum. Kids can enjoy virgin versions, which have a touch of soursop, mango, or banana flavoring. If you arrive between 8 am and 5 pm, you pay an entrance fee of $4 per person, $2 per vehicle; it's free for children under 12. ⊠ *Rte. 35, at end of road on north side of island.*

WHERE TO EAT

Restaurants are spread all over the island, although fewer are found in the west and northwest sections. Most restaurants out of town are easily accessible by taxi and have ample parking. If you dine in Charlotte Amalie, take a taxi. Parking close to restaurants can be difficult to find, and walking around after dark isn't advisable for safety reasons.

Dining on St. Thomas is informal. Few restaurants require a jacket and tie. Still, at dinner in the snazzier places shorts and T-shirts are inappropriate; men would do well to wear slacks and a shirt with buttons. Dress codes on St. Thomas rarely require women to wear skirts, but you can never go wrong with something flowing.

For approximate costs, see the dining and lodging price chart at the beginning of this chapter.

CHARLOTTE AMALIE

$$$$
ECLECTIC
Fodor's Choice
★

✕ **Banana Tree Grille.** The eagle's-eye view of the Charlotte Amalie harbor from this breeze-cooled restaurant is as fantastic as the food. Linen tablecloths, china, and silver place settings combine with subdued lighting to create an elegant feel. To start, try the "seafood cocktail" of lobster, shrimp, scallops, and squid marinated in a savory herb vinaigrette. The signature dish here—and worthy of its fame—is Chef Patrick Bellantoni's New York sirloin seasoned simply with olive oil and garlic and grilled to order. Arrive before 6 pm and watch the cruise ships depart from the harbor while you enjoy a drink at the bar. ⊠ *Bluebeard's Castle, Bluebeard's Hill* ☎ *340/776–4050* ⊕ *www.bananatreegrille.com* ⚏ *Reservations essential* ☾ *Closed Mon. No lunch.*

$$
JAPANESE

✕ **Beni Iguana's Sushi Bar and Restaurant.** Edible art is an apt description for the sushi and sashimi feast that draws visitors and locals alike. The 5-foot-tall reef tank will definitely put you in the mood for seafood. There are nearly 30 vegetarian and seafood rolls to choose from, including avocado, spicy crab, and red snapper. The real favorite here is steamed mussels in a house-made creamy sesame dressing dubbed "iguana sauce," which is, happily, not made from the spiny reptile that roams the island's hillsides and roadways. ⊠ *Havensight Mall, Bldg. IX* ☎ *340/777–8744.*

$$$$
SPANISH
★

✕ **Café Amalia.** A great place to take a break and get a bite while shopping, this open-air café tucked into the alleyway of Palm Passage is owned by Antiguan-born Randolph Maynard and his German wife Helga, and they serve authentic Spanish cuisine. Try tapas such as mussels in brandy sauce, escargots with mushrooms and herb butter, or Galician-style octopus and baby eels served in a sizzling garlic sauce. Paella is a house specialty, as is the caramel flan. Ask for an inside table

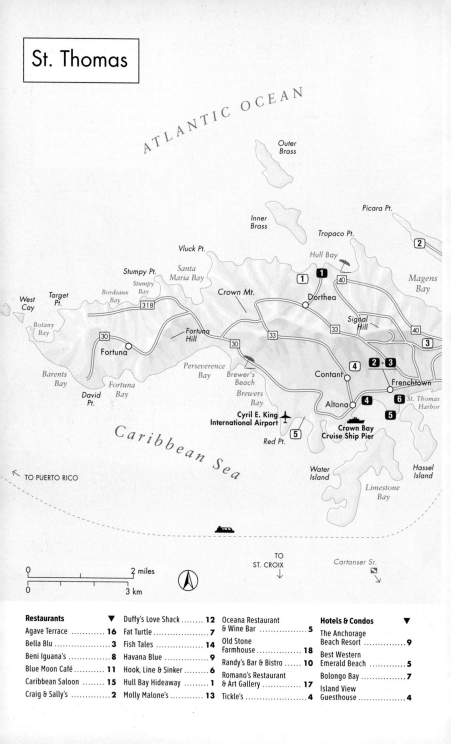

St. Thomas

ATLANTIC OCEAN

Outer Brass

Inner Brass

Picara Pt.

Tropaco Pt.

Vluck Pt.

Hull Bay

Stumpy Pt.

Santa Maria Bay

Stumpy Bay

Bordeaux Bay

Crown Mt.

Magens Bay

⓵ 🄷

40

Dorthea

Signal Hill

West Cay

Target Pt.

318

Fortuna Hill

Botany Bay

30

33

33

40

Fortuna

30

⓷

Barents Bay

Fortuna Bay

Perseverence Bay

Brewer's Beach

⓸ 🄷2 · 🄷3

Contant

Frenchtown

David Pt.

Brewers Bay

🄷4

⓺ St. Thomas Harbor

Cyril E. King International Airport ✈

Altona

Crown Bay Cruise Ship Pier 🛳

🄷5

⓹

Red Pt.

Water Island

Hassel Island

Caribbean Sea

Limestone Bay

← TO PUERTO RICO

🄷2

🄷3

0 —————— 2 miles
0 —————— 3 km

TO ST. CROIX ↓

Cartanser Sr. ◺ ↘

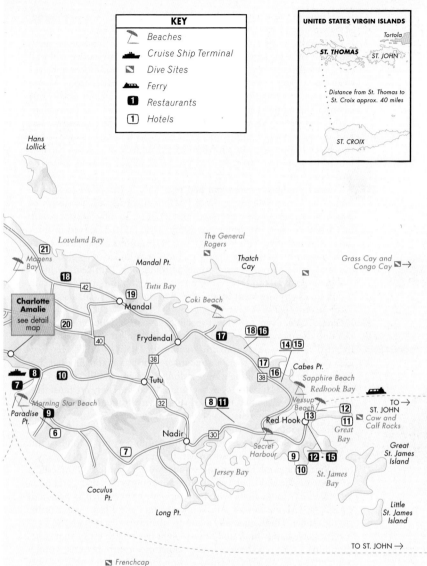

KEY

- Beaches
- Cruise Ship Terminal
- Dive Sites
- Ferry
- **1** Restaurants
- 1 Hotels

UNITED STATES VIRGIN ISLANDS

Tortola

ST. THOMAS ST. JOHN

Distance from St. Thomas to
St. Croix approx. 40 miles

ST. CROIX

Hans
Lollick

Lovelund Bay

The General
Rogers

Grass Cay and
Congo Cay

Magens
Bay

Mandal Pt.

Thatch
Cay

Charlotte
Amalie
see detail
map

Tutu Bay

Coki Beach

Mandal

Frydendal

Cabes Pt.

Sapphire Beach

Redhook Bay

Tutu

Morning Star Beach

Vessup
Beach

TO →
ST. JOHN

Paradise
Pt.

Nadir

Red Hook

Cow and
Calf Rocks

Great
Bay

Great
St. James
Island

Secret
Harbour

Jersey Bay

St. James
Bay

Little
St. James
Island

Coculus
Pt.

Long Pt.

TO ST. JOHN →

Frenchcap

if the idea of passersby checking out your meal isn't too appetizing. ⊠ *Palm Passage, 24 Dronnigens Gade* ☎ *340/714–7373.*

$$ ✗ **Café Amici.** Within the historic stonework and cascading tropical
ITALIAN blossoms of A.H. Riise Alley, this charming open-air eatery will pull you in by the nose and send you straight to the wood-burning brick-oven pizza. Toppings range from everyday to eclectic, from Asiago cheese and portobello mushrooms to tandoori chicken and clams casino. The menu is not all pizza: there are fresh salads (tamarind-barbecued shrimp salad is a definite winner), open-faced sandwiches, and unique pastas made to order. The local business crowd keeps this place hopping for lunch Monday through Friday, so go early or late to be sure of a table. ⊠ *37 Main St.* ☎ *340/776–0444* ⊙ *Closed Sun. No dinner.*

$$$ ✗ **Cuzzin's Caribbean Restaurant and Bar.** This is the place to sample
CARIBBEAN bona fide Virgin Islands cuisine. For lunch, order tender slivers of conch stewed in a rich onion-and-butter sauce, savory braised oxtail, or curried chicken. At dinner the island-style mutton, served in thick gravy and seasoned with locally grown herbs, offers a tasty treat that's deliciously different. Side dishes include peas and rice, boiled green bananas, fried plantains, and potato stuffing. In a 19th-century livery stable on Back Street, this restaurant is hard to find but well worth it if you like sampling local foods. ⊠ *7 Wimmelskafts Gade, also called Back St.* ☎ *340/777–4711.*

$$ ✗ **Gladys' Café.** Even if the local specialties—conch in butter sauce, salt
CARIBBEAN fish and dumplings, hearty red bean soup—didn't make this a recom-
Fodor'sChoice mended café, it would be worth coming for Gladys's smile. Her cozy
★ alleyway restaurant is rich in atmosphere with its mahogany bar and native stone walls, making dining a double delight. While you're here, pick up a $5 or $10 bottle of her special hot sauce. There are mustard-, oil and vinegar–, and tomato-based versions; the tomato-based sauce is the hottest. Only Amex is accepted. ⊠ *Waterfront at Royal Dane Mall* ☎ *340/774–6604* ⊙ *No dinner.*

$$ ✗ **Greenhouse Bar and Restaurant.** The hip and hip-at-heart come to this
AMERICAN bustling waterfront restaurant to eat, listen to music, and play games,
☾ both video and pool. Even the most finicky eater should find something to please on the eight-page menu that offers burgers, salads, and pizza served all day long, along with more upscale entrées such as peel-and-eat shrimp, Maine lobster, Alaskan king crab, and Black Angus prime rib for dinner. This is generally a family-friendly place, though the Two-for-Tuesdays happy hour and Friday-night live reggae music that starts thumping at 10 pm draw a lively, sometimes rambunctious, young-adult crowd. ⊠ *Waterfront Hwy. at Storetvaer Gade* ☎ *340/774–7998* ⊕ *www.thegreenhouserestaurant.com.*

$ ✗ **Jen's Gourmet Café and Deli.** This hole-in-the-wall eatery is the closest
AMERICAN thing you can find to a New York–style Jewish deli. Choose the smoked
Fodor'sChoice salmon platter for breakfast or hot pastrami on rye at lunch. Home-
★ made desserts like chocolate layer cake, apple strudel, and peaches-and-cream-cheese strudel are yummy. There's no parking nearby, so come on foot or by cab. ⊠ *Grand Galleria, 43–46 Norre Gade* ☎ *340/777–4611* ⊕ *www.jensdeli.com* ⊙ *Closed Sun. No dinner.*

CLOSE UP

Where to Shop for Groceries

High food prices in Virgin Islands supermarkets are enough to dull anyone's appetite. According to a report by the U.S. Virgin Islands Department of Labor, food is significantly more expensive than on the mainland.

Although you'll never match the prices back home, you can shop around for the best deals. If you're traveling with a group, it pays to stock up on the basics at warehouse-style stores like Pricesmart (membership required) and Cost-U-Less. Even the nonbulk food items here are sold at lower prices than in the supermarkets or convenience stores. Good buys include beverages, meats, produce, and spirits.

After this, head to supermarkets such as Plaza Extra, Pueblo, and Food Center. Although the prices aren't as good as at the big-box stores, the selection is better.

Finally, if you want to splurge on top-quality meats, exotic produce and spices, and imported cheeses and spirits, finish off your shopping at high-end shops such as Marina Market or Gourmet Gallery.

The Fruit Bowl is the place for fresh produce. The prices and selection are unbeatable.

For really fresh tropical fruits, vegetables, and seasoning herbs, visit the farmers' markets in Smith Bay (daily), at Market Square (daily), at Yacht Haven Grande (first and third Sunday of the month), and in Estate Bordeaux (last Sunday of every month).

$$
BARBECUE
✕**Texas Pit BBQ.** The smell of smoky barbecue ribs, beef brisket, and chicken wafts enticingly from these mobile stands, which set up daily around 4 pm. Austin native and longtime Virgin Islands resident Bill Collins perfected his signature sauce, which received a thumbs-up from the late culinary great James Beard. Your choice of homemade seasoned rice, coleslaw, or potato salad completes the meal. There's no seating, but you can always head over to the nearest beach and make it a picnic. Besides the two Charlotte Amalie branches, you can also find one at the northern end of Red Hook Shopping Center. ⊠ *Waterfront, across from Windward Passage Hotel* ☎ *340/776–9579* ▬ *No credit cards* ⊗ *No lunch. Closed Sun.* ⊠ *Wheatley Center* ☎ *340/714–5775* ▬ *No credit cards* ⊗ *Closed Sun.*

$$$$
ITALIAN
★
✕**Virgilio's.** For the island's best northern Italian cuisine, don't miss this intimate, elegant hideaway tucked on a quiet side street. Eclectic art covers the two-story brick walls, and the sound of opera sets the stage for a memorable meal. Come here for more than 40 homemade pastas topped with superb sauces—capellini with fresh tomatoes and garlic or peasant-style spaghetti in a rich tomato sauce with mushrooms and prosciutto. House specialties include osso buco and tiramisu—expertly crafted by chef Ernesto Garrigos, who has prepared these two dishes on the Discovery Channel's *Great Chefs of the World* series. ⊠ *18 Main St.* ☎ *340/776–4920* ⚸ *Reservations essential* ⊗ *Closed Sun.*

EAST END

$$$$ ✕ **Agave Terrace.** The freshest fish is what reels in the customers to
SEAFOOD this open-air restaurant in the Point Pleasant Resort. The catch of
the day—a steak or a fillet—is served with choices of a dozen sauces,
including teriyaki-mango and lime-ginger. If you get lucky on a sportfishing day charter, the chef will cook your fish if you bring it in by 3
pm. Come early and have a drink at the Lookout Lounge, which has
breathtaking views of the British Virgins. ⊠ *Point Pleasant Resort,
Rte. 38, Estate Smith Bay* ☎ *340/775–4142* ⊕ *www.agaveterrace.com*
🌣 *No lunch.*

$$$ ✕ **Blue Moon Café.** Watch the serene scene of sailboats floating at anchor
AMERICAN while supping; sunsets are especially spectacular here. Enjoy French toast
☕ topped with toasted coconut for breakfast, a grilled mahimahi sandwich
with black olive–caper mayonnaise at lunch, or grilled Long Island duck
breast marinated in lime juice and Cruzan spiced rum for dinner. No-see-
ums, nearly invisible insects with a fierce bite, can be bothersome here
at sunset, so bring bug spray. ⊠ *Secret Harbour Beach Resort, Rte. 32,
Red Hook* ☎ *340/779–2080* ⊕ *www.bluemooncafevi.com.*

$$$ ✕ **Caribbean Saloon.** Dine casually, watch sports on wide-screen TVs,
AMERICAN and listen to live music on the weekends at this hip sports bar that's in
the center of the action in Red Hook. The menu ranges from finger-
licking barbecue ribs to more sophisticated fare such as the signature
filet mignon wrapped in bacon and smothered in melted Gorgonzola
cheese. There's always a catch of the day; the fishing fleet is only steps
away. A late-night menu is available from 10 pm until 4 am. ⊠ *Rte.
32 at American Yacht Harbor, Bldg B., Red Hook* ☎ *340/775–7060*
⊕ *www.caribbeansaloon.com.*

$$ ✕ **Duffy's Love Shack.** If the floating bubbles don't attract you to this
ECLECTIC zany eatery, the lime-green shutters, loud rock music, and fun-loving
waitstaff just might. It's billed as the "ultimate tropical drink shack,"
and the bartenders shake up such exotic concoctions as the Love Shack
Volcano—a 50-ounce flaming extravaganza. The menu has a selec-
tion of burgers, tacos, burritos, and salads. Try the grilled mahimahi
taco salad or jerk Caesar wrap. Wednesday night is usually a theme
party complete with giveaways. ⊠ *Rte. 32, Red Hook* ☎ *340/779–2080*
⊕ *www.duffysloveshack.com* ▭ *No credit cards.*

$$$ ✕ **Fish Tales.** The owners of this restaurant also own a sportfishing oper-
☕ ation, so you know the local fish like tuna, wahoo, mahimahi, and
SEAFOOD "ole wife" (a local white fish) is definitely fresh. The real deal is the
daily Happy Hour from 3 to 6 pm, when you can order fresh oysters
on the half shell for $14 per dozen or $7 per half-dozen. Save room
for the signature Fisherman's Platter—a half-pound each of Alaskan
king crab legs, Dungeness crab, shrimp, and Andouille sausage—which
you can order for lunch or dinner. Farm-raised catfish, three types of
Po Boys (shrimp, oyster, and scallop), and housemade Key lime pie
are all winners. There's also a children's menu. ⊠ *Rte. 32, Red Hook*
☎ *340/714–3188.*

$$$ ✕ **Molly Molone's.** This dockside eatery has a devoted following among
IRISH local boaters, who swear by the traditional American and Irish fare. Opt
☕ for eggs Benedict or rashers of Irish sausages and eggs for breakfast, or

fork into fish-and-chips, Irish stew, or bangers and mash (sausage and mashed potatoes) for lunch or dinner. Beware: the resident iguanas will beg for table scraps—bring your camera. ⊠ *Rte. 32 at American Yacht Harbor, Bldg. D, Red Hook* ☎ *340/775–1270.*

$$$$
ECLECTIC
Fodor's Choice
★
✕ **Old Stone Farmhouse.** Dine in the splendor of a beautifully restored plantation house. Come early and sidle up to the beautiful mahogany bar, where you can choose from an extensive wine list. Then, spoon into French onion soup as an appetizer; move on to executive chef–owner Greg Engelhardt's braised Angus beef short ribs paired with a sautéed local Caribbean lobster tail; and finish with a decadent bananas Foster. Personalized attention makes dining here a delight. ⊠ *Rte. 42, 1 mi (1½ km) west of entrance to Mahogany Run Golf Course, Estate Lovenlund* ☎ *340/777–6277* ⊕ *www.oldstonefarmhouse.com* ⌫ *Reservations essential* ⊗ *Closed Mon.*

$$$$
ITALIAN
★
✕ **Romano's Restaurant and Art Gallery.** Inside this huge old stucco house, superb northern Italian cuisine is served in dining rooms where the walls are lined with whimsical works of art painted by doubly talented owner–chef Tony Romano. Try the pastas, either with a classic ragout or with one of Tony's more unique creations, such as a cream sauce with mushrooms, prosciutto, pine nuts, and Parmesan. There's classic osso bucco and veal scaloppini, too. If you like the food here, know that Romano also offers his personal chef services at villas and condos. ⊠ *Rte. 388 at Coki Point, Estate Frydendal* ☎ *340/775–0045* ⊕ *www.romanosrestaurant.com* ⌫ *Reservations essential* ⊗ *Closed Sun. No lunch.*

SOUTH SHORE

$$$$
ECLECTIC
✕ **Fat Turtle.** Graze on local lobster, burgers, and salads, as well as pizza baked in a stone-floored oven while gazing at the million-dollar megayachts docked right next to this hip seaside eatery. Even if you aren't hungry, stop here on Friday nights for the DJ Dance Party and Laser Light Show. ⊠ *5403 Yacht Haven Grande, Havensight* ☎ *340/714–3566* ⊕ *www.fat-turtle.com.*

$$$$
ECLECTIC
Fodor's Choice
★
✕ **Havana Blue.** The cuisine here is described as Cuban-Asian, but the dining experience is out of this world. A glowing wall of water meets you as you enter, and then you're seated at a table laid with linen and silver that's illuminated in a soft blue light radiating from above. Be sure to sample the mango mojito, made with fresh mango, crushed mint, and limes. Entrées include coconut-chipotle ceviche, sugarcane-glazed pork tenderloin medallions, and the signature dish, miso sea bass. Hand-rolled cigars and aged rums finish the night off in true Cuban style. For something really special, request an exclusive table for two set on Morning Star Beach—you get a seven-course tasting menu, champagne, and your own personal waiter, all for $350 for two. ⊠ *Marriott Morningstar Beach Resort, Rte. 315, Estate Bakkeroe* ☎ *340/715–2583* ⊕ *www.havanabluerestaurant.com* ⌫ *Reservations essential* ⊗ *No lunch.*

$$$$
ECLECTIC
★
✕ **Randy's Bar and Bistro.** There's no view here—even though you're at the top of a hill—but the somewhat hidden location has helped to keep this one of the island's best dining secrets. This wine shop and deli caters to a local lunch crowd. At night, you forget you're tucked

into a nearly windowless building. The tableside bread for starters is a thick, crusty focaccia flavored with nearly 10 different vegetables. Try the Brie-stuffed filet mignon or the rack of lamb. After-dinner cigars and wine complete the experience. ⊠ *Al Cohen's Plaza, atop Raphune Hill, ½ mi (¾ km) east of Charlotte Amalie* ☎ *340/777–3199.*

$ ✕ **Texas Pit BBQ.** The smell of smoky barbecue ribs, beef brisket, and
BARBECUE chicken wafts enticingly from these mobile stands, which set up daily
Ⓒ around 4 pm. Austin native and longtime Virgin Islands resident Bill Collins perfected his signature sauce, which received a thumbs-up from the late culinary great James Beard. Your choice of homemade seasoned rice, coleslaw, or potato salad completes the meal. There's no seating, but you can always head over to the nearest beach and make it a picnic. Besides the Red Hook branch, there are also two branches in Charlotte Amalie. ⊠ *Red Hook Plaza, Red Hook* ☎ *340/774–0610* ▭ *No credit cards* ⊘ *No lunch. Closed Sun.*

WEST END

$$$$ ✕ **Bella Blu.** In a quaint building in Frenchtown, this place has an ever-
MEDITERRANEAN changing display of local art on the walls and delicious specials to
Ⓒ match. Alexander Treml's Mediterranean-inspired menu includes an appetizer platter of hummus, baba ghanoush, and lentils and cracked-wheat fritters served with yogurt sauce. Entrées include such treats as lamb tagine and saffron-and-Parmesan risotto. As a salute to his homeland, Austria-born Treml always has a schnitzel or two on the menu. Lunchtime attracts a business crowd that breaks bread and brokers deals at the same time. ⊠ *Frenchtown Mall, 24-A Honduras St., Frenchtown* ☎ *340/774–4349* ⊘ *Closed Sun.*

$$$$ ✕ **Craig and Sally's.** In the heart of Frenchtown, culinary wizard Sally
ECLECTIC Darash shows off her tasty creativity by never duplicating a menu. Her
Fodor's Choice inspiration is pure local; it may start when a French fisherman shows up
★ on her doorstep with a fish wiggling at the end of his speargun or when a community matriarch brings by bunches of fresh basil and thyme. The result may be a yellowfin tuna ceviche or roasted eggplant cheese-cake with a basil chiffonade. Husband Craig, who has a wry humor, maintains a 300-bottle wine list that's won accolades. ⊠ *22 Honduras St., Frenchtown* ☎ *340/777–9949* ⊕ *www.craigandsallys.com* ⊘ *Closed Mon. and Tues. No lunch weekends.*

$$$ ✕ **Hook, Line and Sinker.** Anchored right on the breezy Frenchtown water-
SEAFOOD front, adjacent to the pastel-painted boats of the local fishing fleet, this
Ⓒ harbor-view eatery serves high-quality fish dishes. The almond-crusted yellowtail snapper is a house specialty. Spicy jerk-seasoned swordfish and grilled tuna topped with a yummy mango-rum sauce are also good bets. This is one of the few independent restaurants serving Sunday brunch. ⊠ *Frenchtown Mall, 2 Honduras St., Frenchtown* ☎ *340/776–9708* ⊕ *www.hooklineandsinkervi.com.*

$$ ✕ **Hull Bay Hideaway.** Here you can find live bands (think rock and
AMERICAN roll and reggae), pool tables, dart tournaments, burgers, barbecue ribs,
Ⓒ chicken, fresh fish, and a fully-stocked bar just steps away from the beach. This family-friendly open-air bar and restaurant is the unofficial home of the Northside French commercial fishing fleet and home of the

Annual Bastille Day Kingfish Tournament in July. ⊠ *Rte. 37, at the end of the road, Estate Hull Bay* ☎ *340/777–1898.*

$$$$
ECLECTIC

✕ **Oceana Restaurant and Wine Bar.** In the old Russian consulate great house at the tip of the Frenchtown peninsula, this restaurant offers superb views along with fresh seafood dishes expertly prepared by longtime Virgin Islands chef Patricia LaCourte and her staff. Specialties include a pan-seared sea bass served on a saffron risotto cake with white-truffle butter, as well as bouillabaisse chockfull of mussels, manila clams, shrimp, and Caribbean lobster simmered in a tomato-saffron broth. Walk off a big meal with a five-minute stroll into nearby Frenchtown, where several bars have a DJ or live music on the weekends. ⊠ *Villa Olga, Frenchtown* ☎ *340/774–4262* ⊕ *www.oceana.vi* ⊗ *No dinner Sun.*

$$
AMERICAN
☺

✕ **Tickle's Dockside Pub.** Nautical types as well as the local working crowd come here for casual fare with homey appeal: chicken-fried steak, meat loaf with mashed potatoes, and baby back ribs. Hearty breakfasts feature eggs and pancakes, and lunch is a full array of burgers, salads, sandwiches, and soups. From November through April, the adjacent marina is full of megayachts that make for some great eye candy while you dine. ⊠ *Crown Bay Marina, Rte. 304, Estate Contant* ☎ *340/776–1595* ⊕ *www.ticklesdocksidepub.com.*

WHERE TO STAY

The island's first hotels were all based in Charlotte Amalie, the hub of action at the time. Most people choose lodgings here to be close to the airport, to experience the charm of the historic district, or for convenience when on business. Over the years, tourism has trickled eastward, and today the major hotel chains have perched their properties on the beach. Those who want a self-contained resort that feels like an island unto itself head here. The location of these resorts makes island-hopping to St. John or the British Virgin Islands a breeze. Private villas dot the island, especially in the less populated north.

For approximate costs, see the dining and lodging price chart at the beginning of this chapter. The following hotel reviews have been condensed for this book. Please go to Fodors.com for expanded reviews of each property.

PRIVATE VILLAS AND CONDOMINIUMS

St. Thomas has a wide range of private villas, from modest two-bedroom houses to luxurious five-bedroom mansions. Most will require that you book for seven nights during high season, five in low season. A minimum stay of up to two weeks is often required during the Christmas season.

You can arrange private villa rentals through various agents that represent luxury residences and usually have both Web sites and brochures that show photos of the properties they represent. Some are suitable for travelers with disabilities, but be sure to ask specific questions regarding your own needs. **Calypso Realty** (✉ *Box 12178* ☎ *340/774–1620 or 800/747–4858* ⊕ *www.calypsorealty.com*) specializes in rental properties around St. Thomas. **McLaughlin-Anderson Luxury Caribbean Villas**

(⌂ *1000 Blackbeard's Hill, Suite 3* ☎ *340/776–0635 or 800/537–6246* ⊕ *www.mclaughlinanderson.com*) handles rental villas throughout the U.S. Virgin Islands, British Virgin Islands, and Grenada. Many villas and condominiums are in complexes on St. Thomas's East End.

CHARLOTTE AMALIE

Accommodations in town and near town offer the benefits of being close to the airport, shopping, and a number of casual and fine-dining restaurants. The downside is that this is the most crowded and noisy area of the island. Crime can also be a problem. Don't go for a stroll at night in the heart of town. Use common sense, and take the same precautions you would in any major city. Properties along the hillsides are less likely to have crime problems; plus, they command a steady breeze from the cool trade winds. This is especially important if you're visiting in summer and early fall.

¢   🏨 **The Green Iguana.** Atop Blackbeard's Hill, this value-priced small hotel

HOTEL   offers the perfect mix of gorgeous harbor views, proximity to shopping (five-minute walk), and secluded privacy provided by the surrounding flamboyant trees and bushy hibiscus. **Pros:** personalized service; near the center of town; laundry on premises. **Cons:** need a car to get around; neighborhood is sketchy at night. ⊠ *37B Blackbeard's Hill* ☎ *340/776–7654 or 800/484–8825* ⊕ *www.thegreeniguana.com* ⇱ *6 rooms* ⚭ *In-room: a/c, no safe, kitchen (some), Wi-Fi. In-hotel: pool, laundry facilities* ⑩ *No meals.*

¢–$ 🏨 **Hotel 1829.** Antique charm—though some may simply call it old—is

B&B/INN   readily apparent in this rambling 19th-century merchant's house, from the hand-painted Moroccan tiles to a Tiffany window. **Pros:** close to attractions; budget-priced; breakfast served on the verandah. **Cons:** small rooms; tour groups during the day; neighborhood dicey at night. ⊠ *Government Hill, Box 1567* ☎ *340/776–1829 or 800/524–2002* ⊕ *www.hotel1829.com* ⇱ *15 rooms* ⚭ *In-room: a/c, no safe, Wi-Fi. In-hotel: bar, pool, some age restrictions* ⑩ *Breakfast.*

¢–$ 🏨 **Mafolie Hotel.** The view and the value are the selling points of this

B&B/INN   hotel perched 700 feet above Charlotte Amalie's harbor. **Pros:** fantastic views; nice restaurant and bar; family-run establishment. **Cons:** tiny pool; on a busy street; need a car to get around. ⊠ *Rte. 35, Box 7091, Estate Mafolie* ☎ *340/774–2790 or 800/225–7035* ⊕ *www.mafolie. com* ⇱ *22 rooms* ⚭ *In-room: a/c, no safe. In-hotel: restaurant, bar, pool* ⑩ *Breakfast.*

$ 🏨 **Villa Santana.** Built by exiled General Antonio López Santa Anna of

HOTEL   Mexico, this 1857 landmark provides a panoramic view of the harbor

Fodor's Choice   and plenty of West Indian charm, which will make you feel as if you're

★   living in a charming slice of Virgin Islands history. **Pros:** historic charm; plenty of privacy. **Cons:** not on a beach; no restaurant; need a car to get around. ⊠ *2D Denmark Hill* ☎ *340/776–1311* ⊕ *www.villasanta. com* ⇱ *6 rooms* ⚭ *In-room: a/c, no safe, kitchen (some), no TV (some), Wi-Fi. In-hotel: pool* ⑩ *No meals.*

$ 🏨 **Windward Passage Hotel.** Business travelers, those on their way to

HOTEL   the British Virgin Islands, or laid-back vacationers who want the convenience of being able to walk to duty-free shopping, sights, and restaurants, stay at this harborfront hotel. **Pros:** walking distance to Charlotte Amalie; nice harbor views. **Cons:** basic rooms; on a busy street; no water sports, but dive shop is on property. ⊠ *Waterfront Hwy., Box 640* ☎ *340/774–5200 or 800/524–7389* ⊕ *www.windwardpassage.com* ➹ *140 rooms, 11 suites* ⚉ *In-room: a/c, Wi-Fi. In-hotel: restaurant, bar, pool, gym* †◯† *No meals.*

EAST END

You can find most of the large, luxurious beachfront resorts on St. Thomas's East End. The downside is that these properties are about a 30-minute drive from town and a 45-minute drive from the airport (substantially longer during peak hours). On the upside, these properties tend to be self-contained; plus, there are a number of good restaurants, shops, and water-sports operators in the area. Once you've settled in, you don't need a car to get around.

$$$ ☖ **The Anchorage Beach Resort.** A beachfront setting and homey conveniences that include full kitchens and washer–dryer units are what attract families to these two- and three-bedroom suites on Cowpet Bay next to the St. Thomas Yacht Club. **Pros:** on the beach; good amenities. **Cons:** small pool; noisy neighbors; need a car to get around. ⊠ *Rte. 317, Estate Nazareth* ✆ *Antilles Resorts, Box 24786, Christiansted, St. Croix 00824-0786* ☎ *800/874–7897* ⊕ *www.antillesresorts.com* ➹ *11 suites* ⚉ *In-room: a/c, no safe, kitchen. In-hotel: bar, tennis courts, pool, gym, beach, laundry facilities* †◯† *No meals.*
RENTAL

$$ ☖ **Pavilions and Pools Villa Hotel.** Although the rates might lead you to believe you're buying resort ambience, the reality is that you get fairly basic accommodations here. **Pros:** intimate atmosphere; friendly host; private pools. **Cons:** some small rooms; on a busy road; long walk to beach. ⊠ *6400 Rte. 38, Estate Smith Bay* ☎ *340/775–6110 or 800/524–2001* ⊕ *www.pavilionsandpools.com* ➹ *25 1-bedroom villas* ⚉ *In-room: a/c, kitchen. In-hotel: restaurant, pools* †◯† *Breakfast.*
RENTAL

$$$ ☖ **Point Pleasant Resort.** Hilltop suites give you an eagle's-eye view of the East End and beyond, and those in a building adjacent to the reception area offer incredible sea views. **Pros:** lush setting; convenient kitchens; pleasant pools. **Cons:** steep climb from beach; need a car to get around; some rooms need refurbishing. ⊠ *6600 Rte. 38, Estate Smith Bay* ☎ *340/775–7200 or 800/524–2300* ⊕ *www.pointpleasantresort. com* ➹ *128 suites* ⚉ *In-room: a/c, kitchen. In-hotel: restaurants, bar, tennis court, pools, gym, beach, laundry facilities, business center* †◯† *No meals.*
RESORT

$$$$ ☖ **Ritz-Carlton, St. Thomas.** Everything sparkles at the island's most luxurious resort, from the in-room furnishings and amenities to the infinity pool, white-sand beach, and turquoise sea beyond. **Pros:** gorgeous views; great water-sports facilities; beautiful beach; airport shuttle. **Cons:** service can sometimes be spotty for such an upscale hotel; food and drink can lack flair and are expensive ($15 hamburger, $9.75 piña colada); half-hour or more drive to town and airport. ⊠ *Rte. 317, Box 6900, Estate Great Bay* ☎ *340/775–3333 or 800/241–3333*
RESORT
Fodor's Choice ★

The Ritz-Carlton, St.Thoma

Villa Santana

⊕ *www.ritzcarlton.com* ⟿ *255 rooms, 20 suites, 2 villas, 81 condos* ⬧ *In-room: a/c, Wi-Fi. In-hotel: restaurants, bars, tennis courts, pools, gym, spa, beach, water sports, children's programs, business center* ⭐ *No meals.*

$$$

RENTAL

⬚ **Sapphire Beach Condominium Resort and Marina.** A beautiful half-mile-long white-sand beach is the real ace here, because accommodations can be hit-or-miss depending on whether you book with a private condo owner (hit) or the management company (miss). **Pros:** beachfront location; water sports abound; near ferries. **Cons:** some rooms need refurbishing; restaurant fare limited; some construction noise. ⊠ *6720 Estate Smith Bay* ☎ *800/524–2090, 340/773–9150, or 800/874–7897* ⊕ *www.antillesresorts.com* ⟿ *171 condos* ⬧ *In-room: a/c, no safe, kitchen (some). In-hotel: restaurant, bar, tennis courts, pool, beach, water sports* ⭐ *No meals.*

$

RENTAL

⬚ **Sapphire Village.** These high-rise towers feel more like apartment buildings than luxury resorts, so if you're looking for a home away from home, this might be the place. **Pros:** within walking distance of Red Hook; nice views; secluded feel. **Cons:** small rooms; limited dining options; noisy neighbors. ⊠ *Rte. 38, Sapphire Bay* ⊕ *Antilles Resorts, Box 24786, Christiansted, St. Croix 00824-0786* ☎ *340/779–1540 or 800/874–7897* ⊕ *www.antillesresorts.com* ⟿ *15 condos* ⬧ *In-room: a/c, no safe, kitchen. In-hotel: restaurant, bar, tennis courts, pools, beach, water sports, laundry facilities* ⭐ *No meals.*

$$$$

RENTAL

⬚ **Sea Star.** Located on the water and accessed via an electronic gate, this villa has hand-painted murals, a fully equipped professional kitchen, and an entertainment center full of the latest electronic gadgets. **Pros:** right on the water; five-minute drive to restaurants, shops, and ferry in Red Hook. **Cons:** rocky waterfront location not the best for swimming; access is hard to find and down a road with many potholes; somewhat secluded. ⊠ *Cabrita Point, East End* ☎ *800/742–4240* ⊕ *stthomasseastar.com* ⟿ *5 bedrooms, 5½ baths* ⬧ *In-room: a/c, no safe, Wi-Fi. In-hotel: pool, beach, laundry facilities* ⭐ *No meals.*

$$–$$$

RENTAL

⬚ **Secret Harbour Beach Resort.** There's not a bad view from these low-rise studio, one-, and two-bedroom condos, which are either beachfront or perched on a hill overlooking an inviting cove. **Pros:** beautiful beach and great snorkeling; good restaurant; secluded location. **Cons:** some rooms are small; car needed to get around; condo owners are territorial about beach chairs. ⊠ *Rte. 317, Box 6280, Estate Nazareth* ☎ *340/775–6550 or 800/524–2250* ⊕ *www.secretharbourvi.com* ⟿ *49 suites* ⬧ *In-room: a/c, no safe, kitchen. In-hotel: restaurant, bar, tennis courts, pool, gym, beach, water sports* ⭐ *Breakfast.*

$$–$$$

RENTAL

⬚ **Tree Tops.** Gaze across to St. John from either of these condo-style villas set high atop a hill. **Pros:** five-minute drive to restaurants, shops, and ferry in Red Hook; good telecommunications, Wi-Fi, and cable TV; owners also have a day-sail operation which makes it easy to get a reservation onboard. **Cons:** flying bugs can be a problem at dusk if you sit outside (but nothing spray can't solve); somewhat hard to find; too small for a large family. ⊠ *Red Hook, St. Thomas, 6501 Red Hook Plaza, Suite 71* ☎ *340/775–4110* ⊕ *www.beachtops.com/treetop.html* ⟿ *2 bedrooms, 2 baths* ⬧ *In-room: a/c, no safe. In-hotel: pool* ⭐ *No meals.*

$$$$ ⌂ **Wyndham Sugar Bay Resort and Spa.** At the only full all-inclusive resort
ALL-INCLUSIVE on St. Thomas, the terra-cotta high-rise buildings are surrounded by
Ⓒ palm trees and lush greenery, but the rooms and the walkways between
FodorsChoice them have a bit of a generic feel. **Pros:** gorgeous pool area; full-service
★ spa; on-site casino. **Cons:** some steps to climb; small beach; limited
dining options. ⊠ *38 Smith Bay, Estate Smith Bay* ☎ *340/777–7100
or 800/927–7100* ⊕ *www.wyndham.com* ⋤ *294 rooms, 7 suites* ⌂ *In-
room: a/c. In-hotel: restaurants, bar, tennis courts, pool, gym, spa,
beach, water sports, children's programs* ¦◯¦ *All-inclusive.*

SOUTH SHORE

The south shore of St. Thomas connects to the east end of the island
via a beautiful road that rambles along the hillside with frequent peeks
between the hills for a view of the ocean and, on a clear day, of St. Croix
some 40 mi (60 km) to the south. The resorts here are on their own
beaches. They offer several opportunities for water sports, as well as
land-based activities, fine dining, and evening entertainment.

$–$$ ⌂ **Bolongo Bay Beach Resort.** All the rooms at this family-run resort
ALL-INCLUSIVE tucked along a 1,000-foot-long palm-lined beach have balconies with
ocean views; down the beach are 12 studio and two-bedroom con-
dos with full kitchens. **Pros:** family-run property; on the beach; water
sports abound. **Cons:** a bit run-down; on a busy road; need a car to
get around. ⊠ *Rte. 30, Box 7150, Estate Bolongo* ☎ *340/775–1800 or
800/524–4746* ⊕ *www.bolongobay.com* ⋤ *65 rooms, 12 condos* ⌂ *In-
room: a/c, kitchen (some). In-hotel: restaurants, bar, tennis courts, pool,
beach, water sports* ¦◯¦ *Multiple meal plans.*

$$$–$$$$ ⌂ **Marriott Frenchman's Reef and Morning Star Beach Resorts.** Set majesti-
RESORT cally on a promontory overlooking the east side of Charlotte Ama-
Ⓒ lie's harbor, Frenchman's Reef is the high-rise full-service superhotel,
whereas Morning Star is the even more upscale boutique property
nestled closer to the fine white-sand beach. **Pros:** beachfront location;
good dining options; plenty of activities. **Cons:** musty smell on lower
levels; long walk between resorts; a crowded cruise-ship feel. ⊠ *Rte.
315, Box 7100, Estate Bakkeroe* ☎ *340/776–8500 or 800/233–6388*
⊕ *www.marriott.com* ⋤ *479 rooms, 27 suites; 220 2- and 3-bedroom
time-share units* ⌂ *In-room: a/c, Wi-Fi. In-hotel: restaurants, bar, ten-
nis courts, pools, gym, spa, beach, children's programs* ¦◯¦ *No meals.*

WEST END

A few properties are in the hills overlooking Charlotte Amalie to the
west or near Frenchtown, which is otherwise primarily residential.

$$–$$$ ⌂ **Best Western Emerald Beach Resort.** You get beachfront ambience at
HOTEL this reasonably priced miniresort tucked beneath the palm trees, but the
tradeoff is that it's directly across from a noisy airport runway. **Pros:**
beachfront location; good value; great Sunday brunch. **Cons:** airport
noise until 10 pm; on a busy road; limited water sports. ⊠ *8070 Lind-
berg Bay* ☎ *340/777–8800 or 800/780–7234* ⊕ *www.emeraldbeach.*

com ⟿ *90 rooms* ⚿ *In-room: a/c, no safe. In-hotel: restaurant, bar, tennis courts, pool, gym, beach* ⏐◎⏐ *Breakfast.*

¢–$ ⊡ **Island View Guesthouse.** Perched 545 feet up the face of Crown Moun-
B&B/INN   tain, this small inn has a homey feel; the hands-on owners can book tours or offer tips about the best sightseeing spots. **Pros:** spectacular views; friendly atmosphere; good value. **Cons:** small pool; need a car to get around. ⊠ *Rte. 332, Box 1903, Estate Contant* ☎ *340/774–4270 or 800/524–2023* ⊕ *www.islandviewstthomas.com* ⟿ *12 rooms, 10 with bath* ⚿ *In-room: a/c (some), no safe, kitchen (some). In-hotel: pool, laundry facilities* ⏐◎⏐ *Breakfast.*

$$$–$$$$ ⊡ **Kyalami.** If the walls could talk, they'd tell about celebrities that
RENTAL   partied the night away in this grand mansion. **Pros:** kitchen has a dishwasher; house has Wi-Fi; there's an on-site manager in case of problems; the location is great—Magens Bay is five minutes away by car. **Cons:** not directly on the beach; requires a car to get around; can be many mosquitoes after fall rains. ⊠ *McLaughlin Anderson Villas, Charlotte Amalie* ⌂ *1000 Blackbeards Hill, Suite 3, St. Thomas 00802* ☎ *340/776–0635 or 800/537–6246* ⊕ *www.mclaughlinanderson.com* ⟿ *2 bedrooms, 2 baths* ⚿ *In-room: a/c, Wi-Fi. In-hotel: pool, laundry facilities, some age restrictions* ⏐◎⏐ *No meals.*

$$$ ⊡ **Sand Dollar Estate.** President Clinton and his family vacationed in this
RENTAL   luxurious villa that can house up to 22 people. **Pros:** beachfront loca-
tion; elegance everywhere; full-time manager on-site. **Cons:** secluded location; need a car to get to restaurants and shops; somewhat dif-
ficult to find. ⊠ *Estate Peterborg, Charlotte Amalie, St. Thomas* ☎ *908/698–2722* ⊕ *www.sanddollarestate.com* ⟿ *8 bedrooms, 8½ baths* ⚿ *In-room: a/c, no safe, Wi-Fi. In-hotel: pool, beach, laundry facilities* ⏐◎⏐ *No meals.*

$$–$$$ ⊡ **Seventh Heaven.** Honeymooners or couples celebrating an anni-
RENTAL   versary will enjoy the comfy-cozy feel of this cottage perched high atop Skyline Drive. **Pros:** five- to 10-minute drive to either beach or town; incredible view; maid service. **Cons:** not directly on the beach; small and suitable for a couple only; need a car to get to shopping and restaurants. ⊠ *McLaughlin Anderson Villas, Charlotte Amalie, 1000 Blackbeards Hill, Suite 3, St. Thomas* ☎ *340/776–0635 or 800/537–6246* ⊕ *www.mclaughlinanderson.com* ⟿ *1 bedroom, 1 bath* ⚿ *In-room: a/c, Wi-Fi. In-hotel: pool, laundry facilities, some age restrictions* ⏐◎⏐ *No meals.*

$$$$ ⊡ **St. James Bay House.** Overlooking barely habited Great St. James
RENTAL   Island, this cliff-side estate has its own white-sand beach 50 feet from the main house. **Pros:** house has Wi-Fi service; sits directly on a private beach; located on its own private island. **Cons:** short private launch trip required to reach; no services such as restaurants or shops on the island; no maid service or chef. *Deck Point, East End, St. Thomas* ☎ *312/643–2740* ⊕ *www.stjamesbayhouse.com* ⟿ *4 bedrooms, 4½ baths* ⚿ *In-room: a/c, no safe, Wi-Fi. In-hotel: pool, beach, laundry facilities, some age restrictions.* ⏐◎⏐ *No meals.*

$–$$ ⊡ **Stone Cottage.** In a gated estate on the island's lush north side, this
RENTAL   one-bedroom villa is perfect for a romantic getaway for two. **Pros:** lush tropical setting; security in gated estate; gorgeous view of the ocean.

Mocko Jumbie Magic

Mocko Jumbies, the island's other-worldly stilt walkers, trace their roots back to West Africa. The steps of the stilt walkers held religious significance in West Africa, but today's West Indian version is more secular—bending backward to gravity-defying lengths and high kicking to the pulsating beat of drums, bells, and whistles.

Today satins and sequins have replaced costumes made of grasses, shells, and feathers. Festive head-pieces—braids of feathers, glitter-ing crowns, tall hats, and even spiky horns—attract plenty of attention

from onlookers. A mask completes the outfit, assuring that the dancer's identity is concealed from spectators, thus maintaining the magic of the Mocko Jumbie.

Beyond Carnival celebrations, the Mocko Jumbie is so popular that it's a mainstay at many hotels. Mocko Jumbie dancers also perform at store openings, when cruise ships dock, or even at weekend beach jams. Old-fashioned or newfangled, Mocko Jumbies will always be loved best for driving away "jumbie spirits," as they say in the islands.

Cons: secluded location and somewhat hard to find; need a car to get to shops and restaurants; can be many mosquitoes after rains in the fall. ⊠ *McLaughlin Anderson Villas, Charlotte Amalie, 1000 Blackbeards Hill, Suite 3, St. Thomas* ☎ *340/776–0635 or 800/537–6246* ⊕ *www. mclaughlinanderson.com* ⇦ *1 bedroom, 1 bath* ♨ *In-room: a/c, Wi-Fi. In-hotel: pool, laundry facilities* ▐◯▌ *No meals.*

$$$$
RENTAL ⌂ **Villa Gardenia.** Perfect for three couples or a family of six, this contemporary villa sits atop a breezy hill. As it is close to Magens Bay and Mahogany Run Golf Course, you couldn't ask for a bet-ter location. **Pros:** daily maid service (weekdays); five-minute drive to beach and 18-hole golf course; lush, cool location. **Cons:** need a car to get to shops and restaurants; mosquitoes can be a problem after fall rains; not on a beach. ⊠ *McLaughlin Anderson Villas, Char-lotte Amalie* ⌂ *1000 Blackbeards Hill, Suite 3, St. Thomas 00802* ☎ *340/776–0635 or 800/537–6246* ⊕ *www.mclaughlinanderson.com* ⇦ *3 bedrooms, 3½ baths* ♨ *In-room: a/c, Wi-Fi. In-hotel: pool, laun-dry facilities* ▐◯▌ *No meals.*

$$–$$$
RENTAL ⌂ **Villa Longview.** Located on a quiet side road less than five minutes drive from the white sandy beach at Magens Bay, this beautifully decorated villa is well-equipped for recreation with a home theater (and large selection of DVDs), fully equipped kitchen, barbecue grill, and private pool. **Pros:** quiet location; five-minute drive to beach; great views of the Atlantic Ocean. **Cons:** not right on the beach; need a car to restau-rants and shops (it's a 15- to 20-minute drive). ⊠ *Calypso Realty, Box 12178, Charlotte Amalie, St. Thomas* ☎ *340/774–1620 or 800/747–4858* ⊕ *www.calypsorealty.com* ⇦ *2 bedrooms, 2 baths* ♨ *In-room: a/c, no safe, Wi-Fi. In-hotel: pool, laundry facilities* ▐◯▌ *No meals.*

DID YOU KNOW?

Mocko jumbie stilt-walkers are a mainstay of Caribbean festivals and celebrations. They originated in West Africa and first appeared in the Caribbean in Trinidad.

Reichold Center for the Arts, across from Brewers Bay.

NIGHTLIFE AND THE ARTS

On any given night, especially in season, you can find steel-pan orchestras, rock and roll, piano music, jazz, broken-bottle dancing (actual dancing atop broken glass), disco, and karaoke. Pick up a free copy of the bright-yellow *St. Thomas–St. John This Week* magazine when you arrive (it can be found at the airport, in stores, and in hotel lobbies). The back pages list who's playing where. The Friday edition of the *Daily News* carries complete listings for the upcoming weekend.

NIGHTLIFE

CHARLOTTE AMALIE

BARS

Greenhouse Bar and Restaurant. This restaurant closes for dinner at 10 pm. Once this favorite eatery puts away the salt-and-pepper shakers, it becomes a rock-and-roll club with a DJ or live reggae bands raising the weary to their feet six nights a week. ⊠ *Waterfront Hwy. at Storetvaer Gade, Charlotte Amalie* ☎ *340/774–7998.*

EAST END

BARS

Agave Terrace. This bar sometimes has an island-style steel-pan band, which is a treat that should not be missed. Steel-pan music resonates after dinner here on Tuesday and Thursday. ⊠ *Point Pleasant Resort, Rte. 38, Estate Smith Bay* ☎ *340/775–4142.*

Duffy's Love Shack. At this island favorite, a live band and dancing under the stars are the big draws for locals and visitors alike. ⊠ *Red Hook Plaza, Red Hook* ☎ *340/779–2080.*

Latitude 18. This popular hot spot hosts an ever-changing lineup of live bands from on-island and from the U.S. mainland. Open Mic night is every Thursday. ⊠ *Vessup Bay Estate Nazareth* ☎ *340/777–4552.*

SOUTH SIDE
BARS
Epernay Bistro. This place is an intimate nightspot with small tables for easy chatting, wine and champagne by the glass, and a spacious dance floor. Mix and mingle with island celebrities. The action runs from 4 pm until the wee hours Monday through Saturday. ⊠ *Frenchtown Mall, 24-A Honduras St., Frenchtown* ☎ *340/774–5348.*

Iggies Beach Bar. Bolongo Bay's beachside bar offers karaoke on Saturday nights, so you can sing along to the sounds of the surf or the latest hits at this beachside lounge. There are live bands on weekends, and you can dance inside or kick up your heels under the stars. Wednesday it's Carnival Night complete with steel-pan music, a limbo show and West Indian Buffet. ⊠ *Bolongo Bay Beach Club & Villas, Rte. 30, Estate Bolongo* ☎ *340/775–1800.*

THE ARTS

SOUTH SIDE
THEATER
Pistarkle Theater. This theater in the Tillett Gardens complex is air-conditioned and has more than 100 seats; it hosts a dozen or more productions annually, plus a children's summer drama camp. ⊠ *Tillett Gardens, Rte. 38, across from Tutu Park Shopping Mall, Estate Tutu* ☎ *340/775–7877.*

Reichhold Center for the Arts. St. Thomas's major performing arts center has an amphitheater, and its more expensive seats are covered by a roof. Schedules vary, so check the paper to see what's on when you're in town. Throughout the year there's an entertaining mix of local plays, dance exhibitions, and music of all types. ⊠ *Rte. 30, across from Brewers Beach, Estate Lindberg Bay* ☎ *340/693–1559.*

SHOPPING

Fodor's Choice
★

St. Thomas lives up to its billing as a duty-free shopping destination. Even if shopping isn't your idea of how to spend a vacation, you still may want to slip in on a quiet day (check the cruise-ship listings—Monday and Sunday are usually the least crowded) to browse. Among the best buys are liquor, linens, china, crystal (most stores will ship), and jewelry. The amount of jewelry available makes this one of the few items for which comparison shopping is worth the effort. Local crafts include shell jewelry, carved calabash bowls, straw brooms, woven baskets, and dolls. Creations by local doll maker Gwendolyn Harley—like her costumed West Indian market woman—have been

Charlotte Amalie is filled with back alleys and interesting shops.

little goodwill ambassadors, bought by visitors from as far away as Asia. Spice mixes, hot sauces, and tropical jams and jellies are other native products.

On St. Thomas, stores on Main Street in Charlotte Amalie are open weekdays and Saturday 9 to 5. The hours of the shops in the Havensight Mall (next to the cruise-ship dock) and the Crown Bay Commercial Center (next to the Crown Bay cruise-ship dock) are the same, though occasionally some stay open until 9 on Friday, depending on how many cruise ships are anchored nearby. You may also find some shops open on Sunday if cruise ships are in port. Hotel shops are usually open evenings, as well.

There's no sales tax in the USVI, and you can take advantage of the $1,600 duty-free allowance per family member (remember to save your receipts). Although you can find the occasional salesclerk who will make a deal, bartering isn't the norm.

CHARLOTTE AMALIE

The prime shopping area in **Charlotte Amalie** is between Post Office and Market squares; it consists of two parallel streets that run east–west (Waterfront Highway and Main Street) and the alleyways that connect them. Particularly attractive are the historic **A.H. Riise Alley, Royal Dane Mall, Palm Passage,** and pastel-painted **International Plaza.**

Vendors Plaza, on the waterfront side of Emancipation Gardens in Charlotte Amalie, is a central location for vendors selling handmade earrings, necklaces, and bracelets; straw baskets and handbags; T-shirts;

fabrics; African artifacts; and local fruits. Look for the many brightly colored umbrellas.

ART GALLERIES

Camille Pissarro Art Gallery. This second-floor gallery is actually in the birthplace of St. Thomas's famous artist, offering a fine collection of original paintings and prints by local and regional artists. ⊠ *14 Main St., Charlotte Amalie* ☎ *340/774–4621.*

Gallery St. Thomas. This gallery has a nice collection of fine art and collectibles in a charming space, including paintings, wood sculpture, glass, and jewelry that are from or inspired by the Virgin Islands. ⊠ *Palm Passage, Charlotte Amalie* ☎ *340/777–6363.*

CAMERAS AND ELECTRONICS

Boolchand's. This store sells brand-name cameras, audio and video equipment, and binoculars. ⊠ *31 Main St., Charlotte Amalie* ☎ *340/776–0794.*

Royal Caribbean. Royal Caribbean stocks a wide selection of cameras, camcorders, stereos, watches, and clocks. There are two branches near each other in Charlotte Amalie. ⊠ *23 Main St., Charlotte Amalie* ☎ *340/776–5449* ⊠ *33 Main St., Charlotte Amalie* ☎ *340/776–4110.*

CHINA AND CRYSTAL

The Crystal Shoppe at A.H. Riise. This retailer specializes in all that glitters, from Swarovski and Waterford crystal to figurines by Hummel, Daum, and Royal Copenhagen, and china by Belleek, Kosta Boda, and several Limoges factories. There's also a large selection of Lladró figurines. ⊠ *37 Main St., at Riise's Alley, Charlotte Amalie* ☎ *340/776–2303.*

Little Switzerland. This popular Caribbean chain carries crystal from Baccarat, Waterford, and Orrefors; and china from Kosta Boda, Rosenthal, and Wedgwood, among others in its two Charlotte Amalie stores. There's also an assortment of Swarovski cut-crystal animals, gemstone globes, and many other affordable collectibles. It also does a booming mail-order business; ask for a catalog. ⊠ *5 Dronningens Gade, across from Emancipation Garden, Charlotte Amalie* ☎ *340/776–2010* ⊠ *3B Main St., Charlotte Amalie* ☎ *340/776–2010.*

CLOTHING

Fresh Produce. This clothing store doesn't sell lime-green mangoes, peachy-pink guavas, or sunny-yellow bananas. But you will find these fun, casual colors in the Fresh Produce clothing line. This is one of only 16 stores to stock 100% of this California-created, tropical-feel line of apparel for women. Find dresses, shirts, slacks, and skirts in small to plus sizes as well as accessories such as bags and hats. ⊠ *Riise's Alley, Charlotte Amalie* ☎ *340/774–0807.*

Local Color. This St. Thomas chain has clothes for men, women, and children among its brand-name wear such as Jams World, Fresh Produce, and Urban Safari. There's also St. John artist Sloop Jones's colorful, hand-painted island designs on cool dresses, T-shirts, and sweaters. Find tropically oriented accessories such as big-brim straw hats, bold-color bags, and casual jewelry. ⊠ *Royal Dane Mall, at Waterfront, Charlotte Amalie* ☎ *340/774–2280.*

Tommy Hilfiger. This outlet for the popular designer specializes in classic American jeans and sportswear, as well as trendy bags, belts, ties, socks, caps, and wallets. ⊠ *Waterfront Hwy. at Trompeter Gade, Charlotte Amalie* ☎ *340/777–1189.*

White House/Black Market. This store boasts sophisticated clothing for women. You'll find just the right party or evening wear look in dresses, tops and bottoms made out of everything from sequins to shimmering and satiny fabrics. Check out the perpetual sale rack in the back for the best deals. ⊠ *24 Main St., at Palm Passage, Charlotte Amalie* ☎ *340/775–8245.*

FOODSTUFFS

☾ **Belgian Chocolate Company.** This store makes its beautiful chocolates before your eyes. Specialties include triple-chocolate rum truffles. You can find imported chocolates here as well. Both the homemade and imported come in decorative boxes, so they make great gifts. ⊠ *Alley, Charlotte Amalie* ☎ *340/777–5247.*

HANDICRAFTS

Native Arts and Crafts Cooperative. This crafts market is made up of a group of more than 40 local artists—including schoolchildren, senior citizens, and people with disabilities—who create the handcrafted items for sale here: African-style jewelry, quilts, calabash bowls, dolls, carved-wood figures, woven baskets, straw brooms, note cards, and cookbooks. This is also the site of the Virgin Islands Welcome Center. ⊠ *Tolbod Gade across from Emancipation Garden, Charlotte Amalie* ☎ *340/777–1153.*

JEWELRY

Cardow Jewelry. This store is a chain—with gold in several lengths, widths, sizes, and styles—along with diamonds, emeralds, and other precious gems. You're guaranteed 40% to 60% savings off U.S. retail prices or your money will be refunded within 30 days of purchase. ⊠ *33 Main St., Charlotte Amalie* ☎ *340/776–1140.*

Diamonds International. At this major chain shop with several outlets on St. Thomas, just choose a diamond, emerald, or tanzanite gem and a mounting, and you can have your dream ring set in an hour. Famous for having the largest inventory of diamonds on the island, this shop welcomes trade-ins, has a U.S. service center, and offers free diamond earrings with every purchase. ⊠ *31 Main St., Charlotte Amalie* ☎ *340/774–3707* ⊠ *3 Drakes Passage, Charlotte Amalie* ☎ *340/775–2010* ⊠ *7AB Drakes Passage, Charlotte Amalie* ☎ *340/774–1516.*

H. Stern Jewelers. At this major Caribbean jeweler, the World Collection of jewels set in modern, fashionable designs and an exclusive sapphire watch have earned this Brazilian jeweler a stellar name. ⊠ *8 Main St., Charlotte Amalie* ☎ *340/776–1939.*

Jewels. This jewelery store sells name-brand jewelry and watches in abundance. Designer jewelry lines include David Yurman, Bulgari, Chopard, and Penny Preville. The selection of watches is extensive, with brand names including Jaeger le Coultre, Tag Heuer, Breitling, Movado, and

Gucci. ⊠ *Main St. at Riise's Alley, Charlotte Amalie* ☎ *340/777–4222* ⊠ *Waterfront at Hibiscus Alley, Charlotte Amalie* ☎ *340/777–4222.*

Rolex Watches at A. H. Riise. A.H. Riise is the Virgin Islands' official Rolex retailer, and this shop offers one of the largest selections of these fine timepieces in the Caribbean. An After Sales Service Center assures that your Rolex keeps on ticking for a lifetime. ⊠ *37 Main St., at Riise's Alley, Charlotte Amalie* ☎ *340/776–2303.*

Trident Jewels and Time. Fine gems and exquisite timepieces are the draw at this second-generation family-owned boutique. You'll find loose diamonds, sapphires, emeralds, and tanzanite as well as name-brand watches such as Ulysse Nardin, Harry Winston, Franck Muller, Bovet, Jaquet Droz, Bell & Ross, U-Boat, Graham and Technomarine. ⊠ *9 Main St., Charlotte Amalie* ☎ *340/776–7152* ⊕ *www.trident-jewels. com* ⊙ *Daily 9–5.*

LEATHER GOODS

Coach Boutique at Little Switzerland. This designer leather store has a full line of fine leather handbags, belts, gloves, and more for women, plus briefcases and wallets for men. Accessories for both sexes include organizers, travel bags, and cell-phone cases. ⊠ *5 Main St., Charlotte Amalie* ☎ *340/776–2010.*

☾ **Zora's.** This store specializes in fine, made-to-order leather sandals. There's also a selection of locally made backpacks, purses, and briefcases in durable, brightly colored canvas. ⊠ *Norre Gade across from Roosevelt Park, Charlotte Amalie* ☎ *340/774–2559.*

LINENS

Fabric in Motion. Fine Italian linens share space with Liberty's of London silky cottons, colorful batiks, cotton prints, ribbons, and accessories at this small shop. ⊠ *Storetvaer Gade, Charlotte Amalie* ☎ *340/774–2006.*

Mr. Tablecloth. This store has prices to please, and the friendly staff will help you choose from the floor-to-ceiling selection of linens, from Tuscany lace tablecloths to Irish linen pillowcases. ⊠ *6–7 Main St., Charlotte Amalie* ☎ *340/774–4343.*

LIQUOR AND TOBACCO

A.H. Riise Liquors and Tobacco. This giant duty-free liquor outlet offers a large selection of tobacco (including imported cigars), as well as cordials, wines, and rare vintage Armagnacs, cognacs, ports, and Madeiras. It also stocks fruits in brandy and barware from England. Enjoy rum samples at the tasting bar. Prices are among the best in St. Thomas. ⊠ *37 Main St., at Riise's Alley, Charlotte Amalie* ☎ *340/776–2303.*

PERFUME

Tropicana Perfume Shoppe. This perfume outlet is in an 18th-century Danish building and offers a large selection of fragrances for men and women, including those locally made by Gail Garrison from the essential oils of tropical fruits and flowers such as mango and jasmine. ⊠ *2 Main St., Charlotte Amalie* ☎ *340/774–0010.*

EAST END

Red Hook has **American Yacht Harbor,** a waterfront shopping area with a dive shop, a tackle store, clothing and jewelry boutiques, a bar, and a few restaurants.

Don't forget **St. John.** A ferry ride (an hour from Charlotte Amalie or 20 minutes from Red Hook) will take you to the charming shops of **Mongoose Junction** and **Wharfside Village,** which specialize in unusual, often island-made articles.

ART GALLERIES

The Color of Joy. This gallery offers locally made arts and crafts, including pottery, batik, hand-painted linen-and-cotton clothing, glass plates and ornaments, and watercolors by owner Corinne Van Rensselaer. There are also original prints by many local artists. ⊠ *Rte. 317, about 100 yards west of Ritz-Carlton, Red Hook* ☎ *340/775–4020.*

CLOTHING

☺ **Keep Left.** This is a friendly shop with something for everyone in the family, including Patagonia dresses, Quiksilver swimwear, Jams World shirts, Watership Trading hats, and NAOT sandals. ⊠ *American Yacht Harbor, Bldg. C, Rte. 32, Red Hook* ☎ *340/775–9964.*

FOODSTUFFS

Food Center. This supermarket sells fresh produce, meats, and seafood. There's also an on-site bakery and deli with hot-and-cold prepared foods, which are the draw here, especially for those renting villas, condos, or charter boats in the East End area. ⊠ *Rte. 32, Estate Frydenhoj* ☎ *340/777–8806.*

Marina Market. This market near the ferry to St. John has the best fresh meat and seafood on the island. ⊠ *Rte. 32 across from Red Hook ferry, Red Hook* ☎ *340/779–2411.*

Pueblo Supermarket. This Caribbean chain carries stateside brands of most products—but at higher prices because of shipping costs to the islands. ⊠ *Sub Base, ½ mi [¾ km] east of Crown Bay Marina, Estate Contant* ☎ *340/774–4200* ⊠ *Rte. 30, 1 mi [1½ km] north of Havensight Mall, Estate Thomas* ☎ *340/774–2695.*

HANDICRAFTS

☺ **Dolphin Dreams.** This crafts store has gaily painted Caribbean-theme Christmas ornaments, art glass from the Mitchell-Larsen studio, and jewelry made from recycled coral. Signature clothing lines include Bimini Bay and Rum Reggae. This boutique is the exclusive Red Hook source for the famous Caribbean Hook Bracelet, originated by the Caribbean Bracelet Company on St. Croix. ⊠ *American Yacht Harbor, Bldg. C, Rte. 32, Red Hook* ☎ *340/775–0549.*

JEWELRY

Diamonds International. At this major chain shop with several outlets on St. Thomas, just choose a diamond, emerald, or tanzanite gem and a mounting, and you can have your dream ring set in an hour. Famous for having the largest inventory of diamonds on the island, this shop welcomes trade-ins, has a U.S. service center, and offers free diamond earrings with every purchase. ⊠ *Wyndham Sugar Bay Beach Club & Resort, Rte. 38, Estate Smith Bay* ☎ *340/714–3248.*

Jewels. This jewelery store sells name-brand jewelry and watches in abundance. Designer jewelry lines include David Yurman, Bulgari, Chopard, and Penny Preville. The selection of watches is extensive, with brand names including Jaeger le Coultre, Tag Heuer, Breitling, Movado, and Gucci. ⊠ *Ritz-Carlton St. Thomas, Rte. 322, Estate Nazareth* ☎ *340/776–7850.*

SOUTH SIDE

West of Charlotte Amalie, the pink-stucco **Nisky Center,** on Harwood Highway about ½ mi (¾ km) east of the airport, is more of a hometown shopping center than a tourist area, but there's a bank, clothing store, and Radio Shack.

At the Crown Bay cruise-ship pier, the **Crown Bay Center,** off the Harwood Highway in Sub Base about ½ mi (¾ km), has quite a few shops.

Havensight Mall, next to the cruise-ship dock, may not be as charming as downtown Charlotte Amalie, but it does have more than 60 shops. It also has an excellent bookstore, a bank, a pharmacy, a gourmet grocery, and smaller branches of many downtown stores. The shops at **Port of $ale,** adjoining Havensight Mall (its buildings are pink instead of brown), sell discount goods. Next door to Port of $ale is the **Yacht Haven Grande** complex, a stunning megayacht marina with beautiful, safe walkways and many upscale shops.

East of Charlotte Amalie on Route 38, **Tillett Gardens** is an oasis of artistic endeavor across from the Tutu Park Shopping Mall. The late Jim and Rhoda Tillett converted this Danish farm into an artists' retreat in 1959. Today you can watch artisans produce silk-screen fabrics, candles, pottery, and other handicrafts. Something special is often happening in the gardens as well: the Classics in the Gardens program is a classical music series presented under the stars, Arts Alive is a semiannual arts-and-crafts fair held in November and May, and the Pistarckle Theater holds its performances here from November through April.

Tutu Park Shopping Mall, across from Tillett Gardens, is the island's one and only enclosed mall. More than 50 stores and a food court are anchored by Kmart and Plaza Extra grocery store. Archaeologists have discovered evidence that Arawak Indians once lived near the grounds.

ART GALLERIES

Mango Tango. This gallery sells and displays works by popular local artists—originals, prints, and note cards. There's a one-person show at least one weekend a month, and the store also has the island's largest humidor and a brand-name cigar gallery. ⊠ *Al Cohen's Plaza, ½ mi [¾ km] east of Charlotte Amalie* ☎ *340/777–3060.*

BOOKS

Dockside Bookshop. This Havensight store is packed with books for children, travelers, cooks, and historians, as well as a good selection of paperback mysteries, best sellers, art books, calendars, and prints. It also carries a selection of books written in and about the Caribbean and the Virgin Islands. ⊠ *Havensight Mall, Bldg. VI, Rte. 30, Havensight* ☎ *340/774–4937.*

CAMERAS AND ELECTRONICS

Boolchand's. This store sells brand-name cameras, audio and video equipment, and binoculars. ⊠ *Havensight Mall, Bldg. II, Rte. 30, Havensight* ☎ *340/776–0302.*

Royal Caribbean. Royal Caribbean stocks a wide selection of cameras, camcorders, stereos, watches, and clocks and has several outlets, both in Charlotte Amalie and elsewhere on St. Thomas. ⊠ *Havensight Mall, Bldg. I, Rte. 30, Havensight* ☎ *340/776–8890* ⊠ *Yacht Haven Grande, Havensight* ☎ *340/779–6364* ⊠ *Crown Bay Commercial Center, Rte. 30, Crown Bay* ☎ *340/779–6372.*

CHINA AND CRYSTAL

Little Switzerland. The major Caribbean duty-free chain carries crystal from Baccarat, Waterford, and Orrefors; and china from Kosta Boda, Rosenthal, and Wedgwood, among others. There's also an assortment of Swarovski cut-crystal animals, gemstone globes, and many other affordable collectibles. It also does a booming mail-order business; ask for a catalog. ⊠ *Havensight Mall, Bldg. II, Rte. 30, Havensight* ☎ *340/776–2198* ⊠ *Yacht Haven Grand, Bldg. C, 38, Havensight* ☎ *340/776–2546.*

Scandinavian Center. The Center has the best of Scandinavia, including Royal Copenhagen, Georg Jensen, Kosta Boda, and Orrefors. Owners Søren and Grace Blak make regular buying trips to northern Europe and are a great source of information on crystal. Online ordering is available if you want to add to your collection once home. ⊠ *Havensight Mall, Bldg. III, Rte. 30, Havensight* ☎ *340/777–8620 or 877/454–8377* ⊠ *Crown Bay Commercial Center, Rte. 30, Crown Bay* ☎ *340/777–8620.*

CLOTHING

☾ **Local Color.** Local Color has clothes for men, women, and children among its brand-name wear such as Jams World, Fresh Produce, and Urban Safari. There's also St. John artist Sloop Jones's colorful, hand-painted island designs on cool dresses, T-shirts, and sweaters. Find tropically oriented accessories such as big-brim straw hats, bold-color bags, and casual jewelry. ⊠ *Havensight Mall, Rte. 30, Havensight* ☎ *340/774–3178.*

White House/Black Market. This boutique sells sophisticated clothing for women. You'll find just the right party or evening wear look in dresses, tops and bottoms made out of everything from sequins to shimmering and satiny fabrics. Check out the perpetual sale rack in the back for the best deals. ⊠ *Yacht Haven Grande, Havensight* ☎ *340/775-8245.*

FOODSTUFFS

Cost-U-Less. Cost-U-Less is the Caribbean equivalent of Costco and Sam's Club and sells everything from soup to nuts, but in giant sizes and case lots—without a membership fee. The meat-and-seafood department, however, has family-size portions. There's a well-stocked fresh-produce section and a case filled with rotisserie chicken. ⊠ *Rte. 38, ¼ mi [½ km] west of Rte. 39 intersection, Estate Donoe* ☎ *340/777–3588.*

Fruit Bowl. This grocery store is the best place on the island to go for fresh fruits and vegetables. There are also many ethnic, vegetarian, and health-food items as well as a fresh meat and seafood department. ⊠ *Wheatley Center, Rtes. 38 and 313 intersection, Charlotte Amalie* ☎ *340/774–8565.*

Gourmet Gallery. This gourmet market is where visiting megayacht owners go to buy their caviar. There's also an excellent and reasonably priced wine selection, as well as specialty ingredients for everything from tacos to curries to chow mein. A full-service deli offers imported meats, cheeses, and in-store prepared foods that are perfect for a gourmet picnic. ⊠ *Crown Bay Marina, Rte. 304, Estate Contant* ☎ *340/776–8555* ⊠ *Havensight Mall, Bldg. VI, Rte. 30, Havensight* ☎ *340/774–4948.*

Plaza Extra. This large, U.S.–style supermarket sells everything you need from produce to meat, including fresh seafood, an excellent deli, and a bakery. There's a liquor department, too. ⊠ *Tutu Park Shopping Mall, Rte. 38, Estate Tutu* ☎ *340/775–5646.*

PriceSmart. This giant emporium carries everything from electronics to housewares in its members-only warehouse-size store. The meat, poultry, and seafood departments are especially popular. A small café in front sells pizzas, hot dogs, and the cheapest bottled water on the island—just $1 a pop. ⊠ *Rte. 38 west of Fort Mylner, Estate Tutu* ☎ *340/777–3430.*

HANDICRAFTS

☺ **Caribbean Marketplace.** This is a great place to buy handicrafts from the Caribbean and elsewhere. Also look for Sunny Caribee spices, teas from Tortola, and coffee from Trinidad. ⊠ *Havensight Mall, Rte. 30, Havensight* ☎ *340/776–5400.*

JEWELRY

Cardow Jewelry. This store is a chain—with gold in several lengths, widths, sizes, and styles—along with diamonds, emeralds, and other precious gems. You're guaranteed 40% to 60% savings off U.S. retail prices or your money will be refunded within 30 days of purchase. ⊠ *Havensight Mall, Bldg. I, Rte. 30, Havensight* ☎ *340/774–0530 or 340/774–5905.*

Diamonds International. At this major chain shop with several outlets on St. Thomas, just choose a diamond, emerald, or tanzanite gem and a mounting, and you can have your dream ring set in an hour. Famous for having the largest inventory of diamonds on the island, this shop welcomes trade-ins, has a U.S. service center, and offers free diamond earrings with every purchase. ⊠ *Havensight Mall, Bldg. II, Rte. 30, Havensight* ☎ *340/776–0040* ⊠ *Crown Bay Center, Rte. 30, Crown Bay* ☎ *340/779–7057.*

H. Stern Jewelers. At this major Caribbean jeweler, the World Collection of jewels set in modern, fashionable designs and an exclusive sapphire watch have earned this Brazilian jeweler a stellar name. ⊠ *Havensight Mall, Bldg. II, Rte. 30, Havensight* ☎ *340/776–1223.*

Jewels. This jewelry store sells name-brand jewelry and watches in abundance. Designer jewelry lines include David Yurman, Bulgari, Chopard, and Penny Preville. The selection of watches is extensive, with brand names including Jaeger le Coultre, Tag Heuer, Breitling, Movado, and Gucci. ⊠ *Havensight Mall, Bldg. II, Rte. 30, Havensight* ☎ *340/776–8590* ⊠ *Yacht Haven Grande, Rte. 38, Havensight* ☎ *340/776–1908.*

Rolex Watches at A.H. Riise. A.H. Riise is the Virgin Islands' official Rolex retailer, and this shop offers one of the largest selections of these fine timepieces in the Caribbean. An After Sales Service Center assures that your Rolex keeps on ticking for a lifetime. ⊠ *Havensight Mall, Bldg. II, Rte. 30, Havensight* ☎ *340/776–4002.*

LIQUOR AND TOBACCO

A.H. Riise Liquors and Tobacco. This giant duty-free liquor outlet offers a large selection of tobacco (including imported cigars), as well as cordials, wines, and rare vintage Armagnacs, cognacs, ports, and Madeiras. It also stocks fruits in brandy and barware from England. Enjoy rum samples at the tasting bar. Prices are among the best in St. Thomas. ⊠ *Havensight Mall, Bldg. I, Rte. 30, Havensight* ☎ *340/776–7713.*

Al Cohen's Discount Liquor. Cohen's has an extremely large wine selection in a warehouse-style store. ⊠ *Rte. 30 across from Havensight Mall, Havensight* ☎ *340/774–3690.*

Tobacco Discounters. This duty-free outlet carries a full line of discounted brand-name cigarettes, cigars, and tobacco accessories. ⊠ *Port of $ale Mall, Rte. 30, next to Havensight Mall, Havensight* ☎ *340/774–2256.*

MUSIC

Music Shoppe II. This is a good place to buy the latest Caribbean releases on CD—steel pan, reggae, and calypso. ⊠ *Rte. 30, Havensight Mall, Bldg. III, Havensight* ☎ *340/774–1900.*

TOYS

Ↄ **Kmart.** This giant discount chain store has five aisles of toys for boys and girls: Barbie dolls, hula hoops, computer games, dollhouses, talking teddies, and more. ⊠ *Tutu Park Shopping Mall, Rte. 38, Estate Tutu* ☎ *340/714–5839* ⊠ *Lockhart Gardens, Rte. 38, Estate Long Bay* ☎ *340/774–4046.*

SPORTS AND THE OUTDOORS

AIR TOURS

On the Charlotte Amalie waterfront next to Tortola Wharf, **Air Center Helicopters** (⊠ *Waterfront, Charlotte Amalie* ☎ *340/775–7335 or 800/619–0013* ⊕ *www.aircenterhelicopters.com*) offers a minimum 30-minute tour that includes St. Thomas, St. John, and Jost Van Dyke priced at $750 for up to 6 people. If you can afford the splurge, it's a nice ride, but in truth, you can see most of the aerial sights from Paradise Point, and there's no place you can't reach easily by car or boat.

BOATING AND SAILING

Calm seas, crystal waters, and nearby islands (perfect for picnicking, snorkeling, and exploring) make St. Thomas a favorite jumping-off spot for day- or weeklong sails or powerboat adventures. With more than 100 vessels from which to choose, St. Thomas is the charter-boat center of the U.S. Virgin Islands. You can go through a broker to book a sailing vessel with a crew or contact a charter company directly. Crewed charters start at approximately $2,600 per person per week, while bareboat charters can start at as little as $1,200 per person for a 50- to 55-foot sailboat (but this doesn't include provisioning, fuel, and optional add-ons like rental of water toys), which can comfortably accommodate up to six people. If you want to rent your own boat, hire a captain. Most local captains are excellent tour guides.

Single-day charters are also a possibility. You can hire smaller boats for the day, including the services of a captain if you wish to have someone take you on a guided snorkel trip around the islands.

Awesome Powerboat Rentals (⊠ *6100 Red Hook Quarter, Red Hook* ☎ *340/775–0860* ⊕ *www.powerboatrentalsvi.com*) at "P" dock offers 26-foot twin-engine catamarans for day charters. Rates range from $345 to $385 for a half or full day. A captain can be hired for $125 for a day.

Island Yachts (⊠ *6100 Red Hook Quarter, 18B, Red Hook* ☎ *340/775–6666 or 800/524–2019* ⊕ *www.iyc.vi*) offers sail- or powerboats with or without crews.

Luxury is the word at **Magic Moments** (⊠ *American Yacht Harbor, Red Hook* ☎ *340/775–5066* ⊕ *www.yachtmagicmoments.com*), where the crew of a 45-foot Sea Ray offers a pampered island-hopping snorkeling cruise. Nice touches include icy-cold eucalyptus-infused washcloths to freshen up with and a gourmet wine and lobster lunch.

Nauti Nymph (⊠ *6501 Red Hook Plaza, Suite 201, Red Hook* ☎ *540/775–5066 or 800/734–7345* ⊕ *www.nautinymph.com*) has a large selection of 25- to 32-foot powerboats and power catamarans. Rates vary from $325 to $620 a day, including snorkeling gear, water skis, and outriggers, but not including fuel. You can hire a captain for $115 more.

Stewart Yacht Charters (⊠ *6501 Red Hook Plaza, Suite 20, Red Hook* ☎ *340/775–1358 or 800/432–6118* ⊕ *www.stewartyachtcharters.com*) is run by longtime sailor Ellen Stewart, who is an expert at matching clients with yachts for weeklong crewed charter holidays.

Bareboat sail- and powerboats, including a selection of stable trawlers, are available at **VIP Yacht Charters** (⊠ *South off Rte. 32, Estate Frydenhoj* ☎ *340/774–9224 or 866/847–9224* ⊕ *www.vipyachts.com*), at Compass Point Marina.

BICYCLING

Water Island Adventures (⊠ *Water Island* ☎ *340/714–2186 or 340/775–5770* ⊕ *www.waterislandadventures.com*) offers a cycling adventure to the USVI's "newest" Virgin. You take a ferry ride from Crown Bay to Water Island before jumping on a Cannondale mountain bike for a 90-minute tour over rolling hills on dirt and paved roads. On cruise-ship days, a direct ferry goes from the West India Company Docks, but this is only for cruise passengers who have booked the bike tour. Explore the remains of the Sea Cliff Hotel, reputedly the inspiration for Herman Wouk's book *Don't Stop the Carnival,* and then take a cooling swim at beautiful Honeymoon Beach. Helmets, water, guides, and ferry fare are included in the $65 cost. Bike rentals are available on days when no tours are scheduled: call for details.

DIVING AND SNORKELING

Popular dive sites include such wrecks as the *Cartanser Sr.,* a beautifully encrusted World War II cargo ship sitting in 35 feet of water, and the *General Rogers,* a Coast Guard cutter resting at 65 feet. Here you can find a gigantic resident barracuda. Reef dives offer hidden caves and archways at **Cow and Calf Rocks,** coral-covered pinnacles at **Frenchcap,** and tunnels where you can explore undersea from the Caribbean to the Atlantic at **Thatch Cay, Grass Cay,** and **Congo Cay.** Many resorts and charter yachts offer dive packages. A one-tank dive starts at $90; two-tank dives are $110 and up. Call the USVI Department of Tourism to obtain a free eight-page guide to Virgin Islands dive sites. There are plenty of snorkeling possibilities, too.

☾ **Admiralty Dive Center** (⊠ *Windward Passage Hotel, Waterfront Hwy., Charlotte Amalie* ☎ *340/777–9802 or 888/900–3483* ⊕ *www.admiraltydive.com*) provides boat dives, rental equipment, and a retail store. Four-tank to 12-tank packages are available if you want to dive over several days.

Blue Island Divers (⊠ *Crown Bay Marina, Rte. 304, Estate Contant* ☎ *340/774–2001* ⊕ *www.blueislanddivers.com*) is a full-service dive shop that offers both day and night dives to wrecks and reefs and specializes in custom dive charters.

B.O.S.S. Underwater Adventure (⊠ *Crown Bay Marina, Rte. 304, Charlotte Amalie* ☎ *340/777–3549* ⊕ *www.bossusvi.com*) offers an alternative to traditional diving in the form of an underwater motor scooter called BOSS, or Breathing Observation Submersible Scooter. A 3½-hour tour, including snorkel equipment, rum punch, and towels, is $100 per person.

☾ **Coki Beach Dive Club** (⊠ *Rte. 388, at Coki Point, Estate Frydendal* ☎ *340/775–4220* ⊕ *www.cokidive.com*) is a PADI Gold Palm outfit run by avid diver Peter Jackson. Snorkeling and dive tours in the fish-filled reefs off Coki Beach are available, as are classes from beginner to underwater photography.

Snuba of St. Thomas (⊠ *Rte. 388, at Coki Point, Estate Smith Bay* ☎ *340/693–8063* ⊕ *www.visnuba.com*) offers something for nondivers, a cross between snorkeling and scuba diving: a 20-foot air hose con-

CLOSE UP

Made in St. Thomas

Justin Todman, aka the Broom Man, keeps the dying art of broom making alive. It's a skill he learned at the age of six from his father. From the fronds of the date palm, Todman delicately cuts, strips, and dries the leaves, a process that can take up to a week. Then he creatively weaves the leaves into distinctively shaped brooms with birch-berry wood for handles. There are feather brooms, cane brooms, multicolor yarn brooms, tiny brooms to fit into a child's hand, and tall long-handled brooms to reach cobwebs on the ceiling. Some customers buy Todman's brooms—sold at the Native Arts & Crafts Cooperative—not for cleaning but rather for celebrating their nuptials. It's an old African custom for the bride and groom to jump over a horizontally laid broom to start their new life.

Gail Garrison puts the essence of local flowers, fruits, and leaves into perfumes, powders, and body splashes. Her Island Fragrances line includes frangipani-, white ginger-, and jasmine-scented perfumes; aromatic mango, lime, and coconut body splashes; and bay rum aftershave for men. Garrison compounds, mixes, and bottles the products herself in second-floor offices on Charlotte Amalie's Main Street. You can buy the products in the Tropicana Perfume Shop.

Gwendolyn Harley preserves Virgin Islands culture in the personalities of her hand-sewn, softly sculptured historic dolls for sale at the Native Arts & Crafts Cooperative. There are quadrille dancers clad in long, colorful skirts; Frenchwomen with their neat peaked bonnets; and farmers sporting handwoven straw hats. Each one-of-kind design is named using the last syllable of Harley's first name; the dolls have names like Joycelyn, Vitalyn, and Iselyn.

Cheryl Miller cooks up ingredients like sun-sweetened papayas, fiery Scotch bonnet peppers, and aromatic basil leaves into the jams, jellies, and hot sauces she sells in her Cheryl's Taste of Paradise line. Five of Miller's products—Caribbean Mustango Sauce, Caribbean Sunburn, Mango Momma Jam, Mango Chutney, and Hot Green Pepper Jelly—have won awards at the National Fiery Foods Show in Albuquerque, New Mexico.

Jason Budsan traps the enticing aromas of the islands into sumptuous candles he sells at his Tillett Gardens workshop. Among the scents are Ripe Mango, Night Jasmine, Lime in de Coconut, Frenchie Connection (with vanilla and lavender), and Ripe Pineapple.

2

---

nects you to the surface. The cost is $52. Children must be eight or older to participate.

St. Thomas Diving Club (✉ *Bolongo Bay Beach Resort, Rte. 30, Box 7150, Estate Bolongo* ☎ *340/776–2381* ⊕ *www.stthomasdivingclub.com*) is another PADI five-star center that offers boat dives to the reefs around Buck Island and nearby offshore wrecks as well as multiday dive packages.

DID YOU KNOW?

The waters around St. Thomas are renowned for game fish. The U.S. Virgin Islands Game Fishing Club sponsors nine game-fishing events throughout the year between July and November.

FISHING

★ Fishing here is synonymous with blue marlin angling—especially from June through October. Four 1,000-pound-plus blues, including three world records, have been caught on the famous North Drop, about 20 mi (32 km) north of St. Thomas. A day charter for marlin with up to six anglers costs $1,600 for the day. If you're not into marlin fishing, try hooking sailfish in winter, dolphin (the fish, not the mammal) in spring, and wahoo in fall. Inshore trips for two to four hours range from $350 to $550, respectively. To find the trip that will best suit you, walk down the docks at either American Yacht Harbor or Sapphire Beach Marina in the late afternoon and chat with the captains and crews.

An excellent choice is **Captain Rob Richards** (⊠ *Westin, St. John, dock, Great Bay, St. John* ☏ *340/513–0389* ⊕ *www.sportfishingstjohn.com*), who runs the 32-foot center console Mixed Bag I and 40-foot Luhrs Express Mixed Bag II, and who enjoys beginners—especially kids—as well as fishing with experienced anglers.

☙ For marlin, Captain Red Bailey's **Abigail III** (⊠ *Rte. 38, Sapphire Bay* ☏ *340/775–6024* ⊕ *www.visportfish.com*) operates out of the Sapphire Beach Resort & Marina.

The **Charter Boat Center** (⊠ *6300 Red Hook Plaza, Red Hook* ☏ *340/775–7990* ⊕ *www.charterboat.vi*) is a major source for sportfishing charters, both marlin and inshore.

For inshore or offshore trips, **Double Header Sportfishing** (⊠ *Sapphire Bay Marina, Rte. 38 Sapphire Bay* ☏ *340/775–5274* ⊕ *www. doubleheadersportfishing.net*) offers trips out to the North Drop on its 40-foot sportfisher and half-day reef and bay trips aboard its two speedy 35-foot center consoles.

Captain Eddie Morrison, aboard the 45-foot Viking **Marlin Prince** (⊠ *American Yacht Harbor, Red Hook* ☏ *340/693–5929* ⊕ *www.marlinprince. com*), is one of the most experienced charter operators in St. Thomas and specializes in fly-fishing for blue marlin.

GOLF

★ The **Mahogany Run Golf Course** (⊠ *Rte. 42, Estate Lovenlund* ☏ *340/777–6006 or 800/253–7103* ⊕ *www.mahoganyrungolf.com*) attracts golfers for its spectacular view of the British Virgin Islands and the challenging three-hole Devil's Triangle. At this Tom and George Fazio–designed, par-70, 18-hole course, there's a fully stocked pro shop, snack bar, and open-air clubhouse. Greens fees and half-cart fees for 18 holes are $150. The course is open daily, and there are frequently informal weekend tournaments. It's the only course on St. Thomas.

GUIDED TOURS

VI Taxi Association St. Thomas City-Island Tour (☏ *340/774–4550* ⊕ *www. vitaxi.com*) gives a two-hour tour for two people in an open-air safari bus or enclosed van; aimed at cruise-ship passengers, this $29 tour includes stops at Drake's Seat and Mountain Top. Other tours include a three-hour trip to Coki Beach with a shopping stop in downtown Charlotte Amalie for $435 per person, a three-hour trip to the Coral World Ocean Park for $45 per person, and a five-hour beach tour to St. John for $75 per person. For $35 to $40 for two, you can hire a taxi for a customized three-hour drive around the island. Make sure to see Mountain Top, as the view is wonderful.

HORSE RACING

The **Clinton Phipps Racetrack** (✉ *Rte. 30, Estate Nadir* ☎ *340/775–4555*) schedules races—especially on local holidays—with sanctioned betting. Be prepared for large crowds.

PARASAILING

The waters are so clear around St. Thomas that the outlines of coral reefs are visible from the air. Parasailers sit in a harness attached to a parachute that lifts them off a boat deck until they're sailing through the sky. Parasailing trips average a 10-minute ride in the sky that costs $75 per person. Friends who want to ride along pay $20 for the boat trip.

Caribbean Watersports and Tours (✉ *6501 Red Hook Plaza, Red Hook* ☎ *340/775–9360* ⊕ *www.viwatersports.com*) makes parasailing pick-ups from 10 locations around the island, including many major beach-front resorts. A parasail costs $75 per person. The company also rents Jet Skis, kayaks, and floating battery-power chairs.

SEA EXCURSIONS

Landlubbers and seafarers alike will enjoy the wind in their hair and salt spray in the air while exploring the waters surrounding St. Thomas. Several businesses can book you on a snorkel-and-sail to a deserted cay for a half day that starts at $85 per person or a full day that begins at $125 per person. An excursion over to the British Virgin Islands starts at $125 per person, not including customs fees. A luxury daylong motor-yacht cruise complete with gourmet lunch is $375 or more per person.

For a soup-to-nuts choice of sea tours, contact the **Adventure Center** (✉ *Marriott's Frenchman's Reef Hotel, Rte. 315, Estate Bakkeroe* ☎ *340/774–2992 or 866/868–7784* ⊕ *www.adventurecenters.net*).

The **Charter Boat Center** (✉ *6300 Red Hook Plaza, Red Hook* ☎ *340/775–7990* ⊕ *www.charterboat.vi*) specializes in day trips to the British Virgin Islands and day- or weeklong sailing charters.

Limnos Charters (✉ *Compass Point Marina, Rte. 32, Estate Frydenhoj* ☎ *340/775–3203* ⊕ *www.limnoscharters.com*) offers one of the most popular British Virgin Islands day trips, complete with lunch, open bar, and snorkeling gear. Destinations include the Baths in Virgin Gorda and the sparsely inhabited island of Jost Van Dyke.

Jimmy Loveland at **Treasure Isle Cruises** (✉ *Rte. 32, Estate Nadir* ☎ *340/775–9500* ⊕ *www.treasureislecruises.com*) can set you up with everything from a half-day sail to a seven-day U.S. and British Virgin Islands trip that combines sailing with accommodations and sightseeing trips onshore.

SEA KAYAKING

☺ Fish dart, birds sing, and iguanas lounge on the limbs of dense mangrove trees deep within a marine sanctuary on St. Thomas's southeast shore. Learn about the natural history here in a guided kayak-snorkel tour to Patricia Cay or via an inflatable boat tour to Cas Cay for snorkeling and hiking. Both are 2½ hours long. The cost is $75 per person.

Mangrove Adventures (⊠ *Rte. 32, Estate Nadir* ☎ *340/779–2155* ⊕ *www.viecotours.com*) rents its two-person sit-atop ocean kayaks and inflatable boats for self-guided exploring as well as for a three-hour guided tour to historic Hassel Island, which includes a visit to some of the historic forts and military structures on the island, a short hike to a breathtaking vista and swim off a deserted beach. The cost is $89 per person. In addition, many resorts on St. Thomas's East End also rent kayaks.

TENNIS

The Caribbean sun is hot, so be sure to hit the courts before 10 am or after 5 pm. (Many courts are lighted.) You can indulge in a set or two even if you're staying in a guesthouse without courts; most hotels rent time to nonguests.

Marriott Frenchman's Reef and Morning Star Beach Resorts (⊠ *Rte. 315, Estate Bakkeroe* ☎ *340/776–8500 Ext. 6818*) has two courts. Nonguests play for $20 per hour.

Two courts are available at the **Ritz-Carlton, St. Thomas** (⊠ *Rte. 317, Box 6900, Estate Great Bay* ☎ *340/775–3333*), where nonguests can take lessons for $90 per hour and $45 per half hour.

Sapphire Beach Resort & Marina (⊠ *Sapphire Bay* ☎ *340/775–6100 Ext. 8135*) has four courts that fill up fast in the cool early-morning hours. The cost for nonguests is $20 per hour.

At **Wyndham Sugar Bay Beach Club and Resort** (⊠ *Rte. 38, Box 6500, Estate Smith Bay* ☎ *340/777–7100*) nonguests can rent any of the four courts for $20 per hour. Lessons start at $45 for a half hour.

Lindberg Bay Park (⊠ *Rte. 302, Estate Lindberg Bay,*) has two courts that are open to the public; it's opposite Cyril E. King Airport.

There are two public tennis courts at **Sub Base** (⊠ *Rte. 306, next to Water and Power Authority, Estate Contant*), open on a first-come, first-served basis at no cost. Lights are on until 10 pm.

WINDSURFING

☺ Expect some spills, anticipate the thrills, and try your luck clipping through the seas. Most beachfront resorts rent Windsurfers and offer one-hour lessons for about $120.

If you want to learn, try Paul Stoeken's **Island Sol** (⊠ *Ritz-Carlton St. Thomas, Estate Nazareth* ☎ *340/776–9463* ⊕ *www.islandsol.net*). The two-time Olympic athlete charges $120 per hour for private lessons, $85 per hour for group lessons. There's a free windsurfing clinic every Tuesday at 9:30 am.

One of the island's best-known independent windsurfing companies is **West Indies Windsurfing** (⊠ *Vessup Beach, No. 9, Estate Nazareth* ☎ *340/775–6530*). Owner John Phillips is the board buff who introduced the sport of kiteboarding to the USVI; it entails using a kite to lift a sailboard off the water for an airborne ride. A private kiteboarding lesson costs $100 per hour for the land portion and $200 for a two-hour private lesson on the water. Phillips also rents stand-up paddleboards (SUP), the latest water-sports rage, for $30 per hour or $175 to $225 per day based on the quality of the board. There's usually calm water, which is perfect for SUP right off Vessup Beach or around the peninsula in Great Bay.

St. John

WORD OF MOUTH

"I like how scenic the island is and how much there is to do, all of the beaches and hiking trails, the boats anchored out everywhere, the views, the great food. It was an all-around great island."

—Kristen1206

WELCOME TO ST. JOHN

TOP REASONS TO GO

★ **Beach-Hopping:** Fill your cooler with cold drinks, grab the snorkeling gear, and stash your beach chair in the back of your car for a day spent at the beaches along St. John's North Shore Road.

★ **Hiking Reef Bay:** Opt for a trip with a ranger in Virgin Islands National Park. A safari bus takes you to the trailhead, and a boat brings you back.

★ **Snorkeling at Trunk Bay:** Trunk Bay is St. John's most popular snorkeling spot, and for good reason. A snorkeling trail teaches you about the local marine life.

★ **Relaxing in a Villa:** There are about 500 vacation villas across the island in all sizes, prices, and locations; most will give you all the comforts of home.

★ **Exploring Cruz Bay:** Spend a half-day poking around Cruz Bay's varied stores, shopping for that perfect gift for the folks back home.

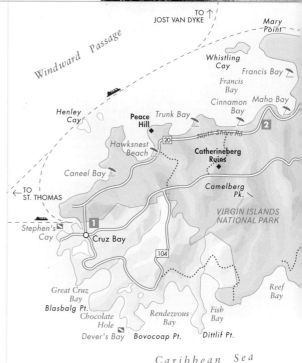

1 Cruz Bay and Environs. St. John's main town is where you go for both dining and nightlife. Most of the shopping is here, as well as the ferry dock, where all island visitors arriving by ferry arrive. Its environs include the area around the Westin Resort and Villas, Fish Bay, and Gifft Hill.

2 North Shore. Caneel Bay, Maho Bay Camps, and the Cinnamon Bay campground can all be found along North Shore Road. Some of the island's best beaches, including those at Caneel and Trunk Bay, are accessible here.

3 Coral Bay and Environs. The island's second town is about a half-hour drive from Cruz Bay. You'll find a collection of businesses here, including a half-dozen-plus places to eat and a slew of vacation villas. If you head to the northern edge of Coral Bay, the East

3

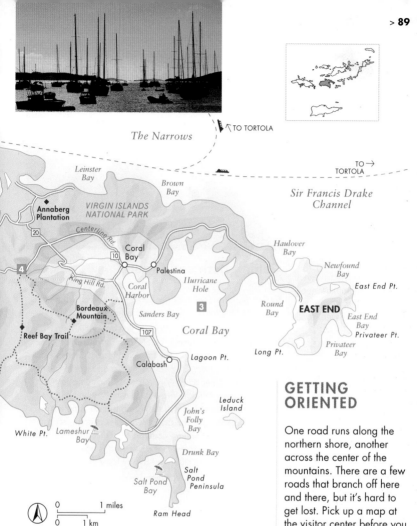

The Narrows

↖ TO TORTOLA

TO →
TORTOLA

Leinster Bay

Brown Bay

Sir Francis Drake Channel

◆ **Annaberg Plantation**

VIRGIN ISLANDS NATIONAL PARK

20

Centerline Rd.

10

Coral Bay

Palestina

Hurricane Hole

Haulover Bay

Newfound Bay

East End Pt.

4

King Hill Rd.

Coral Harbor

Sanders Bay

3

Round Bay

EAST END

East End Bay

Privateer Pt.

◆ **Bordeaux Mountain**

107

Coral Bay

Privateer Bay

• Reef Bay Trail

Calabash

Lagoon Pt.

Long Pt.

Leduck Island

White Pt.

Lameshur Bay

John's Folly Bay

Drunk Bay

Salt Pond Bay

Salt Pond Peninsula

Ram Head

0   1 miles
0   1 km

GETTING ORIENTED

One road runs along the northern shore, another across the center of the mountains. There are a few roads that branch off here and there, but it's hard to get lost. Pick up a map at the visitor center before you start out and you'll have no problems. Few residents remember the route numbers, so have your map in hand if you stop to ask for directions. There are lunch spots at Cinnamon Bay and in Coral Bay, or you can do what the locals do—find a secluded spot for a picnic. The grocery stores in Cruz Bay sell Styrofoam coolers just for this purpose.

End offers little in the way of civilization, but Vie's Snack Shack is a good place to stop for lunch if you want to enjoy the deserted beach here. On the southern edge, Salt Pond Bay Beach has some interesting tide pools to explore, and Lameshur Bay Beach is one of the island's better snorkeling spots.

4 Mid Island. The center part of the island stretches along Centerline Road (Rte. 10) from outside Cruz Bay past Reef Bay to Bordeaux. There are a couple of spots to take in the views, and a stop at the Catherineberg Ruins makes a nice break.

ST. JOHN PLANNER

Do You Need a Car?

You will almost certainly need a car if you are staying in a villa or in Coral Bay, but you might be able to get by with taxis if you are staying elsewhere. A four-wheel-drive SUV is your best bet. You'll be able to safely drive on the hilly roads when it rains, and you'll probably need one to get up that steep (and in some cases, unpaved) road to your villa.

CAR RENTALS

All the car-rental companies in St. John are locally owned, and most are just a short walk from the ferry dock in Cruz Bay, and those located a bit farther away will pick you up.

Contacts **Best** (📞 340/693–8177). **Cool Breeze** (📞 340/776–6588 ⊕ www.coolbreeze carrental.com). **Courtesy** (📞 340/776–6650 ⊕ www.courtesy carrental.com). **Delbert Hill Taxi & Jeep Rental Service** (📞 340/776–6637). **Denzil Clyne** (📞 340/776–6715). **O'Connor Car Rental** (📞 340/776–6343 ⊕ www.oconnorcarrental.com). **St.John Car Rental** (📞 340/776–6103 ⊕ www.stjohncar rental.com). **Spencer's Jeep** (📞 340/693–8784 or 888/776–6628 ⊕ www.spencerjeep rentals.com).

Getting Here and Around

By Air: St. John does not have an airport, so you will need to fly into St. Thomas and then take a ferry over.

By Ferry: There's frequent daily service from both Red Hook and Charlotte Amalie on St. Thomas to Cruz Bay (the more frequent ferry is the one from Red Hook). There's also frequent service from Cruz Bay to Tortola and less frequent service to the other British Virgin Islands, including Jost Van Dyke (some via Tortola). Virgin Islands ferry schedules are published on the web site of the Virgin Islands Vacation Guide & Community. The actual schedules change, so you should check with the ferry companies to determine the current schedules. Remember that a passport is now required to travel between the USVI and BVI by ferry.

Contacts **Virgin Islands Vacation Guide and Community** (⊕ www.vinow.com).

By Bus: Modern Vitran buses on St. John run from the Cruz Bay ferry dock through Coral Bay to the far eastern end of the island at Salt Pond, making numerous stops in between. The fare is $1 to any point, but the service is slow and not always reliable.

By Taxi: Taxis meet ferries arriving in Cruz Bay. Most drivers use vans or open-air safari buses. You can find them congregated at the dock and at hotel parking lots. You can also hail them anywhere on the road. Almost all trips will be shared, and prices are per person. Paradise Taxi will pick you up if you call, but most drivers don't provide that service. If you need one to pick you up at your rental villa, ask the villa manager who you might call or arrange a ride in advance.

Contacts **Paradise Taxi** (📞 340/714–7913).

Where to Stay

St. John doesn't have many beachfront hotels, but that's a small price to pay for all the pristine sand. The island's two excellent resorts—Caneel Bay Resort and the Westin St. John Resort & Villas—are on the beach. Most villas are in the residential south-shore area, a 15-minute drive from the north-shore beaches. If you head east you come to the laid-back community of Coral Bay, where there are growing numbers of villas and cottages. If you're looking for West Indian village charm, there are a few inns in Cruz Bay. Your choice of accommodations also includes condominiums and cottages near town; two campgrounds, both at the edges of beautiful beaches (bring bug repellent); ecoresorts; and luxurious villas, often with a pool or a hot tub (sometimes both) and a stunning view.

Where to Eat

The cuisine on St. John seems to get better every year, with culinary-school-trained chefs vying to see who can come up with the most imaginative dishes. There are restaurants to suit every taste and budget—from the elegant establishments at Caneel Bay Resort (where men may be required to wear a jacket at dinner) to the casual in-town eateries of Cruz Bay. For quick lunches, try the West Indian food stands in Cruz Bay Park and across from the post office. Some restaurants close for vacation in September and even October. If you have your heart set on a special place, call ahead to make sure it's open during these months.

HOTEL AND RESTAURANT PRICES

Restaurant prices are for a main course at dinner and include any taxes or service charges. Hotel prices are per night for a double room in high season, excluding taxes, service charges, and meal plans (except at all-inclusives).

WHAT IT COSTS IN U.S. DOLLARS

	¢	$	$$	$$$	$$$$
Restaurants	under $8	$8–$12	$13–$20	$21–$30	over $30
Hotels		under $150	$150–$275	$276–$375	$376–$475	over $475

Essentials

Banks St. John has two banks. First Bank is one block up from the ferry dock, and Scotia Bank is at the Marketplace on Route 104.

Safety Although crime is not as prevalent on St. John as it is on St. Thomas and St. Croix, it does exist. Keep your hotel or vacation villa door locked at all times, even during the day if you are, say, out by the pool. Stick to well-lighted streets at night, and use the same kind of street sense that you would in any unfamiliar territory. It's not a good idea to walk around Cruz Bay late at night. If you don't have a car, plan on taking a taxi, which you should arrange in advance.

Tour Options On St. John taxi drivers provide tours of the island, making stops at various sites, including Trunk Bay and Annaberg Plantation for about $25 a person. Rangers at the **V.I. National Park Visitors Center** (⊠ *Cruz Bay* ☎ *340/776–6201* ⊕ *www.nps. gov/viis*) give several guided tours on- and offshore (some requiring reservations).

Visitor Information USVI Division of Tourism (⊠ *Henry Samuel St., next to post office, Cruz Bay* ☎ *340/776–6450* ⊕ *www. usvitourism.vi*). **Virgin Islands Hotel & Tourism Association** (☎ *340/774–6835* ⊕ *www. virgin-islands-hotels.com*).

By Lynda Lohr

Only 3 miles from St. Thomas but still a world apart, St. John is the least developed of the U.S. Virgin Islands. While two-thirds of its tropical hills remain protected as national parkland, a bit of hustle and bustle has come to Cruz Bay, the island's main town. Accommodations range from world-class luxury resorts to top-notch vacation villas to back-to-basics campgrounds.

St. John's heart is Virgin Islands National Park, a treasure that takes up a full two-thirds of St. John's 20 square mi (53 square km). The park was spearheaded by Laurance S. Rockefeller and Frank Stick and was finally handed over to the Department of Interior in 1956. The park helps keep the island's interior in its pristine and undisturbed state, but if you go at midday you'll probably have to share your stretch of beach with others, particularly at Trunk Bay.

The island is booming, and it can get a tad crowded at the ever-popular Trunk Bay Beach during the busy winter season; parking woes plague the island's main town of Cruz Bay, but you won't find traffic jams or pollution. It's easy to escape from the fray, however: just head off on a hike or go early or late to the beach. The sun won't be as strong, and you may have that perfect crescent of white sand all to yourself.

St. John doesn't have a grand agrarian past like her sister island, St. Croix, but if you're hiking in the dry season, you can probably stumble upon the stone ruins of old plantations. The less adventuresome can visit the repaired ruins at the park's Annaberg Plantation and Caneel Bay resort.

In 1675 Jorgen Iverson claimed the unsettled island for Denmark. By 1733 there were more than 1,000 slaves working more than 100 plantations. In that year the island was hit by a drought, hurricanes, and a plague of insects that destroyed the summer crops. With famine a real threat and the planters keeping them under tight reign, the slaves revolted on November 23, 1733. They captured the fort at Coral Bay, took control of the island, and held on to it for six months. During this period, about 20% of the island's total population was killed, the tragedy affecting both black and white residents in equal percentages. The rebellion was eventually put down with the help of French troops from Martinique. Slavery continued until 1848, when slaves in St. Croix marched on Frederiksted to demand their freedom from the Danish government. This time it was granted. After emancipation, St. John fell into decline, its inhabitants eking out a living on small farms. Life continued in much the same way until the national park opened in 1956 and tourism became an industry.

Of the three U.S. Virgin Islands, St. John, which has 5,000 residents, has the strongest sense of community, which is primarily rooted in a desire to protect the island's natural beauty. Despite the growth, there are still many pockets of tranquillity. Here you can truly escape the pressures of modern life for a day, a week—perhaps, forever.

> **DRIVING IN ST. JOHN**
>
> The terrain in St. John is very hilly, the roads are winding, and the blind curves numerous. Major roads are well paved, but once you get off a specific route, dirt roads filled with potholes are common. For such driving, a four-wheel-drive vehicle is your best bet. Be aware that you can't bring all rental cars over to St. John from St. Thomas. Even more important, the barge service is very busy, so you can't always get a space.

EXPLORING ST. JOHN

CRUZ BAY

St. John's main town may be compact (it consists of only several blocks), but it's definitely a hub: the ferries from St. Thomas and the British Virgin Islands pull in here, and it's where you can get a taxi or rent a car to travel around the island. There are plenty of shops in which to browse, a number of watering holes where you can stop for a breather, many restaurants, and a grassy square with benches where you can sit back and take everything in. Look for the current edition of the handy, amusing "St. John Map" featuring Max the Mongoose.

Elaine Ione Sprauve Library. On the hill just above Cruz Bay is the Enighed Estate great house, built in 1757. *Enighed* is Danish for "concord" (unity or peace). The great house and its outbuildings (a sugar factory and horse-driven mill) were destroyed by fire and hurricanes, and the house sat in ruins until 1982. The library offers Internet access for $2 an hour. ⊠ *Rte. 104, make a right past Texaco station, Cruz Bay* ☎ *340/776–6359* ⚑ *Free* ☺ *Weekdays 9–5.*

V.I. National Park Visitors Center. To pick up a useful guide to St. John's hiking trails, see various large maps of the island, and find out about current Park Service programs, including guided walks and cultural demonstrations, stop by the park visitor center, which is open daily from 8 to 4:30. ⊠ *Near baseball field, Cruz Bay* ☎ *340/776–6201* ⊕ *www.nps.gov/viis.*

DID YOU KNOW?

Trunk Bay is the most popular beach on St. John and is in Virgin Islands National Park. The fee is $4.

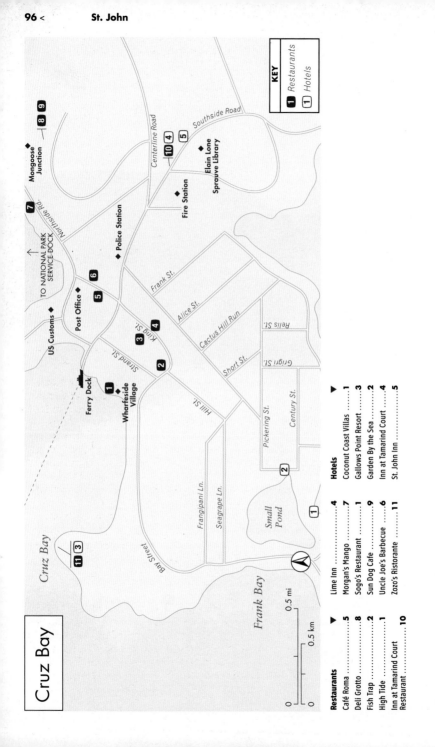

Cruz Bay

KEY
- ▮ Restaurants
- ① Hotels

Restaurants ▶

Café Roma 5
Deli Grotto 8
Fish Trap 2
High Tide 1
Inn at Tamarind Court
Restaurant 10
Lime Inn 4
Morgan's Mango 7
Sogo's Restaurant 1
Sun Dog Cafe 9
Uncle Joe's Barbecue ...6
Zozo's Ristorante 11

Hotels ▶

Coconut Coast Villas 1
Gallows Point Resort 3
Garden By the Sea 2
Inn at Tamarind Court 4
St. John Inn 5

0.5 mi

0.5 km

Sugar mill ruins at Annaberg Plantation.

NORTH SHORE

Fodor's Choice ★ **Annaberg Plantation.** In the 18th century, sugar plantations dotted the steep hills of this island. Slaves and free Danes and Dutchmen toiled to harvest the cane that was used to create sugar, molasses, and rum for export. Built in the 1780s, the partially restored plantation at Leinster Bay was once an important sugar mill. Although there are no official visiting hours, the National Park Service has regular tours, and some well-informed taxi drivers will show you around. Occasionally you may see a living-history demonstration—someone making johnnycake or weaving baskets. For information on tours and cultural events, contact the V.I. National Park Visitors Center. ⊠ *Leinster Bay Rd., Annaberg* ☎ *340/776–6201* ⊕ *www.nps.gov/viis* ☒ *Free* ☉ *Daily dawn–dusk.*

Peace Hill. It's worth stopping at this spot just past the Hawksnest Bay overlook for great views of St. John, St. Thomas, and the BVI. On the flat promontory is an old sugar mill. ⊠ *Off Rte. 20, Denis Bay.*

MID ISLAND

★ **Bordeaux Mountain.** St. John's highest peak rises to 1,277 feet. Route 10 passes near enough to the top to offer breathtaking vistas. Don't stray into the road here—cars whiz by at a good clip along this section. Instead, drive nearly to the end of the dirt road that heads off next to the restaurant and gift shop for spectacular views at Picture Point and the trailhead of the hike downhill to Lameshur. Get a trail map from the park service before you start. ⊠ *Rte. 10, Bordeaux.*

CLOSE UP

St. John Archaeology

Archaeologists continue to unravel St. John's past through excavations at Trunk Bay and Cinnamon Bay, both prime tourist destinations within Virgin Islands National Park.

Work began back in the early 1990s, when the park wanted to build new bathhouses at the popular Trunk Bay. In preparation for that project, the archaeologists began to dig, turning up artifacts and the remains of structures that date to AD 900. The site was once a village occupied by the Taino, a peaceful group that lived in the area for many centuries. A similar but not quite as ancient village was discovered at Cinnamon Bay.

By the time the Taino got to Cinnamon Bay—they lived in the area from about AD 1000 to 1500—their society had developed to include chiefs, commoners, workers, and slaves. The location of the national park's busy Cinnamon Bay campground was once a Taino temple that belonged to a king or chief. When archaeologists began digging in 1998, they uncovered several dozen *zemis*, which are small clay gods used in ceremonial activities, as well as beads, pots, and many other artifacts.

Near the end of the Cinnamon Bay dig archaeologists turned up another less ancient but still surprising discovery. A burned layer indicated that a plantation slave village had also stood near Cinnamon Bay campground; it was torched during the 1733 revolt because its slave inhabitants had been loyal to the planters. Since the 1970s, bones from slaves buried in the area have been uncovered at the water's edge by beach erosion.

Catherineberg Ruins. At this fine example of an 18th-century sugar and rum factory, there's a storage vault beneath the windmill. Across the road, look for the round mill, which was later used to hold water. In the 1733 slave revolt Catherineberg served as headquarters for the Amina warriors, a tribe of Africans captured into slavery. ⊠ *Rte. 10, Catherineberg.*

Fodor's Choice ★

Reef Bay Trail. This is one of the most interesting hikes on St. John, but unless you're a rugged individualist who wants a physical challenge (and that describes a lot of people who stay on St. John), you can probably get the most out of the trip if you join a hike led by a park service ranger who can identify the trees and plants on the hike down, fill you in on the history of the Reef Bay Plantation, and tell you about the petroglyphs on the rocks at the bottom of the trail. A side trail takes you to the plantation's greathouse, a gutted but mostly intact structure that maintains vestiges of its former beauty. Take the safari bus from the park's visitor center. A boat takes you from the beach at Reef Bay back to the visitor center, saving you the uphill climb. You can make advance reservations for this trip, and it's a good idea during the high season. You should call a couple of weeks in advance, especially during February and March, to make sure that the trips haven't filled up, but a spot on the waiting list will suffice at most since since there are often no-shows. ⊠ *Rte. 10, Reef Bay* ☎ *340/776–6201 Ext. 238 for reservations* ⊕ *www.nps.gov/viis* ✆ *Free, safari bus $6, return boat trip to Cruz Bay $15* ⊘ *Tours at 9:30 am, days change seasonally.*

CORAL BAY AND ENVIRONS

Coral Bay. This laid-back community at the island's dry, eastern end is named for its shape rather than for its underwater life—the word *coral* comes from *kraul,* Dutch for "corral." Coral Bay is growing fast, but it's still a small, neighborly place. You'll probably need a four-wheel-drive vehicle if you plan to stay at this end of the island, as some of the rental houses are up unpaved roads that wind around the mountain. If you come just for lunch, a regular car will be fine.

3

BEACHES

St. John is blessed with many beaches, and all of them fall into the good, great, and don't-tell-anyone-else-about-this-place categories. Those along the north shore are all within the national park. Some are more developed than others—and many are crowded on weekends, holidays, and in high season—but by and large they're still pristine. Beaches along the south and eastern shores are quiet and isolated.

NORTH SHORE

Cinnamon Bay Beach. This long, sandy beach faces beautiful cays and abuts the national park campground. The facilities are open to the public and include cool showers, toilets, a commissary, and a restaurant. You can rent water-sports equipment here—a good thing, because there's excellent snorkeling off the point to the right; look for the big angelfish and large schools of purple triggerfish. Afternoons on Cinnamon Bay can be windy—a boon for windsurfers but an annoyance for sunbathers—so arrive early to beat the gusts. The Cinnamon Bay hiking trail begins across the road from the beach parking lot; ruins mark the trailhead. There are actually two paths here: a level nature trail (signs along it identify the flora) that loops through the woods and passes an old Danish cemetery, and a steep trail that starts where the road bends past the ruins and heads straight up to Route 10. Restrooms are on the main path from the commissary to the beach and scattered around the campground. ⊠ *North Shore Rd., Rte. 20, Cinnamon Bay, about 4 mi (6 km) east of Cruz Bay.*

Francis Bay Beach. Because there's little shade, this beach gets toasty warm in the afternoon when the sun comes around to the west, but the rest of the day it's a delightful stretch of white sand. The only facilities are a few picnic tables tucked among the trees and a portable restroom, but folks come here to watch the birds that live in the swampy area behind the beach. The park offers bird-watching hikes here on Sunday morning; sign up at the visitor center in Cruz Bay. To get here, turn left at the Annaberg intersection. ⊠ *North Shore Rd., Rte. 20, Francis Bay, ¼ mi (½ km) from Annaberg intersection.*

★ **Hawksnest Beach.** Sea grape and waving palm trees line this narrow beach, and there are restrooms, cooking grills, and a covered shed for picnicking. A patchy reef just offshore means snorkeling is an easy swim away, but the best underwater views are reserved for ambitious snorkelers who head farther to the east along the bay's fringes. Watch out for boat traffic—a channel guides dinghies to the beach, but the occasional boater strays into the swim area. It's the closest drivable beach to Cruz Bay, so it's often crowded with locals and visitors. ⊠ *North Shore Rd., Rte. 20, Hawksnest Bay, about 2 mi (3 km) east of Cruz Bay.*

Maho Bay Beach. This popular beach is below Maho Bay Camps, a wonderful hillside enclave of tent cabins. The campground offers breakfast and dinner at its Pavilion Restaurant, water-sports equipment rentals at the beach, and restrooms. After a five-minute hike down a long flight of stairs to the beach, snorkelers head off along rocky outcroppings for a look at all manner of colorful fish. Watch for a sea turtle or two to cross your path. Another lovely strip of sand with the same name sits right along the North Shore Road. Turn left at the Annaberg intersection and follow the signs about 1 mi (1½ km) for Maho Bay Camps. ⊠ *Off North Shore Rd., Rte. 20, Maho Bay.*

Fodor's Choice ★ **Trunk Bay Beach.** St. John's most-photographed beach is also the preferred spot for beginning snorkelers because of its underwater trail. (Cruise-ship passengers interested in snorkeling for a day flock here, so if you're looking for seclusion, arrive early or late in the day.) Crowded or not, this stunning beach is one of the island's most beautiful. There are changing rooms with showers, bathrooms, a snack bar, picnic tables, a gift shop, phones, lockers, and snorkeling-equipment rentals. The parking lot often overflows, but you can park along the road. ⊠ *North Shore Rd., Rte. 20, Trunk Bay, about 2½ mi (4 km) east of Cruz Bay.*

CORAL BAY AND ENVIRONS

Lameshur Bay Beach. This sea grape–fringed beach is toward the end of a partially paved road on the southeast coast. The reward for your long drive is solitude, good snorkeling, and a chance to spy on some pelicans. The beach has a couple of picnic tables, rusting barbecue grills, and a portable restroom. The ruins of the old plantation are a five-minute walk down the road past the beach. The area has good hiking trails, including a trek (more than a mile) up Bordeaux Mountain before an easy walk to Yawzi Point. ⊠ *Off Rte. 107, about 1½ mi (2½ km) from Salt Pond, Lameshur Bay.*

Salt Pond Bay Beach. If you're adventurous, this rocky beach on the scenic southeastern coast—next to Coral Bay and rugged Drunk Bay—is worth exploring. It's a short hike down a hill from the parking lot, and the only facilities are an outhouse and a few picnic tables scattered about. Tide pools are filled with all sorts of marine creatures, and the snorkeling is good, particularly along the bay's edges. A short walk takes you to a pond where salt crystals collect around the edges. Hike farther uphill past cactus gardens to Ram Head for see-forever views. Leave nothing valuable in your car, as reports of thefts are common. ⊠ *Rte. 107, Salt Pond Bay, about 3 mi (5 km) south of Coral Bay.*

WHERE TO EAT

With the exception of the grown-on-the-island greens, which you can find in salads at a wide variety of local restaurants, and an occasional catch of local fish, almost all the food served here is imported from the mainland. This means that you may find prices on restaurant menus and supermarket shelves on the high side, since the shipping costs are passed along to the consumer.

For approximate costs, see the dining and lodging price chart at the beginning of this chapter.

3

CRUZ BAY

$$$$ ✕ **Asolare.** Contemporary Asian cuisine dominates the menu at this ele-
PAN-ASIAN gant open-air eatery in an old St. John house. Come early and relax over
★ drinks while you enjoy the sunset lighting up the harbor. Start with an appetizer such as seared scallops with smoked bacon and a habanero vinegar sauce, then move on to entrées such as grilled pork tenderloin with a chipotle hoisin barbecue sauce or sesame-seared tuna served with a carrot ginger slaw. If you still have room for dessert, try the mimosa-poached pears with honey. ✉ *Rte. 20 on Caneel Hill, Estate Lindholm* ☎ *340/779–4747* ☙ *No lunch.*

$$$ ✕ **Café Roma.** This second-floor restaurant in the heart of Cruz Bay is *the*
ITALIAN place for traditional Italian cuisine: lasagna, spaghetti and meatballs,
☯ and three-cheese manicotti. Small pizzas are available at the table, but larger ones are for takeout or at the bar. Rum-caramel bread pudding is a dessert specialty. This casual eatery can get crowded in winter, so show up early. ✉ *Vesta Gade, Cruz Bay* ☎ *340/776–6524* ⊕ *www.stjohn-caferoma.com* ☙ *No lunch.*

$ ✕ **Deli Grotto.** At this air-conditioned (but no-frills) sandwich shop you
ECLECTIC place your order at the counter and wait for it to be delivered to your table or for takeout. The portobello panini with savory sautéed onions is a favorite, but the other sandwiches such as the smoked turkey and artichoke get rave reviews. Order a delicious brownie or cookie for dessert. ✉ *Mongoose Junction Shopping Center, North Shore Rd., Cruz Bay* ☎ *340/777–3061* ⊟ *No credit cards* ☙ *No dinner.*

$$$ ✕ **Fish Trap Restaurant and Seafood Market.** The main dining room here
ECLECTIC is open to the breezes and buzzes with a mix of locals and visitors, but
☯ the back room has air-conditioning. Start with a tasty appetizer such as conch fritters or fish chowder (a creamy combination of snapper, white wine, paprika, and secret spices). You can always find steak and chicken dishes, as well as the interesting fish of the day. ✉ *Bay and Strand Sts., next to Our Lady of Mount Carmel Church, Cruz Bay* ☎ *340/693–9994* ⊕ *www.thefishtrap.com* ☙ *Closed Mon. No lunch.*

$$$ ✕ **High Tide.** This casual spot right at Cruz Bay Beach serves every-
ECLECTIC thing from hamburgers and mahimahi sandwiches to a fish of the
☯ day with sauces like mango chutney or island salsa. The kids' menu includes favorites like chicken tenders and grilled-cheese sandwiches. ✉ *Wharfside Village, Strand St., Cruz Bay* ☎ *340/714–6169* ⊕ *www.hightidevi.com.*

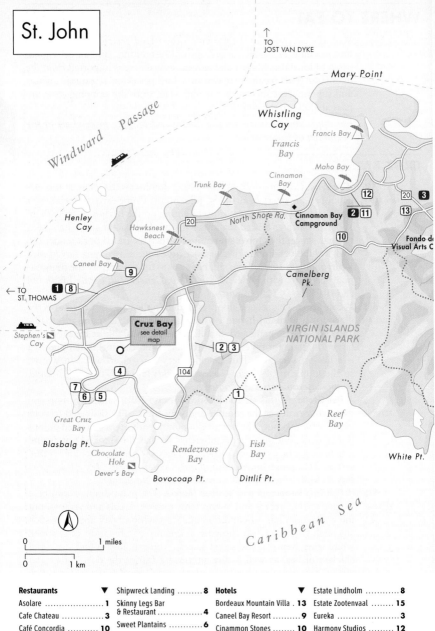

St. John

TO
JOST VAN DYKE

Mary Point

Windward Passage

Whistling
Cay

Francis Bay

Francis
Bay

Maho Bay

Trunk Bay

Cinnamon
Bay

Henley
Cay

Hawksnest
Beach

North Shore Rd.

Cinnamon Bay
Campground

12

2 **11**

20 **3**

13

10

Fondo de
Visual Arts C

20

Caneel Bay

9

Camelberg
Pk.

← TO
ST. THOMAS

1 **8**

Stephen's
Cay

Cruz Bay
see detail
map

VIRGIN ISLANDS
NATIONAL PARK

2 **3**

4

104

7

6 **5**

1

Great Cruz
Bay

Reef
Bay

Blasbalg Pt.

Chocolate
Hole

Rendezvous
Bay

Fish
Bay

White Pt.

Dever's Bay

Bovocoap Pt.

Dittlif Pt.

Caribbean Sea

0   1 miles
0   1 km

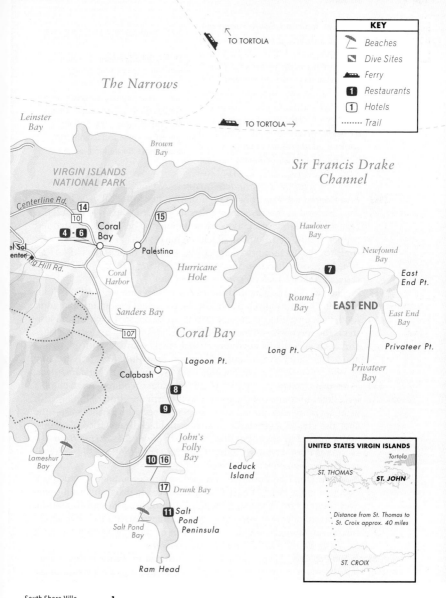

KEY

- Beaches
- Dive Sites
- Ferry
- **1** Restaurants
- 1 Hotels
- .... Trail

TO TORTOLA

TO TORTOLA →

The Narrows

Leinster Bay

Brown Bay

Sir Francis Drake Channel

VIRGIN ISLANDS NATIONAL PARK

Centerline Rd.

14

10

4 - **6**

Coral Bay

Haulover Bay

Newfound Bay

East End Pt.

15

el Sol enter

g Hill Rd.

Palestina

Coral Harbor

Hurricane Hole

7

Round Bay

EAST END

East End Bay

Sanders Bay

107

Coral Bay

Long Pt.

Privateer Pt.

Privateer Bay

Calabash

Lagoon Pt.

8

9

John's Folly Bay

Leduck Island

Lameshur Bay

10 **16**

17 *Drunk Bay*

11 *Salt Pond Peninsula*

Salt Pond Bay

Ram Head

UNITED STATES VIRGIN ISLANDS

Tortola

ST. THOMAS **ST. JOHN**

Distance from St. Thomas to St. Croix approx. 40 miles

ST. CROIX

$$ ✕ **Inn at Tamarind Court Restaurant.**
ECLECTIC   There's a different chef—each with
a unique style—here every night,
which makes for an eclectic menu.
On Monday schoolteacher Val
serves up gyros and spanakopita
from her native Greece. On other
nights you might find Mexican, bis-
tro-style, or down-home American
cooking, depending on who's in the
kitchen. ⊠ *Inn at Tamarind Court,
Rte. 104, Cruz Bay* ☎ *340/776–
6378* ⊕ *www.innattamarindcourt.com* ⊗ *No lunch.*

$$$$ ✕ **La Plancha del Mer.** Cooked on a searing hot iron grill called a *plan-*
MEDITERRANEAN   *cha,* the food at this restaurant takes its cues from Spain and southern
France. The house specialty is steak with garlic herb fries, roasted red
pepper coulis, and homemade chimichurri aioli. Locals and visitors
come for the bargain-priced appetizers at happy hour at the bar. ⊠ *Rte.
104, Mongoose Junction Shopping Center, Cruz Bay* ☎ *340/777–7333*
⊕ *www.laplanchadelmar.com* ⊗ *Closed Sun.*

$$ ✕ **Lime Inn.** Vacationers and mainland transplants who call St. John
CONTINENTAL   home flock to this alfresco spot for the congenial hospitality and good
food, including all-you-can-eat shrimp on Wednesday night. Fresh lobster is the specialty, and the menu also includes shrimp-and-steak dishes
and such specials as coconut-crusted chicken breast with plantains
and a Thai curry–cream sauce. ⊠ *Lemon Tree Mall, King St., Cruz Bay*
☎ *340/776–6425* ⊕ *www.limeinn.com* ⊗ *No lunch Sat. No dinner Sun.*

$$$ ✕ **Morgan's Mango.** A visit to this alfresco eatery requires you to climb a
CONTINENTAL   long flight of stairs, but the food is well worth the effort. Although fish
is the specialty—try the voodoo snapper topped with a fruity salsa—the
chef also creates a vegetarian platter with black beans, fried plantains,
and a mound of sweet potatoes. ⊠ *North Shore Rd., across from V.I.
National Park Visitors Center, Cruz Bay* ☎ *340/693–8141* ⊕ *www.
morgansmango.com* ⊗ *No lunch.*

$$ ✕ **Sogo's.** Don't be put off by the pedestrian decor. Sogo's, which can
CARIBBEAN   be found in the heart of busy Cruz Bay, serves up delightful, traditional
West Indian fare. The menu includes such dishes as kingfish, mutton,
and curried goat that you won't find at other restaurants. Less adven-
turous eaters might like the jerk chicken or the conch fritters. ⊠ *King
St., Cruz Bay* ☎ *340/779–4404* ⊗ *Closed Sun.*

$$ ✕ **Sun Dog Café.** There's an unusual assortment of dishes at this charm-
ECLECTIC   ing alfresco restaurant, which you'll find tucked into a courtyard in the
upper reaches of the Mongoose Junction shopping center. Kudos to the
white pizza with artichoke hearts, roasted garlic, mozzarella cheese, and
capers. The Jamaican jerk chicken salad and the black-bean quesadilla are
also good choices. ⊠ *Mongoose Junction Shopping Center, North Shore
Rd., Cruz Bay* ☎ *340/693–8340* ⊕ *www.sundogcafe.com* ⊗ *No dinner.*

$ ✕ **Uncle Joe's Barbecue.** Juicy ribs and tasty chicken legs dripping with
BARBECUE   the house barbecue sauce make for one of St. John's best dining deals.
⟳   An ear of corn, rice, and a generous scoop of macaroni salad or cole

slaw round out the plate. This casual spot crowds the edge of a busy sidewalk in the heart of Cruz Bay. Even though there are a few open-air tables for dining "in," the ambience is more than a tad on the pedestrian side, so takeout is a better bet. ⊠ *North Shore Rd., across from post office, Cruz Bay* ☎ *340/693–8806* ⊟ *No credit cards.*

$$$$ ✕ **Zozo's Ristorante.** Creative takes on old standards coupled with lovely

ITALIAN   presentations draw the crowds to this restaurant at Gallows Point

Fodor'sChoice   Resort. Start with crispy fried calamari served with a pesto mayonnaise.

★   The chef dresses up roasted mahimahi with a pine-nut crust and serves it with a warm goat cheese–and-arugula salad. The slow-simmered osso buco comes with prosciutto-wrapped asparagus and saffron risotto. The sunset views will take your breath away. ⊠ *Gallows Point Resort, Bay St., Cruz Bay* ☎ *340/693–9200* ✆ *No lunch.*

NORTH SHORE

$$ ✕ **Pavillion Restaurant.** At the end of a long, partially paved road at Maho

ECLECTIC   Bay Camps, this casual open-air restaurant is worth the drive. The menu

☺   changes daily, but there's always a handful of seafood, chicken, and vegetarian entrées. Give your order at the counter. While you wait for it to be cooked—the chef calls your name when it's done—help yourself to the salad bar, rolls, and iced tea included with your dinner. Arrive early to enjoy the spectacular sunset views. ⊠ *Maho Bay Camps, off Rte. 20, Maho Bay* ☎ *340/776–6226* ⊕ *www.maho.org* ✆ *No lunch.*

MID ISLAND

$ ✕ **Café Chateau.** Your hamburgers and sweet potato fries come with

AMERICAN   a side of fabulous views of Coral Bay and the British Virgin Islands.

★   Located at the popular Bordeaux overlook, this restaurant also serves salads made with local greens and fish sandwiches. The adjacent ice cream shop blends up some delicious fruit smoothies. ⊠ *Rte. 10, Bordeaux* ☎ *340/776–6611* ✆ *No dinner.*

CORAL BAY AND ENVIRONS

$$$ ✕ **Café Concordia.** A stellar view and delightful food are good reasons

CONTINENTAL   to drive all the way out to Concordia for dinner. There's no wait ser-

Fodor'sChoice   vice—just give your order to the bartender—but that helps keep costs

★   down. The menu changes daily, but the fishermen's platter with shrimp, mussels, conch, and squid is a good bet if it's on the menu. Or come by for drinks and something from the "little bites" menu. Try the flatbread with smoked Gouda, figs, and toasted almonds. ⊠ *Off Route 107, Estate Concordia* ✆ *P.O. Box 310, Cruz Bay, St. John 00831* ☎ *340/693–5855* ⊕ *www.maho.org.*

$$ ✕ **Donkey Diner.** In an odd combination that works well for Coral Bay

ECLECTIC   visitors and residents, this tiny spot along the main road through Coral Bay sells yummy breakfasts and pizza. Breakfasts can be as ordinary or as innovative as you like, with the menu running from fried eggs with bacon to blueberry pancakes to scrambled tofu served with home fries. Pizzas are equally eclectic, with toppings that include everything from the usual pepperoni and mushrooms to more exotic corn, raisins, and kalamata olives, but they are only available Wednesday through Friday and Sunday. ⊠ *Rte. 10, Coral Bay* ☎ *340/693–5240* ⊕ *www. donkeydiner.com* ⊟ *No credit cards.*

$$$
CARIBBEAN
★

✕ **Miss Lucy's Restaurant.** Sitting seaside at remote Friis Bay, Miss Lucy's dishes up Caribbean food with a contemporary flair. Dishes such as tender conch fritters, a spicy West Indian stew called callaloo, and fried fish make up most of the menu, but you also find a generous paella filled with seafood, sausage, and chicken on the menu. Sunday brunches are legendary, and if you're around when the moon is full, stop by for the monthly full-moon party. The handful of small tables near the water is the nicest, but if they're taken or the mosquitoes are swarming, the indoor tables do nicely. ⊠ *Rte. 107, Friis Bay* ☎ *340/693–5244* ☉ *Closed Mon. No dinner Sun.*

$$$
AMERICAN

✕ **Shipwreck Landing.** A favorite with locals and visitors, this alfresco restaurant serves up tasty food in a casual setting. Opt for the tables closest to the road for the best breezes and water views. The menu includes lots of seafood, but the chicken and beef dishes ensure that everyone's satisfied. If it's a day when the chef made homemade soup, try at least a cup. For lunch, the grilled mahimahi sandwich is always a good bet. ⊠ *Route 107, between Coral Bay and Salt Pond, Freeman's Ground* ☎ *340/693–5640.*

$
AMERICAN
★

✕ **Skinny Legs Bar and Restaurant.** Sailors who live aboard boats anchored offshore and an eclectic coterie of residents gather for lunch and dinner at this funky spot in the middle of a boatyard-cum–shopping complex. If owner Moe Chabuz is around, take a gander at his gams; you'll see where the restaurant got its name. It's a great place for burgers, fish sandwiches, and whatever sports event is on the satellite TV. ⊠ *Rte. 10, Coral Bay* ☎ *340/779–4982* ⊕ *www.skinnylegs.com.*

$$$
CARIBBEAN

✕ **Sweet Plantains.** The food here is a sophisticated take on Caribbean cuisine. The fish of the day—it could be mahimahi or grouper—is served with a Caribbean flair and is always especially good, or try one of the curries if you don't want seafood. For a real local taste, start with the saltfish cakes served with shredded cabbage and mango puree. The coconut flan for dessert is another Caribbean favorite. ⊠ *Rte. 107, Coral Bay* ☎ *340/777–4653* ⊕ *www.sweetplantains-stjohn.com* ☉ *Closed Tues.*

$
ECLECTIC

✕ **Tourist Trap.** Lobster rolls in traditional crustless buns are the main event at this roadside eatery—really just a roadside shack—but the fish sandwiches, hot dogs with homemade chili, meatball subs, and nachos with homemade roasted tomatillo sauce, make for a tasty lunch or snack. ⊠ *Rte. 107, Concordia* ☎ *340/774–0912* ⊕ *www.wedontneednostinkingwebsite. com* ⊟ *No credit cards* ☉ *Closed Sun. and Mon. No dinner.*

$
CARIBBEAN
★

✕ **Vie's Snack Shack.** Stop by Vie's when you're out exploring the island. Although it's just a shack by the side of the road, Vie's serves up some great cooking. The garlic chicken legs are crisp and tasty, and the conch fritters are really something to write home about. Plump and filled with fresh herbs, a plateful will keep you going for the rest of the afternoon. Save room for a wedge of coconut pie—called a tart in this neck of the woods. When you're finished eating, a spectacular white-sand beach down the road beckons. ⊠ *Rte. 10, Hansen Bay* ☎ *340/693–5033* ⊟ *No credit cards* ☉ *Closed Sun. and Mon. No dinner.*

CAMPING IN ST. JOHN

For those on a really tight budget, St. John has a handful of camping spots. The best of these is probably the basic Cinnamon Bay Campground in the national park, but others are more elaborate like the "eco-tents" at Condordia and Maho. They appeal to those who don't mind bringing their own beach towels from home or busing their own tables at dinner. If you want your piña colada delivered beachside by a smiling waiter, you'd be better off elsewhere.

Cinnamon Bay Campground
(✉ *Rte. 20, Cinnamon Bay*
☎ *340/776–6330 or 800/539–9998*
⊕ *www.cinnamonbay.com*) sits in the heart of Virgin Islands National Park, a stellar location right at the beach. Tents, rustic cottages, and bare sites are nestled in the trees that stretch behind the shore, and you have easy access to hiking, water sports, and ranger-led evening programs.

The amenities are basic, but include propane stoves, cooking equipment, and bed linens with the cottages ($126–$163) and tents ($92); reserve early if you'd like a cottage right behind the beach. Other cottages, tents, and bare sites sit a short walk away. Only the screened cottages have electric lights; those using the already erected tents depend on propane lanterns. With bare sites ($32), you must bring all your own equipment. Showers and flush toilets, as well as a restaurant and a small store, are a short walk away from the camping area. The area can be buggy, the showers are cold, and there can be some traffic noise, but the beachfront site is nice, and there are hiking trails and activities close by. Reservations for one of the 55 permanent tents, 40 cottages, or 31 tent sites are essential in winter and recommended at other times. The campground is closed in September and October.

WHERE TO STAY

St. John attracts so many different kinds of travelers because accommodations come in all price ranges. Folks on a budget can sleep at Cinnamon Bay Campground. Cruz Bay has a few moderately priced guesthouses and no-frills vacation villas. Those with fatter wallets will have no trouble finding a room at the island's resorts or luxury vacation villas.

CONDOMINIUM RESORTS AND COTTAGES

St. John does have several resort-style condo complexes. Many of the island's condos are just minutes from the hustle and bustle of Cruz Bay, but you can find more scattered around the island.

PRIVATE CONDOS AND VILLAS

Here and there between Cruz Bay and Coral Bay are about 500 private villas and condos (prices range from $ to $$$$). With pools or hot tubs, full kitchens, and living areas, these lodgings provide a fully functional home away from home. They're perfect for couples and extended groups of family or friends. You need a car, since most lodgings are in the hills and very few at the beach. Villa managers usually pick you up at the dock, arrange for your rental car, and answer questions upon arrival as well as during your stay. Prices drop in the summer season, which is generally after April 15. Some companies begin off-season pricing a week or two later, so be sure to ask.

If you want to be close to Cruz Bay's restaurants and boutiques, a villa in the Chocolate Hole and Great Cruz Bay areas will put you a few minutes away. The Coral Bay area has a growing number of villas, but you'll be about 20 minutes from Cruz Bay. Beaches string out along the north shore, so you won't be more than 15 minutes from the water no matter where you stay.

RENTAL AGENTS

Book-It VI (⌂ *5000 Estate Enighed, PMB 15, Cruz Bay 00831* ☎ *340/693–8555 or 800/416–1205* ⊕ *www.bookitvi.com*) handles villas all across St. John.

Carefree Get-Aways (⌂ *Box 1626, Cruz Bay 00831* ☎ *340/779–4070 or 888/643–6002* ⊕ *www.carefreegetaways.com*) manages vacation villas on the island's southern and western edges.

Caribbean Villas & Resorts (⌂ *Box 458, Cruz Bay 00831* ☎ *340/776–6152 or 800/338–0987* ⊕ *www.caribbeanvilla.com*) handles condo rentals for Cruz Views and Gallow's Point Resort, as well as for many private villas.

Caribe Havens (✉ *Box 455, Cruz Bay* ☎ *340/776–6518* ⊕ *www.caribehavens.com*) has mainly budget properties scattered around the island.

Catered to Vacation Homes (✉ *Marketplace Suite 206, 5206 Enighed, Cruz Bay* ☎ *340/776–6641 or 800/424–6641* ⊕ *www.cateredto.com*) has luxury homes, mainly in the middle of the island and on the western edge.

Cloud 9 Villas (✉ *Box 102, Cruz Bay* ☎ *340/693–8495 or 866/693–8496* ⊕ *www.cloud9villas.com*) has several homes, with most in the Gifft Hill and Chocolate Hole area.

Great Caribbean Getaways (⌂ *Box 8317, Cruz Bay 00831* ☎ *340/693–8692 or 800/341–2532* ⊕ *www.greatcaribbeangetaways.com*) handles private villas from Cruz Bay to Coral Bay.

Island Getaways (⌂ *Box 1504, Cruz Bay 00831* ☎ *340/693–7676 or 888/693–7676* ⊕ *www.islandgetawaysinc.com*) has villas in the Great Cruz Bay–Chocolate Hole area, with a few others scattered around the island.

On-Line Vacations (⌂ *Box 9901, Emmaus 00831* ☎ *340/776–6036 or 888/842–6632* ⊕ *www.onlinevacations.com*) books vacation villas around St. John.

Private Homes for Private Vacations (✉ *7605 Mamey Peak, Coral Bay* ☎ *340/776–6876* ⊕ *www.privatehomesvi.com*) has homes across the island.

Seaview Vacation Homes (⌂ *Box 644, Cruz Bay 00831* ☎ *340/776–6805 or 888/625–2963* ⊕ *www.seaviewhomes.com*) handles homes with views of the ocean in the Chocolate Hole, Great Cruz Bay, and Fish Bay areas.

Star Villas (⌂ *1202 Gallows Point, Cruz Bay 00831* ☎ *340/776–6704* ⊕ *www.starvillas.com*) has cozy villas just outside Cruz Bay.

St. John Ultimate Villas (✆ *Box 1324, Cruz Bay 00831* ☎ *340/776–4703 or 888/851–7588* ⊕ *www.stjohnultimatevillas.com*) manages villas across the island.

Vacation Vistas (✆ *Box 476, Cruz Bay 00831* ☎ *340/776–6462* ⊕ *www. vacationvistas.com*) manages villas mainly in the Chocolate Hole, Great Cruz Bay, and Rendezvous areas.

Windspree (✉ *7924 Emmaus, Cruz Bay* ☎ *340/693–5423 or 888/742– 0357* ⊕ *www.windspree.com*) handles villas mainly in the Coral Bay area.

For approximate costs, see the dining and lodging price chart at the beginning of this chapter. The following hotel reviews have been condensed for this book. Please go to Fodors.com for expanded reviews of each property.

CRUZ BAY AND ENVIRONS

$$$ 🏠 **Cloud Nine.** Step out of bed and into the pool at this casual villa in the
RENTAL   residential Gifft Hill neighborhood. **Pros:** great views; spacious deck; lovely pool. **Cons:** need car to get around; bland decor. ✉ *Off Gifft Hill Rd., Gifft Hill* ⊕ *www.cloud9villas.com* 🛏 *3 bedrooms, 3 bathrooms* ⚙ *In-room: a/c, Wi-Fi. In-hotel: pool, laundry facilities* ☞ *7-night minimum* �� *No meals.*

$$–$$$ 🏠 **Coconut Coast Villas.** This small condominium complex with stu-
RENTAL   dio, two-, and three-bedroom apartments is a 10-minute walk from Cruz Bay, but is insulated from the town's noise in a sleepy suburban neighborhood. **Pros:** good snorkeling; full kitchens; walk to Cruz Bay. **Cons:** small beach; some uphill walks; nearby utility plant can be noisy. ✉ *Turner Bay* ✆ *Box 618, Cruz Bay 00831* ☎ *340/693–9100 or 800/858–7989* ⊕ *www.coconutcoast.com* 🛏 *9 units* ⚙ *In-room: a/c, no safe, kitchen, Wi-Fi. In-hotel: pool, beach, business center* ⓓ *No meals.*

$$–$$$ 🏠 **Estate Lindholm Bed and Breakfast.** Built among old stone ruins on a lushly
B&B/INN   planted hill overlooking Cruz Bay, Estate Lindholm has an enchanting setting. **Pros:** lush landscaping; gracious host; pleasant decor. **Cons:** can be noisy; some uphill walks; on a busy road. ✉ *Rte. 20 on Caneel Hill, Estate Lindholm* ✆ *Box 1360, Cruz Bay 00831* ☎ *340/776–6121 or 800/322– 6335* ⊕ *www.estatelindholm.com* 🛏 *14 rooms* ⚙ *In-room: a/c, no safe. In-hotel: restaurant, pool, gym, some age restrictions* ⓓ *Breakfast.*

$ 🏠 **Eureka.** With views of Chocolate Hole and beyond, Eureka provides
RENTAL   casual living at budget prices. **Pros:** close to shops and restaurants; inexpensive. **Cons:** few frills; no a/c; need a car to get around. ✉ *Off Gifft Hill Rd., Gifft Hill* ⊕ *www.caribehavens.com* 🛏 *2 bedrooms, 2 baths* ⚙ *In-room: no a/c, no safe. In-hotel: laundry facilities* ▬ *No credit cards* ☞ *7-night minimum* ⓓ *No meals.*

$$$–$$$$ 🏠 **Gallows Point Resort.** You're a short walk from restaurants and shops
RESORT   at this waterfront location just outside Cruz Bay, but once you step into your condo, the hustle and bustle are left behind. **Pros:** walk to shopping; excellent restaurant; comfortably furnished rooms. **Cons:** some rooms can be noisy; mediocre beach; insufficient parking. ✉ *Gallows Point, Bay St., Cruz Bay* ✆ *Box 58, Cruz Bay* ☎ *340/776–6434 or 800/323–7229* ⊕ *www.gallowspointresort.com* 🛏 *60 units* ⚙ *In-room: a/c, kitchen, Wi-Fi. In-hotel: restaurant, pool, beach, water sports, business center* ⓓ *No meals.*

$
B&B/INN

⊡ **Garden by the Sea Bed and Breakfast.** A stay here will allow you to live like a local in a middle-class residential neighborhood near a bird-filled salt pond. **Pros:** homey atmosphere; great breakfasts; breathtaking view from deck. **Cons:** noise from nearby power substation; some uphill walks; basic amenities. ⊠ *Enighed* ⌂ *Box 37, Cruz Bay 00831* ☎ *340/779–4731* ⊕ *www.gardenbythesea.com* ⟿ *3 rooms* ☖ *In-room: a/c, no safe, no TV, Wi-Fi* ▭ No credit cards ⦿ *Breakfast.*

¢
B&B/INN

⊡ **Inn at Tamarind Court.** If money is a concern—and you don't want to go camping—opt for the Inn at Tamarind Court. **Pros:** walk to restaurants and shops; good breakfasts; convivial atmosphere. **Cons:** on a busy road; bland decor; need a car to get around. ⊠ *Rte. 104, Cruz Bay* ⌂ *Box 350, Cruz Bay* ☎ *340/776–6378 or 800/221–1637* ⊕ *www. innattamarindcourt.com* ⟿ *20 rooms* ☖ *In-room: a/c, no safe, kitchen (some), Wi-Fi. In-hotel: restaurant.* ⦿ *Breakfast.*

$$$$
RENTAL

⊡ **Ristaba.** Big families or couples who travel together will enjoy Ristaba's abundant space. **Pros:** pleasant neighborhood; lots of space; great pool. **Cons:** other houses nearby; need car to get around; no a/c in common areas. ⊠ *465 Rock Ridge Rd., Chocolate Hole North* ⊕ *www.vacationvistas.com* ⟿ *6 bedrooms, 6 bathrooms* ☖ *In-room: a/c (some), no safe, Wi-Fi. In-hotel: pool, laundry facilities* ▭ No credit cards ⟳ *7-night minimum* ⦿ *No meals.*

$-$$
RENTAL

⊡ **Serendip.** This complex offers modern apartments on lush grounds with lovely views and makes a great pick for a budget stay in a residential locale. **Pros:** comfortable accommodations; good views; nice neighborhood. **Cons:** no beach; need car to get around; nearby construction. ⊠ *Off Rte. 104, Enighed* ⌂ *Box 273, Cruz Bay 00831* ☎ *340/776–6646 or 888/800–6445* ⊕ *www.serendipstjohn.com* ⟿ *10 apartments* ☖ *In-room: a/c, no safe, kitchen, Wi-Fi. In-hotel: pool, laundry facilities* ⦿ *No meals.*

$$$$
RENTAL

⊡ **South Shore Villa.** When it seems you've been driving forever, you'll reach this spacious villa up in the clouds above the island's south shore. **Pros:** stellar view, great pool, top-notch kitchen. **Cons:** need car to get around, isolated location. ⊠ *Skytop, Fish Bay* ⊕ *www.seaviewhomes. com* ⟿ *4 bedrooms, 4½ bathrooms* ☖ *In-room: a/c, Wi-Fi. In-hotel: pool, laundry facilities, some age restrictions* ▭ No credit cards ⟳ *7-night minimum* ⦿ *No meals.*

$$$–$$$$
RENTAL

⊡ **Splash.** You can't beat this location. Splash sits right on the water near the Westin Resort and Villas, giving you the option of strolling over for dinner. **Pros:** waterfront location; lovely furnishings; close to restaurants. **Cons:** need car to get around; other houses nearby; indoor pool not good for families with kids. ⊠ *Great Cruz Bay Rd., Great Cruz Bay* ⊕ *www. caribbeanvilla.com* ☖ *In-room: a/c (some), Wi-Fi. In-hotel: pool, laundry facilities* ▭ No credit cards ⟳ *7-night minimum* ⦿ *No meals.*

$
B&B/INN

⊡ **St. John Inn.** A stay here gives you a bit of style at what passes for budget prices in St. John. **Pros:** walk to restaurants and shops; convivial atmosphere; pretty pool. **Cons:** need car to get around; noisy location; insufficient parking. ⊠ *Off Rte. 104, Cruz Bay* ⌂ *Box 37, Cruz Bay* ☎ *340/693–8688 or 800/666–7688* ⊕ *www.stjohninn.com* ⟿ *11 units* ☖ *In-room: a/c, no safe, kitchen (some), Wi-Fi. In-hotel: pool* ⦿ *Breakfast.*

$$$$ 🖭 **Westin St. John Resort and Villas.** The island's largest resort provides a
RESORT nice beachfront location and enough activities to keep you busy. **Pros:**
entertaining children's programs; pretty pool area; many activities.
Cons: mediocre beach; long walk to some parts of the resort; need car
to get around. ✉ *Rte. 104, Great Cruz Bay* ✆ *Box 8310, Cruz Bay*
00831 ☎ *340/693–8000 or 800/808–5020* ⊕ *www.westinresortstjohn.*
com ⤴ *175 rooms, 146 villas* ⚙ *In-room: a/c, kitchen (some), refrig-*
erator, Internet, Wi-Fi. In-hotel: restaurants, tennis courts, pool, gym,
beach, water sports, children's programs ⦿ *No meals.*

NORTH SHORE

$$$$ 🖭 **Caneel Bay Resort.** Well-heeled honeymooners, couples celebrating
RESORT anniversaries, and extended families all enjoy Caneel Bay Resort's laid-
Fodor'sChoice back luxury. **Pros:** lovely beaches; gorgeous rooms; lots of amenities.
★ **Cons:** staff can be chilly; isolated location; rates are pricey. ✉ *Rte. 20,*
Caneel Bay ✆ *Box 720, Cruz Bay 00831* ☎ *340/776–6111 or 888/767–*
3966 ⊕ *www.caneelbay.com* ⤴ *166 rooms* ⚙ *In-room: a/c, no safe, no*
TV, Wi-Fi. In-hotel: restaurants, tennis courts, pool, spa, beach, water
sports, children's programs, business center ⦿ *Breakfast.*

$ 🖭 **Harmony Studios.** An ecologically correct environment is one of the
RESORT draws at these condominium-style units that sit hillside at Maho Bay.
Pros: convivial atmosphere; near beach; comfortable units. **Cons:** lots
of stairs; no air-conditioning; need car to get around. ✉ *Maho Bay*
✆ *Box 310, Cruz Bay 00831* ☎ *340/776–6240 or 800/392–9004*
⊕ *www.maho.org* ⤴ *12 units* ⚙ *In-room: no a/c, no safe, kitchen, no*
TV. In-hotel: restaurant, beach, water sports, children's programs,
business center ⦿ *No meals.*

¢ 🖭 **Maho Bay Camps.** Tucked into the greenery along the island's North
RESORT Shore, eco-conscious Maho Bay Camps attracts a sociable crowd that
☾ likes to explore the undersea world off the campground's beach or
Fodor'sChoice attend on-site seminars. **Pros:** friendly atmosphere; tasty food; real eco-
★ resort. **Cons:** many stairs to climb; can be buggy; need a car to get
around. ✉ *Maho Bay* ✆ *Box 310, Cruz Bay 00831* ☎ *340/776–6240*
or 800/392–9004 ⊕ *www.maho.org* ⤴ *114 tent cottages with shared*
baths ⚙ *In-room: no a/c, no safe, no TV. In-hotel: restaurant, beach,*
water sports, children's programs, business center ⦿ *No meals.*

MID ISLAND

$$$$ 🖭 **Bordeaux Mountain Villa.** With many pieces of antique furniture, lots of
RENTAL stone walls and four-poster beds, this gracious villa exudes charm. It has
plenty of room for large groups to spread out in both good weather and
bad. Guests can step right into the heated pool from the indoor/outdoor
room on the villa's lower level, or they can gather to enjoy the media
room on the upper level. The Bordeaux area can be a bit chilly during
the winter, but the rain-forest climate keeps guests cool during the summer months. **Pros:** lots of charm; cool in summer. **Cons:** need car to get
around; not on the beach; chilly in winter. ✉ *Off Rte. 107, Bordeaux*
⊕ *www.stjohnultimatevillas.com* ⤴ *4 bedrooms 4½ baths* ⚙ *In-room:*
a/c (some), no safe, Wi-Fi. In-hotel: pool, laundry facilities ⦿ *No meals.*

3

Caneel Bay Resort

Maho Bay Camps & Estate Concordia Preserve

$$$$ ⚏ **Cinnamon Stones.** The stunning view of the north shore and the islands
RENTAL beyond is the first thing you notice at this graciously appointed villa
Fodor'sChoice in the prestigious Catherineberg area. **Pros:** stellar view; good layout;
★ quiet setting. **Cons:** need car to get around; long drive to restaurants and
shops; can be damp. ⊠ *Wattapama Rd., Catherineberg* ⌂ *Island Get-*
aways Inc., P.O. Box 1504, Cruz Bay 00831⊕ *www.islandgetawaysinc.*
com ⟿ *3 bedrooms, 4½ bathrooms* ⚭ *In-room: no a/c, Wi-Fi. In-hotel:*
pool, laundry facilities ▬ *No credit cards* ⊗ *Closed Jan.–Mar. and Sept.*
⟿ *6-night minimum* †○| *No meals.*

CORAL BAY AND ENVIRONS

$ ⚏ **Concordia Studios and Eco-tents.** This off-the-beaten-path resort—under
RENTAL the same management as Maho Bay Camps—is on the remote Salt Pond
Fodor'sChoice peninsula. **Pros:** good views; ecofriendly environment; beach nearby.
★ **Cons:** need car to get around; lots of stairs. ⊠ *Estate Concordia* ⌂ *Box*
310, Cruz Bay 00831 ☎ *340/693–5855 or 800/392–9004* ⊕ *www.maho.*
org ⟿ *9 studios, 25 tents* ⚭ *In-room: no a/c, no safe, kitchen (some), no*
TV. In-hotel: restaurant, pool †○| *No meals.*

$$$$ ⚏ **Coral Cove.** You'll smell the sea wherever you are at Coral Cove. **Pros:**
RENTAL on the water; lots of amenities; lovely pool. **Cons:** need a car to get
around; on busy road. ⊠ *Rte 107, John's Folly* ⊕ *www.cateredto.com*
⟿ *4 bedrooms, 4½ bathrooms* ⚭ *In-room: a/c (some), Wi-Fi. In-hotel:*
pool, gym, laundry facilities, some pets allowed, some age restrictions
⊗ *Closed Sept.* ⟿ *7-night minimum* †○| *No meals.*

$$$–$$$$ ⚏ **Estate Zootenvaal.** Comfortable and casual, this small cottage colony
RENTAL gives you the perfect place to relax. **Pros:** quiet beach; private; near res-
taurants. **Cons:** some traffic noise; no air-conditioning. ⊠ *Rte. 10, Hur-*
ricane Hole, Zootenvaal ☎ *340/776–6321* ⊕ *www.estatezootenvaal.*
com ⟿ *4 units* ⚭ *In-room: no a/c, no safe (some), kitchen, no TV*
(some). In-hotel: beach ▬ *No credit cards* †○| *No meals.*

$$$ ⚏ **Villa Margherita.** With two bedrooms at opposite ends of the house,
RENTAL Villa Margherita is a good choice for two couples vacationing together.
Pros: plenty of space; pleasant hot tub; nice neighborhood. **Cons:** no
beach; need car to get around; so-so view. ⊠ *Majestic Mile, Upper Caro-*
lina ⊕ *www.windspree.com/homes* ⟿ *2½ bedrooms, 2½ bathrooms*
⚭ *In-room: a/c, no safe, Wi-Fi. In-hotel: laundry facilities* ⊗ *Closed*
Sept. †○| *No meals.*

NIGHTLIFE

St. John isn't the place to go for glitter and all-night partying. Still, after-
hours Cruz Bay can be a lively little town in which to dine, drink, dance,
or flirt. Notices posted on the bulletin board outside the Connections
telephone center—up the street from the ferry dock—or listings in the
island's two newspapers (the *St. John Sun Times* and *Tradewinds*) will
keep you apprised of local events.

CRUZ BAY

Fred's. There's calypso and reggae on Friday night at this popular night-spot. ⊠ *King St., Cruz Bay* ☎ *340/776–6363.*

Woody's. Young folks like to gather here, where sidewalk tables provide a close-up view of Cruz Bay's action. ⊠ *Near ferry dock and First Bank, Cruz Bay* ☎ *340/779–4625.*

Zozo's Ristorante. After a sunset drink at this restaurant, which is up the hill from Cruz Bay, you can stroll around town (much is clustered around the small waterfront park). Many of the young people from the U.S. mainland who live and work on St. John will be out sipping and socializing, too. ⊠ *Gallows Point Resort, Bay St., Cruz Bay* ☎ *340/693–9200.*

CORAL BAY AND ENVIRONS

Island Blues. As its name implies, this is the hot place to go for music at the eastern end of the island. ⊠ *Rte. 107, Coral Bay* ☎ *340/776–6800.*

Skinny Legs Bar and Restaurant. On the far side of the island, landlubbers and old salts listen to music and swap stories at this popular casual restaurant and bar. ⊠ *Rte. 10, Coral Bay* ☎ *340/779–4982.*

SHOPPING

CRUZ BAY

Luxury goods and handicrafts can be found on St. John. Most shops carry a little of this and a bit of that, so it pays to poke around. The main Cruz Bay shopping district runs from **Wharfside Village,** just around the corner from the ferry dock, to **Mongoose Junction,** an inviting shopping center on North Shore Road. (The name of this upscale shopping mall, by the way, is a holdover from a time when those furry island creatures gathered at a nearby garbage bin.) Out on Route 104 stop in at the **Marketplace** to explore its gift and crafts shops. On St. John, store hours run from 9 or 10 to 5 or 6. Wharfside Village and Mongoose Junction shops in Cruz Bay are often open into the evening.

ART GALLERIES

Fodor's Choice
★
Bajo el Sol. Bajo el Sol sells works by owner Livy Hitchcock, plus pieces from a roster of the island's best artists. Shop for oil and acrylics, sculptures, and ceramics. ⊠ *Mongoose Junction Shopping Center, North Shore Rd., Cruz Bay* ☎ *340/693–7070.*

Caravan Gallery. This gallery owned by Radha Speer sells unusual jewelry that Radha has traveled the world to find. And the more you look, the more you see—wood carvings, tribal art, and masks for sale cover the walls and tables, making this a great place to browse. ⊠ *Mongoose Junction Shopping Center, North Shore Rd., Cruz Bay* ☎ *340/779–4566.*

Coconut Coast Studios. This waterside shop is a five-minute walk from the center of Cruz Bay and showcases the work of Elaine Estern. She specializes in undersea scenes. ⊠ *Frank Bay, Cruz Bay* ☎ *340/776–6944.*

Continued on page 124

BELOW THE WAVES By Lynda Lohr

Colorful reefs and wrecks rife with corals and tropical fish make the islands as interesting underwater as above. Brilliantly colored reef fish vie for your attention with corals in wondrous shapes. Scuba diving gets you up close and personal with the world below the waves.

Bright blue tangs and darting blue-headed wrasses. Corals in wondrous shapes—some look like brains, others like elk antlers. Colorful, bulbous sponges. All these and more can be spotted along the myriad reefs of the U.S. and British Virgin Islands. You might see a pink conch making its way along the ocean bottom in areas with seagrass beds. If you're really lucky, a turtle may swim into view, or a lobster may poke its antennae out of a hole in the reef or rocks. If you do a night dive, you might run into an octopus. But you may be surprised at how much you can see by simply hovering just below the surface, with nothing more than a mask and snorkel. It's a bird's-eye view, but an excellent one. Whether scuba diving or snorkeling, take along an underwater camera to capture memories of your exciting adventure. You can buy disposable ones at most dive shops or bring one from home.

DIVE AND SNORKELING SITES IN BRITISH VIRGIN ISLANDS

TORTOLA

Although a major base for dive operations in the BVI (due to its proximity to so many exceptional dive sites), Tortola itself doesn't have as much to offer divers. However, there are still some noteworthy destinations. The massive **Brewer's Bay Pinnacles** grow 70 feet high to within 30 feet of the surface; the rock mazes are only for advanced divers because of strong currents and they are not always acces-

sible. Abundant reefs close to shore make **Brewer's Bay** popular with snorkelers, as are **Frenchman's Cay** and **Long Bay Beef Island. Diamond Reef,** between Great Camanoe and Scrub Island, is a small wall about 200 yards long. **Shark Point,** off the northeast coast of Scrub Island, does have resident sharks. Though isolated in open ocean, the wreck of the **Chikuzen,** a Japanese refrigerator ship, is a popular site.

THE ISLANDS OF THE SIR FRANCIS DRAKE CHANNEL

Southeast of Tortola lie a string of islands with some of the BVI's finest dive sites, some world famous. The wreck of the royal mail ship **Rhone** is between Peter and Salt islands and is, perhaps, the most famous dive site in the BVI. **Wreck Alley,** consisting of three sunken modern ships, is between Salt and Cooper islands. At **Alice in Wonderland,** south of

Ginger Island, giant, mushroom-shaped corals shelter reef fish, moray eels, and crustaceans. **Alice's Backside,** off the northwestern tip of Ginger Island, is usually smooth enough for snorkeling and shallow enough so that beginner divers can get a good look at the myriad sealife and sponges.

The Chikuzen

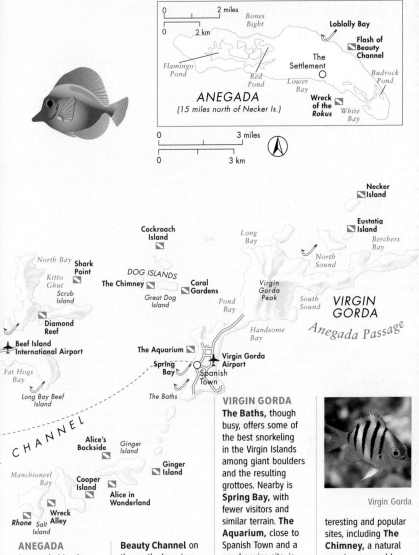

Virgin Gorda

VIRGIN GORDA

The Baths, though busy, offers some of the best snorkeling in the Virgin Islands among giant boulders and the resulting grottoes. Nearby is **Spring Bay,** with fewer visitors and similar terrain. **The Aquarium,** close to Spanish Town and a good novice site, is so called because of the abundance of reef fish that swim around the submerged granite boulders that are similar to those of The Baths. Further west of Virgin Gorda, the Dog Islands have some in-

teresting and popular sites, including **The Chimney,** a natural opening covered by sponges off Great Dog. South of Great Dog, **Coral Gardens** has a large coral reef with a submerged airplane wreck nearby. Fish are drawn to nearby **Cockroach Island.**

ANEGADA

Surrounded by the third-largest barrier reef in the world, Anegada has great snorkeling from virtually any beach on the island. But there are also some notable dive sites as well. The **Flash of**

Beauty Channel on the north shore is a great open-water dive, but only suitable for experienced divers. But even novices can enjoy diving at the **Wreck of the *Rokus*,** a Greek cargo ship off the island's southern shore.

DIVE AND SNORKELING SITES
IN U.S. VIRGIN ISLANDS

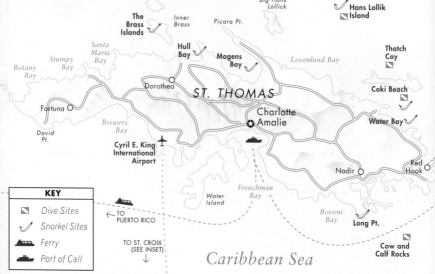

ST. THOMAS

St. Thomas has at least 40 popular dive sites, most shallow. Favorite reef dives off St. Thomas include **Cow and Calf Rocks,** which barely break water off the southeast coast of St. Thomas; the coral-covered pinnacles of **Frenchcap** south of St. Thomas; and tunnels where you can explore undersea from the Caribbean to the Atlantic at **Thatch Cay** (where the Coast Guard cutter *General Rogers* rests at 65 feet). **Grass Cay** and **Mingo Cay** between St. Thomas and St. John are also popular dive sites. **Coki Beach** offers the best off-the-beach snorkeling in St. Thomas. Nearby Coral World offers a dive-helmet walk for the untrained, and Snuba of St. Thomas has tethered shallow dives for non-certified divers. **Magens Bay,** the most popular beach on St. Thomas, provides lovely snorkeling if you head along the edges. You're likely to see some colorful sponges, darting fish, and maybe even a turtle if you're lucky. This is a stop on every island tour.

ST. JOHN

St. John is particularly known for its myriad good snorkeling spots—certainly more than for its diving opportunities, though there are many dive sites within easy reach of Cruz Bay. **Trunk Bay** often receives the most attention because of its underwater snorkeling trail created by the National Park Service; signs let you know what you're seeing in terms of coral and other underwater features. And the beach is easy to reach since taxis leave on demand from Cruz Bay. A patchy reef just offshore means good snorkeling at **Hawksnest Beach.** Additionally, **Cinnamon Bay** and **Leinster Bay** also get their fair share of praise as snorkeling spots. That's not to say that you can't find good dive sites near St. John. **Deaver's Bay** is a short boat ride around the point from Cruz Bay, where you can see angelfish, southern stingrays, and triggerfish feeding at 30 to 50 feet. **The Leaf** is a large coral reef off St. John's southern shore.

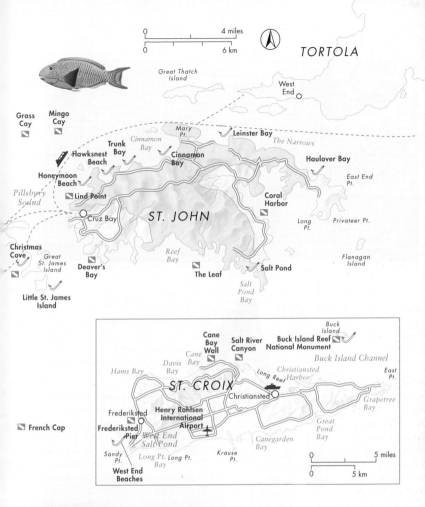

Map labels

TORTOLA

Great Thatch Island

West End

Grass Cay

Mingo Cay

Mary Pt.

Leinster Bay

The Narrows

Cinnamon Bay

Trunk Bay

Cinnamon Bay

Haulover Bay

Hawksnest Beach

Honeymoon Beach

East End Pt.

Pillsbury Sound

Lind Point

Coral Harbor

ST. JOHN

Cruz Bay

Long Pt.

Privateer Pt.

Christmas Cove

Great St. James Island

Reef Bay

Deaver's Bay

The Leaf

Salt Pond

Flanagan Island

Little St. James Island

Salt Pond Bay

Buck Island

Cane Bay Wall

Salt River Canyon

Buck Island Reef National Monument

Cane Bay

Buck Island Channel

Davis Bay

Hams Bay

Long Reef

Christiansted Harbor

East Pt.

ST. CROIX

Christiansted

Grapetree Bay

French Cap

Frederiksted

Henry Rohlsen International Airport

Great Pond Bay

Frederiksted Pier

West End Salt Pond

Canegarden Bay

Sandy Pt.

Long Pt. Bay

Long Pt.

Krause Pt.

West End Beaches

0   4 miles
0   6 km

0   5 miles
0   5 km

Coral near St. Croix

ST. CROIX

The largest of the U.S. Virgin Islands is a favorite of both divers and snorkelers and offers something for everyone. Snorkelers are often fascinated by the marked snorkeling trail at **Buck Island Reef,** which is a short boat ride from the island's east end; it's a U.S. national monument. Divers are drawn to the north shore, especially the **Cane Bay Wall,** a spectacular drop-off that's reachable from the beach, though usually reached by boat. Another north-shore site is the **Salt River Canyon,** where you can float downward through a canyon filled with colorful fish and coral. On the island's west end, **Frederiksted Pier** is home to a colony of sea horses, creatures seldom seen in the waters of the Virgin Islands. Casual snorkelers would also enjoy snorkeling at the **West End Beaches.**

SCUBA DIVING

St.Croix

If you've never been diving, start with an introductory lesson—often called a "resort course"—run by any one of the Virgin Islands' dive shops. All meet stringent safety standards. If they didn't, they'd soon be out of business. If you're staying at a hotel, you can often find the dive shop on-site; otherwise, your hotel probably has an arrangement with one nearby. If you're on a cruise, cruise-ship companies offer shore excursions that include transportation to and from the ship as well as the resort course. Certification requires much more study and practice, but it is required to rent air tanks, get air refills, and join others on guided dives virtually anywhere in the world.

The number one rule of diving is safety. The basic rules for safe diving are simple, and fools ignore them at their own peril. Serious diving accidents are becoming increasingly rare these days, thanks to the high level of diver training. However, they do still occur occasionally. Surfacing too rapidly without exhaling—or going too deep for too long—can result in an air embolism or a case of the bends. Roy L. Schneider Hospital in St. Thomas has a decompression chamber that serves all the Virgin Islands. If you get the bends, you'll be whisked to the hospital for this necessary treatment.

Fauna is another concern. Though sharks, barracuda, and moray eels are on the most-feared list, more often it's sea urchins and fire coral that cause pain when you accidentally bump them. Part of any scuba-training

Divers learn how to jump in from a boat

St.Croix

program is a review of sea life and the importance of respecting the new world you're exploring. Dive professionals recognize the value of protecting fragile reefs and ecosystems in tropical waters, and instructors emphasize look-don't-touch diving (the unofficial motto is: take only pictures, leave only bubbles). Government control and protection of dive sites is increasing, especially in such heavily used areas as the Virgin Islands.

While you can scuba dive off a beach—and you can find shops renting scuba equipment and providing airfills at the most popular beaches—a trip aboard a dive boat provides a more extensive glimpse into this wonderful undersea world. Since the dive shops can provide all equipment, there's no need to lug heavy weights and a bulky BC in your luggage. For the most comfort, you might want to bring your own regulator if you have one. The dive-boat captains and guides know the best dive locations, can find alternatives when the seas are rough, and will help you deal with heavy tanks and cumbersome equipment. Trips are easy to organize.

Dive shops on all islands make frequent excursions to a wide variety of diving spots, and your hotel, villa manager, or cruise-ship staff will help you make arrangements.

If you fly too soon after diving, you're at risk for decompression sickness, which occurs when nitrogen trapped in your bloodstream doesn't escape. This creates a painful and sometimes fatal condition called the bends, not a sickness you want to develop while you're winging your way home after a fun-filled beach vacation. Opinions vary, but as a rule of thumb, wait at least 12 hours after a single dive to fly. However, if you've made multiple dives or dived several days in a row, you should wait at least 18 hours. If you've made dives that required decompression stops, you should also wait at least 24 hours before flying. To be safe, consult with your physician.

The Virgin Islands offer a plethora of dive sites, and you'll be taken to some of the best if you sign on to a dive trip run by one of the many dive operations scattered around the islands.

DIVER TRAINING

Good to know: Divers can become certified through PADI *(www.padi.com)*, NAUI *(www.naui.org)*, or SSI *(www.divessi.com)*. The requirements for all three are similar, and if you do the classroom instruction and pool training with a dive shop associated with one organization, the referral for the open water dives will be honored by most dive shops. Note that you should not fly for at least 24 hours after a dive, because residual nitrogen in the body can pose health risks upon decompression. While there are no rigid rules on diving after flying, make sure you're well-hydrated before hitting the water.

Cost: The four-day cost for classroom dive training can range from $300 to $500, but be sure to ask if equipment, instruction manuals, and log books are extra. Some dive shops have relationships with hotels, so check for dive/stay packages. Referral dives (a collaborative effort among training agencies) run from $400 to $300 and discover scuba runs around $120 to $200.

SNUBA

Beyond snorkeling or the requirements of scuba, you also have the option of "Snuba." The word is a trademarked portmanteau or combo of snorkel and scuba. Marketed as easy-to-learn family fun, Snuba lets you breathe underwater via tubes from an air-supplied vessel above, with no prior diving or snorkel experience required.

NOT CERTIFIED?

Not sure if you want to commit the time and money to become certified? Not a problem. Most dive shops and many resorts will offer a discover scuba day-long course. In the morning, the instructor will teach you the basics of scuba diving: how to clear your mask, how to come to the surface in the unlikely event you lose your air supply, etc. In the afternoon, instructors will take you out for a dive in relatively shallow water—less than 30 feet. Be sure to ask where the dive will take place. Jumping into the water off a shallow beach may not be as fun as actually going out to the coral. If you decide that diving is something you want to pursue, the open dive may count toward your certification.

■**TIP→** You can often book discover dives at the last minute. It may not be worth it to go out on a windy day when the currents are stronger. Also the underwater world looks a whole lot brighter on sunny days.

(top) Underwater shot of tropical reef, (bottom) Diver silhouette, Cane Bay, St Croix

Sea Urchin	Tiger Grouper	Foureye Butterflyfish
Parrotfish	Blue Tang	Hogfish
Spottle Eagle Ray	Bonefish	Green Sea Turtle
Dolphin (mahi mahi)	Snook	French Angelfish

3

IN FOCUS BELOW THE WAVES

REEF FISH IN THE VIRGIN ISLANDS

From the striped sergeant majors to bright blue tangs, the reefs of the Virgin Islands are teeming with fish, though not nearly as many as in eons past. Warming waters and pollution have taken their toll on both coral and fish species. But many reefs in the Virgin Islands still thrive; you'll also see sponges, crustaceans, perhaps a sea turtle or two, and bigger game fish like grouper and barracuda; sharks are seen but are rarely a problem for divers. Beware of fire corals, which are not really corals but rather a relative of the jellyfish and have a painful sting; if you brush up against a fire coral, spread vinegar on the wound as soon as possible to minimize the pain.

CLOSE UP

Local St. John Celebrations

Although the U.S. Virgin Islands mark all of the same federal holidays as the mainland, they have a few of their own. Transfer Day, on March 31, commemorates Denmark's sale of the territory to the United States in 1917. Emancipation Day, on July 3, marks the date slavery was abolished in the Danish West Indies in 1848. Liberty Day, on November 1, honors David Hamilton Jackson, who secured freedom of the press and assembly from King Christian X of Denmark.

While you're on St. John, don't hesitate to attend local events like the annual Memorial Day and Veterans Day celebrations sponsored by the American Legion. These small parades give a poignant glimpse into island life. The St. Patrick's Day Parade is another blink-and-you'll-miss-it event. It's fun to join the islanders who come out decked in green. The annual Friends of Virgin Islands National Park meeting in January is another place to mix and mingle with the locals.

Fodor's Choice
★

Friends of the Park Store. Find purses made out of license plates, flip-flops made of coconut husks and recycled rubber, and more at this store run by the nonprofit group that raises money for Virgin Islands National Park. It's a great spot to buy educational materials for kids and books about the island. ⊠ *Mongoose Junction Shopping Center, North Shore Rd., Cruz Bay* ☎ *340/779–8700* ⊕ *www.friendsvinp.org.*

BOOKS

National Park Headquarters Bookstore. The bookshop at Virgin Islands National Park Headquarters sells several good histories of St. John, including *St. John Back Time* by Ruth Hull Low and Rafael Lito Valls and, for intrepid explorers, longtime resident Pam Gaffin's *Feet, Fins and Four-Wheel Drive*). ⊠ *Cruz Bay* ☎ *340/776–6201.*

CLOTHING

Big Planet Adventure Outfitters. You knew when you arrived that someplace on St. John would cater to the outdoor enthusiasts who hike up and down the island's trails. This store sells flip-flops and Reef footwear, along with colorful and durable cotton clothing and accessories by Billabong. The store also sells children's clothes. ⊠ *Mongoose Junction Shopping Center, North Shore Rd., Cruz Bay* ☎ *340/776–6638.*

Bougainvillea Boutique. This store is your destination if you want to look as if you've stepped out of the pages of the resort-wear spread in an upscale travel magazine. Owner Susan Stair carries very chic men's and women's resort wear, straw hats, leather handbags, and fine gifts. ⊠ *Mongoose Junction Shopping Center, North Shore Rd., Cruz Bay* ☎ *340/693–7190.*

St. John Editions. This boutique specializes in swimsuits and nifty cotton dresses that go from beach to dinner with a change of shoes and accessories. Owner Molly Soper also carries attractive straw hats and inexpensive jewelry. ⊠ *North Shore Rd., Cruz Bay* ☎ *340/693–8444.*

FOOD

If you're renting a villa, condo, or cottage and doing your own cooking, there are several good places to shop for food, particularly in Cruz Bay; just be aware that prices are much higher than those at home.

PARKING IN CRUZ BAY

Cruz Bay's parking problem is maddening. Your best bet is to rent a car from a company that allows you to park in its lot. Make sure you ask before you sign on the dotted line if you plan to spend time in Cruz Bay.

Dolphin Market. This small store in Cruz Bay is a good source for fresh produce, deli items, and all the basics. ⊠ *Boulon Center, Rte. 10, Cruz Bay* ☎ *340/776–5322.*

FOOD

St. John Market. This store has good prices (for St. John) and a nice selection of fruits, veggies, and the basics plus items you don't find at other stores like soy flour. ⊠ *Rte. 104 near the Westin Resort and Villas, Great Cruz Bay* ☎ *340/776-6001.*

★ **Starfish Market.** The island's largest store usually has the best selection of meat, fish, and produce. ⊠ *The Marketplace, Rte. 104, Cruz Bay* ☎ *340/779–4949.*

GIFTS

Bamboula. This multicultural boutique carries unusual housewares, rugs, bedspreads, accessories, and men's and women's clothes and shoes that owner Jo Sterling has found on her world travels. ⊠ *Mongoose Junction Shopping Center, North Shore Rd., Cruz Bay* ☎ *340/693–8699.*

Best of Both Worlds. The store sells and displays the pricey metal sculptures and attractive artworks that hang from its walls; the nicest are small glass decorations shaped like mermaids and sea horses. ⊠ *Mongoose Junction Shopping Center, North Shore Rd., Cruz Bay* ☎ *340/693–7005.*

Donald Schnell Studio. You'll find unusual handblown glass, wind chimes, kaleidoscopes, fanciful fountains, and more in addition to pottery bowls and more here. Your purchases can be shipped worldwide. ⊠ *Amore Center, Rte. 104 near roundabout, Cruz Bay* ☎ *340/776–6420.*

Every Ting. As its name implies, the store at Gallows Point Resort has a bit of this and a bit of that. Shop for Caribbean books and CDs, picture frames decorated with shells, and T-shirts with tropical motifs. Residents and visitors also drop by to have a cup of coffee. ⊠ *Gallows Point Resort, Bay St., Cruz Bay* ☎ *340/693–5820.*

Fabric Mill. Fabric Mill has a good selection of women's clothing in tropical brights, as well as lingerie, sandals, and batik wraps. Or take home several yards of colorful batik fabric and make your own dress. ⊠ *Mongoose Junction Shopping Center, North Shore Rd., Cruz Bay* ☎ *340/776–6194.*

Nest and Company. This small shop carries perfect take-home gifts in colors that reflect the sea. Shop here for soaps in tropical scents, dinnerware, and much more. ⊠ *Marketplace Shopping Center, Rte. 108, Cruz Bay* ☎ *340/715–2552.*

★ **Pink Papaya.** Pink Papaya is where you can find the well-known work of longtime Virgin Islands resident and painter M.L. Etre, plus a huge collection of one-of-a-kind gifts, including bright tableware, unusual trays, and unique tropical jewelry. ⊠ *Lemon Tree Mall, King St., Cruz Bay* ☎ *340/693–8535.*

JEWELRY

Free Bird Creations. This is your on-island destination for special hand-crafted jewelry—earrings, bracelets, pendants, chains—as well as a good selection of water-resistant watches for your beach excursions. ⊠ *Dockside Mall, next to ferry dock, Cruz Bay* ☎ *340/693–8625.*

Jewels. A branch of the St. Thomas store, Jewels carries emeralds, diamonds, and other jewels in attractive yellow- and white-gold settings, as well as strings of creamy pearls, watches, and other designer jewelry. ⊠ *Mongoose Junction Shopping Center, North Shore Rd., Cruz Bay* ☎ *340/776–6007.*

R&I Patton Goldsmiths. This store is owned by Rudy and Irene Patton, who design most of the lovely silver and gold jewelry on display. The rest comes from various designer friends. Sea fans (those large, lacy plants that sway with the ocean's currents) in filigreed silver, starfish and hibiscus pendants in silver or gold, and gold sand-dollar-shaped charms and earrings are choice selections. ⊠ *Mongoose Junction, North Shore Rd., Cruz Bay* ☎ *340/776–6548.*

Verace. This store is filled with jewelry from such well-known designers as Toby Pomeroy and Patrick Murphy. Murphy's stunning gold sailboats with gems for hulls will catch your attention. ⊠ *Wharfside Village, Strand St., Cruz Bay* ☎ *340/693–7599.*

MID ISLAND

JEWELRY

Tutu Much. This jewelry boutique carries larimar jewelry set in sterling silver by craftsmen in Bali that is designed by owner Tutu Singer. While larimar, mined in the Dominican Republic, is the star, other pieces are made from shells. Still others have the petroglyph design that reflects St. John's past. The tiny shop also carries attractive woven grass purses made in Colombia. ⊠ *Bordeaux Overlook, Rte. 10, Centerline Rd., Bordeaux* ☎ *340/779–4709.*

CORAL BAY AND ENVIRONS

At the island's East end, there are a few stores—selling clothes, jewelry, and artwork—here and there from the village of **Coral Bay** to the small complex at **Shipwreck Landing.**

CLOTHING

Jolly Dog. Jolly Dog is a place where you can stock up on the stuff you forgot to pack. Sarongs in cotton and rayon, beach towels with tropical motifs, and hats and T-shirts sporting the "Jolly Dog" logo fill the shelves. ⊠ *Shipwreck Landing, Rte. 107, Sanders Bay*

☎ 340/693–5333 ✉ *Skinny Legs Shopping Complex, Rte. 10, Coral Bay* ☎ 340/693–5900.

Sloop Jones. This store is worth the trip all the way out to the island's east end to shop for made-on-the-premises clothing and pillows, in fabrics splashed with tropical colors. Fabrics are in cotton and linen, and are supremely comfortable. ✉ *Off Rte. 10, East End* ☎ 340/779–4001.

FOOD

Lily's Gourmet Market. This small store in Coral Bay carries the basics plus meat, fish, and produce. ✉ *Cocoloba Shopping Center, Rte. 107, Coral Bay* ☎ 340/777–3335.

Love City Mini Mart. The store may not look like much, but it's one of the very few places to shop in Coral Bay and has a surprising selection. ✉ *Off Rte. 107, Coral Bay* ☎ 340/693–5790.

GIFTS

Awl Made Here. This store on the East End specializes in locally made leather goods. Owner Tracey Keating creates lovely journal covers, wallets, and belts, but she also does special orders. The store carries other locally made items such as imaginative jewelry and hand-painted wineglasses. ✉ *Skinny Legs Shopping Complex, Rte. 10, Coral Bay* ☎ 340/777–5757.

Mumbo Jumbo. With what may be the best prices in St. John, Mumbo Jumbo carries everything from tropical clothing to stuffed sea creatures in a cozy little shop. ✉ *Skinny Legs Shopping Complex, Rte. 10, Coral Bay* ☎ 340/779–4277.

SPORTS AND THE OUTDOORS

BOATING AND SAILING

If you're staying at a hotel, your activities desk will usually be able to help you arrange a sailing excursion aboard a nearby boat. Most day sails leaving Cruz Bay head out along St. John's north coast. Those that depart from Coral Bay might drop anchor at some remote cay off the island's east end or even in the nearby British Virgin Islands. Your trip usually includes lunch, beverages, and at least one snorkeling stop. Keep in mind that inclement weather could interfere with your plans, though most boats will still go out if rain isn't too heavy.

★ **St. John Concierge Service** (✉ *Across from post office, Cruz Bay* ☎ 340/777–2665 or 800/808–6025 ⊕ *www.stjohnconciergeservice.com*). The capable staff can find a charter sail or power boat that fits your style and pocketbook. The company also books fishing and scuba trips.

For a speedier trip to the cays and remote beaches off St. John, you can rent a powerboat from **Ocean Runner** (✉ *On waterfront, Cruz Bay* ☎ 340/693–8809 ⊕ *www.oceanrunnerusvi.com*). The company rents one- and two-engine boats for $375 to $705 per day. Gas and oil will run you $100 to $300 a day extra, depending on how far you're going. It's a good idea to have some skill with powerboats for this self-drive adventure, but if you don't, you can hire a boat with a captain for $430 to $705 a day.

Even novice sailors can take off in a small sailboat from Cruz Bay Beach with **Sail Safaris** (⊠ *On waterfront, Cruz Bay* ☎ *340/626–8181 or 866/820–6906* ⊕ *www.sailsafaris.net*) to one of the small islands off St. John. Guided half-day tours on small or large boats start at $70 per person. Rentals run $47 per hour.

DIVING AND SNORKELING

Although just about every beach has nice snorkeling—Trunk Bay, Cinnamon Bay, and Waterlemon Cay at Leinster Bay get the most praise—you need a boat to head out to the more remote snorkeling locations and the best scuba spots. Sign on with any of the island's water-sports operators to get to spots farther from St. John. If you use the one at your hotel, just stroll down to the dock to hop aboard. Their boats will take you to hot spots between St. John and St. Thomas, including the tunnels at **Thatch Cay,** the ledges at **Congo Cay,** and the wreck of the *General Rogers*. Dive off St. John at **Stephens Cay,** a short boat ride out of Cruz Bay, where fish swim around the reefs as you float downward. At **Devers Bay,** on St. John's south shore, fish dart about in colorful schools. **Carval Rock,** shaped like an old-time ship, has gorgeous rock formations, coral gardens, and lots of fish. It can be too rough here in winter, though. Count on paying $85 for a one-tank dive and $100 for a two-tank dive. Rates include equipment and a tour. If you've never dived before, try an introductory course, called a resort course. Or if certification is in your vacation plans, the island's dive shops can help you get your card.

Cruz Bay Watersports (⊠ *Lumberyard Shopping Complex, Cruz Bay* ☎ *340/776–6234* ⊠ *Westin St. John, Great Cruz Bay* ☎ *340/776–6234* ⊕ *www.divestjohn.com*) actually has two locations: in Cruz Bay at the Lumberyard Shopping Complex and at the Westin St. John Resort. Owners Marcus and Patty Johnston offer regular reef, wreck, and night dives and USVI and BVI snorkel tours. The company holds both PADI five-star-facility and NAUI-Dream-Resort status.

Low Key Watersports (⊠ *Wharfside Village, Strand St., Cruz Bay* ☎ *340/693–8999 or 800/835–7718* ⊕ *www.divelowkey.com*) offers two-tank dives and specialty courses. It's certified as a PADI five-star training facility.

FISHING

Well-kept charter boats—approved by the U.S. Coast Guard—head out to the north and south drops or troll along the inshore reefs, depending on the season and what's biting. The captains usually provide bait, drinks, and lunch, but you need to bring your own hat and sunscreen. Fishing charters run about $1,400 for the full-day trip.

Captain Byron Oliver (☎ *340/693–8339*) takes you out to the north and south drops.

An excellent choice for fishing charters is **Captain Rob Richards** (⊠ *Westin, St. John, Great Bay* ☎ *340/513–0389* ⊕ *www.sportfishingstjohn.com*),

who runs the 32-foot center console *Mixed Bag I* and 40-foot Luhrs Express *Mixed Bag II,* and who enjoys beginners—especially kids—as well as fishing with experienced anglers. He will pick up parties in St. Thomas even though he is based in St. John.

GUIDED TOURS

In St. John, taxi drivers provide tours of the island, making stops at various sites, including Trunk Bay and Annaberg Plantation. Prices run around $15 a person. The taxi drivers congregate near the ferry in Cruz Bay. The dispatcher will find you a driver for your tour. Along with providing trail maps and brochures about Virgin Islands National Park, the park service also gives several guided tours on- and offshore. Some are offered only during particular times of the year, and some require reservations. For more information, contact the **V.I. National Park Visitors Center** (✉ *Cruz Bay* ☎ *340/776–6201* ⊕ *www.nps.gov/viis*).

HIKING

Although it's fun to go hiking with a Virgin Islands National Park guide, don't be afraid to head out on your own. To find a hike that suits your ability, stop by the park's visitor center in Cruz Bay and pick up the free trail guide; it details points of interest, trail lengths, and estimated hiking times, as well as any dangers you might encounter. Although the park staff recommends long pants to protect against thorns and insects, most people hike in shorts because it can get very hot. Wear sturdy shoes or hiking boots even if you're hiking to the beach. Don't forget to bring water and insect repellent.

Fodor's Choice ★   The **Virgin Islands National Park** (✉ *1300 Cruz Bay Creek, St. John* ☎ *340/776–6201* ⊕ *www.nps.gov/viis*) maintains more than 20 trails on the north and south shores and offers guided hikes along popular routes. A full-day trip to Reef Bay is a must; it's an easy hike through lush and dry forest, past the ruins of an old plantation, and to a sugar factory adjacent to the beach. It can be a bit arduous for young kids, however. Take the $6 safari bus from the park's visitor center to the trailhead, where you can meet a ranger who'll serve as your guide. The park provides a boat ride back to Cruz Bay for $15 to save you the walk back up the mountain. The schedule changes from season to season; call for times and reservations, which are essential.

HORSEBACK RIDING

Clip-clop along the island's byways for a slower-pace tour of St. John. **Carolina Corral** (☎ *340/693–5778*) offers horseback trips and wagon rides down scenic roads with owner Dana Barlett. She has a way with horses and calms even the most novice riders. Rates start at $65 for a one-hour ride.

SEA KAYAKING

Poke around crystal bays and explore undersea life from a sea kayak. Rates run about $110 for a full day in a double kayak. Tours start at $65 for a half day.

On the Cruz Bay side of the island, **Arawak Expeditions** (✉ *Mongoose Juction Shopping Center, North Shore Rd., Cruz Bay* ☎ *340/693–8312 or 800/238–8687* ⊕ *www.arawakexp.com*) has professional guides who use traditional and sit-on-top kayaks to ply coastal waters. The company also rents single and double kayaks, so you can head independently to nearby islands such as Stephen's Cay.

Explore Coral Bay Harbor and Hurricane Hole on the eastern end of the island in a sea kayak from **Crabby's Watersports** (✉ *Rte. 107, next to Cocoloba shopping center, Coral Bay* ☎ *340/714–2415* ⊕ *www.crabbyswatersports.com*). If you don't want to paddle into the wind to get out of Coral Bay Harbor, the staff will drop you off in Hurricane Hole so you can paddle downwind back to Coral Bay. Crabby's also rents snorkel gear, beach chairs, umbrellas, coolers, and floats.

Hidden Reef EcoTours (✉ *Rte. 10, Round Bay* ☎ *340/513–9613 or 877/529–2575* ⊕ *www.kayaksj.com*) offers two- and three-hour, full-day and full-moon kayak tours through Coral Reef National Monument and its environs. This pristine area is home to coral reefs, mangroves, and lush sea-grass beds filled with marine life.

WINDSURFING

Steady breezes and expert instruction make learning to windsurf a snap. Try **Cinnamon Bay Campground** (✉ *Rte. 20, Cinnamon Bay* ☎ *340/693–5902 or 340/626–4769*), where rentals are $50 to $100 per hour. Lessons are available right at the waterfront; just look for the Windsurfers stacked up on the beach. The cost for a one-hour lesson starts at $60, plus the cost of the board rental. You can also rent kayaks, stand-up paddle boards, Boogie boards, small sailboats, and surfboards.

St. Croix

WORD OF MOUTH

"I have been to Maui, Barbados, St. Martin, and St. Barths, but St. Croix is now my favorite. I don't know whether it is my stage of life or the fact that I really needed a vacation, but I fell head over heels in love with the island. It just has the right combination of charm, beauty, rusticism, and flavor without a lot of artificial glitz."
—Birdie

WELCOME TO ST. CROIX

TOP REASONS TO GO

★ **Sailing to Buck Island:** The beach at the western end of the island is a great spot to relax after a snorkeling adventure or a hike up the hill to take in the stunning view.

★ **Diving the Wall:** Every dive boat in St. Croix makes a trip to the Wall, one of the Caribbean's best diving experiences, but you can also enjoy great diving from Cane Bay Beach.

★ **Exploring Fort Christiansvaern:** History buffs flock to Christiansted National Historic Site. Head to the upper ramparts of Fort Christiansvaern to ponder how life was for early settlers.

★ **Experiencing plantation life:** Whim Plantation showcases St. Croix's agrarian past. The estate has been lovingly restored.

★ **Strolling around Christiansted:** You can easily while away the better part of a day in Christiansted, St. Croix's main town. The shops carry everything from one-of-a-kind artworks to handcrafted jewelry to simple souvenirs.

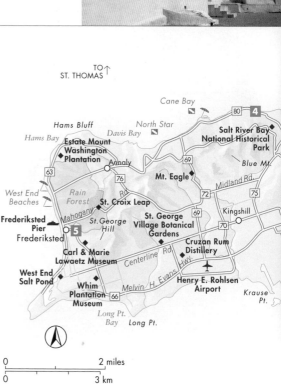

1 Christiansted. The island's main town has restaurants, shops, and a few places to stay.

2 West of Christiansted. This busy area includes a handful of condos and restaurants in Estates Golden Rock and Princesse.

3 East End. Most of the larger resorts are on the East End of St. Croix, but there are also some hidden treasures to explore.

4 North Shore. Divers head to Cane Bay; while Salt River Bay has excellent kayaking and diving opportunities.

4

Buck Island

Buck Island Reef National Monument

Salt River Bay

◆ **Judith's Fancy**

Green Cay

Long Reef

Pull Pt. *Coakley Bay*

Christiansted Harbor

2

Tamarind Reef Beach

Christiansted

East End Rd. [82]

Teague Bay

Cramer's Park

Cottongarden Pt.

Sugarloaf Hill

◆ **Point Udall**

Northside Rd.

Little Princess Estate

Gallow's Bay

6

Sunny Isle

1

3

Isaacs Bay

Grapetree Bay

South Side Rd. [60]

Grassy Pt.

Recovery Hill

Prospect Hill

Robin Bay

HOVENSA Oil Refinery

South Side Rd. [62]

Great Pond Bay

Milord Pt.

◆

Manchenil Bay

Canegarden Bay

C a r i b b e a n   S e a

GETTING ORIENTED

5 Frederiksted. The island's westernmost settlement has a smattering of stores, restaurants, activities, and the island's cruise pier.

6 Mid Island. This extensive area includes a small patch of rain forest, a handful of historic sites, the island's biggest shopping center at Sunny Isles, and a bed-and-breakfast.

Although there are things to see and do in St. Croix's two towns, Christiansted and Frederiksted (both named after Danish kings), there are lots of interesting spots in between them and to the east of Christiansted. Just be sure you have a map in hand (pick one up at a rental-car agency, or stop by the tourist office for an excellent one that's free). Many secondary roads remain unmarked; if you get confused, ask for help. Locals are always ready to point you in the right direction.

ST. CROIX PLANNER

Do You Need a Car?

More than on most of the other Virgin Islands, the answer is yes. Even if you are staying in or near Christiansted, you might want to rent a car for a day or two so you can explore the island.

CAR RENTALS

Atlas is outside Christiansted but provides pickups at hotels. Avis is at Henry Rohlsen Airport and at the seaplane ramp in Christiansted. Budget has branches at the airport, in the King Christian Hotel in Christiansted, and at the Renaissance Carambola Beach Resort. Judi of Croix delivers vehicles to your hotel. Midwest is outside Frederiksted, but arranges pickup at hotels. Olympic and Thrifty are outside Christiansted, but will pick up at hotels.

Getting Here and Around

By Air: While St. Croix is not as well served as St. Thomas when it comes to nonstop flights from the United States, you will still be able to fly nonstop from Atlanta (on Delta) or Miami (on American Airlines). You can also get connecting service through San Juan or St. Thomas. Cape Air flies from San Juan and St. Thomas and offers code-share arrangements with all major airlines, so your luggage can transfer seamlessly. Seaborne Airlines flies between St. Thomas, St. Croix, and San Juan.

Airports Henry Rohlsen Airport (✉ *St. Croix* ☎ *340/778–1012* ⊕ *www.viport.com*).

By Ferry: A ferry run by V.I. SeaTrans connects St. Thomas and St. Croix Friday through Monday. Departure times depend on the day of the week, with the earliest leaving St. Thomas at 7:45 am on Friday and the latest at 4:15 pm on Friday and Saturday. From St. Croix, the earliest departs at 10 am Friday and the latest at 6:15 pm Friday and Saturday. This ferry is often cancelled in the slow fall months.

Ferry Contacts V.I. SeaTrans (✉ *St. Thomas* ☎ *340/776–5494* ⊕ *www.goviseatrans.com*).

By Bus: Privately owned taxi vans crisscross St. Croix regularly, providing reliable service between Frederiksted and Christiansted along Route 70. This inexpensive ($1.50 one way) mode of transportation is favored by locals, and though the many stops on the 20-mi (32-km) drive between the two main towns make the ride slow, it's never dull. Vitran public buses aren't the quickest way to get around the island, but they're comfortable and affordable. The fare is $1 between Christiansted and Frederiksted or to places in between.

By Taxi: Taxis are available in downtown Christiansted, at the Henry E. Rohlsen Airport, and at the Frederiksted pier during cruise-ship arrivals, or they can be called. In Frederiksted, all the shops are a short walk away, as is a great beach, so there's no need for a taxi if you are staying in town. Most cruise-ship passengers visit Christiansted on a tour since a taxi will cost $25 for one or two people (one way).

Contacts Antilles Taxi Service (☎ *340/773–5020*). **St. Croix Taxi Association** (☎ *340/778–1088*).

Where to Stay

You can find everything from plush resorts to simple beachfront digs in St. Croix. If you sleep in either the Christiansted or Frederiksted area, you'll be closest to shopping, restaurants, and nightlife. Most of the island's other hotels will put you just steps from the beach. St. Croix has several small but special properties that offer personalized service. If you like all the comforts of home, you may prefer to stay in a condominium or villa. Whether you stay in a hotel, a condominium, or a villa, you'll enjoy up-to-date amenities. Most properties have room TVs, but at some bed-and-breakfasts there might be one only in the common room.

Where to Eat

Seven flags have flown over St. Croix, and each has left its legacy in the island's cuisine. You can feast on Italian, French, and American dishes; there are even Chinese and Mexican restaurants in Christiansted. Fresh local seafood is plentiful and always good; wahoo, mahimahi, and conch are most popular. Island chefs often add Caribbean twists to familiar dishes. For a true island experience, stop at a local restaurant for goat stew, curried chicken, or fried pork chops. Regardless where you eat, your meal will be an informal affair. As is the case everywhere in the Caribbean, prices are higher than you'd pay on the mainland. Some restaurants may close for a week or two in September or October, so if you're traveling during these months it's best to call ahead.

HOTEL AND RESTAURANT PRICES

Restaurant prices are for a main course at dinner and include any taxes or service charges. Hotel prices are per night for a double room in high season, excluding taxes, service charges, and meal plans (except at all-inclusives).

WHAT IT COSTS IN U.S. DOLLARS

	¢	$	$$	$$$	$$$$
Restaurants	under $8	$8–$12	$13–$20	$21–$30	over $30
Hotels		under $150	$150–$275	$276–$375	$376–$475	over $475

Essentials

Banks St. Croix has branches of Banco Popular in the Orange Grove and Sunny Isle shopping centers. V.I. Community Bank is in Sunny Isle, Frederiksted, Estate Diamond, Orange Grove Shopping Center, and in downtown Christiansted. Scotia Bank has branches in Sunny Isle, Frederiksted, Christiansted, and Sunshine Mall.

Scuba Diving Emergencies Roy L. Schneider Hospital (⊠ *Sugar Estate, St. Thomas* ☎ *340/776–8311*) has a hyperbaric chamber.

Safety Don't wander the streets of Christiansted or Frederiksted alone at night. Don't leave valuables in your car, and keep it locked wherever you park. Don't leave cameras, purses, and other valuables lying on the beach while you snorkel for an hour (or even for a minute).

Tour Options **St. Croix Safari Tours** (☎ *340/773–6700* ⊕ *www. gotostcroix.com/safaritours*) offers van tours of St. Croix. Excursions depart from Christiansted and last about five hours starting at $60 per person. **St. Croix Transit** (☎ *340/772–3333*) offers van tours of St. Croix. Tours depart from Carambola Beach Resort, last about three hours, and cost from $65 per person.

Visitor Information USVI Division of Tourism (☎ *340/772–0357* ⊕ *www.usvitourism.vi*).

4

By Lynda Lohr   The largest of the USVI, St. Croix is 40 mi (64 km) south of St. Thomas. Plantation ruins, reminiscent of the days when St. Croix was a great producer of sugar, dot the island. Its northwest is covered by a lush rain forest, its drier east end spotted with cacti. The restored Danish port of Christiansted and the more Victorian-looking Frederiksted are its main towns; Buck Island, off the island's northeast shore, attracts many day visitors.

Until 1917 Denmark owned St. Croix and her sister Virgin Islands, an aspect of the island's past that is reflected in street names in the main towns of Christiansted and Frederiksted, as well as the surnames of many island residents. Those early settlers from Denmark and other European nations left behind slews of 18th- and 19th-century ruins, all of them worked by slaves brought over on ships from Africa, their descendants, and white indentured servants lured to St. Croix to pay off their debt to society. Some of these ruins—such as the Christiansted National Historic site, Whim Plantation, the ruins at St. George Village Botanical Garden, the Nature Conservancy's property at Estate Princess, and the ruins at Estate Mount Washington and Judith's Fancy—are open for easy exploration. Others are on private land, but a drive around the island passes the ruins of 100 plantations here and there on St. Croix's 84 square mi. Their windmills, great houses, and factories are all that's left of the 224 plantations that once grew sugarcane, tobacco, and other agricultural products at the height of the island's plantation glory.

The downturn began in 1801, when the British occupied the island. The demise of the slave trade in 1803, another British occupation from 1807 to 1815, droughts, the development of the sugar-beet industry in Europe, political upheaval, and a depression sent the island on a downward economic spiral.

St. Croix never recovered from these blows. The freeing of all of the Virgin Islands' slaves in 1848, followed by labor riots, fires, hurricanes, and an earthquake during the last half of the 19th century, brought what was left of the island's economy to its knees. The start of Prohibition in 1922 called a halt to the island's rum industry, further crippling the economy. The situation remained dire—so bad that President Herbert Hoover called the territory an "effective poorhouse" during a 1931 visit—until the rise of tourism in the late 1950s and 1960s. With tourism came economic improvements coupled with an influx of residents from other Caribbean islands and the mainland, but St. Croix still depends partly on industries like the huge oil refinery outside Frederiksted to provide employment.

Today suburban subdivisions fill the fields where sugarcane once waved in the tropical breeze. Condominium complexes line the beaches along the north coast outside Christiansted. Homes that are more elaborate dot the rolling hillsides. Modern strip malls and shopping centers sit along major roads, and it's as easy to find a McDonald's as it is Caribbean fare.

Although St. Croix sits definitely in the 21st century, with only a little effort you can easily step back into the island's past.

EXPLORING ST. CROIX

CHRISTIANSTED

Christiansted is a historic Danish-style town that always served as St. Croix's commercial center. Your best bet is to see the historic sights in the morning, when it's still cool. Break for lunch at an open-air restaurant before spending as much time as you like shopping.

In the 1700s and 1800s Christiansted was a trading center for sugar, rum, and molasses. Today there are law offices, tourist shops, and restaurants, but many of the buildings, which start at the harbor and go up the gently sloped hillsides, still date from the 18th century. You can't get lost. All streets lead back downhill to the water.

St. Croix Visitor Center. If you want some friendly advice, stop by weekdays between 8 and 5 for maps and brochures. ⊠ *Government House, King St.* ☎ *340/773–1404* ⊕ *www. visitusvi.com.*

Apothecary Hall. If you're strolling downtown Christiansted's streets, it's worth a peek into the Christiansted Apothecary Hall. Although the exhibits are behind Plexiglas, they give you a glimpse into a 19-century pharmacy. This tiny museum is at the original location of a pharmacy that operated from 1816 to 1970. ⊠ *Company*

DRIVING IN ST. CROIX

Unlike St. Thomas and St. John, where narrow roads wind through hillsides, St. Croix is relatively flat, and it even has a four-lane highway. The speed limit on the Melvin H. Evans Highway is 55 mph (88 kph) and elsewhere between 35 to 40 mph (55 to 65 kph). Roads are often unmarked, so be patient—sometimes getting lost is half the fun. On St. Croix, with its big HOVENSA refinery, gas prices are much closer to what you might expect to pay stateside. You still drive on the left.

DID YOU KNOW?

Some of St. Croix's best beaches are on the west end of the island north and south of Frederiksted. You can have lunch at the Sunset Grill and then walk right into the water.

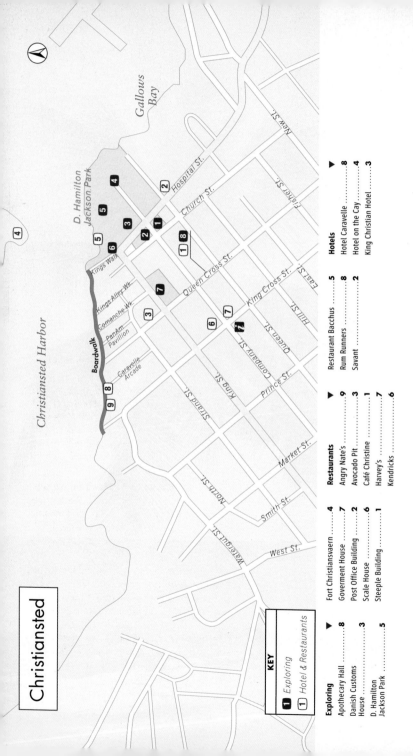

Christiansted

KEY

▶ ① Exploring

① Hotel & Restaurants

Exploring ▶

Apothecary Hall	8
Danish Customs House	3
D. Hamilton Jackson Park	5
Fort Christiansvaern	4
Goverment House	7
Post Office Building	2
Scale House	6
Steeple Building	1

Restaurants ▶

Angry Nate's	9
Avocado Pit	3
Café Christine	1
Harvey's	7
Kendricks	6
Restaurant Bacchus	5
Rum Runners	8
Savant	2

Hotels ▶

Hotel Caravelle	8
Hotel on the Cay	4
King Christian Hotel	3

Fort Christiansvaern, a national historic site.

and Queen Sts. ☎ *No phone* ⊕ *www.stcroixlandmarks.com* ✉ *Free* ⊗ *Mon.–Sat. 10–5.*

D. Hamilton Jackson Park. When you're tired of sightseeing, stop at this shady park on the street side of Fort Christiansvaern for a rest. It's named for a famed labor leader, judge, and journalist who started the first newspaper not under the thumb of the Danish crown (his birthday, November 1, is a territorial holiday celebrated with much fanfare in St. Croix). ✉ *Between Fort Christiansvaern and Danish Customs House.*

Danish Customs House. Built in 1830 on foundations that date from a century earlier, the historic building, which is near Ft. Christiansvaern, originally served as both a customshouse and a post office. In 1926 it became the Christiansted Library, and it's been a national park facility since 1972. It's closed to the public, but the sweeping front steps make a nice place to take a break. ✉ *King St.* ☎ *340/773–1460* ⊕ *www.nps.gov/chri.*

⟳ **Ft. Christiansvaern.** The large yellow fortress dominates the waterfront.
Fodor's Choice ★ Because it's so easy to spot, it makes a good place to begin a walking tour. In 1749 the Danish built the fort to protect the harbor, but the structure was repeatedly damaged by hurricane-force winds and had to be partially rebuilt in 1771. It's now a national historic site, the best preserved of the few remaining Danish-built forts in the Virgin Islands. The park's visitor center is here. Rangers are on hand to answer questions. ✉ *Hospital St.* ☎ *340/773–1460* ⊕ *www.nps.gov/chri* ✉ *$3 (includes Steeple Building)* ⊗ *Weekdays 8–4:30, weekends 9–4:30.*

Government House. One of the town's most elegant structures was built as a home for a Danish merchant in 1747. Today it houses offices. If you're here weekdays from 8 to 4:30, slip into the peaceful inner courtyard to admire the still pools and gardens. A sweeping staircase leads you to a second-story ballroom, still used for official government functions. ⊠ *King St.* ☎ *340/773–1404.*

Post Office Building. Built in 1749, Christiansted's former post office was once the Danish West India & Guinea Company warehouse. It now serves as the park's administrative building. ⊠ *Church St.*

Scale House. Constructed in 1856, this was once the spot where goods passing through the port were weighed and inspected. Park staffers now sell a good selection of books about St. Croix history and its flora and fauna. ⊠ *King St.* ☎ *340/773–1460* ⊕ *www.nps.gov/chri* ⊘ *Weekdays 8–4:30, weekends 9–4:30.*

Steeple Building. Built by the Danes in 1753, the former church was the first Danish Lutheran church on St. Croix. It's now a museum containing exhibits on the island's Indian inhabitants. It's worth the short walk to see the building's collection of archaeological artifacts, displays on plantation life, and exhibits on the architectural development of Christiansted, the early history of the church, and Alexander Hamilton, the first secretary of the U.S. Treasury, who grew up in St. Croix. Hours are irregular, so ask at the visitor center. ⊠ *Church St.* ☎ *340/773–1460* ☞ *$3 (includes Ft. Christiansvaern).*

EAST END

An easy drive (roads are flat and well marked) to St. Croix's eastern end takes you through some choice real estate. Ruins of old sugar estates dot the landscape. You can make the entire loop on the road that circles the island in about an hour, a good way to end the day. If you want to spend a full day exploring, you can find some nice beaches and easy walks with places to stop for lunch.

★ **Buck Island Reef National Monument.** Buck Island has pristine beaches that are just right for sunbathing, but there's also some shade for those who don't want to fry. The snorkeling trail set in the reef allows close-up study of coral formations and tropical fish. Overly warm seawater temperatures have led to a condition called coral bleaching that has killed some of the coral. The reefs are starting to recover, but how long it will take is anyone's guess. There's an easy hiking trail to the island's highest point, where you can be rewarded for your efforts by spectacular views of St. John. Charter-boat trips leave daily from the Christiansted waterfront or from Green Cay Marina, about 2 mi (3 km) east of Christiansted. Check with your hotel for recommendations. ⊠ *Off North Shore of St. Croix* ☎ *340/773–1460* ⊕ *www.nps.gov/buis.*

> ### BIG EVENT
>
> St. Croix celebrates Carnival in late December with the St. Croix Christmas Festival. If you don't book far ahead, it can be hard to find a room because of the influx of visitors from around the region and around the world.

Sea turtles nest in several places on St. Croix.

Point Udall. This rocky promontory, the easternmost point in the United States, is about a half-hour drive from Christiansted. A paved road takes you to an overlook with glorious views. More adventurous folks can hike down to the pristine beach below. On the way back, look for the castle, an enormous mansion that can only be described as a cross between a Moorish mosque and the Taj Mahal. It was built by an extravagant recluse known only as the Contessa. Point Udall is sometimes a popular spot for thieves. Residents advise taking your valuables with you and leaving your car unlocked so they won't break into it to look inside. ⊠ *Rte. 82, Et Stykkeland.*

MID ISLAND

A drive through the countryside between Christiansted and Frederiksted will take you past ruins of old plantations, many bearing whimsical names (Morningstar, Solitude, Upper Love) bestowed by early owners. The traffic moves quickly—by island standards—on the main roads, but you can pause and poke around if you head down some side lanes. It's easy to find your way west, but driving from north to south requires good navigation. Don't leave your hotel without a map. Allow an entire day for this trip, so you'll have enough time for a swim at a north-shore beach. Although you can find lots of casual eateries on the main roads, pick up a picnic lunch if you plan to head off the beaten path.

Cruzan Rum Distillery. A tour of the company's factory, established in 1760, culminates in a tasting of its products, all sold here at bargain prices. It's worth a stop to look at the distillery's charming old buildings even

CLOSE UP

Turtles on St. Croix

Like creatures from the prehistoric past, green, leatherback, and hawksbill turtles crawl ashore during the annual April-to-November turtle nesting season to lay their eggs. They return from their life at sea every two to seven years to the beach where they were born. Since turtles can live for up to 100 years, they may return many times to nest in St. Croix.

The leatherbacks like Sandy Point National Wildlife Refuge and other spots on St. Croix's western end, but the hawksbills prefer Buck Island and the East End. Green turtles are also found primarily on the East End.

All are endangered species that face numerous predators, some natural, some the result of the human presence. Particularly in the Frederiksted area, dogs and cats prey on the nests and eat the hatchlings. Occasionally

a dog will attack a turtle about to lay its eggs, and cats train their kittens to hunt at turtle nests, creating successive generations of turtle-egg hunters. In addition, turtles have often been hit by fast-moving boats that leave large slices in their shells if they don't kill them outright.

The leatherbacks are the subject of a project by the international group Earthwatch. Each summer teams arrive at Sandy Point National Wildlife Refuge to ensure that poachers, both natural and human, don't attack the turtles as they crawl up the beach. The teams also relocate nests that are laid in areas prone to erosion. When the eggs hatch, teams stand by to make sure the turtles make it safely to the sea, and scientists tag them so they can monitor their return to St. Croix.

---

if you're not a rum connoisseur. ⊠ *West Airport Rd., Estate Diamond* ☎ *340/692–2280* ⊕ *www.cruzanrum.com* ✉ *$5* ⊙ *Weekdays 9–4.*

Fodor's Choice ★ **St. George Village Botanical Garden.** At this 17-acre estate, fragrant flora grows amid the ruins of a 19th-century sugarcane plantation village. There are miniature versions of each ecosystem on St. Croix, from a semiarid cactus grove to a verdant rain forest. The small museum is also well worth a visit. ⊠ *Rte. 70, turn north at sign, St. George* ☎ *340/692–2874* ⊕ *www.sgvbg.org* ✉ *$8* ⊙ *Daily 9–5.*

☺ **Whim Plantation Museum.** The lovingly restored estate, with a windmill, **Fodor's**Choice ★ cook house, and other buildings, will give you a sense of what life was like on St. Croix's sugar plantations in the 1800s. The oval-shaped greathouse has high ceilings and antique furniture and utensils. Notice its fresh, airy atmosphere—the waterless stone moat around the greathouse was used not for defense but for gathering cooling air. If you have kids, the grounds are the perfect place for them to run around, perhaps while you browse in the museum gift shop. It's just outside of Frederiksted. ⊠ *Rte. 70, Estate Whim* ☎ *340/772–0598* ⊕ *www.stcroixlandmarks.com* ✉ *$10* ⊙ *Mon.–Sat. 10–4.*

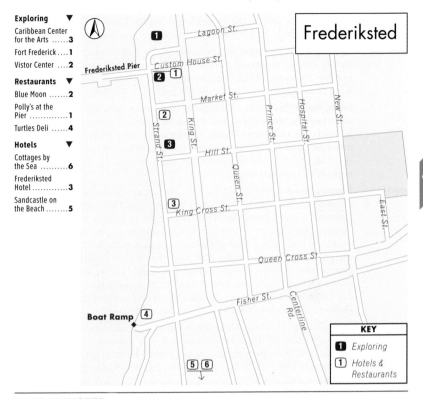

FREDERIKSTED

St. Croix's second-largest town, Frederiksted, was founded in 1751. While Christiansted is noted for its Danish buildings, Frederiksted is better known for its Victorian architecture. One long cruise-ship pier juts into the sparkling sea. It's the perfect place to start a tour of this quaint city. A stroll around its historic sights will take you no more than an hour. Allow a little more time if you want to duck into the few small shops.

Caribbean Museum Center for the Arts. Sitting across from the waterfront in a historic building, this small museum hosts an always-changing roster of exhibits. Many are cutting-edge multimedia efforts that you might be surprised to find in such an out-of-the way location. The openings are popular events. ⊠ *10 Strand St.* ☎ *340/772–2622* ⊕ *www.cmcarts. org* ☝ *Free* ☾ *Tues.–Sat. (and any cruise-ship day) 10–4.*

☾ **Fort Frederik.** On July 3, 1848, 8,000 slaves marched on this fort to demand their freedom. Danish governor Peter von Scholten, fearing they would burn the town to the ground, stood up in his carriage parked in front of the fort and granted their wish. The fort, completed in 1760, houses an art gallery and a number of interesting historical exhibits, including some focusing on the 1848 Emancipation and the 1917 transfer of the Virgin Islands from Denmark to the United States.

It's within earshot of the Frederiksted Visitor Center. ⊠ *Waterfront* ☎ *340/772–2021* ✉ *$3* ☉ *Weekdays (and any cruise-ship day) 8:30–4.*

Frederiksted Visitor Center. Across from the pier, Federiksted's visitor center has brochures from numerous St. Croix businesses, as well as a few exhibits about the island. You can stop in weekdays from 8 to 5. ⊠ *321 King St., Frederiksted Mall* ☎ *340/772–0357* ☉ *Weekdays 8–5.*

Estate Mount Washington Plantation. Several years ago, while surveying the property, the owners discovered the ruins of a sugar plantation beneath the rain-forest brush. The grounds have since been cleared and opened to the public. You can take a self-guided walking tour of the mill, the rum factory, and other ruins. ⊠ *Rte. 63, Mount Washington* ☉ *Daily dawn–dusk.*

Fodor's Choice ★ **Lawaetz Museum.** For a trip back in time, tour this circa-1750 farm. Owned by the prominent Lawaetz family since 1896, just after Carl Lawaetz arrived from Denmark, the lovely two-story house is in a valley at La Grange. A Lawaetz family member shows you the four-poster mahogany bed Carl and Marie shared, the china Marie painted, the family portraits, and the fruit trees that fed the family for several generations. Initially a sugar plantation, it was subsequently used to raise cattle and grow produce. ⊠ *Rte. 76, Mahogany Rd., Estate Little La Grange* ☎ *340/772–1539* ⊕ *www.stcroixlandmarks.com* ✉ *$10* ☉ *Tues., Thurs., Sat. (and any cruise-ship day) 10–4.*

St. Croix Leap. This workshop sits in the heart of the rain forest, about a 15-minute drive from Frederiksted. It sells mirrors, tables, bread-boards, and mahogany jewelry boxes crafted by local artisans. ⊠ *Rte. 76, Brooks Hill* ☎ *340/772–0421* ☉ *Weekdays 9–5, Sat. 10–5.*

West End Salt Pond. A bird-watcher's delight, this salt pond attracts a large number of winged creatures, including flamingos. ⊠ *Veteran's Shore Dr., Hesselberg.*

NORTH SHORE

Judith's Fancy. In this upscale neighborhood are the ruins of an old greathouse and tower of the same name, both remnants of a circa-1750 Danish sugar plantation. The "Judith" comes from the first name of a woman buried on the property. From the guardhouse at the neighborhood entrance, follow Hamilton Drive past some of St. Croix's loveliest homes. At the end of Hamilton Drive the road overlooks Salt River Bay, where Christopher Columbus anchored in 1493. On the way back, make a detour left off Hamilton Drive onto Caribe Road for a close look at the ruins. The million-dollar villas are something to behold, too. ⊠ *Turn north onto Rte. 751, off Rte. 75, Judith's Fancy.*

Mt. Eagle. At 1,165 feet, this is St. Croix's highest peak. Leaving Cane Bay and passing North Star Beach, follow the coastal road that dips briefly into a forest; then turn left on Route 69. Just after you make the turn, the pavement is marked with the words "The Beast" and a set of giant paw prints. The hill you're about to climb is the famous Beast of

CLOSE UP

Marching on Frederiksted

On July 3, 1848, more than 8,000 slaves demanding their freedom marched half a mile from LaGrange to Frederiksted. Their actions forever changed the course of history. Gov. General Peter von Scholten stood up in his carriage in front of Fort Frederick to declare: "You are now free. You are hereby emancipated. Go home peacefully."

Von Scholten was relieved of his position and charged with dereliction of duty by the Danish government. He departed from St. Croix on July 14, leaving behind his lover, a free black woman named Anna Heegaard. He never returned, and died in Denmark in 1852.

The revolt had its roots in the 1834 emancipation of slaves in Great Britain's Caribbean colonies, including what are now called the British Virgin Islands. The Danish government,

sensing what was coming, began to improve the working conditions for its slaves. These efforts, however, failed to satisfy the slaves who wanted full freedom.

On July 28, 1847, Danish King Christian VIII ruled that slavery would continue a dozen more years, but those born during those 12 years would be free. This further angered the island's slaves. On July 2, 1848, a conch shell sounded, signifying that the slaves should start gathering. The die was cast, and the rest, as they say, is history.

After emancipation, the former slaves were forced to sign yearly contracts with plantation owners. Those contracts could only be renegotiated on October 1, still called Contract Day. This angered the plantation workers and gave rise to other uprisings throughout the late 1800s.

the St. Croix Half Ironman Triathlon, an annual event during which participants must cycle up this intimidating slope. ⊠ *Rte. 69.*

Salt River Bay National Historical Park and Ecological Preserve. This joint national and local park commemorates the area where Christopher Columbus's men skirmished with the Carib Indians in 1493 on his second visit to the New World. The peninsula on the bay's east side is named for the event: Cabo de las Flechas (Cape of the Arrows). Although the park is just in the developing stages, it has several sights with cultural significance. A ball court, used by the Caribs in religious ceremonies, was discovered at the spot where the taxis park. Take a short hike up the dirt road to the ruins of an old earthen fort for great views of Salt River Bay. The area also encompasses a coastal estuary with the region's largest remaining mangrove forest, a submarine canyon, and several endangered species, including the hawksbill turtle and the roseate tern. A visitor center, open winter only, sits just uphill to the west. The water at the beach can be on the rough side, but it's a nice place for sunning. ⊠ *Rte. 75 to Rte. 80, Salt River* ☎ *340/773–1460* ⊕ *www.nps.gov/sari* ☉ *Nov.–June, Tues.–Thurs. 9–4.*

BEACHES

EAST END

Fodor's Choice ★ **Buck Island.** Part of Buck Island Reef National Monument, this is a must-see for anyone in St. Croix. The beach is beautiful, but its finest treasures are those you can see when you plop off the boat and adjust your mask, snorkel, and fins to swim over colorful coral and darting fish. Don't know how to snorkel? No problem—the boat crew will have you outfitted and in the water in no time. Take care not to step on those black-pointed spiny sea urchins or touch the mustard-color fire coral, which can cause a nasty burn. Most charter-boat trips start with a snorkel over the lovely reef before a stop at the island's beach. An easy 20-minute hike leads uphill to an overlook for a bird's-eye view of the reef below. Find restrooms at the beach. ⊠ *5 mi (8 km) north of St. Croix* ☎ *340/773–1460* ⊕ *www.nps.gov/buis.*

NORTH SHORE

Cane Bay. On the island's breezy North Shore, Cane Bay does not always have gentle waters, but there are seldom many people around, and the scuba diving and snorkeling are wondrous. You can see elkhorn and brain corals, and less than 200 yards out is the drop-off called Cane Bay Wall. Cane Bay can be an all-day destination. You can rent kayaks and snorkeling and scuba gear at water-sports shops across the road, and a couple of casual restaurants beckon when the sun gets too hot. The beach has no public restrooms. ⊠ *Rte. 80, about 4 mi (6 km) west of Salt River, Cane Bay.*

FREDERIKSTED

West End beaches. There are several unnamed beaches along the coast road north of Frederiksted, but it's best if you don't stray too far from civilization. For safety's sake, most vacationers plop down their towel near one of the casual restaurants spread out along Route 63. The beach at the Rainbow Beach Club, a five-minute drive outside Frederiksted, has a bar, a casual restaurant, water sports, and volleyball. If you want to be close to the cruise-ship pier, just stroll on over to the adjacent sandy beach in front of Ft. Frederik. On the way south out of Frederiksted, the stretch near Sandcastle on the Beach hotel is also lovely. ⊠ *Rte. 63, north and south of Frederiksted.*

WHERE TO EAT

St. Croix has restaurants scattered from one end to the other, so it's usually not hard to find a place to stop when you're exploring the island. Most travelers eat dinner near their hotel so as to avoid long drives on dark, unfamiliar roads. Christiansted has the island's widest selection of restaurants. Don't rule out Frederiksted, especially if you're out exploring the island. It has a handful of delightful restaurants.

For approximate costs, see the dining and lodging price chart at the beginning of this chapter.

CHRISTIANSTED

$$ ✕**Angry Nates.** Serving breakfast, lunch, and dinner, Angry Nates has
ECLECTIC something for everyone on its extensive menu. Dinner can be as fancy as tilapia and garlic shrimp with mushrooms, white white, and garlic butter, or as basic as a burger or chicken sandwich. If your taste buds run to hot, try the shrimp pistolette—a hallowed-out baguette filled with shrimp and laced with really hot sauce. ⊠ *King Cross St. at the Boardwalk* ☎ *340/692–6283* ⊕ *www.angrynates.com.*

$ ✕**Avocado Pitt.** Locals gather at this Christiansted waterfront spot for
ECLECTIC the breakfast and lunch specials as well as for a bit of gossip. Breakfast runs to stick-to-the-ribs dishes like oatmeal and pancakes. Lunches include such dressed-up basics as the Yard Bird on a Bun, a chicken-breast sandwich tarted up with a liberal dose of hot sauce. The yellowfin tuna sandwich is made from fresh fish and gives a new taste to a standard lunchtime favorite. ⊠ *King Christian Hotel, 59 Kings Wharf* ☎ *340/773–9843* ☉ *No dinner.*

$$ ✕**Café Christine.** At this favorite with the professionals who work in
FRENCH downtown Christiansted the presentations are as dazzling as the food.
★ The small menu changes daily, but look for dishes such as shrimp-and-asparagus salad drizzled with a lovely vinaigrette or a vegetarian plate with quiche, salad, and lentils. Desserts are perfection. If the pear pie topped with chocolate is on the menu, don't hesitate. This tiny restaurant has tables in both the air-conditioned dining room and on the outside porch that overlooks historic buildings. ⊠ *Apothecary Hall Courtyard, 4 Company St.* ☎ *340/713–1500* ⊟ *No credit cards* ☉ *Closed weekends and July–mid-Nov. No dinner.*

$ ✕**Harvey's.** The dining room is plain, even dowdy, and plastic lace
CARIBBEAN tablecloths constitute the sole attempt at decor—but who cares? The food is delicious. Daily specials, such as mouthwatering goat stew and tender conch in butter, served with big helpings of rice and vegetables, are listed on the blackboard. Genial owner Sarah Harvey takes great pride in her kitchen, bustling out from behind the stove to chat and urge you to eat up. ⊠ *11B Company St.* ☎ *340/773–3433* ☉ *Closed Sun. No dinner.*

$$$$ ✕**Kendricks.** The chef at this open-air restaurant—a longtime favorite
CONTINENTAL among locals—conjures up creative contemporary cuisine. To start, try
★ the Alaskan king crab cakes with habanero aioli or the warm chipotle pepper with a garlic and onion soup. Move on to the house specialty: herb-crusted rack of lamb with roasted garlic and fresh thyme

4

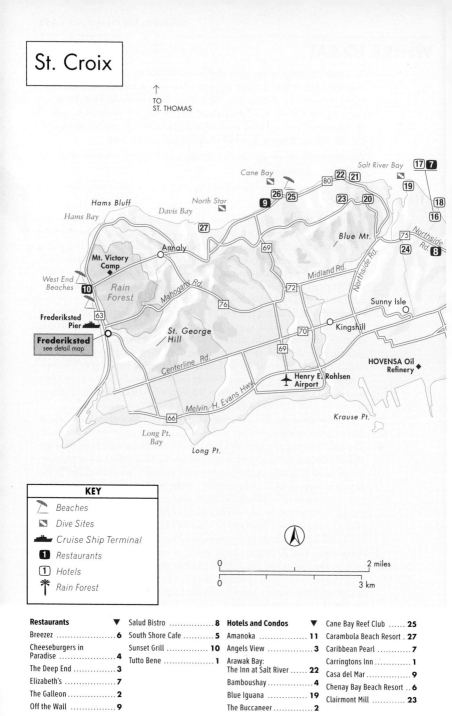

St. Croix

↑
TO
ST. THOMAS

Salt River Bay

Cane Bay

North Star

Hams Bluff
Davis Bay
Hams Bay

80 **22** **21** **17** **7**

26 **25** **19**

9 **23** **20** **18**

16

27 Blue Mt.

Annaly

69 **75** Northside Rd. **24** **8**

Mt. Victory
Camp

West End
Beaches

Rain
Forest

Mahogany Rd.

Midland Rd.

Northside Rd.

72

Sunny Isle

10 **76**

Frederiksted
Pier

63

St. George
Hill

70 Kingshill

Frederiksted
see detail map

Centerline Rd.

69

HOVENSA Oil
Refinery ◆

Henry E. Rohlsen
Airport

Melvin H. Evans Hwy

Krause Pt.

66

Long Pt.
Bay

Long Pt.

KEY

⚓ Beaches
◧ Dive Sites
🚢 Cruise Ship Terminal
■ Restaurants
□ Hotels
✳ Rain Forest

0 _____ 2 miles
0 _____ 3 km

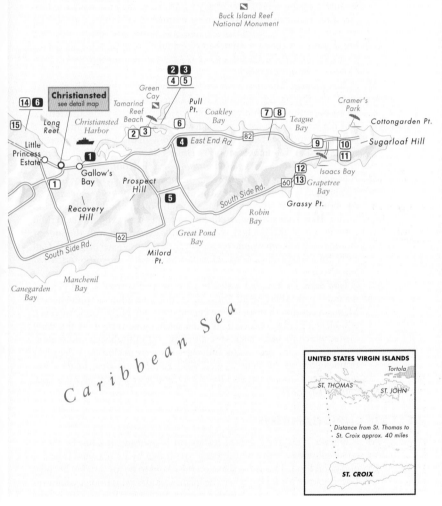

Buck Island

Buck Island Reef
National Monument

Christiansted
see detail map

14 6
15
Long
Reef
Little
Princess
Estate
Christiansted
Harbor
Gallow's
Bay
1
Prospect
Hill
Recovery
Hill
62
South Side Rd.

Green
Cay
Tamarind
Reef
Beach
2 3

2 3
4 5

6

Pull
Pt.
Coakley
Bay
4 East End Rd.
82
5
South Side Rd.
Great Pond
Bay
Milord
Pt.
Robin
Bay

7 8
Teague
Bay

Cramer's
Park
Cottongarden Pt.
9
10 Sugarloaf Hill
11
12 Isaacs Bay
60 13 Grapetree
Bay
Grassy Pt.

Manchenil
Bay
Canegarden
Bay

Caribbean Sea

UNITED STATES VIRGIN ISLANDS
Tortola
ST. THOMAS
ST. JOHN

*Distance from St. Thomas to
St. Croix approx. 40 miles*

ST. CROIX

sauce. ⊠ *Company St. and King Cross St.* ☎ *340/773–9199* ⊕ *www. kendricksdining.com* ☙ *Closed Sun. No lunch.*

$$$$ ✕ **Restaurant Bacchus.** On the chic side, this restaurant is as notable
CONTINENTAL for its extensive wine list as it is for its food. The menu changes
★ regularly, but often includes favorites such as chopped tuna in a soy-sesame dressing served over crispy wontons. Such entrées as local lobster and fresh fish, steak swimming in mushroom sauce, and the filet mignon with Gorgonzola and a foie gras butter are always popular. For dessert, try the rum-drenched sourdough bread pudding. ⊠ *Queen Cross St. off King St.* ☎ *340/692–9922* ⊕ *www.restaurantbacchus.com* ☙ *Closed Mon. No lunch.*

$$ ✕ **Rum Runners.** The view is as stellar as the food at this highly popular
CONTINENTAL local standby. Sitting right on Christiansted boardwalk, Rum Runners
☙ serves everything, including a to-die-for salad of crispy romaine lettuce
Fodor'sChoice and tender grilled lobster drizzled with lemongrass vinaigrette. More
★ hearty fare includes baby back ribs cooked with the restaurant's special spice blend and Guinness stout. ⊠ *Hotel Caravelle, 44A Queen Cross St.* ☎ *340/773–6585* ⊕ *www.rumrunnersstcroix.com.*

$$$ ✕ **Savant.** Savant is one of those small but special spots that locals love.
ECLECTIC The cuisine is a fusion of Mexican, Thai, and Caribbean—an unusual
★ combination that works surprisingly well. You can find anything from fresh fish to Thai curry with chicken to maple-teriyaki pork tenderloin coming out of the kitchen. With 20 tables crammed into the indoor dining room and small courtyard, this little place can get crowded. Call early for reservations. ⊠ *4C Hospital St.* ☎ *340/713–8666* ☙ *Closed Sun. No lunch.*

$$$ ✕ **Tutto Bene.** Its muraled walls, brightly striped cushions, and painted
ITALIAN trompe-l'oeil tables make Tutto Bene look more like a sophisticated Mexican cantina than an Italian cucina. One bite of the food, however, will clear up any confusion. Written on hanging mirrors is the daily menu, which includes such specialties as veal saltimbocca and scaloppine of veal with prosciutto and sage. Desserts, including a decadent tiramisu, are on the menu as well. ⊠ *Hospital St., in Boardwalk shopping center, Gallows Bay* ☎ *340/773–5229* ⊕ *www.tuttobenerestaurant. com* ☙ *No lunch.*

WEST OF CHRISTIANSTED

$$$ ✕ **Breezez.** This aptly named restaurant is poolside at Club St. Croix
ECLECTIC condominiums. Visitors and locals are drawn by its reasonable prices
☙ and good food. This is *the* place on the island to be for Sunday brunch.
Locals gather for lunch, when the menu includes everything from burgers to blackened prime rib with a horseradish sauce. For dessert, try the Amaretto cheesecake with either chocolate or fruit topping. ⊠ *Club St. Croix, 3220 Golden Rock, off Rte. 752, Golden Rock* ☎ *340/718–7077.*

$$$ ✕ **Elizabeth's at H2O.** With a lovely beachfront location and stellar
ECLECTIC food, this restaurant has developed quite a following. Lunch brings
Fodor'sChoice out lots of locals for the West Indian buffet that features mahimahi
★ creole-style. Dinner entrées include surf and turf with mashed potatoes. ⊠ *Hibiscus Beach Resort, off Rte. 752, Estate Princess* ☎ *4131*

La Grand Princess, Christiansted 00820 ☎ *340/718–0735* ⊕ *www. elizabethsath2o.com.*

$$$ ✕ **Salud Bistro.** This eatery's imaginative menu takes its cue from the
ITALIAN fresh flavors of the Mediterranean. Start with the savory cheese plate served with homemade bread and crostini before moving on to fresh fish or the grilled duck with a hibiscus confit. ⊠ *Princess Shopping Center, Rte. 75, La Grande Princess* ☎ *340/718–7900* ⊕ *www.saludbistro. com* ☺ *Closed Sun.*

EAST END

$$ ✕ **Cheeseburgers in Paradise.** A perennial favorite with local and visit-
AMERICAN– ing families, this open-air restaurant in the middle of a field serves
CASUAL up terrific New York strip steak, burgers with toppings that run from
☺ mushrooms to fried onions, and, of course, cheeseburgers. There's room for kids to run around before dinner. ⊠ *Rte. 82, Southgate* ☎ *340/773–1119.*

$$ ✕ **The Deep End.** A favorite with locals and vacationers, this poolside
ECLECTIC restaurant serves up terrific crab-cake sandwiches, London broil with onions and mushrooms, and delicious pasta in various styles. To get here from Christiansted, take Route 82 and turn left at the sign for Green Cay Marina. ⊠ *Tamarind Reef Hotel, Annas Hope* ☎ *340/713–7071.*

$$$$ ✕ **The Galleon.** This popular dockside restaurant is always busy. Start
ECLECTIC with the Caesar salad or perhaps a grilled lamb lollipop with a tamarind glaze. The chef's signature dish is a tender filet mignon topped with fresh local lobster. Fish lovers should try the grilled mahimahi with an artichoke and tomato salad. Take Route 82 out of Christiansted, and then turn left at the sign for Green Cay Marina. ⊠ *Green Cay Marina, Annas Hope* ☎ *340/773–9949* ⊕ *www.galleonrestaurant. com* ☺ *No lunch.*

$$$ ✕ **South Shore Café.** This casual bistro, popular with locals for its good
ECLECTIC food, sits on the island's south shore near the Great Salt Pond. The restaurant's menu includes dishes drawn from several different cuisines. Meat lovers and vegetarians can find common ground with a menu that ranges from handmade pasta to lamb and seafood. The selection isn't extensive, but the chef puts together a blackboard full of specials every day. ⊠ *South Shore Rd., near Great Pond* ☎ *340/773–9311* ☺ *Closed Mon. and Tues. No lunch.*

NORTH SHORE

$$ ✕ **Off the Wall.** Divers fresh from a plunge at the North Shore's popular
ECLECTIC Cane Bay Wall gather at this breezy spot on the beach. If you want to sit a spell before you order, a hammock beckons. Deli sandwiches, served with delicious chips, make up most of the menu. Pizza and salads are also available. ⊠ *Rte. 80, Cane Bay* ☎ *340/778–4771* ⊕ *www. otwstx.com.*

FREDERIKSTED

$$ ✕ **Beach Side Café.** Sunday brunch is big, but locals and visitors flock
ECLECTIC to this oceanfront bistro at Sandcastle on the Beach resort for lunch
and dinner. Both menus include burgers and flatbread pizza, but at
dinner the grilled pork chop with mango salsa shines. For lunch, the
hummus plate is a good bet. ⊠ *Sandcastle on the Beach, 127 Smith-
field* ☎ *340/772–1205* ⊕ *www.sandcastleonthebeach.com* ☺ *Closed
Tues.–Thurs.*

$$$ ✕ **Blue Moon.** This terrific little bistro, which has a loyal local follow-
ECLECTIC ing, offers a changing menu that draws on Cajun and Caribbean fla-
Fodor'sChoice vors. Try the spicy gumbo with andouille sausage or crab cakes with
★ a spicy aioli for your appetizer. A grilled chicken breast served with
spinach and artichoke hearts and topped with Parmesan and cheddar
cheeses makes a good entrée. The Almond Joy sundae should be your
choice for dessert. There's live jazz on Wednesday and Friday. ⊠ *7
Strand St.* ☎ *340/772–2222* ⊕ *www.bluemoonstcroix.com* ☺ *Closed
Mon.*

$ ✕ **Polly's at the Pier.** With an emphasis on fresh ingredients, this very
ECLECTIC casual spot right on the waterfront serves yummy fare. The gourmet
grilled cheese sandwich comes with your choice of three cheeses as
well as delicious additions like basil, fresh Bosc pears, and avocado.
Salads are a specialty, and many are made with local greens like bibb
lettuce and organic mixed greens. ⊠ *3 Strand St.* ☎ *340/719–9434*
☺ *No dinner.*

$ ✕ **Turtles Deli.** You can eat outside at this tiny spot just as you enter
ECLECTIC downtown Frederiksted. Lunches are as basic as a corned beef on rye
☺ or as imaginative as the Raven (turkey breast with bacon, tomato,
and melted cheddar cheese on French bread). Also good is the Beast,
named after the grueling hill that challenges bikers in the annual triathlon. It's piled high with hot roast beef, raw onion, and melted
Swiss cheese with horseradish and mayonnaise. Early risers stop by
for cinnamon buns and espresso. ⊠ *38 Strand St., at Prince Passage*
☎ *340/772–3676* ⊕ *www.turtlesdeli.com* ▭ *No credit cards* ☺ *Closed
Sun. No dinner.*

WHERE TO STAY

Although a stay right in historic Christiansted may mean putting up
with a little urban noise, you probably won't have trouble sleeping.
Christiansted rolls up the sidewalks fairly early, and humming air-
conditioners drown out any noise. Solitude is guaranteed at hotels and
inns outside Christiansted and on the outskirts of sleepy Frederiksted.

Families and groups may find more value in a condo that allows you to
do a bit of cooking but still have access to a pool or a limited array of
resort-style amenities. There are a lot of condos and apartment buildings on St. Croix, particularly along the North Shore and East End. If
you want to be close to the island's restaurants and shopping, look for
a condominium in the hills above Christiansted or on either side of the
town. An East End location gets you out of Christiansted's hustle and

bustle, but you're still only 15 minutes from town. North Shore locations are lovely, with gorgeous sea views and lots of peace and quiet.

PRIVATE CONDOS AND VILLAS

St. Croix has more than 350 private villas scattered all over the island from modest two-bedroom houses with just the basics to lavish and luxurious five-bedroom compounds with every imaginable amenity. But most are located in the center or on the East End. Renting a villa gives you all the convenience of home as well as top-notch amenities. Many have pools, hot tubs, and deluxe furnishings. Most companies meet you at the airport, arrange for a rental car, and provide helpful information about the island.

If you want to be close to the island's restaurants and shopping, look for a condominium or villa in the hills above Christiansted or on either side of the town. An East End location gets you out of Christiansted's hustle and bustle, but you're still only 15 minutes from town. North Shore locations are lovely, with gorgeous sea views and lots of peace and quiet.

RENTAL AGENTS

Vacation St. Croix (☎ 340/718–0361 or 877/788–0361 ⊕ www.vacation-stcroix.com) has villas all around the island.

For approximate costs, see the dining and lodging price chart at the beginning of this chapter. The following hotel reviews have been condensed for this book. Please go to Fodors.com for expanded reviews of each property.

CHRISTIANSTED

¢ 🏨 **Company House Hotel.** With an elegant lobby, including a grand piano,
HOTEL and attractive rooms, this hotel provides comfortable and affordable accommodations in the heart of Christiansted. **Pros:** convenient location; attractive rooms. **Cons:** no parking; no beach; busy neighborhood. ⊠ *2 Company St.* ☎ *340/773–1377* ⊕ *www.companyhousehotel.com* 🛏 *31 rooms, 2 suites* ⚿ *In-room: a/c, no safe, Wi-Fi. In-hotel: bar, pool, business center* ⑩ *No meals.*

$ 🏨 **Hotel Caravelle.** Near the harbor, at the waterfront end of a pleasant
HOTEL shopping arcade, the Caravelle's in-town location puts you steps away from shops and restaurants. **Pros:** good restaurant; convenient location; convenient parking. **Cons:** no beach; busy in-town neighborhood. ⊠ *44A Queen Cross St.* ☎ *340/773–0687 or 800/524–0410* ⊕ *www.hotelcaravelle.com* 🛏 *43 rooms, 1 suite* ⚿ *In-room: a/c, no safe, Wi-Fi. In-hotel: restaurant, bar, pool, business center* ⑩ *No meals.*

$ 🏨 **Hotel on the Cay.** Hop on the free ferry to reach this peaceful lodging in
RESORT the middle of Christiansted Harbor. **Pros:** quiet atmosphere; convenient location; lovely beach. **Cons:** accessible only by ferry; no parking available; Wi-Fi in upstairs terrace only. ⊠ *Protestant Cay* ☎ *340/773–2035 or 800/524–2035* ⊕ *www.hotelonthecay.com* 🛏 *53 rooms* ⚿ *In-room: a/c, no safe. In-hotel: restaurant, pool, beach, water sports, business center* ⑩ *No meals.*

¢–$ 🏨 **King Christian Hotel.** A stay at the King Christian puts you right in the
HOTEL heart of Christiansted's historic district. **Pros:** rooms have ocean views; car rental in lobby; convenient location. **Cons:** no beach; need to take

a taxi at night; no parking lot. ⊠ *57 King St., Box 24467* ☎ *340/773–6330 or 800/524–2012* ⊕ *www.kingchristian.com* ↘ *39 rooms* ⚴ *In-room: a/c, no safe (some), Wi-Fi (some). In-hotel: restaurant, pool, business center* ⏐◎⏐ *Breakfast.*

WEST OF CHRISTIANSTED

¢–$ ⌂ **Carringtons Inn.** Hands-on owners Claudia and Roger Carrington are
B&B/INN the real reason to stay here, and they conjure up delicious breakfasts—
Fodor'sChoice rum-soaked French toast is a house specialty—dole out advice, and
★ make you feel right at home. **Pros:** welcoming hosts; tasteful rooms; great breakfasts. **Cons:** no beach; need car to get around. ⊠ *4001 Estate Hermon Hill, Christiansted* ☎ *340/713–0508 or 877/658–0508* ⊕ *www.carringtonsinn.com* ↘ *5 rooms* ⚴ *In-room: a/c, no safe, no TV, Wi-Fi. In-hotel: pool, business center* ⏐◎⏐ *Breakfast.*

$–$$ ⌂ **Club St. Croix.** Sitting beachfront just outside Christiansted, this mod-
RENTAL ern condominium complex faces a lovely sandy beach. **Pros:** beachfront
♺ location; good restaurant; full kitchens. **Cons:** need car to get around; sketchy neighborhood. ⊠ *Rte. 752, Estate Golden Rock* ☎ *340/718–9150 or 800/524–2025* ⊕ *www.antillesresorts.com* ↘ *53 apartments* ⚴ *In-room: a/c, no safe, kitchen, Wi-Fi. In-hotel: restaurant, tennis courts, pool, beach, business center* ⏐◎⏐ *No meals.*

$ ⌂ **Colony Cove.** In a string of condominium complexes, Colony Cove
RENTAL lets you experience comfortable beachfront living. **Pros:** beachfront
♺ location; comfortable units; good views. **Cons:** sketchy neighbor-hood; need car to get around. ⊠ *Rte. 752, Estate Golden Rock* ☎ *340/718–1965 or 800/524–2025* ⊕ *www.antillesresorts.com* ↘ *62 apartments* ⚴ *In-room: a/c, no safe, kitchen, Wi-Fi. In-hotel: pool, beach* ⏐◎⏐ *No meals.*

$ ⌂ **Hibiscus Beach Hotel.** This hotel is on a lovely beach—the best reason
RESORT to stay here. **Pros:** nice beach; good restaurant; close to Christiansted. **Cons:** dated decor; sketchy neighborhood; need car to get around. ⊠ *4131 Estate La Grande Princesse, off Rte. 752, La Grande Princesse* ☎ *340/718–4042 or 800/442–0121* ⊕ *www.hibiscusbeachresort.com* ↘ *38 rooms* ⚴ *In-room: a/c, Wi-Fi, In-hotel: restaurant, pool, beach, water sports, business center* ⏐◎⏐ *Breakfast.*

$–$$ ⌂ **The Palms at Pelican Cove.** A 10-minute drive from Christiansted's
RESORT interesting shopping and restaurants, this resort with its mixed bag of guests has a gorgeous strand of white sand at its doorstep. **Pros:** nice beach; good dining options; friendly staff. **Cons:** need car to get out and about; neighborhood not the best. ⊠ *Off Rte. 752, La Grande Princesse* ☎ *340/718–8920 or 800/548–4460* ⊕ *www.palmspelicancove.com* ↘ *40 rooms* ⚴ *In-room: a/c. In-hotel: restaurant, tennis courts, pool, beach, water sports, business center* ⏐◎⏐ *Breakfast.*

$$ ⌂ **Sugar Beach.** With all the conveniences of home, Sugar Beach has
RENTAL apartments that are immaculate and breezy. **Pros:** pleasant beach; full
♺ kitchens; space to spread out. **Cons:** sketchy neighborhood; need car to get around. ⊠ *Rte. 752, Estate Golden Rock* ☎ *340/718–5345 or 800/524–2049* ⊕ *www.sugarbeachstcroix.com* ↘ *46 apartments* ⚴ *In-room: a/c, no safe, kitchen, Wi-Fi (some). In-hotel: tennis courts, pool, beach, business center* ⏐◎⏐ *No meals.*

EAST END

$$ RENTAL **Amanoka.** Amanoka, a spacious villa with gorgeous sea views of Teague Bay and Buck Island, is elegant yet still very tropical. **Pros:** lots of space; sea views. **Cons:** must drive to beach; need car to get around. *Off Rte. 82, Teague Bay www.vacationstcroix.com 4 bedrooms, 4½ baths In-room: a/c (some), no safe, Wi-Fi. In-hotel: pool, laundry facilities No meals.*

$$$–$$$$ RENTAL **Angels View.** With the Buccaneer Golf Course just a five-minute drive away, this gracious villa is perfect for vacationers who want to combine rounds of golf with their relaxation. **Pros:** close to golf; lovely views **Cons:** not on the beach; need car to get around. *Off Rte. 82, Shoys www.vacationstcroix.com 3 bedroom, 3 bath In-room: a/c (some), no safe, Wi-Fi. In-hotel: pool, laundry facilities No meals.*

$$$ RENTAL **Bamboushay.** With bright, tropical colors and comfortable wicker and rattan furniture, Villa Bamboushay is a wonderful spot to settle in with your extended family. **Pros:** spacious; views of Green Cay. **Cons:** not on the beach; need car to get around. *Off Rte. 82, Mt. Pleasant www.vacationstcroix.com 3 bedroom, 3½ bath In-room: a/c (some), no safe, Wi-Fi. In-hotel: pool, laundry facilities No meals.*

$$$–$$$$ RESORT **The Buccaneer.** For travelers who want everything at their fingertips, this resort has sandy beaches, swimming pools, and extensive sports facilities. **Pros:** beachfront location; numerous activities; nice golf course. **Cons:** pricey rates; insular environment; need car to get around. *Rte. 82, Box 25200, Shoys 340/712–2100 or 800/255–3881 www.thebuccaneer.com 138 rooms In-room: a/c, Wi-Fi. In-hotel: restaurants, bar, golf course, tennis courts, pools, gym, spa, beach, water sports, children's programs, business center Breakfast.*

$$ RENTAL **Caribbean Pearl.** This comfortable villa has glass doors that lead from the great room to the pool deck, making indoor–outdoor living a breeze. **Pros:** good views; nice decor; lovely garden. **Cons:** not on the beach; need car to get around. *Off East End Rd., Cotton Valley www.vacationstcroix.com 3 bedrooms, 3 bathrooms In-room: a/c (some), no safe, Wi-Fi. In-hotel: pool, laundry facilities 5-night minimum No meals.*

$$$–$$$$ RENTAL **Casa del Mar.** With an elegant and sophisticated vibe, this waterfront home has plenty of room for families or friends to spread out in. **Pros:** good views; nice kitchen; good snorkeling. **Cons:** on busy road; need car to get around. *East End Rd., Teague Bay www.vacationstcroix.com 3 bedrooms, 3 bathrooms In-room: a/c, no safe, Internet. In-hotel: pool, beach, laundry facilities 5-night minimum No meals.*

$ RESORT **Chenay Bay Beach Resort.** The seaside setting and complimentary tennis and water-sports equipment make this resort a real find, particularly for families with active kids. **Pros:** beachfront location; good children's program; wide array of water sports. **Cons:** need car to get around; lacks pizzazz; Wi-Fi in lobby and restaurant only. *Rte. 82, Green Cay Box 24600, Christiansted 00824 340/773–2918 or 800/548–4457 www.chenaybay.com 50 rooms In-room: a/c,*

4

no safe, kitchen. In-hotel: restaurant, bar, tennis courts, pool, beach, water sports, children's programs †○| *No meals.*

$$-$$$
ALL-INCLUSIVE

⊞ **Divi Carina Bay Resort.** An oceanfront location, the island's only casino, and plenty of activities make this resort a good bet. **Pros:** spacious beach; good restaurant; on-site casino. **Cons:** need car to get around; many stairs to climb; staff can seem chilly. ⊠ *25 Rte. 60, Estate Turner Hole* ☎ *340/773–9700 or 877/773–9700* ⊕ *www.divicarina.com* ⇆ *146 rooms, 2 suites, 20 villas* ⚭ *In-room: a/c, Internet, Wi-Fi (some). In-hotel: restaurants, bars, golf course, tennis courts, pool, gym, beach, water sports, business center* †○| *All-inclusive.*

$-$$
RENTAL
Fodor'sChoice
★

⊞ **Lymin' Beach House.** "Limin'" means relaxing in local parlance, and that's exactly what you can do at this beachfront villa on St. Croix's south side. **Pros:** beachfront location; well-planned layout; near restaurants and nightlife. **Cons:** near busy road; need car to get around. ⊠ *South Shore Rd., Estate Turner's Hole* ⊕ *www.vacationstcroix.com* ⇆ *2 bedrooms, 2 bathrooms* ⚭ *In-room: a/c (some). In-hotel: beach, laundry facilities, some age restrictions* ⚭ *5-night minimum* †○| *No meals.*

$$$-$$$$
RENTAL

⊞ **Reef Watch.** Watch boats sail off to Buck Island from Reef Watch's spacious deck or simply spend time relaxing in the hammock with a good book from the villa's library. This home has an understated tropical elegance with rattan and wood furniture and subdued colors. Two bedrooms flank the great room, while a third is in its own cottage, offering more privacy for couples traveling together. **Pros:** plenty of space for six adults or a large family; good views. **Cons:** must drive to the beach; need car to get around. ⊠ *Off Rte. 82, Cotton Valley* ⊕ *www.vacationstcroix.com* ⇆ *3 bedrooms, 3 bathrooms* ⚭ *In-room: a/c (some), no safe, Wi-Fi. In-hotel: pool, laundry facilities* †○| *No meals.*

$-$$
HOTEL

⊞ **Tamarind Reef Hotel.** Spread out along a sandy beach, these low-slung buildings offer casual comfort. **Pros:** good snorkeling; tasty restaurant; rooms have kitchenettes. **Cons:** need car to get around; motel-style rooms. ⊠ *5001 Tamarind Reef, off Rte. 82, Annas Hope* ☎ *340/773–4455 or 800/619–0014* ⊕ *www.tamarindreefhotel.com* ⇆ *39 rooms* ⚭ *In-room: a/c, Wi-Fi (some). In-hotel: restaurant, pool, water sports* †○| *No meals.*

$$
RENTAL
★

⊞ **Villa Madeleine.** If you like privacy and your own private pool, you'll like Villa Madeleine. **Pros:** pleasant decor; full kitchens; private pools. **Cons:** lower units sometimes lack views; need car to get around; no beachfront. ⊠ *Off Rte. 82, Teague Bay* ⚭ *5014 Villa Madeleine, Christiansted 00820* ☎ *340/718–0361 or 877/788–0361* ⊕ *www.vacationstcroix.com* ⇆ *43 villas* ⚭ *In-room: a/c, no safe, kitchen, Internet (some), Wi-Fi (some). In-hotel: tennis court, pools* †○| *No meals.*

FREDERIKSTED

$
RENTAL

⊞ **Cottages by the Sea.** Step out your door and onto a stunning stretch of white beach. This string of cottages beneath towering palm trees have quaint names beginning with the letter C—Cruzan, Conch, and Castaway, to name a few. **Pros:** beachfront location; delightful decor; friendly hosts. **Cons:** neighborhood sketchy at night; need car to get

CAMPING IN ST. CROIX

Out on the west end, where few tourists stay, **Mount Victory Camp** (✉ *Creque Dam Rd., Frederiksted* ☎ *340/772–1651 or 866/772–1651* ⊕ *www.mtvictorycamp.com*) offers a remarkable quietude that distinguishes this out-of-the-way spread on 8 acres in the island's rain forest. If you really want to commune with nature, you'll be hard-pressed to find a better way to do it on St. Croix. Hosts Bruce and Mathilde Wilson are on hand to explain the environment. You sleep in screened-in tent-cottages ($95–$125) perched on a raised platform and covered by a roof. Each has electricity and a rudimentary outdoor kitchen. There are also some bare tent sites for $30 per night. The shared, spotlessly clean bathhouse is an easy stroll away. The location feels remote, but a lovely sand beach and the Sunset Grill restaurant are a 2-mi (3-km) drive down the hill. In another 10 minutes you're in Frederiksted. Reservations are essential, and this is a cash-only place.

around; some rooms need freshening. ✉ *127A Smithfield, Rte. 71* ☎ *340/772–0495 or 800/323–7252* ⊕ *www.caribbeancottages.com* ⤳ *22 cottages* ⚭ *In-room: a/c, no safe, kitchen, Wi-Fi. In-hotel: beach, water sports, laundry facilities* ⏸ *No meals.*

¢ 🏨 **Frederiksted Hotel.** The Frederiksted Hotel offers basic but comfortable
HOTEL waterfront rooms for budget travelers. **Pros:** close to restaurants; walk to public beach; reasonable rates. **Cons:** neighborhood sketchy at night; need car to get around. ✉ *442 Strand St.* ☎ *340/772–0500* ⊕ *www.frederikstedhotel.com* ⤳ *37 rooms* ⚭ *In-room: a/c, no safe, kitchen (some), Wi-Fi. In-hotel: restaurant, pool* ⏸ *No meals.*

$ 🏨 **Sandcastle on the Beach.** Right on a gorgeous stretch of white beach,
HOTEL this hotel caters primarily to gay men and lesbians, but everyone is welcome. **Pros:** lovely beach; close to restaurants; gay-friendly vibe. **Cons:** neighborhood sketchy at night; need car to get around; no children's activities. ✉ *127 Smithfield, Rte. 71, Frederiksted* ☎ *340/772–1205 or 800/524–2018* ⊕ *www.sandcastleonthebeach.com* ⤳ *8 rooms, 8 suites, 5 villas* ⚭ *In-room: a/c, kitchen (some), Wi-Fi (some). In-hotel: restaurant, pools, gym, beach, water sports, laundry facilities, business center* ⏸ *Breakfast.*

NORTH SHORE

¢ 🏨 **Arawak Bay: The Inn at Salt River.** With stellar views of St. Croix's North
INN/B&B Shore and an affable host, this small inn allows you to settle into island life at a price that doesn't break the bank. **Pros:** 20 minutes from Christiansted; budget prices. **Cons:** no beach nearby; can be some road noise. ✉ *Rte. 80, Salt River* ✉ *Box 3475, Kingshill 00851* ☎ *340/772–1684* ⊕ *www.arawakbaysaltriver.co.vi* ⤳ *14 rooms* ⚭ *In-room: a/c, no safe, Wi-Fi. In-hotel: pool, business center* ⏸ *Breakfast.*

$$–$$$ 🏨 **Blue Iguana.** This modern villa sits just behind a stand of sea-grape
RENTAL trees, giving you easy access to the sandy beach and a casual beach vaca-
★ tion. **Pros:** good neighborhood; beachfront location; good views. **Cons:** no shade in yard; need car to get around. ✉ *Jefferson Way, Judith's*

Fancy ⊕ *www.vacationstcroix.com* ⇔ *3 bedrooms, 3 bathrooms* ♿ *In-room: a/c (some), no safe, Wi-Fi. In-hotel: pool, beach, laundry facilities* ✆ *5-night minimum* ⏹ *No meals.*

$$$$ ⌂ **Clairmont Mill.** A one-of-a-kind property once featured in Architec-
RENTAL   tural Digest, Clairmont Mill's centerpiece is an old plantation-era sugar
Fodor's Choice   mill. **Pros:** historic setting; great views; interesting decor. **Cons:** isolated
★   location; need car to get around. ⊠ *Off Northside Rd., Estate Clair-mont* ⊕ *www.vacationstcroix.com* ⇔ *5 bedrooms, 5½ bathrooms* ♿ *In-room: a/c (some), no safe, Wi-Fi. In-hotel: pool, gym, laundry facilities* ✆ *5-night minimum* ⏹ *No meals.*

$$$ ⌂ **Renaissance St. Croix Carambola Beach Resort and Spa.** We like this
★   resort's stellar beachfront setting and peaceful ambience. **Pros:** lovely
RESORT   beach; relaxing atmosphere; close to golf. **Cons:** ongoing renovation;
still some dated rooms; need car to get around. ⊠ *Rte. 80, Davis Bay* ✆ *Box 3031, Kingshill 00851* ☎ *340/778–3800 or 888/503–8760* ⊕ *www.marriott.com* ⇔ *151 rooms* ♿ *In-room: a/c, kitchen (some), Internet, Wi-Fi (some). In-hotel: restaurants, tennis courts, pool, gym, spa, beach, water sports, business center* ⏹ *No meals.*

$$$$ ⌂ **Sugar Bay House.** With four bedrooms scattered around this spacious
RENTAL   villa, there's room for big families or several couples who enjoy vacation-ing together. **Pros:** good views; comfy decor; spacious kitchen. **Cons:** need car to get around; caretaker lives on the property. ⊠ *Off North Shore Rd., Estate Salt River* ⊕ *www.vacationstcroix.com* ⇔ *4 bedrooms, 4½ bathrooms* ♿ *In-room: a/c (some), no safe, Internet, Wi-Fi. In-hotel: pool, laundry facilities* ✆ *5-night minimum* ⏹ *No meals.*

$ ⌂ **Villa Margarita.** This quiet retreat provides a particularly good base
RENTAL   if you want to admire the dramatic views of the windswept coast. **ros:** friendly host; great views; snorkeling nearby. **Cons:** isolated location; need car to get around; limited amenities. ⊠ *Off Rte. 80, Salt River* ✆ *9024 Salt River, Christiansted 00820* ☎ *340/713–1930* ⊕ *www.villamargarita.com* ⇔ *3 units* ♿ *In-room: a/c, no safe, kitchen, Wi-Fi. In-hotel: pool, some age restrictions* ⏹ *No meals.*

$ ⌂ **Waves at Cane Bay.** St. Croix's famed Cane Bay Wall is just offshore from
HOTEL   this hotel, giving it an enviable location. **Pros:** great diving; restaurants nearby; beaches nearby. **Cons:** need car to get around; on main road; bland decor. ⊠ *Rte. 80, Cane Bay* ✆ *Box 1749, Kingshill 00851* ☎ *340/718–1815 or 800/545–0603* ⊕ *www.canebaystcroix.com* ⇔ *12 rooms* ♿ *In-room: a/c, no safe, kitchen, Wi-Fi. In-hotel: restaurant, bar, pool* ⏹ *No meals.*

MID ISLAND

$–$$ ⌂ **Villa Greenleaf.** This spacious B&B is all about the details—four-
B&B/INN   poster beds with elegant duvets, towels folded just so, hand-stenciled
Fodor's Choice   trim on the walls, and gardens tastefully planted. **Pros:** tasteful decor;
★   convivial atmosphere; car included in rate. **Cons:** no beach; no restau-rants nearby; need car to get around. ⊠ *Island Center Rd., Montpelier* ✆ *Box 675, Christiansted 00821* ☎ *340/719–1958 or 888/282–1001* ⊕ *www.villagreenleaf.com* ⇔ *5 rooms* ♿ *In-room: a/c, Wi-Fi. In-hotel: pool* ⏹ *Breakfast.*

Villa Greenleaf

NIGHTLIFE AND THE ARTS

The island's nightlife is ever-changing, and its arts scene is eclectic—ranging from Christmastime performances of *The Nutcracker* to any locally organized shows. Folk-art traditions, such as quadrille dancers, are making a comeback. To find out what's happening, pick up the local newspapers—*V.I. Daily News* and *St. Croix Avis*—available at newsstands. Christiansted has a lively and eminently casual club scene near the waterfront. Frederiksted has a couple of restaurants and clubs offering weekend entertainment.

CHRISTIANSTED

NIGHTLIFE

Fort Christian Brew Pub. This pub is where locals and visitors listen to live music Wednesday, Friday, and Saturday. ⊠ *Boardwalk at end of Kings Alley, Christiansted* ☎ *340/713-9820* ⊕ *www.fortchristianbrewpub.com.*

Hotel on the Cay. This off-shore resort hosts a West Indian buffet on Tuesday night in the winter season, when you can watch a broken-bottle dancer (a dancer who braves a carpet of shattered glass) and mocko jumbie (stilt-dancing) characters. ⊠ *Protestant Cay, Christiansted* ☎ *340/773-2035.*

EAST END

NIGHTLIFE

Divi Carina Bay Resort. Although you can gamble at the island's only casino, it's really the nightly music that draws big crowds to this resort. ⊠ *25 Rte. 60, Estate Turner Hole* ☎ *340/773-7529.*

MID ISLAND

THE ARTS

Whim Plantation Museum. The museum outside Frederiksted hosts classical music concerts in winter. ⊠ *Rte. 70, Estate Whim* ☎ *340/772-0598.*

FREDERIKSTED

NIGHTLIFE

Fodor'sChoice ★ **Blue Moon.** Blue Moon is a popular waterfront restaurant in Frederiksted, and it's the place to be for live jazz on Wednesday and Friday, one of the few nightlife options on this end of the island. ⊠ *7 Strand St., Frederiksted* ☎ *340/772-2222.*

Fodor'sChoice ★ **Sunset Jazz.** This outdoor event has become the hot ticket in Frederiksted, drawing crowds of both visitors and locals at 6 pm on the third Friday of every month to watch the sun go down and hear good music. ⊠ *Waterfront, Frederiksted* ☎ *340/690-0617.*

SHOPPING

Although the shopping on St. Croix isn't as varied or extensive as that on St. Thomas, the island does have several small stores with unusual merchandise. St. Croix shop hours are usually Monday through Saturday 9 to 5, but there are some shops in Christiansted open in the evening. Stores are often closed on Sunday.

If you've rented a condominium or a villa, you'll appreciate St. Croix's excellent stateside-style supermarkets (albeit with prices that are at least 30% higher than on the U.S. mainland). Fresh vegetables, fruits, and meats arrive frequently. Try the open-air stands strung out along Route 70 for island produce.

CHRISTIANSTED

AREAS AND MALLS

In Christiansted the best shopping areas are the **Pan Am Pavilion** and **Caravelle Arcade,** off Strand Street, and along **King** and **Company streets.** These streets give way to arcades filled with boutiques. **Gallows Bay** has a blossoming shopping area in a quiet neighborhood.

ART GALLERIES

Danica Art Gallery. This gallery displays and sells the modernist paintings of owner Danica David; jewelry, pottery, and other works by various artists also fill this gallery. ⌂ *6 Company St., Christiansted* ☎ *340/719–6000.*

Undercover Books. This well-stocked independent bookseller sells Caribbean-themed books as well as the latest good reads. The store is across from the post office in the Gallows Bay shopping area. ⌂ *5030 Anchor Way, Gallows Bay* ☎ *340/719–1567.*

CLOTHING

Fodor's Choice
★ **Coconut Vine.** This is a great place to pop into at the start of your vacation. You'll leave with enough comfy cotton or rayon batik men's and women's clothes to make you look like a local. Although the tropical designs and colors originated in Indonesia, they're perfect for the Caribbean. ⌂ *1111 Strand St., Christiansted* ☎ *340/773–1991.*

From the Gecko. This store sells the hippest clothes on St. Croix, including superb island-style clothing and other items. ⌂ *1233 Queen Cross St., Christiansted* ☎ *340/778–9433.*

Hot Heads. This small store sells hats, hats, and more hats, which are often perched on top of cotton shifts, comfortable shirts, and other tropical wear. If you forgot your bathing suit, this store has a good selection. ⌂ *Kings Alley Walk, Christiansted* ☎ *340/773–7888.*

Pacificotton. Pacificotton will let you round out your tropical wardrobe with something new. Shifts, tops, and pants in Caribbean colors as well as bags and hats fill the racks. ⌂ *1110 Strand St., Christiansted* ☎ *340/773–2125.*

GIFTS

Cache of the Day. This tiny store sells whatever its sea theme has tossed up. Mermaid dolls recline on shelves next to dishtowels printed with shapes of the sea. The sea-themed books make for good beach reads and the cards are perfect for take home gifts. ⊠ *55 Company St., Christiansted* ☎ *340/773–1377.*

★ **Gone Tropical.** This store offers an eclectic collection of special gifts. On her travels about the world, Margo Meacham keeps her eye out for special delights for her shop—from tablecloths and napkins in bright Caribbean colors to unique fashion accessories. ⊠ *5 Company St., Christiansted* ☎ *340/773–4696.*

Many Hands. This shop sells pottery in bright colors, paintings of St. Croix and the Caribbean, prints, and maps—all made by local artists—and all making for perfect take-home gifts. If your purchase is too cumbersome to carry, the owners ship all over the world. ⊠ *21 Pan Am Pavilion, Strand St., Christiansted* ☎ *340/773–1990.*

Mitchell-Larsen Studio. This glass gallery offers an interesting amalgam of carefully crafted glass plates, sun-catchers, and more. All pieces are made on-site by a St. Croix glassmaker, and they are often whimsically adorned with tropical fish, flora, and fauna. ⊠ *200 Company St., Christiansted* ☎ *340/719–1000.*

Fodor's Choice **Royal Poinciana.** An attractive shop, Royal Poinciana is filled with island
★ seasonings and hot sauces, West Indian crafts, bath gels, and herbal teas. Shop here for tablecloths and paper goods in tropical brights. ⊠ *1111 Strand St., Christiansted* ☎ *340/773–9892.*

Tesoro. Tesoro is crowded with an eclectic range of colorful and boldly painted merchandise. Shop for metal sculptures made from retired steel pans, mahogany bowls, and hand-painted place mats in bright tropical colors. ⊠ *36C Strand St., Christiansted* ☎ *340/773–1212.*

HOUSEWARES

Designworks. This store and gallery sells furniture as well as one of the largest selections of local art, along with Caribbean-inspired bric-a-brac in all price ranges. If a mahogany armoire or cane-back rocker catches your fancy, the staff will arrange to have it shipped to your home at no charge from its mainland warehouse. ⊠ *6 Company St., Christiansted* ☎ *340/713–8102.*

JEWELRY

Crucian Gold. Crucian Gold carries the unique gold creations of St. Croix native Brian Bishop. His trademark piece is the Turk's Head ring (a knot of interwoven gold strands), but jewelry made of shards of plantation-era china set in gold are just lovely. ⊠ *1112 Strand St., Christiansted* ☎ *340/773–5241.*

Gold Worker. This shop specializes in handcrafted jewelry in silver and gold that will remind you of the Caribbean. Hummingbirds dangle from silver chains, and sand dollars adorn gold necklaces. The sugar mills in silver and gold speak of St. Croix's past. ⊠ *3 Company St., Christiansted* ☎ *340/516–6042.*

ib Designs. This small shop showcases the handcrafted jewelry of local craftsman Whealan Massicott. In both silver and gold, the designs are simply elegant. ⊠ *Company St. at Queen Cross St., Christiansted* ☎ *340/773–4322.*

Nelthropp and Low. Nelthropp and Low specializes in gold jewelry but also carries diamonds, emeralds, rubies, and sapphires. Jewelers will create one-of-a-kind pieces to your design. ⊠ *1102 Strand St., Christiansted* ☎ *340/773–0365 or 800/416–9078.*

Sonya's. This store is owned and operated by Sonya Hough, who invented the popular hook bracelet. She has added an interesting decoration to these bracelets: the swirling symbol used in weather forecasts to indicate hurricanes. ⊠ *1 Company St., Christiansted* ☎ *340/778–8605.*

4

LIQUOR AND TOBACCO
Baci Duty Free Liquor and Tobacco. This large duty-free store has a walk-in humidor with a good selection of Arturo Fuente, Partagas, and Macanudo cigars. It also carries sleek Swiss-made watches and collectables. ⊠ *1235 Queen Cross St., Christiansted* ☎ *340/773–5040.*

PERFUMES
Violette Boutique. Violette sells perfumes, cosmetics, and skin-care products. ⊠ *Caravelle Arcade, 38 Strand St., Christiansted* ☎ *340/773–2148.*

WEST OF CHRISTIANSED

FOOD
Pueblo. This stateside-style market has two branches, though prices are still more than what you would pay back home. ⊠ *Orange Grove Shopping Center, Rte. 75, Christiansted* ☎ *340/773–0118.*

EAST END

FOOD
Schooner Bay Market. Although it's on the smallish side, this market has good-quality deli items. ⊠ *Rte. 82, Mount Welcome* ☎ *340/773–3232.*

MID ISLAND

FOOD
Cost-U-Less. This warehouse-type store is great for visitors because it doesn't charge a membership fee. It's east of Sunny Isle Shopping Center. ⊠ *Rte. 70, Sunny Isle* ☎ *340/719–4442.*

Plaza Extra. This supermarket chain has a good selection of Middle Eastern foods in addition to the usual grocery-store items. ⊠ *United Shopping Plaza, Rte. 70, Sion Farm* ☎ *340/778–6240* ⊠ *Rte. 70, Mount Pleasant* ☎ *340/719–1870.*

Pueblo. This stateside-style market has two branches, though prices are still more than what you would pay back home. ⊠ *Villa La Reine Shopping Center, Rte. 75, La Reine* ☎ *340/778–1272.*

LIQUOR AND TOBACCO

Kmart. The U.S. discount chain has two branches on St. Croix, both of which carry a huge line of deep discounted, duty-free liquor, among many other items. ⊠ *Sunshine Mall, Rte. 70, Frederiksted* ☎ *340/692–5848* ⊠ *Sunny Isle Shopping Center, Rte. 70, Sunny Isle* ☎ *340/719–9190.*

FREDERIKSTED

AREAS AND MALLS

The best shopping in Frederiksted is along **Strand Street** and in the side streets and alleyways that connect it with **King Street.** Most stores close on Sunday, except when a cruise ship is in port. One caveat: Frederiksted has a reputation for muggings, so for safety's sake stick to populated areas of Strand and King streets, where there are few—if any—problems.

SPORTS AND THE OUTDOORS

BOAT TOURS

Almost everyone takes a day trip to Buck Island aboard a charter boat. Most leave from the Christiansted waterfront or from Green Cay Marina and stop for a snorkel at the island's eastern end before dropping anchor off a gorgeous sandy beach for a swim, a hike, and lunch. Sailboats can often stop right at the beach; a larger boat might have to anchor a bit farther offshore. A full-day sail runs about $100, with lunch included on most trips. A half-day sail costs about $70.

Big Beard's Adventure Tours (⊠ *Christiansted* ☎ *340/773–4482* ⊕ *www. bigbeards.com*) takes you on catamarans, either the *Renegade* or the *Adventure,* from the Christiansted waterfront to Buck Island for snorkeling before dropping anchor at a private beach for a barbecue lunch.

Caribbean Sea Adventures (⊠ *Christiansted* ☎ *340/773–2628* ⊕ *www. caribbeanseaadventures.com*) departs from the Christiansted waterfront for half- and full-day trips.

Teroro Charters (⊠ *Green Cay Marina, Annas Hope* ☎ *340/773–3161* ⊕ *www.gotostcroix.com/heinz/index.php*) offers charters on two trimarans, *Teroro II* and *Dragonfly,* which leave Green Cay Marina for full- or half-day sails. Bring your own lunch.

DIVING AND SNORKELING

Fodor'sChoice
★ At **Buck Island,** a short boat ride from Christiansted or Green Cay Marina, the reef is so nice that it's been named a national monument. You can dive right off the beach at **Cane Bay,** which has a spectacular drop-off called the Cane Bay Wall. Dive operators also do boat trips along the Wall, usually leaving from Salt River or Christiansted. **Frederiksted Pier** is home to a colony of sea horses, creatures seldom seen in the waters of the Virgin Islands. At **Green Cay,** just outside Green Cay Marina in the East End, you can see colorful fish swimming

DID YOU KNOW?

Buck Island Reef National Monument has one of the most powder-soft beaches to be found in St. Croix. You can take a sailing trip to the island for a half- or full day.

Divers love the sponge-encrusted Rosa Maria, off the west end of St. Croix.

around the reefs and rocks. Two exceptional North Shore sites are **North Star** and **Salt River,** which you can reach only by boat. At Salt River you can float downward through a canyon filled with colorful fish and coral.

The island's dive shops take you out for one- or two-tank dives. Plan to pay about $70 for a one-tank dive and $95 for a two-tank dive, including equipment and an underwater tour. All companies offer certification and introductory courses called resort dives for novices.

Which dive outfit you pick usually depends on where you're staying. Your hotel may have one on-site. If so, you're just a short stroll away from the dock. If not, other companies are close by. Where the dive boat goes on a particular day depends on the weather, but in any case, all St. Croix's dive sites are special. All shops are affiliated with PADI, the Professional Association of Diving Instructors.

Folks staying in the Judith's Fancy area are closest to **Anchor Dive Center** (⊠ *Salt River Marina, Rte. 80, Salt River* ☎ *340/778–1522 or 800/532–3483* ⊕ *www.anchordivestcroix.com*). The company also has facilities at the Buccaneer hotel. Anchor takes divers to more than 35 sites, including the Wall at Salt River Canyon.

Cane Bay Dive Shop (⊠ *Rte. 80, Cane Bay* ☎ *340/773–9913 or 800/338–3843* ⊕ *www.canebayscuba.com*) is the place to go if you want to do a beach dive or boat dive along the North Shore. The famed Cane Bay Wall is 200 yards from the five-star PADI facility. This company also has shops at Pan Am Pavilion in Christiansted, on Strand Street in Frederiksted, at the Carambola Beach Resort, and at the Divi Carina Bay Resort.

Deep-sea fishing in St. Croix's coastal waters.

If you're staying in Christiansted, **Dive Experience** (✉ *1111 Strand St., Christiansted* ☎ *340/773–3307 or 800/235–9047* ⊕ *www.divexp.com*) has PADI five-star status and runs trips to the North Shore walls and reefs in addition to offering the usual certification and introductory classes.

In Frederiksted, **N2 the Blue** (✉ *Frederiksted Pier, Rte. 631, Frederiksted* ☎ *340/772–3483 or 888/789–3483* ⊕ *www.n2theblue.com*) takes divers right off the beach near Coconuts restaurant, on night dives off the Frederiksted Pier, or on boat trips to wrecks and reefs.

St. Croix Ultimate Bluewater Adventures (✉ *Queen Cross St., Christiansted* ☎ *340/773–5994 or 877/567–1367* ⊕ *www.stcroixscuba.com*) can take you to your choice of more than 75 sites; it also offers a variety of packages that include hotel stays.

FISHING

Since the early 1980s some 20 world records—many for blue marlin—have been set in these waters. Sailfish, skipjack, bonito, tuna (allison, blackfin, and yellowfin), and wahoo are abundant. A charter runs about $500 for a half day (for up to six people), with most boats going out for four-, six-, or eight-hour trips.

Caribbean Sea Adventures (✉ *59 Kings Wharf, Christiansted* ☎ *340/773–2628* ⊕ *www.caribbeanseaadventures.com*) will take you out on a 38-foot powerboat. **Gone Ketchin'** (✉ *Salt River Marina, Rte. 80, Salt River* ☎ *340/713–1175* ⊕ *www.goneketchin.com*) arranges trips with old salt Captain Grizz.

GOLF

St. Croix's courses welcome you with spectacular vistas and well-kept greens. Check with your hotel or the tourist board to determine when major celebrity tournaments will be held. There's often an opportunity to play with the pros.

Fodor's Choice **Buccaneer Golf Course.** The Buccaneer Resort has an 18-hole course. It's
★ close to Christiansted, so it's convenient for those staying in or near town. Greens fees are $90, with an additional $20 for cart rental. ⊠ *Rte. 82, Shoys* 🕾 *340/712–2144* ⊕ *www.thebuccaneer.com.*

★ **Carambola Golf Club.** The spectacular 18-hole course at the Renaissance St. Croix Carambola Resort, in the northwest valley, was designed by Robert Trent Jones Sr. It sits near Carambola Beach Resort. Greens fees are $140 for 18 holes, which includes the use of a golf cart. ⊠ *Remaissance St. Croix Carambola Resort, Rte. 18, Davis Bay* 🕾 *340/778–5638* ⊕ *www.golfcarambola.com.*

The Links at Divi St. Croix. This attractive mini-golf course is just across from the Divi Carina Bay Resort. ⊠ *Rte. 60, Turner Hole* 🕾 *340/773–9700* ⊕ *www.divicarina.com* 🔊 *$8* ☉ *Daily noon–8.*

Reef Golf Course. This public course on the island's east end has 9 holes. Greens fees are $20, and cart rental is $15. ⊠ *Teague Bay* 🕾 *340/773–8844.*

GUIDED TOURS

St. Croix Safari Tours (🕾 *340/773–6700* ⊕ *www.gotostcroix.com/safaritours*) offers van tours of St. Croix. Excursions depart from Christiansted and last about five hours. Costs run from $60 per person, including admission fees to attractions.

St. Croix Transit (🕾 *340/772–3333*) offers van tours of St. Croix. Tours depart from Carambola Beach Resort, last about three hours, and cost from $65 per person, including the admission fees to all attractions visited on the tour.

HIKING

Although you can set off by yourself on a hike through a rain forest or along a shore, a guide will point out what's important and tell you why.

Ay-Ay Eco Hike and Tours Association (🖅 *Box 2435, Kingshill 00851* 🕾 *340/772–4079*), run by Ras Lumumba Corriette, takes hikers up hill and down dale in some of St. Croix's most remote places, including the rain forest and Mt. Victory. Some hikes include stops at places such as the Lawaetz Museum and old ruins. The cost is $60 per person for a three- or four-hour hike. There's a three-person minimum. A full-day jeep tour through the rain forest runs $120 per person.

Horseback riding in the island's rain forest.

HORSEBACK RIDING

Well-kept roads and expert guides make horseback riding on St. Croix pleasurable. At Sprat Hall, just north of Frederiksted, Jill Hurd runs **Paul and Jill's Equestrian Stables** (⊠ *Rte. 58, Frederiksted* ☎ *340/772–2880 or 340/332–0417* ⊕ *www.paulandjills.com*). She will take you through the rain forest, across the pastures, along the beaches, and through valleys—explaining the flora, fauna, and ruins on the way. A 1½-hour ride costs $90.

KAYAKING

Caribbean Adventure Tours (⊠ *Salt River Marina, Rte. 80, Salt River* ☎ *340/778–1522* ⊕ *www.stcroixkayak.com*) takes you on trips through Salt River Bay National Historical Park and Ecological Preserve, one of the island's most pristine areas. All tours run $450.

Virgin Kayak Tours (⊠ *Rte. 80, Cane Bay* ☎ *340/778–0071* ⊕ *www. virginkayaktours.com*) runs guided kayak trips on the Salt River and rents kayaks so you can tour around the Cane Bay area by yourself. All tours are $45. Kayak rentals are $40 for the entire day.

TENNIS

The public courts in Frederiksted and out east at Cramer Park are in questionable shape. It's better to pay a fee and play at one of the hotel courts. Costs vary by resort, but count on paying up to $8 an hour per person.

The Buccaneer (⊠ *Rte. 82, Shoys* ☎ *340/773–3036*) has eight courts (two lighted), plus a pro and a full tennis shop.

Carambola Beach Resort (⊠ *Rte. 80, Davis Bay* ☎ *340/778–3800*) has one lighted court.

Chenay Bay Beach Resort (⊠ *Rte. 82, Green Cay* ☎ *340/773–2918*) has two courts.

Club St. Croix (⊠ *Rte. 752, Estate Golden Rock* ☎ *340/718–4800*) has two tennis courts, one with lights.

WATER SPORTS

St. Croix Watersports (⊠ *Hotel on Cay, Protestant Cay, Christiansted* ☎ *340/773–7060* ⊕ *www.stcroixwatersports.com*) rents WaveRunners for $55 per half hour that will allow you to zip around Christiansted's harbor in style.

Tortola

WORD OF MOUTH

"I love Tortola and have been there many times as I had friends who lived on the island. I would typically stay there for one to three weeks, so I got to know the island very well. There is a lot to do and there are plenty of beaches to suit all sorts of personalities."

—eurotraveller

WELCOME TO TORTOLA

TOP REASONS TO GO

★ **Charter a Boat:** Tortola is the charter yacht capital of the Caribbean and a popular destination for boaters.

★ **Hit the Road:** You'll get the real flavor of the island by heading out in whatever direction you choose. The views are dramatic, and the traffic is light enough to allow for easy driving.

★ **Shop in Road Town:** The island's largest community is also home to an eclectic collection of stores.

★ **Hit the Trail:** Tortola is home to Sage Mountain National Park, a small but quite nice nature reserve.

★ **Get Wet:** Dive trips to spectacular locations leave from Tortola. If you're not certified to dive, an introductory course can teach you the basics and whet your appetite for more adventures under the sea.

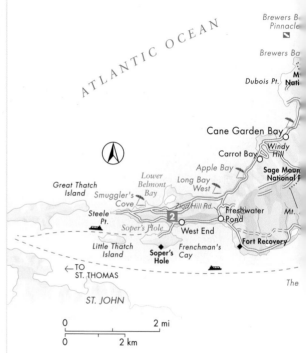

ATLANTIC OCEAN

Brewers B
Pinnacle

Brewers Ba

Dubois Pt.   M
Nati

Cane Garden Bay

Windy
Hill
Carrot Bay

Apple Bay   Sage Mour
National F
Lower   Long Bay
Belmont   West
Great Thatch   Bay
Island   Smuggler's
Cove   Zion Hill Rd.   Freshwater
Steele   Pond   Mt.
Pt.   Soper's Hole   West End
Little Thatch   Frenchman's   Fort Recovery
Island   Soper's   Cay
Hole
← TO
ST. THOMAS
The

ST. JOHN

0   2 mi
0   2 km

1 Road Town and environs. In the middle of the island's south coast, the capital is a hub for shopping, dining, and ferries, which dock here.

2 West End. In addition to some resorts and private villas, the west end of Tortola has a major ferry pier, a few good beaches, and some shops and restaurants.

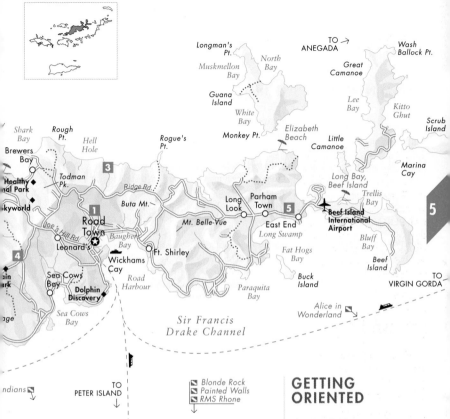

Longman's Pt.

North Bay

TO → ANEGADA

Wash Ballock Pt.

Muskmellon Bay

Great Camanoe

Guana Island

Lee Bay

Kitto Ghut

White Bay

Elizabeth Beach

Little Camanoe

Scrub Island

Shark Bay

Rough Pt.

Hell Hole

Rogue's Pt.

Monkey Pt.

Marina Cay

Brewers Bay

3

Long Bay, Beef Island

Trellis Bay

5

Healthy nal Park

Todman Pk.

Ridge Rd.

Buta Mt.

Long Look

Parham Town

5

Beef Island International Airport

kyworld

Mt. Belle-Vue

East End

Long Swamp

Bluff Bay

Road Town

Baughers Bay

Beef Island

TO VIRGIN GORDA

Joe's Hill Rd.

Leonard's

Ft. Shirley

Fat Hogs Bay

4

Wickhams Cay

Road Harbour

Buck Island

Paraquita Bay

ain rk

Sea Cows Bay

Dolphin Discovery

Alice in Wonderland

age

Sea Cows Bay

Sir Francis Drake Channel

ndians

TO PETER ISLAND ↓

Blonde Rock
Painted Walls
RMS Rhone

GETTING ORIENTED

The North Shore is where all the best beaches are found. Road Town, the island's tiny metropolis, has several restaurants and shops, as well as a smattering of historic sights and hotels. West End also has a concentration of establishments and a ferry pier. East End is isolated. Getting around is pretty easy, but the island's roads are extraordinarily steep and twisting, making driving demanding. It's best to explore the island a bit at a time.

3 North Shore. The best beaches and some good resorts (mostly concentrated in Cane Garden Bay and Brewer's Bay) can be found on the North Shore.

4 Mid-Island. Tortola's steep mid-section is home to several restaurants, national parks, and slews of villas.

5 East End. Both the airport (on Beef Island) and several resorts are on the more isolated east end of Tortola. There are also a few good beaches here.

TORTOLA PLANNER

Do You Need a Car?

You might get by with taxis, especially if you are staying in Road Town, but if you are in a villa or an isolated resort, a car is a necessity here.

CAR RENTALS

Only Hertz and National have offices at the airport, but most companies will pick you up. It's usually best to reserve a car in advance.

Contacts Avis (⊠ *Opposite Police Station, Road Town* ☎ *284/494-3322* ⊠ *Towers, West End* ☎ *284/495-4973*). **D&D** (⊠ *West End Rd., West End* ☎ *284/495-4765*). **Dollar** (⊠ *Long Bay Beach Resort, Long Bay* ☎ *284/495-4252 Ext. 2017* ⊠ *East End* ☎ *284/494-6093*). **Hertz** (⊠ *West End* ☎ *284/495-4405* ⊠ *Airport, Beef Island* ☎ *284/495-6600* ⊠ *Road Town* ☎ *284/494-6228*). **Itgo Car Rental** (⊠ *Wickham's Cay I, Road Town* ☎ *284/494-2639*). **National** (⊠ *Airport, Beef Island* ☎ *284/495-2626* ⊠ *Duffs Bottom, Road Town* ☎ *284/494-3197*).

Getting Here and Around

By Air: There's no nonstop air service from the continental United States to Tortola; connections are usually made through San Juan, Puerto Rico, or St. Thomas.

By Ferry: Frequent daily ferries connect Tortola with St. Thomas, which many vacationers decide to use as their main air gateway. Ferries go to and from both Charlotte Amalie and Red Hook. There's huge competition between the Tortola-based ferry companies on the St. Thomas–Tortola runs, with boats leaving close together. As you enter the ferry terminal to buy your ticket, crews may try to convince you to take their ferry. Ferries also link Tortola to St. John, where all Red Hook–bound ferries stop in Cruz Bay to clear customs and immigration. Ferries also link Tortola with Jost Van Dyke, Peter Island, and Virgin Gorda. Tortola has two ferry terminals—one at West End and one in Road Town—so make sure you hop a ferry that disembarks closest to where you want to go. Ferry schedules vary, and not all companies make daily trips. The BVI Tourist Board Web site has links to all the ferry companies.

By Taxi: Taxi rates aren't set on Tortola, so you should negotiate the fare with your driver before you start your trip. Fares are per destination, not per person here, so it's cheaper to travel in groups, because the fare will be the same whether you have one, two, or three passengers. On Tortola the BVI Taxi Association has stands in Road Town near Wickham's Cay I. The Waterfront Taxi Association picks up passengers from the Road Town ferry dock. The Airport Taxi Association operates at the Terrance B. Lettsome Airport on Beef Island. You can also usually find a West End Taxi Association taxi at the West End ferry dock.

Contacts Airport Taxi Association (☎ *284/495-1982*). **BVI Taxi Association** (☎ *284/494-3942*). **West End Taxi Association** (☎ *284/495-4934*). **Waterfront Taxi Association** (☎ *284/494-6362*).

Where to Stay

Tortola resorts are intimate—only a handful have more than 50 rooms. Guests are treated as more than just room numbers, and many return year after year. This can make booking a room at popular resorts difficult, even off-season, despite the fact that more than half the island's visitors stay aboard their own or chartered boats. Hotels in Road Town don't have beaches, but they do have pools and are within walking distance of restaurants, bars, and shops. Accommodations outside Road Town are relatively isolated, but most face the ocean. Some places close during the peak of hurricane season—August through October—to give their owners a much-needed break.

Where to Eat

Local seafood is plentiful on Tortola, and although other fresh ingredients are scarce, the island's chefs are a creative lot who apply their skills to whatever the boat delivers. Contemporary American dishes with Caribbean influences are very popular, but you can find French and Italian fare as well. The more expensive restaurants have dress codes: long pants and collared shirts for men and elegant but casual resort wear for women. Prices are often a bit higher than you'd expect to pay back home, and the service can sometimes be a tad on the slow side, but enjoy the chance to linger over the view.

HOTEL AND RESTAURANT PRICES

Restaurant prices are for a main course at dinner and include any taxes or service charges. Hotel prices are per night for a double room in high season, excluding taxes, service charges, and meal plans (except at all-inclusives).

WHAT IT COSTS IN U.S. DOLLARS

	¢	$	$$	$$$	$$$$
Restaurants	under $8	$8–$12	$13–$20	$21–$30	over $30
Hotels	under $150	$150–$275	$276–$375	$376–$475	over $475

Essentials

Banks On Tortola banks are near the waterfront at Wickham's Cay I. All have ATM machines. Look for First Caribbean International Bank, First Bank, and Scotia Bank, among others.

Internet Many hotels offer Internet access to their guests, but there are fewer cybercafés. **Trellis Kitchen Cybercafé** (⊠ *Trellis Bay* ☎ *284/495–2447*) is on the east end of the island, near the airport. **Myett's** (⊠ *Cane Garden Bay* ☎ *284/495–9649*) has a communications center where you can check email.

Safety Although crime is rare, use common sense: don't leave your camera on the beach while you take a dip or your wallet on a hotel dresser when you go for a walk.

Tour Options Romney Associates/Travel Plan Tours (☎ *284/494–4000*) can arrange island tours, boat tours, snorkeling and scuba-diving trips, dolphin swims, and yacht charters from its Tortola base.

Visitor Information BVI Tourist Board (⊠ *Ferry Terminal, Road Town* ☎ *284/494–3134* ⊕ *www.bvitourism.com*).

5

By Lynda Lohr   A day might not be enough to tour this island—all 21 square mi of it—not because there's so much to see and do but because you're meant to relax while you're here. Time stands still even in Road Town, the island's biggest community (though not as still as it did even in the early 1990s), where the hands of the central square's clock occasionally move but never tell the right time. The harbor, however, is busy with sailboats—this is the charter-boat capital of the Caribbean. Tortola's roads dip and curve around the island and lead to lovely, secluded accommodations.

Tortola is definitely busy these days, particularly when several cruise ships tie up at the Road Town dock. Passengers crowd the streets and shops, and open-air jitneys filled with cruise-ship passengers create bottlenecks on the island's byways. That said, most folks visit Tortola to relax on its deserted sands or linger over lunch at one of its many delightful restaurants. Beaches are never more than a few miles away, and the steep green hills that form Tortola's spine are fanned by gentle trade winds. The neighboring islands glimmer like emeralds in a sea of sapphire. It can be a world far removed from the hustle of modern life, but it simply doesn't compare to Virgin Gorda in terms of beautiful beaches—or even luxury resorts, for that matter.

Still a British colonial outpost, the island's economy depends on tourism and its offshore financial-services businesses. With a population of around 24,000 people, most people work in those industries or for the local government. You'll hear lots of crisp British accents thanks to a large number of expats who call the island home, but the melodic West Indian accent still predominates.

Initially settled by Taino Indians, Tortola saw a string of visitors over the years. Christopher Columbus sailed by in 1493 on his second voyage to the new world, and Spain, Holland, and France made periodic visits about a century later. Sir Francis Drake arrived in 1595, leaving his name on the passage between Tortola and St. John. Pirates and buccaneers followed, the British finally laying claim to the island in the late 1600s. In 1741 John Pickering became the first lieutenant governor of Tortola, and the seat of the British government moved from Virgin Gorda to Tortola. As the agrarian economy continued to grow, slaves were imported from Africa. The slave trade was abolished in 1807, but slaves in Tortola and the rest of the BVI did not gain their freedom until August 1, 1834, when the Emancipation Proclamation was read at Sunday Morning Well in Road Town. That date is celebrated every year with the island's annual Carnival.

BVI FERRIES

BVI ferries can be confusing for newcomers. Ferries depart from three different places—Road Town, West End, and Beef Island. Sometimes boats bound for Jost Van Dyke, Virgin Gorda, Anegada, St. Thomas, and St. John depart minutes apart, other times the schedule is skimpy. Departures can be suddenly canceled, particularly in the summer. Sometimes ferries make unscheduled stops. It's always wise to confirm your departure by phone in the morning, and you can always check with the locals catching a ferry if you're still not sure.

Visitors have a choice of accommodations, but most fall into the small and smaller still category. Only Long Bay Resort on Tortola's north shore qualifies as a resort, but even some of the smaller properties add amenities occasionally. A couple of new hotel projects are in the works, so look for more growth in the island's hotel industry over the next decade.

EXPLORING TORTOLA

Tortola doesn't have many historic sights, but it does have lots of spectacular natural scenery and beautiful beaches. Although you could explore the island's 21 square mi (56 square km) in a few hours, opting for such a whirlwind tour would be a mistake. There's no need to live in the fast lane when you're surrounded by some of the Caribbean's most breathtaking panoramas. In any event, you come to Tortola to relax, read in the hammock, and spend hours at dinner, not to dash madly around the island ticking yet another sight off your list. Except for the Dolphin Discovery, where advance booking is recommended, the other island sights are best seen when you stumble upon them on your round-the-island drive.

ROAD TOWN AND ENVIRONS

The bustling capital of the BVI looks out over Road Harbour. It takes only an hour or so to stroll down Main Street and along the waterfront, checking out the traditional West Indian buildings painted in pastel colors and with corrugated-tin roofs, bright shutters, and delicate fretwork trim. For sightseeing brochures and the latest information on everything from taxi rates to ferry schedules, stop in the BVI Tourist Board office. Or just choose a seat on one of the benches in Sir Olva Georges Square,

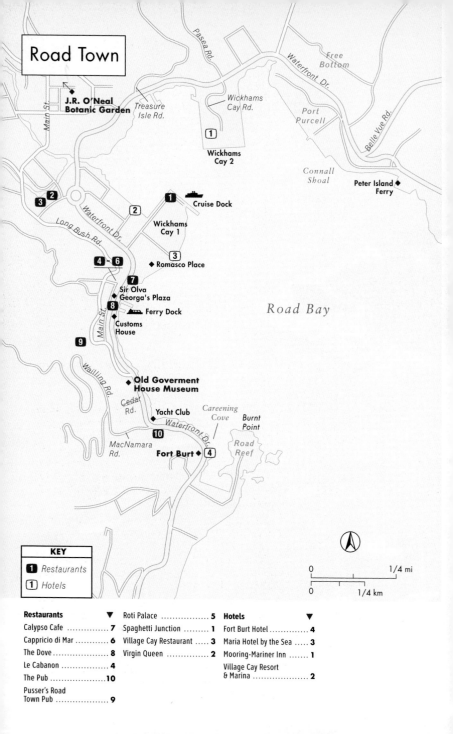

Road Town

J.R. O'Neal
Botanic Garden

Treasure Isle Rd.

Pasea Rd.

Waterfront Dr.

Free Bottom

Wickhams Cay Rd.

Port Purcell

Belle Vue Rd.

□1 **Wickhams Cay 2**

Connall Shoal

Peter Island ◆ Ferry

■1 **Cruise Dock**

□2 **Wickhams Cay 1**

■3 ■2

Waterfront Dr.

Long Bush Rd.

■4 – ■6

■3 ◆ **Romasco Place**

Road Bay

■7 **Sir Olva Georga's Plaza** ◆

■8 ⚓ **Ferry Dock**

◆ **Customs House**

Main St.

■9

Wailling Rd.

◆ **Old Goverment House Museum**

Cedar Rd.

◆ **Yacht Club**

Careening Cove

Burnt Point

Waterfront Dr.

■10

MacNamara Rd.

Fort Burt ◆ □4

Road Reef

Old Government House Museum, Road Town.

on Waterfront Drive, and watch the people come and go from the ferry dock and customs office across the street.

WHAT TO SEE

Dolphin Discovery. Get up close and personal with dolphins as they swim in a spacious seaside pen. There are three different programs that provide a range of experiences. In the Royal Swim, dolphins tow participants around the pen. The less expensive Adventure and Discovery programs allow you to touch the dolphins. ⊠ *Prospect Reef Resort, Road Town* ☎ *284/494–7675* ⊕ *www.dolphindiscovery.com* ⌧ *Royal Swim $149, Adventure $99, Discovery $79* ⊗ *Royal Swim daily at 10, noon, 2, and 4. Adventure and Discovery daily at 11 and 1.*

Ft. Burt. The most intact historic ruin on Tortola was built by the Dutch in the early 17th century to safeguard Road Harbour. It sits on a hill at the western edge of Road Town and is now the site of a small hotel and restaurant. The foundations and magazine remain, and the structure offers a commanding view of the harbor. ⊠ *Waterfront Dr., Road Town* ☎ *No phone* ⌧ *Free* ⊗ *Daily dawn–dusk.*

★ **J.R. O'Neal Botanic Gardens.** Take a walk through this 4-acre showcase of lush plant life. There are sections devoted to prickly cacti and succulents, hothouses for ferns and orchids, gardens of medicinal herbs, and plants and trees indigenous to the seashore. From the tourist office in Road Town, cross Waterfront Drive and walk one block over to Main Street and turn right. Keep walking until you see the high school. The gardens are on your left. ⊠ *Botanic Station, Road Town* ☎ *284/494–3904* ⌧ *$3* ⊗ *Mon.–Sat. 8:30–4:30.*

Fodor's Choice
★

Old Government House Museum. The official government residence until 1997, this gracious building now displays a nice collection of artifacts from Tortola's past. The rooms are filled with period furniture, hand-painted china, books signed by Queen Elizabeth II on her 1966 and 1977 visits, and numerous items reflecting Tortola's seafaring legacy. ⊠ *Waterfront Dr., Road Town* ☎ *284/494–4091* 🖻 *$3* ⊙ *Weekdays 9–3, Sat. 9–1.*

Ft. Recovery. The unrestored ruins of a 17th-century Dutch fort sit amid a profusion of tropical greenery on the grounds of Villas of Fort Recovery Estates. There's not much to see here, and there are no guided tours, but you're welcome to stop by and poke around. ⊠ *Waterfront Dr., Pockwood Pond* ☎ *284/485–4467* 🖻 *Free.*

> **NO PARKING**
>
> Road Town's traffic and parking can be horrific, so avoid driving along Waterfront Drive during morning and afternoon rush hours. It's longer—but often quicker—to drive through the hills above Road Town. (And the views are great as well.) Parking can also be very difficult in Road Town, particularly during high season. There's parking along the waterfront and on the inland side on the eastern end of downtown, but if you're planning a day of shopping, go early to make sure you snag a space.

Soper's Hole. On this little island connected by a causeway to Tortola's western end, you can find a marina and a captivating complex of pastel West Indian–style buildings with shady balconies, shuttered windows, and gingerbread trim that house art galleries, boutiques, and restaurants. Pusser's Landing is a lively place to stop for a cold drink (many are made with Pusser's famous rum) and a sandwich and to watch the boats in the harbor. ⊠ *Soper's Hole.*

NORTH SHORE

Cane Garden Bay. Once a sleepy village, Cane Garden Bay is growing into one of Tortola's most important destinations. Stay here at a small hotel or guesthouse, or stop by for lunch, dinner, or drinks at a seaside restaurant. You can find a few small stores selling clothing and basics such as suntan lotion, and, of course, one of Tortola's most popular beaches is at your feet. The roads in and out of this area are dauntingly steep, so use caution when driving.

Mount Healthy National Park. The remains of an 18th-century sugar plantation can be seen here. The windmill structure has been restored, and you can see the ruins of a mill, a factory with boiling houses, storage areas, stables, a hospital, and many dwellings. It's a nice place to picnic. ⊠ *Ridge Rd., Todman Peak* ☎ *No phone* 🖻 *Free* ⊙ *Daily dawn–dusk.*

★ **Sage Mountain National Park.** At 1,716 feet, Sage Mountain is the highest peak in the BVI. From the parking area, a trail leads you in a loop not only to the peak itself (and extraordinary views) but also to a small rain forest that is sometimes shrouded in mist. Most of the forest was cut down over the centuries to clear land for sugarcane, cotton, and other crops; to create pastureland; or simply to use the stands of timber. In 1964 this park was established to preserve what remained. Up here you can see mahogany trees, white cedars, mountain guavas, elephant-ear vines, mamey trees, and giant bullet woods, to say nothing of such birds as mountain doves and thrushes. Take a taxi from Road Town or drive up Joe's Hill Road and make a left onto Ridge Road toward Chalwell and Doty villages. The road dead-ends at the park. ⊠ *Ridge Rd., Sage Mountain* ☎ *284/494–3904* ☎ *$3* ⊙ *Daily dawn–dusk.*

DRIVING IN TORTOLA

Tortola's main roads are well paved, for the most part, but there are exceptionally steep hills and sharp curves; driving demands your complete attention. A main road circles the island, and several roads cross it, mostly through mountainous terrain.

★ **Skyworld.** Drive up here and climb the observation tower for a stunning 360-degree view of numerous islands and cays. On a clear day you can even see St. Croix (40 mi [64 km] away) and Anegada (20 mi [32 km] away). ⊠ *Ridge Rd., Joe's Hill* ☎ *No phone* ☎ *Free.*

5

BEACHES

Beaches in the BVI are less developed than those on St. Thomas or St. Croix, but they are also less inviting. The best BVI beaches are on deserted islands reachable only by boat, so take a snorkeling or sailing trip at least once. Tortola's north side has several palm-fringed, white-sand beaches that curl around turquoise bays and coves, but none really achieves greatness. Nearly all are accessible by car (preferably a four-wheel-drive vehicle), albeit down bumpy roads that corkscrew precipitously. Some of these beaches are lined with bars and restaurants as well as water-sports-equipment stalls; others have absolutely nothing.

WEST END

Long Bay West. This beach is a stunning, mile-long stretch of white sand; have your camera ready to snap the breathtaking approach. Although Long Bay Resort sprawls along part of it, the entire beach is open to the public. The water isn't as calm here as at Cane Garden or Brewers Bay, but it's still swimmable. Rent water-sports equipment and enjoy the beachfront restaurant at the resort. Turn left at Zion Hill Road; then travel about half a mile. ⊠ *Long Bay Rd.*

Smuggler's Cove. A beautiful, palm-fringed beach, Smuggler's Cove is down a pothole-filled dirt road. After bouncing your way down, you'll feel as if you've found a hidden piece of the island. You probably won't be alone on weekends, though, when the beach fills with snorkelers and sunbathers. There's a fine view of Jost Van Dyke from the shore. The beach is popular with Long Bay Resort guests who want a change of scenery, but there are no amenities. Follow Long Bay Road past Long Bay Resort, keeping to the roads nearest the water until you reach the beach. It's about a mile past the resort. ⊠ *Long Bay Rd.*

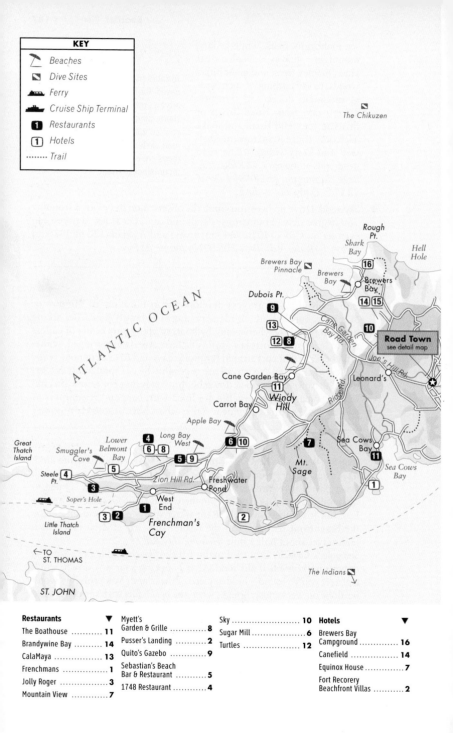

KEY

- Beaches
- Dive Sites
- Ferry
- Cruise Ship Terminal
- **1** Restaurants
- **1** Hotels
- .... Trail

The Chikuzen

Rough Pt.

Shark Bay

Hell Hole

Brewers Bay Pinnacle

Brewers Bay

16

Brewers Bay

Dubois Pt.

9

14 **15**

13

Cane Garden Bay Rd.

10

12 **8**

Road Town
see detail map

Joe's Hill Rd.

Cane Garden Bay

11

Leonard's

Windy Hill

Carrot Bay

Apple Bay

Long Bay West

4

6 **8**

6 **10**

Sea Cows Bay

7

11

5 **9**

Mt. Sage

Sea Cows Bay

Great Thatch Island

Smuggler's Cove

Lower Belmont Bay

4

5

Steele Pt.

4

Zion Hill Rd.

Freshwater Pond

1

3

Soper's Hole

West End

3 **2**

1

Frenchman's Cay

2

Little Thatch Island

ATLANTIC OCEAN

← TO ST. THOMAS

The Indians

ST. JOHN

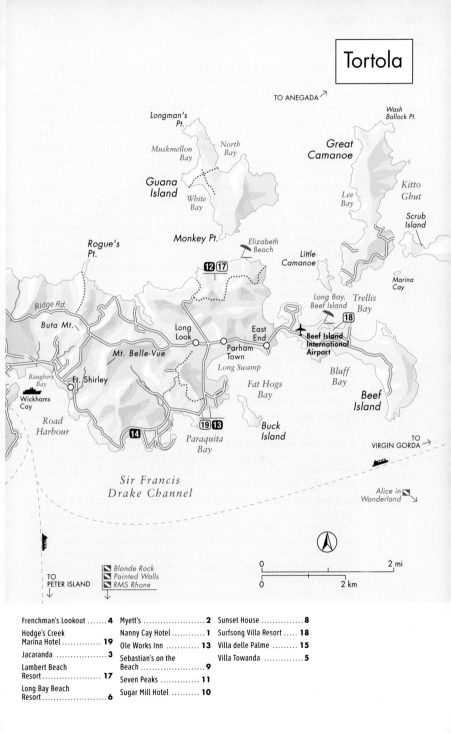

Tortola

TO ANEGADA

Wash
Ballock Pt.

Longman's
Pt.

Muskmellon
Bay

North
Bay

Great
Camanoe

Guana
Island

White
Bay

Kitto
Ghut

Lee
Bay

Scrub
Island

Monkey Pt.

Elizabeth
Beach

Little
Camanoe

Rogue's
Pt.

Marina
Cay

12 **17**

Long Bay,
Beef Island

Trellis
Bay

Ridge Rd.

18

Buta Mt.

Long
Look

Beef Island
International
Airport

Mt. Belle-Vue

Parham
Town

East
End

Bluff
Bay

Long Swamp

Baughers
Bay

Ft. Shirley

Fat Hogs
Bay

Beef
Island

Wickhams
Cay

19 **13**

Buck
Island

Road
Harbour

14

Paraquita
Bay

TO
VIRGIN GORDA

Sir Francis
Drake Channel

Alice in
Wonderland

TO
PETER ISLAND

Blonde Rock
Painted Walls
RMS Rhone

0   2 mi

0   2 km

NORTH SHORE

Apple Bay. Including nearby Little Apple Bay and Capoon's Bay, this is your spot if you want to surf—although the white, sandy beach itself is narrow. Sebastian's, a casual hotel, caters to those in search of the perfect wave. The legendary Bomba's Surfside Shack—a landmark festooned with all manner of flotsam and jetsam—serves drinks and casual food. Otherwise, there's nothing else in the way of amenities. Good waves are never a sure thing, but you're more apt to find them in January and February. If you're swimming and the waves are up, take care not to get dashed on the rocks. ⊠ *North Shore Rd. at Zion Hill Rd.*

Brewers Bay. Brewers Bay is good for snorkeling, and you can find a campground with showers and bathrooms and beach bar tucked in the foliage right behind the beach. An old sugar mill and ruins of a rum distillery are off the beach along the road. The beach is easy to find, but the steep, twisting paved roads leading down the hill to it can be a bit daunting. You can actually reach the beach from either Brewers Bay Road East or Brewers Bay Road West. ⊠ *Brewers Bay Rd. E off Cane Garden Bay Rd.*

Cane Garden Bay. A silky stretch of sand, Cane Garden Bay has exceptionally calm, crystalline waters—except when storms at sea turn the water murky. Snorkeling is good along the edges. Casual guesthouses, restaurants, bars, and even shops are steps from the beach in the growing village of the same name. The beach is a laid-back, even somewhat funky place to put down your towel. It's the closest beach to Road Town—one steep uphill and downhill drive—and one of the BVI's best-known anchorages (unfortunately, it can be very crowded). Watersports shops rent equipment. ⊠ *Cane Garden Bay Rd. off Ridge Rd.*

Elizabeth Beach. Home to Lambert Beach Resort, Elizabeth Beach is a palm-lined, wide, and sandy beach with parking along its steep downhill access road. Other than at the hotel, which welcomes nonguests, there are no amenities aside from peace and quiet. Turn at the sign for Lambert Beach Resort. If you miss it, you wind up at Her Majesty's Prison. ⊠ *Lambert Rd. off Ridge Rd., on eastern end of island.*

★ **Long Bay, Beef Island.** Long Bay on Beef Island has superlative scenery: the beach stretches seemingly forever, and you can catch a glimpse of Little Camanoe and Great Camanoe islands. If you walk around the bend to the right, you can see little Marina Cay and Scrub Island. Long Bay is also a good place to search for seashells. Swim out to wherever you see a dark patch for some nice snorkeling. There are no amenities, so come prepared with your own drinks and snacks. Turn left shortly after crossing the bridge to Beef Island. ⊠ *Beef Island Rd., Beef Island.*

DID YOU KNOW?

Beef Island, on the east end of Tortola, is where you'll find the island's airport; it also has one of the best beaches. There are no facilities, so you just need to relax and enjoy.

WHERE TO EAT

Restaurants are scattered from one end of the island to another, so you're never far from a good meal. Cane Garden Bay, with a handful of restaurants along the beach, is a popular dining destination. Eateries in Road Town are a short stroll from each other, making it easy to find a place that pleases everyone. Most hotels have restaurants that welcome nonguests.

ROAD TOWN

$$
ECLECTIC

✕ **The Boat House.** A popular spot for local yachties, this open-air restaurant dishes up tasty food at very reasonable prices. Try the Caribbean lobster cake served with a curried tartar sauce as an appetizer. The offerings range from a grilled-vegetable-and-feta-cheese sandwich to a pan-seared duck breast served with vegetables. The blueberry-pineapple cheesecake is divine. ⊠ *Manuel Reef Marina, Waterfront Dr., Sea Cow's Bay* ☎ *284/495–0007* ⊕ *www.boathouse.com* ⊘ *Closed Sun.*

$$$$
ITALIAN
Fodor's Choice
★

✕ **Brandywine Bay.** At this restaurant in Brandywine Bay, candlelit outdoor tables have sweeping views of nearby islands. Owner Davide Pugliese prepares foods with lots of fresh herbs. The remarkable menu may include duck with a mango sauce, beef carpaccio, grilled swordfish, and veal chop with ricotta and sun-dried tomatoes. The homemade mozzarella is another standout. The wine list is excellent, and the lemon tart and the tiramisu are irresistible. If you want something lighter, the lounge serves a tapas menu. ⊠ *Sir Francis Drake Hwy., east of Road Town, Brandywine Bay* ⌂ *Box 2914, East End VG1120* ☎ *284/495–2301* ⊕ *www.brandywinebay.com* ⌆ *Reservations essential* ⊘ *Closed Sun.*

$$$
ECLECTIC

✕ **Calypso Café.** Don't be put off by the pedestrian decor. The chef at this shopping-center spot conjures up delicious dishes that run the gamut from burgers to fresh fish to chicken alfredo. It's the place to go for pizza smothered with everything from the standard cheese and tomato to the more unusual chicken and bacon. In winter the staff will deliver anything from its menu straight to your hotel. ⊠ *Wickham's Cay I, Waterfront Dr.* ☎ *284/494–7412.*

$
ITALIAN
Fodor's Choice
★

✕ **Capriccio di Mare.** The owners of the well-known Brandywine Bay restaurant also run this casual, authentic Italian outdoor café. Stop by for an espresso, a fresh pastry, a bowl of perfectly cooked penne, or a crispy tomato-and-mozzarella pizza. Drink specialties include a mango Bellini, an adaptation of the famous cocktail served at Harry's Bar in Venice. ⊠ *Waterfront Dr., Road Town* ☎ *284/494–5369* ⌆ *Reservations not accepted* ⊘ *Closed Sun.*

$$$
ECLECTIC

✕ **The Dove.** Here's a two-in-one restaurant that can meet your needs regardless of the meal you're craving. When you want something more casual or just a few bites along with some drinks, head upstairs for something from the Dove's tapas menu—the sushi plate, pad thai noodles, and duck nachos are especially tasty. For more formal dining, you can eat downstairs and try some of the Dove's innovative cuisine—including five-spice duck breast served in a red-wine-and-ginger sauce, which comes with an apple-and-cabbage mixture and a sweet potato. ⊠ *Waterfront Dr., Road Town* ☎ *284/494–0313* ⊘ *Closed Sun. and Mon. No lunch.*

A Road Town marina at sunrise.

$$$ ✕ **Le Cabanon.** Birds and bougainvillea brighten the patio of this breezy
FRENCH   French restaurant and bar, a popular gathering spot for locals and
visitors alike. French onion soup and smoked salmon salad are good
appetizer choices. From there, move on to the grilled tuna with wasabi
sauce, sole in a brown butter sauce, or beef tenderloin with green pep-
percorn sauce. Save room for such tasty desserts as chocolate cake and
crème brûlée, or opt for a platter of French cheeses. ⊠ *Waterfront Dr.,
Road Town* ☎ *284/494–8660* ⊘ *Closed Sun.*

$$ ✕ **The Pub.** At this lively waterfront spot, tables are arranged along a ter-
AMERICAN–   race facing a small marina and the harbor in Road Town. Hamburgers,
CASUAL   salads, and sandwiches are typical lunch offerings. In the evening you
can also choose grilled fish, sautéed conch, sizzling steaks, or barbe-
cued ribs. There's live entertainment Thursday and Friday, and locals
gather here nightly for spirited games at the pool table. ⊠ *Waterfront
Dr.* ☎ *284/494–2608* ⚔ *Reservations not accepted* ⊘ *No lunch Sun.*

$$ ✕ **Pusser's Road Town Pub.** Almost everyone who visits Tortola stops here
AMERICAN   at least once to have a bite to eat and to sample the famous Pusser's
☾   Rum Painkiller (fruit juices and rum). The nonthreatening menu includes
cheesy pizza, shepherd's pie, fish-and-chips, and hamburgers. Dine inside
in air-conditioned comfort or outside on the verandah, which looks out
on the harbor. ⊠ *Waterfront Dr.* ☎ *284/494–3897* ⊕ *www.pussers.com.*

$$ ✕ **Roti Palace.** You might be tempted to pass this tiny spot on Road
CARIBBEAN   Town's Main Street when you see the plastic tablecloths and fake flow-
★   ers, but owner Jean Leonard's reputation for dishing up fantastic roti is
known far and wide. Flatbread is filled with curried potatoes, onions,
and either chicken, beef, conch, goat, or vegetables. Ask for the bone
out if you order the chicken, to save yourself the trouble of fishing them

out of your mouth. ⊠ *Main St., Road Town* ☎ *284/494–4196* ▤ *No credit cards* ⊙ *Closed Sun. No dinner.*

$$ ✕ **Spaghetti Junction.** Popular with the boating crowd, this longtime favorite
ITALIAN serves up such West Indian dishes as stewed oxtail along with Italian favor-
★ ites like penne smothered in a spicy tomato sauce, spinach-mushroom lasa-
gna, and angel-hair pasta with shellfish. For something that combines a
bit of both, try the spicy jambalaya pasta. You can also find old-fashioned
favorites such as osso bucco on the menu. ⊠ *Wickhams Cay I, Road Town*
☎ *284/494–4880* ⊕ *www.spaghettijunction.net* ⊙ *Closed Sun.*

$$$ ✕ **Village Cay Restaurant.** Docked sailboats stretch nearly as far as the
CARIBBEAN eye can see at this busy Road Town restaurant. For lunch, try the grou-
per club sandwich with an ancho chili mayonnaise. Dinner offerings
run to fish served a variety of ways, including West Indian–style with
okra, onions, and peppers, as well as a seafood jambalaya with lobster,
crayfish, shrimp, mussels, crab, and fish in a mango-passion-fruit sauce.
⊠ *Wickhams Cay I, Road Town* ☎ *284/494–2771.*

$$ ✕ **Virgin Queen.** The sailing and rugby crowds head here to play darts,
ECLECTIC drink beer, and eat Queen's Pizza—a crusty, cheesy pie topped with
sausage, onions, green peppers, and mushrooms. Also on the menu
is excellent West Indian and English fare: barbecued ribs with beans
and rice, bangers and mash, shepherd's pie, and grilled sirloin steak
⊠ *Fleming St.* ☎ *284/494–2310* ⊕ *www.virginqueenbvi.com* ⊙ *Closed
Sun. No lunch Sat.*

WEST END

$$$ ✕ **Jolly Roger Restaurant.** This casual, open-air restaurant near the ferry
ECLECTIC terminal is as popular with locals as it is with visitors. The menu ranges
from burgers to rib-eye steaks to the island favorite, local lobster. Try
the savory fritters filled with tender local conch and herbs for a good
start to your dinner. End it with a slice of sweet key lime pie. ⊠ *West
End* ☎ *284/495–4559* ⊕ *www.jollyrogerbvi.com.*

$$$ ✕ **Pusser's Landing.** Yachters navigate their way to this waterfront restau-
AMERICAN rant. Downstairs, from late morning to well into the evening, you can
ℭ belly up to the outdoor mahogany bar or sit downstairs for sandwiches,
fish-and-chips, and pizzas. At dinnertime head upstairs for a harbor
view and a quiet alfresco meal of grilled steak or fresh fish. ⊠ *Soper's
Hole* ☎ *284/495–4554* ⊕ *www.pussers.com.*

NORTH SHORE

$$$ ✕ **1748 Restaurant.** Relax over dinner in this open-air eatery at Long Bay
CONTINENTAL Beach Resort. Tables are well spaced, offering enough privacy for inti-
mate conversations. The menu changes daily, but several dishes show
up regularly. Start your meal with smoked salmon with green mussels,
creamy seafood soup, or a Caesar salad. Entrées include baby back ribs
in a tangy barbecue sauce served with peas and rice, plantains and corn
on the cob, pan-seared red snapper with vegetables, and for vegetarians, vegetable spring rolls with lo-mein noodles. There are always at
least five desserts to choose from, which might include Belgian chocolate mousse, strawberry cheesecake, or a fluffy lemon-and-coconut

cake. ⊠ *Long Bay Beach Resort, Long Bay* ☎ *284/495–4252* ⊕ *www. longbay.com.*

$$
CARIBBEAN
✕ **Myett's Garden and Grille.** Right on the beach, this bi-level restaurant and bar is hopping day and night. Chowder made with fresh conch is the specialty here, although the menu includes everything from vegetarian dishes to grilled shrimp, steak, and tuna. There's live entertainment every night in winter. ⊠ *Cane Garden Bay* ☎ *284/495–9649.*

$$$
CARIBBEAN
✕ **Quito's Bar and Restaurant.** This rustic beachside bar and restaurant is owned and operated by island native Quito Rymer, a multitalented recording star who plays and sings solo on Tuesday and Thursday and performs with his reggae band on Friday. The menu is Caribbean, with an emphasis on fresh fish, but you should try the conch fritters or the barbecue chicken. ⊠ *Cane Garden Bay* ☎ *284/495–9051* ⊕ *www. quitorymer.com* ⊗ *No lunch.*

$$$
ECLECTIC
✕ **Sebastian's Beach Bar and Restaurant.** The waves practically lap at your feet at this beachfront restaurant on Tortola's North Shore. The menu emphasizes seafood—especially lobster, conch, and local fish—but you can also find dishes such as ginger chicken and filet mignon. It's a perfect spot to stop for lunch on your around-the-island tour. Try the grilled dolphinfish sandwich, served on a soft roll with an oniony tartar sauce. Finish off with a cup of Sebastian's coffee spiked with home-brewed rum. ⊠ *North Coast Rd., Apple Bay* ☎ *284/494–4212* ⊕ *www. sebastiansbvi.com.*

$$$$
ECLECTIC
Fodor's Choice
★
✕ **Sugar Mill Restaurant.** Candles gleam, and the background music is peaceful in this romantic restaurant inside a 17th-century sugar mill. Well-prepared selections on the à la carte menu, which changes nightly, include some pasta and vegetarian entrées. Lobster bisque with basil croutons and a creamy conch chowder are good starters. Favorite entrées include fresh fish with soba noodles, shiitake mushrooms, and a scallion broth; filet mignon topped with an herb-cream sauce; butter-poached shrimp with creamy polenta; and pumpkin-and-black-bean lasagna. ⊠ *Sugar Mill Hotel, Apple Bay* ☎ *284/495–4355* ⊗ *No lunch.*

EAST END

$$$
ECLECTIC
✕ **CalaMaya.** Casual fare is what you can find at this waterfront restaurant. You can always order a burger or Caesar salad; the chicken wrap with sweet-and-sour sauce is a tasty alternative. For dinner, try the mahimahi with sautéed vegetables and rice. ⊠ *Hodge's Creek Marina, Blackburn Hwy.* ☎ *284/495–2126.*

$$$
ECLECTIC
✕ **Turtles.** If you're touring the island, Turtles is a good place to stop for lunch or dinner. Sitting near the ocean at Lambert Beach Resort, this casual place provides a relaxing respite from the rigors of navigating mountain roads. At dinner you might find tiger shrimp in a curry sauce or rack of lamb with a raspberry glaze. Lunch favorites include fried shrimp, fresh tuna on a bun, and some vegetarian dishes. ⊠ *Lambert Beach Resort, Lambert Bay, East End* ☎ *284/495–2877.*

MID-ISLAND

$$$
ECLECTIC
Fodor'sChoice
★

✕ Mountain View. It's worth the drive up Sage Mountain for lunch or dinner at this casual restaurant. The view is spectacular—one of the best on Tortola. The small menu includes dishes such as veal with a ginger sauce and grilled mahimahi in a lime-onion sauce. The lobster-salad sandwich is the house lunch specialty. If it's on the menu, don't pass up the fish sandwich with fries. ⊠ *Sage Mountain* ✆ *Box 4036, Road Town VG1110* ☎ *284/495–9536.*

TORTOLA'S CARNIVAL

Tortola celebrates Carnival on and around August 1 to mark the anniversary of the end of slavery in 1834. A slew of activities culminating with a parade through the streets take place in Road Town. Hotels fill up fast, so make sure to reserve your room and rental car well in advance.

$$
ASIAN

✕ Sky. The top of a mountain is the location for this casually elegant dining room with a menu that features sushi, sashimi, and similar dishes. You'll find the usual tuna, sea bass, and shrimp on the sushi menu, but locals like the tropical-style sushi with smoked salmon and mango. If you like some heat, try the Hurricane. If you're renting a villa in the area, the take-out menu will save you some kitchen chores. ⊠ *Ridge Rd., Joe's Hill* ☎ *284/494–3567* ⊗ *No lunch.*

WHERE TO STAY

Luxury on Tortola is more about a certain state of mind—serenity, seclusion, gentility, and a bit of Britain in the Caribbean—than about state-of-the-art amenities and fabulous facilities. Some properties, especially the vacation villas, are catching up with current trends, but others seem stuck in the 1980s. But don't let a bit of rust on the screen door or a chip in the paint on the balcony railing mar your appreciation of the ambience. You will likely spend most of your time outside, so the location, size, or price of a hotel should be more of a factor to you than the decor.

A stay at any one of the hotels and guesthouses on Tortola's north side will put you closer to the beach, but not to worry: it doesn't take that long to get from one side of the island to the other. Visitors who want to be closer to Road Town's restaurants and shops can find a handful of places in and around the island's main town.

PRIVATE VILLAS

Renting a villa is growing in popularity. Vacationers like the privacy, the space to spread out, and the opportunity to cook meals. As is true everywhere, the most important thing is location. If you want to be close to the beach, opt for a villa on the north shore. If you want to dine out in Road Town every night, a villa closer to town may be a better bet. Prices per week during the winter season run from around $2,000 for a one- or two-bedroom villa up to $10,000 for a five-room beachfront villa. Rates in summer are substantially less. Most, but not all, villas accept credit cards.

RENTAL AGENCIES

Areana Villas (⬡ *Box 263, Road Town VG1110* ☎ *284/494–5864* ⊕ *www. areanavillas.com*) represents top-of-the-line properties. Pastel-color villas with one to six bedrooms can accommodate up to 10 guests. Many have pools, whirlpool tubs, and tiled courtyards.

The St. Thomas–based **McLaughlin-Anderson Luxury Villas** (⬡ *1000 Blackbeard's Hill, Suite 3, St. Thomas, U.S. Virgin Islands 00802-6739* ☎ *340/776–0635 or 800/537–6246* ⊕ *www.mclaughlinanderson.com*) manages nearly three dozen properties around Tortola. Villas range in size from one to six bedrooms and come with full kitchens and stellar views. Most have pools. The company can hire a chef and stock your kitchen with groceries.

Smiths Gore (⬡ *Box 135, Road Town VG1110* ☎ *284/494–2446* ⊕ *www. smithsgore.com*) has properties all over the island, but many are in the Smuggler's Cove area. They range in size from two to five bedrooms. They all have stellar views, lovely furnishings, and lush landscaping.

5

For approximate costs, see the dining and lodging price chart at the beginning of this chapter. The following hotel reviews have been condensed for this book. Please go to Fodors.com for expanded reviews of each property.

ROAD TOWN

$
HOTEL
🏨 **Fort Burt Hotel.** The Fort Burt Hotel surrounds the ruins of an old Dutch fort, giving you a sense of history along with a night's sleep. **Pros:** nice views; historic site; walk to shops and restaurants. **Cons:** little parking; long walk to Road Town; need car to get around; Wi-Fi only in public areas. ✉ *Waterfront Dr., Box 3380* ☎ *284/494–2587* ⊕ *www. fortburt.com* 🛏 *10 rooms, 8 suites* ⚭ *In-room: a/c, no safe, kitchen (some). In-hotel: restaurant, bar, pool* ⦿*No meals.*

$
HOTEL
🏨 **Maria's Hotel by the Sea.** Sitting near the water in busy Road Town, Maria's Hotel by the Sea is perfect for budget travelers who want to be near shops and restaurants but who don't need many frills. **Pros:** good location; spacious rooms; walk to shops and restaurants. **Cons:** busy street; little parking; need car to get around; Wi-Fi only in public areas. ✉ *Waterfront Dr., Box 2364* ☎ *284/494–2595* ⊕ *www.mariasbythesea.com* 🛏 *40 rooms* ⚭ *In-room: a/c, no safe. In-hotel: restaurant, bar, pool* ⦿*No meals.*

$$
B&B/INN
🏨 **Moorings-Mariner Inn.** If you enjoy the camaraderie of a busy marina, this inn on the edge of Road Town may appeal to you. **Pros:** good dining options; friendly guests; excellent spot to charter boats. **Cons:** busy location; long walk to Road Town; need car to get around. ✉ *Waterfront Dr., Box 139* ☎ *284/494–2333 or 800/535–7289* ⊕ *www. bvimarinerinnhotel.com* 🛏 *32 rooms, 7 suites* ⚭ *In-room: a/c, no safe. In-hotel: restaurant, bar, pool, business center* ⦿*No meals.*

$
HOTEL
🏨 **Nanny Cay Hotel.** This quiet oasis is far enough from Road Town to give it a secluded feel but close enough to make shops and restaurants convenient. **Pros:** nearby shops and restaurant; pleasant rooms; marina atmosphere. **Cons:** busy location; need car to get around. ✉ *Nanny Cay* ⬡ *Box 281, Road Town VG1110* ☎ *284/494–2512* ⊕ *www.nannycay. com* 🛏 *38 rooms* ⚭ *In-room: a/c, no safe, kitchen (some). In-hotel: restaurants, tennis court, pool, business center* ⦿*No meals.*

American or British?

Yes, the Union Jack flutters overhead in the tropical breeze, schools operate on the British system, place names have British spellings, Queen Elizabeth II appoints the governor—and the queen's picture hangs on many walls. Indeed, residents celebrate the queen's birthday every June with a public ceremony. You can overhear that charming English accent from a good handful of expats when you're lunching at Road Town restaurants, and you can buy British biscuits—which Americans call cookies—in the supermarkets.

But you can pay for your lunch and the biscuits with American money, because the U.S. dollar is legal tender here. The unusual circumstance is a matter of geography. The practice started in the mid-20th century, when BVI residents went to work in the nearby USVI. On trips home, they brought their U.S. dollars with them. Soon they abandoned the barter system, and in 1959 the U.S. dollar became the official currency. Interestingly, the government sells stamps for use only in the BVI that often carry pictures of Queen Elizabeth II and other royalty with the monetary value in U.S. dollars and cents.

The American influence continued to grow when Americans began to open businesses in the BVI because they preferred its quieter ambience to the hustle and bustle of St. Thomas. Inevitably, cable and satellite TV's U.S.–based programming, along with Hollywood-made movies, further influenced life in the BVI. And most goods are shipped from St. Thomas in the USVI, meaning you can find more American-made Oreos than British-produced Peak Freens on the supermarket shelves.

¢–$ **Village Cay Resort and Marina.** If you want to be able to walk to restaurants and shops, you simply can't beat Village Cay's prime location in the heart of Road Town. **Pros:** prime location; shops and restaurants nearby; nautical ambience. **Cons:** little parking; busy street; need car to get around. ⊠ *Wickham's Cay I, Box 145* ☎ *284/494–2771* ⊕ *www.villagecayhotelandmarina.com* ⤴ *17 rooms, 5 suites* ⚖ *In-room: a/c, no safe, kitchen (some), Internet. In-hotel: restaurant, bar, pool, spa, business center* ⦿ *No meals.*

HOTEL

WEST END

$$ **Fort Recovery Beachfront Villas.** This is one of those small but special properties distinguished by friendly service and the chance to get to know your fellow guests rather than the poshness of the rooms and the upscale amenities. **Pros:** beautiful beach; spacious units; historic site. **Cons:** need car to get around; isolated location. ⊠ *Waterfront Dr., Box 239, Pockwood Pond* ☎ *284/495–4467 or 800/367–8455* ⊕ *www.fortrecovery.com* ⤴ *29 suites, 1 villa* ⚖ *In-room: a/c, no safe, kitchen (some), Wi-Fi. In-hotel: pool, gym, beach, water sports, business center* ⦿ *Breakfast.*

RENTAL ☾ ★

$$$–$$$$ **Frenchmans.** Relaxation is the main event at this comfortable resort on Tortola's West End. **Pros:** beautiful, modern decor; easy walk to Soper's Hole. **Cons:** need a car to get around; lots of steps. ⊠ *Off Sir*

RESORT

Francis Drake Hwy., West End ⚓ P.O. Box 3169, PMB 318, Tortola, BVI VG1130 ☎ 284/494–8811 ⊕ www.frenchmansbvi.com ⇥ 3 1-bedroom, 3 2-bedroom, 3 villas ⚿ In-room: a/c (some), kitchen, Wi-Fi. In-hotel: restaurant, tennis court, pool, beach, water sports, parking, some age restrictions ⦿ No meals.

$$$$ ⌂ **Frenchman's Lookout.** Sitting on a promontory at Tortola's West End,
RENTAL   this stunning villa has stellar views of St. John's green hills. **Pros:** stunning views; high-end amenities; walk to the restaurants and shops. **Cons:** expensive rate; need car to get around; not on the beach; on partially unpaved road. ⊠ *Frenchman's Cay ⊕ www.frenchmanslookout. com ⇥ 5 bedrooms, 5 bathrooms ⚿ In-room: a/c (some), Wi-Fi. In-hotel: pool, gym ⌦ 5-night minimum ⦿ Breakfast.*

$$$$ ⌂ **Jacaranda.** Walk to the shops and restaurants at Soper's Hole from the
RENTAL   spacious villa in the gated community at Frenchman's Cay. **Pros:** great views; lots of outdoor space; comfortable ambience. **Cons:** need car to get out and about; unpaved sections of the road; bedroom on lowest level is small. ⊠ *Dolphin Estate, Frenchman's Cay ⊕ www.smithsgore. com ⇥ 4 bedrooms, 4½ bathrooms ⚿ In-room: a/c (some), Wi-Fi. In-hotel: pool, laundry facilities ▤ No credit cards ⌦ 5-night minimum ⦿ No meals.*

NORTH SHORE

$$$ ⌂ **Equinox House.** With Mediterranean-style architecture, a spacious
RENTAL   pool deck, and lovely sunset views, this villa has it all. **Pros:** great views; lots of outdoor space; near hotel facilities. **Cons:** need car to get around; can be hot in the afternoon. ⊠ *Off North Coast Rd., Belmont ⊕ www. areanavillas.com ⇥ 3 bedrooms, 3 bathrooms ⚿ In-room: a/c, Internet. In-hotel: pool, laundry facilities ⌦ 5-night minimum ⦿ No meals.*

$$–$$$ ⌂ **Long Bay Beach Resort.** Long Bay Beach Resort is Tortola's only choice
RESORT   if you want all the resort amenities, including a beach, scads of water sports, tennis courts, and even a pitch-and-putt golf course. **Pros:** resort atmosphere; good restaurants; many activities. **Cons:** need car to get around; sometimes curt staff; uphill hike to some rooms. ⊠ *Long Bay ⚓ Box 433, Road Town VG1130 ☎ 284/495–4252 or 800/345–0271 ⊕ www.longbay.com ⇥ 53 rooms, 37 suites, 26 villas ⚿ In-room: a/c, kitchen (some). In-hotel: restaurants, bars, tennis courts, pool, gym, spa, beach, water sports, business center ⦿ No meals.*

$–$$ ⌂ **Myett's.** Tucked away in a beachfront garden, this tiny hotel puts you
HOTEL   right in the middle of Cane Garden Bay's busy hustle and bustle. **os:** beautiful beach; good restaurant; shops nearby. **Cons:** busy location; need car to get around. ⊠ *Cane Garden Bay ⚓ Box 556, Cane Garden Bay VG1130 ☎ 284/495–9649 ⊕ www.myettent.com ⇥ 6 rooms, 4 cottages, 1 villa ⚿ In-room: a/c, no safe, kitchen (some). In-hotel: restaurant, spa, beach, business center ⦿ No meals.*

¢–$ ⌂ **Ole Works Inn.** The small hotel's location on busy Cane Garden Bay
HOTEL   and the fact that it's owned by Quito Rymer, one of the island's most popular musicians, guarantee that it's not a quiet retreat. If you don't mind strolling a short distance to the beach, want to eat in the nearby casual restaurants, and enjoy mixing and mingling with the locals at the village's numerous bars, this is a good choice. Rooms are dated, and

some have carpeting rather than tile. Opt for a beach-facing room for the best views. **Pros:** near bars and restaurants; near beach; good restaurant. **Cons:** busy location; loud music; need car to get around; Wi-Fi only in public areas. ✉ *Cane Garden Bay* 📫 *Box 560, Road Town VG1110* ☎ *284/495–4837* 🌐 *www.quitorymer.com* *13 rooms, 5 suites* *In-room: a/c, no safe, kitchen (some). In-hotel: pool* 🍴 *No meals.*

$ HOTEL **Sebastian's on the Beach.** Sitting on the island's north coast, Sebastian's definitely has a beachy feel, and that's its primary charm. **Pros:** nice beach; good restaurants; beachfront rooms. **Cons:** on busy road; some rooms nicer than others; need car to get around. ✉ *Apple Bay* 📫 *Box 441, Road Town VG1110* ☎ *284/495–4212 or 800/336–4870* 🌐 *www.sebastiansbvi.com* *26 rooms, 9 villas* *In-room: a/c, no safe, no TV (some). In-hotel: restaurant, bar, beach, business center* 🍴 *No meals.*

$$$$ RENTAL **Seven Peaks.** As its name suggests, this spacious waterfront villa is capped with seven lavender peaks. **Pros:** nearby beach; great views; lots of outdoor space. **Cons:** need car to get around; loud music at nearby resort. ✉ *Off North Coast Rd., Cane Garden Bay* 🌐 *www.smithsgore.com* *3 bedrooms, 2 bathrooms* *In-room: a/c (some), Wi-Fi. In-hotel: pool* *No credit cards* ☞ *7-night minimum* 🍴 *No meals.*

$$–$$$ HOTEL Fodor's Choice ★ **Sugar Mill Hotel.** Though it's not a sprawling resort, the Sugar Mill Hotel has a Caribbean cachet that's hard to beat, and it's our favorite place to stay on Tortola. **os:** lovely rooms; excellent restaurant; nice views. **Cons:** on busy road; small beach; need car to get around. ✉ *Apple Bay* 📫 *Box 425, Road Town VG1130* ☎ *284/495–4355 or 800/462–8834* 🌐 *www.sugarmillhotel.com* *19 rooms, 2 suites, 1 villa, 1 cottage* *In-room: a/c, no safe, kitchen (some), no TV (some), Wi-Fi. In-hotel: restaurants, bar, pool, beach, water sports, business center* 🍴 *No meals.*

$$$$ RENTAL **Sunset House.** Stunning sunset views distinguish this aptly named house in a residential neighborhood near Long Bay Beach Resort. **Pros:** great views; lots of outdoor space; near hotel facilities. **Cons:** need car to get around; near busy road; can be hot in the afternoon. ✉ *Off North Coast Rd., Long Bay* 🌐 *www.areanavillas.com* *5 bedrooms, 5 bathrooms* *In-room: a/c (some), Internet. In-hotel: pool, laundry facilities* ☞ *5-night minimum* 🍴 *No meals.*

$$$$ RENTAL ★ **Villa Towanda.** The architecture of this spacious villa is reminiscent of an old plantation house. Painted a deep rusty red, the interior is equally attractive. **Pros:** great views; lots of outdoor space; near hotel facilities. **Cons:** need car to get around; can be hot in the afternoon. ✉ *Off North Coast Rd., Belmont* 🌐 *www.areanavillas.com* *3 bedrooms, 3 bathrooms* *In-room: no a/c, Internet. In-hotel: pool, laundry facilities* ☞ *5-night minimum* 🍴 *No meals.*

MID-ISLAND

$$$$ RENTAL **Canefield.** With three large bedrooms, this lovely villa is a good bet for couples who like to vacation together. **Pros:** gracious ambience; great views; lots of outdoor space. **Cons:** need car to get out and about; restaurants and shops a good drive away. ✉ *Off Ridge Road, Greenbank* 🌐 *www.smithsgore.com* *3 bedrooms, 3½ bathrooms* *In-room: a/c (some), Wi-Fi. In-hotel: pool, laundry facilities* 🍴 *No meals.*

$$$$ ⌂ **Villa Delle Palme.** More formal than most vacation villas, Quantock
RENTAL House is a comfortable place to settle in for a week or more. **Pros:** gracious ambience; beautiful views; lots of outdoor space. **Cons:** need car to get around; not near beach. ⊠ *Off Ridge Rd., Greenbank* ⊕ *www. smithsgore.com* ↰ *4 bedrooms, 4½ bathrooms* ♿ *In-room: a/c (some), Wi-Fi. In-hotel: pool, laundry facilities* ▤ *No credit cards* ☞ *5-night minimum* ⍾ *No meals.*

EAST END

¢–$ ⌂ **Hodge's Creek Marina Hotel.** Sitting marina-side on the island's East
HOTEL End, this hotel puts you in the middle of the nautical action. **Pros:** marina atmosphere; good restaurant; some shopping. **Cons:** bland rooms; need car to get around. ⊠ *Hodge's Creek* ⌂ *Box 663, Road Town VG1110* ☎ *284/494–5000* ⊕ *www.pennhotels.com* ↰ *33 rooms* ♿ *In-room: a/c, no safe. In-hotel: restaurant, pool, business center* ⍾ *No meals.*

$$ ⌂ **Lambert Beach Resort.** Although this isolated location on the north-
RESORT east coast puts you far from Road Town, Lambert Bay is one of the island's loveliest stretches of sand and the main reason to recommend this resort. os: lovely beach; beautiful setting; good restaurant. **Cons:** bland rooms; isolated location; need car to get around. ⊠ *Lambert Bay, Box 534, East End* ☎ *284/495–2877* ⊕ *www.lambertresort.com* ↰ *38 rooms, 2 villas, 27 condos* ♿ *In-room: a/c, no safe, kitchen (some), Wi-Fi (some). In-hotel: restaurant, bar, tennis court, pool, spa, beach, water sports, business center* ⍾ *No meals.*

$$$ ⌂ **Surfsong Villa Resort.** Nested in lush foliage right at the water's edge,
RESORT this small resort on Beef Island provides a pleasant respite for vacation-
Fodor's Choice ers who want a villa atmosphere with some hotel amenities. **Pros:** lovely
★ rooms; beautiful beach; chef on call. **Cons:** need car to get around; no restaurants nearby. ⊠ *Beef Island* ⌂ *Box 606, Road Town VG1110* ☎ *284/495–1864* ⊕ *www.surfsong.net* ↰ *1 suite, 7 villas* ♿ *In-room: a/c (some), kitchen, Wi-Fi. In-hotel: beach, water sports, business center, some age restrictions* ⍾ *No meals.*

NIGHTLIFE AND THE ARTS

Like any other good sailing destination, Tortola has watering holes that are popular with salty and not-so-salty dogs. Many offer entertainment; check the weekly *Limin' Times* for schedules and up-to-date information. The local beverage is the Painkiller, an innocent-tasting mixture of fruit juices and rums. It goes down smoothly but packs quite a punch, so give yourself time to recover before you order another.

ROAD TOWN

THE ARTS

Performing Arts Series. Musicians from around the world take to the stage during the island's Performing Arts Series, held from October to May each year. Past artists have included Britain's premier a cappella group, Black Voices; the Leipzig String Quartet; and pianist Richard Ormand.

⊠ *H. Lavity Stoutt Community College, Paraquita Bay* ☎ *284/494–4994* ⊕ *www.hlscc.edu.vg.*

NIGHTLIFE

Pub. At this popular watering hole, there's a happy hour from 5 to 7 every day and live music on Thursday and Friday. ⊠ *Waterfront St., Road Town* ☎ *284/494–2608.*

Pusser's Road Town Pub. Courage is what people are seeking here—John Courage by the pint. Or try Pusser's famous mixed drink, called the Painkiller, and snack on the excellent pizza. ⊠ *Waterfront St., Road Town* ☎ *284/494–3897.*

WEST END

NIGHTLIFE

Jolly Roger. At the Jolly Roger, an ever-changing roster of local and down-island bands plays everything from rhythm and blues to reggae and rock every Friday and Saturday—and sometimes Sunday—starting at 8. ⊠ *West End* ☎ *284/495–4559.*

NORTH COAST

NIGHTLIFE

Bomba's Surfside Shack. By day, you can see that Bomba's, which is covered with everything from crepe-paper leis to ancient license plates to spicy graffiti, looks like a pile of junk; by night it's one of Tortola's liveliest spots. There's a fish fry and a live band every Wednesday and Sunday. People flock here from all over on the full moon, when bands play all night long. ⊠ *Apple Bay* ☎ *284/495–4148.*

Fodor's Choice ★ **Myett's.** Local bands play at this popular spot, which has live music during happy hour, and there's usually a lively dance crowd. ⊠ *Cane Garden Bay* ☎ *284/495–9649.*

Quito's Bar and Restaurant. BVI recording star Quito Rhymer sings island ballads and love songs at his rustic beachside bar–restaurant. Solo shows are on Tuesday and Thursday at 8:30; on Friday at 9:30 Quito performs with his band. ⊠ *Cane Garden Bay* ☎ *284/495–9051.*

Sebastian's. There's often live music at Sebastian's on Thursday and Sunday evenings, and you can dance under the stars. ⊠ *Apple Bay* ☎ *284/495–4212.*

THE ARTS

Fodor's Choice ★ **BVI Music Festival.** Every May hordes of people head to Tortola for this three-day popular festival to listen to reggae, gospel, blues, and salsa music by musicians from around the Caribbean and the U.S. mainland. ⊠ *Cane Garden Bay* ⊕ *www.bvimusicfestival.com.*

SHOPPING

The BVI aren't really a shopper's delight, but there are many shops showcasing original wares—from jams and spices to resort wear to excellent artwork.

ROAD TOWN AND ENVIRONS

Many shops and boutiques are clustered along and just off Road Town's **Main Street.** You can shop in Road Town's **Wickham's Cay I** adjacent to the marina. The **Crafts Alive Market** on the Road Town waterfront is a collection of colorful West Indian–style buildings with shops that carry items made in the BVI. You might find pretty baskets or interesting pottery or perhaps a bottle of home-brewed hot sauce.

ART

Allamanda Gallery. Allamanda carries photography by owner Amanda Baker. ⊠ *124 Main St., Road Town* ☎ *284/494–6680.*

Sunny Caribbee. This gallery has many paintings, prints, and watercolors by artists from around the Caribbean. ⊠ *Main St., Road Town* ☎ *284/494–2178.*

CLOTHES AND TEXTILES

Arawak. This boutique carries batik sundresses, sportswear, and resort wear for men and women. There's also a selection of children's clothing. ⊠ *On dock, Nanny Cay* ☎ *284/494–3983.*

Hucksters. Hucksters sells nifty souvenirs as well as unusual items for the home. ⊠ *Main St., Road Town* ☎ *284/494–7165.*

Latitude 18°. This store sells Maui Jim, Smith, and Oakley sunglasses; Freestyle watches; and a fine collection of beach towels, sandals, Crocs, sundresses, and sarongs. ⊠ *Main St., Road Town* ☎ *284/494–6196.*

Pusser's Company Store. The Road Town Pusser's sells nautical memorabilia, ship models, and marine paintings. There's also an entire line of clothing for both men and women, handsome decorator bottles of Pusser's rum, and gift items bearing the Pusser's logo. ⊠ *Main St. at Waterfront Rd., Road Town* ☎ *284/494–2467.*

FOODSTUFFS

Ample Hamper. This grocer has an outstanding collection of cheeses, wines, fresh fruits, and canned goods from the United Kingdom and the United States. The staff will stock your yacht or rental villa. ⊠ *Inner Harbour Marina, Road Town* ☎ *284/494–2494* ⊕ *www.amplehamper.com.*

Best of British. This boutique has lots of nifty British food you won't find elsewhere. Shop here for Marmite, Vegemite, shortbread, frozen meat pies, and delightful Christmas crackers filled with surprises. ⊠ *Wickham's Cay I, Road Town* ☎ *284/494–3462.*

RiteWay. This market carries a good selection of the usual supplies, but don't expect an inventory like your hometown supermarket. RiteWay will stock villas and yachts. ⊠ *Waterfront Dr. at Pasea Estate, Road Town* ☎ *284/494–2263* ⊠ *Fleming St., Road Town* ☎ *284/494–2263* ⊕ *www.rtwbvi.com.*

5

Most of Tortola's shops are in Road Town.

GIFTS

Fodor's Choice ★ **Bamboushay.** Bamboushay sells handcrafted Tortola-made pottery in shades that reflect the sea. ⊠ *Nanny Cay Marina, Nanny Cay* ☎ *284/494–0393.*

Sunny Caribbee. In a brightly painted West Indian house, this store packages its own herbs, teas, coffees, vinegars, hot sauces, soaps, skin and suntan lotions, and exotic concoctions—Arawak Love Potion and Island Hangover Cure, for example. ⊠ *Main St., Road Town* ☎ *284/494–2178.*

JEWELRY

Colombian Emeralds International. This Caribbean chain caters to the cruise-ship crowd and is the source for duty-free emeralds and other gems in gold and silver settings. ⊠ *Wickham's Cay I, Road Town* ☎ *284/494–7477.*

D'Zandra's. This store carries mostly black-coral items set in gold and silver. Many pieces reflect Caribbean and sea themes. ⊠ *Wickham's Cay I, Road Town* ☎ *284/494–8330.*

Samarkand. Samarkand crafts charming gold-and-silver pendants, earrings, bracelets, and pins, many with island themes such as seashells, lizards, pelicans, and palm trees. There are also reproduction Spanish pieces of eight (old Spanish coins) that were found on sunken galleons. ⊠ *Main St., Road Town* ☎ *284/494–6415.*

PERFUMES AND COSMETICS

Flamboyance. Flamboyance carries designer fragrances and upscale cosmetics. ⊠ *Palm Grove Shopping Center, Waterfront Dr., Road Town* ☏ *284/494–4099.*

STAMPS

BVI Post Office. The BVI's post office is a philatelist's dream. It has a worldwide reputation for exquisite stamps in all sorts of designs. Although the stamps carry U.S. monetary designations, they can be used for postage only in the BVI. ⊠ *Blackburn Rd., Road Town* ☏ *284/494–3701.*

WEST END

There's an ever-growing number of art and clothing stores at **Soper's Hole** in West End.

CLOTHES AND TEXTILES

Pusser's Company Store. Pusser's West End store sells nautical memorabilia, ship models, and marine paintings. There's also an entire line of clothing for both men and women, handsome decorator bottles of Pusser's rum, and gift items bearing the Pusser's logo. ⊠ *Soper's Hole Marina, West End* ☏ *284/495–4599.*

Zenaida's of West End. Zenaida's displays the fabric finds of Argentine Vivian Jenik Helm, who travels through South America, Africa, and India in search of batiks, hand-painted and hand-blocked fabrics, and interesting weaves that can be made into pareus (women's wraps) or wall hangings. The shop also sells unusual bags, belts, sarongs, scarves, and ethnic jewelry. ⊠ *Soper's Hole Marina, West End* ☏ *284/495–4867.*

FOODSTUFFS

Ample Hamper. This market has an outstanding collection of cheeses, wines, fresh fruits, and canned goods from the United Kingdom and the United States. The staff will stock your yacht or rental villa. ⊠ *Frenchman's Cay Marina, West End* ☏ *284/495–4684* ⊕ *www.amplehamper.com.*

SPORTS AND THE OUTDOORS

DIVING AND SNORKELING

Fodor's Choice
★

Clear waters and numerous reefs afford some wonderful opportunities for underwater exploration. In some spots visibility reaches 100 feet, but colorful reefs teeming with fish are often just a few feet below the sea surface. The BVI's system of marine parks means the underwater life visible through your mask will stay protected.

There are several popular dive spots around the islands. **Alice in Wonderland** is a deep dive south of Ginger Island, with a wall that slopes gently from 15 feet to 100 feet. It's an area overrun with huge mushroom-shape coral, hence its name. Crabs, lobsters, and shimmering fan corals make their homes in the tunnels, ledges, and overhangs of **Blonde Rock**, a pinnacle that goes from 15 feet below the surface to 60 feet deep. It's between Dead Chest and Salt Island. When the currents aren't too strong, **Brewers Bay**

Rocking the Bay

Cane Garden Bay is the place to go for live music, with Quito Rhymer frequently delighting the crowds at his Quito's Bar and Restaurant. Myett's is also a happening place some nights. The entire village really jams come May, when the BVI Music Fest gets going. Thousands of people arrive from around the Caribbean and around the world to listen to the best of the Caribbean's reggae, blues, and soca musicians.

Cane Garden Bay is a small but growing community on Tortola's North Shore. There are no chain hotels or sprawling resorts here—all the places to stay are small and locally owned. In addition to the handful of properties on the beach, there are plenty of others up on the hillsides that have eye-popping views. The area has plenty of places to eat, with lobster the specialty on many a menu.

The area fairly bustles on cruise-ship days as busload after busload of round-the-island tour groups disembark to snap a few pictures. Once they're gone, however, a modicum of peace returns to the village.

Pinnacle (20 to 90 feet down) teems with sea life. At the **Indians,** near Pelican Island, colorful corals decorate canyons and grottoes created by four large, jagged pinnacles that rise 50 feet from the ocean floor. The **Painted Walls** is a shallow dive site where corals and sponges create a kaleidoscope of colors on the walls of four long gullies. It's northeast of Dead Chest.

The *Chikuzen,* sunk northwest of Brewers Bay in 1981, is a 246-foot vessel in 75 feet of water; it's home to thousands of fish, colorful corals, and big rays. In 1867 the **RMS** *Rhone,* a 310-foot royal mail steamer, split in two when it sank in a devastating hurricane. It's so well preserved that it was used as an underwater prop in the movie *The Deep.* You can see the crow's nest and bowsprit, the cargo hold in the bow, and the engine and enormous propeller shaft in the stern. Its four parts are at various depths from 30 to 80 feet. Get yourself some snorkeling gear and hop aboard a dive boat to this wreck near Salt Island (across the channel from Road Town). Every dive outfit in the BVI runs scuba and snorkel tours to this part of the BVI National Parks Trust; if you only have time for one trip, make it this one. Rates start at around $70 for a one-tank dive and $100 for a two-tank dive.

Your hotel probably has a dive company right on the premises. If not, the staff can recommend one nearby. Using your hotel's dive company makes a trip to the offshore dive and snorkel sites a breeze. Just stroll down to the dock and hop aboard. All dive companies are certified by PADI, the Professional Association of Diving Instructors, which ensures that your instructors are qualified to safely take vacationers diving. The boats are also inspected to make sure they're seaworthy. If you've never dived, try a short introductory dive, often called a resort course, which teaches you enough to get you underwater. In the unlikely event you get a case of the bends, a condition that can happen when you rise to the surface too fast, your dive team will whisk you to the decompression chamber at Roy L. Schneider Regional Medical Center Hospital in nearby St. Thomas.

Continued on page 214

TRY A YACHT CHARTER

IT'S SURPRISINGLY AFFORDABLE

Savoring a freshly brewed mug of coffee, I sat on the front deck of our chartered 43-foot catamaran and watched the morning show. Laserlike rays of sunlight streamed through a cottony cloud bank, bringing life to the emerald islands and turquoise seas. What would it have been like to sail with Columbus and chart these waters for the first time? How would it feel to cast about the deserted beaches for the perfect place to bury plundered treasure? The aroma of freshly made banana pancakes roused me from my reverie.

Once considered an outward-bound adventure or exclusive domain of the rich and famous, chartering a boat can be a surprisingly affordable and attractive vacation alternative. Perhaps you're already a sailor and want to explore beyond your own lake, river, or bay. Or maybe your idea of sailing has always been on a cruise ship, and now you're ready for a more intimate voyage. Or perhaps you've never sailed before, but you are now curious to cast off and explore a whole new world.

By Carol M. Bareuther

CREWED CHARTER

On a crewed charter, you sit back and relax while the crew provides for your every want and need. Captains are licensed by the U.S. Coast Guard or the equivalent in the British maritime system. Cooks—preferring to be called chefs—have skills that go far beyond peanut butter and jelly sandwiches. There are four meals a day, and many chefs boast certificates from culinary schools ranging from the Culinary Institute of America in New York to the Cordon Bleu in Paris.

The advantage of a crewed yacht charter, with captain and cook, is that it takes every bit of stress out of the vacation. With a captain who knows the local waters, you get to see some of the coves and anchorages that are not necessarily in the guidebooks. Your meals are prepared, cabins cleaned, beds made up every day—and turned down at night, too. Plus, you can sail and take the helm as often as you like. But at the end of the day, the captain is the one who will take responsibility for anchoring safely for the night while the chef goes below and whips up a gourmet meal.

COSTS

$3,850–$6,200 for 2 people for 5 days

$4,900–$7,900 for 2 people for 7 days

$7,000–$12,500 for 6 people for 5 days

$9,000–$16,000 for 6 people for 7 days

Prices are all-inclusive for a 50- to 55-foot yacht in high season except for 10%–15% gratuity.

PROS

■ Passengers just have to lay back and relax with no work (unless they want to help sail)

■ Most crewed charter yachts are catamarans, offering more space than monohulls

■ You have an experienced, local hand on board if something goes wrong

■ Water toys and other extras are often included

CONS

■ More expensive than a bareboat, especially if you get a catamaran

■ Less privacy for your group than on a bareboat

■ Captain makes ultimate decisions about the course

■ Chance for personality conflicts: you have to get along with the captain and chef

(top) Family sailing in the British Virgin Islands

BAREBOAT

If you'd like to bareboat, don't be intimidated. It's a myth that you must be a graduate of a sailing school in order to pilot your own charter boat. A bareboat company will ask you to fill out a resume. The company checks for prior boat-handling experience, the type of craft you've sailed (whether powerboat or sailboat), and in what type of waters. Real-life experience, meaning all those day and weekend trips close to home, count as valuable know-how. If you've done a bit of boating, you may be more qualified than you think to take out a bareboat.

Costs can be very similar for a bareboat and crewed charter, depending on the time of year and size of the boat. You'll pay the highest rates between Christmas and New Year's, when you may not be allowed to do a charter of less than a week. But there are more than 800 bareboats between the USVI and BVI, so regardless of your budget, you should be able to find something in your price range. Plus, you might save a bit by chartering an older boat from a smaller company instead of the most state-of-the-art yacht from a larger company.

COSTS	PROS	CONS
$2,600–$4,400 for a small monohull (2–3 cabins)	■ The ultimate freedom to set the yacht's course	■ Must be able to pass a sailing test
$4,400–$8,000 for a large monohull (4–5 cabins)	■ A chance to test your sailing skills	■ Those unfamiliar with the region may not find the best anchorages
$4,000–$5,000 for a small catamaran (2 cabins)	■ Usually a broader range of boats and prices to choose from	■ You have to cook for and clean up after yourself
$6,000–$12,000 for a large catamaran (4 cabins)	■ More flexibility for meals (you can always go ashore if you don't feel like cooking)	■ You have to do your own provisioning and planning for meals
Prices exclude food, beverages, fuel, and other supplies. Most bareboat rates do not include water toys, taxes, insurance, and permits.	■ You can always hire a captain for a few days	■ If something goes wrong, there isn't an experienced hand onboard

Three women rigging the sails.

WHAT TO CONSIDER

Whether bareboat or a crewed yacht, there are a few points to ponder when selecting your boat.

HOW BIG IS YOUR GROUP?

As a general rule, count on one cabin for every two people. Most people also prefer to have one head (bathroom) per cabin. A multihull, also called a catamaran, offers more space and more equal-size cabins than a monohull sailboat.

WHAT TYPE OF BOAT?

If you want to do some good old traditional sailing, where you're heeling over with the seas at your rails, monohulls are a good option. On the other hand, multihulls are more stable, easier to board, and have a big salon for families. They're also ideal if some people get seasick or aren't as gung-ho for the more traditional sailing experience. If you'd like to cover more ground, choose a motor yacht.

DO YOU HAVE A SPECIAL INTEREST?

Some crewed charter boats specialize in certain types of charters. Among these are learn-to-sail excursions, honeymoon cruises, scuba-diving adventures, and family-friendly trips. Your broker can steer you to the boats that fit your specific needs.

WHAT KIND OF EQUIPMENT DO YOU WANT ONBOARD?

Most charter boats have satellite navigation systems and autopilots, as well as regulation safety gear, dinghies with motors, and even stereos and entertainment systems. But do you want a generator or battery-drive refrigeration system? How about a/c? Do you want a satellite phone? Do you want water toys like kayaks, boogie boards, and Windsurfers?

Now that you've decided on bareboat versus crewed charter and selected your craft, all you need to do is confirm the availability of the date with the company or broker and pay a nonrefundable deposit equal to 50% of the charter price.

TO SAIL OR NOT TO SAIL?

If you're not sure whether a charter yacht vacation is right for you, consider this: would you enjoy a floating hotel room where the scenery outside your window changed according to your desires? A "yes" may entice wary companions to try chartering. A single one-week trip will have them hooked.

Two catamaran sailboats seen from behind.

CHOOSING A CHARTER

CATAMARANS
Multihulls are more stable, easier to board and have a big salon for families. Seasickness is less of an issue.

MOTOR YACHT
Best if you want to cover more ground, but costs a lot more than a sailboat.

MONOHULLS
Good for more traditional and active sailing, but the movement may not appeal to non-sailors.

Information on charters is much easier to find now than even a decade ago. Web sites for bareboat companies show photos of different types of boats—both interiors and exteriors—as well as layout schematics, lists of equipment and amenities, and sample itineraries. Many sites will allow you to book a charter directly, while others give you the option of calling a toll-free number to speak with an agent first.

There are two types of Web sites for crewed charters. If you just want some information, the **Virgin Islands Charteryacht League** (⊕ www.vicl.org) and the **Charter Yacht Society of the British Virgin Islands** (⊕ www.bvicrewedyachts.com) both help you understand what to look for in a crewed charter, from the size of the boat to the amenities. You can't reserve on these sites, but they link to the sites of brokers, who are the sales force for the charter yacht industry. Most brokers, whether they're based in the Caribbean, the United States, or Europe, attend annual charter yacht shows in St. Thomas, Tortola, and Antigua. At these shows, brokers visit the boats and meet the crews. This is what gives brokers their depth of knowledge for "matchmaking," or linking you with a boat that will meet your personality and preferences.

The charter companies also maintain Web sites. About 30% of the crewed charter yachts based out of the U.S. and British Virgin Islands can be booked directly. This saves the commission an owner has to pay to the broker. But while "going direct" might seem advantageous, there is usually little difference in pricing, and if you use a broker, he or she can help troubleshoot if something goes wrong or find a replacement boat if the boat owner has to cancel.

Timing also matters. Companies may offer last-minute specials that are available only online. These special rates—usually for specific dates, destinations, and boats—are updated weekly or even daily.

PREPARING FOR YOUR CHARTER

British Virgin Islands - anchorage in a tropical sea with breakfast on board.

PROVISIONING

Bareboaters must do their own provisioning. It's a good idea to arrange provisioning at least a week in advance.

Bobby's Market Place ⊠ Wickham's Cay I, Road Town, Tortola ☎ 284/494–2189 ⊕ www.bobbysmarketplace.com) offers packages from $18 to $28 per person per day. **Ample Hamper** (⊠ Inner Harbour Marina, Road Town, Tortola ☎ 284/494–2494 ⊠ Frenchmans Cay Marina, West End, Tortola ☎ 284/495–4684 ⊕ www.amplehamper.com) offers more than 1,200 items but no pre-arranged packages.

Provisioning packages from the charter company are usually a bit more expensive, at $25 to $35 per person per day, but they save you the hassle of planning the details. You can also shop on arrival. Both St. Thomas and Tortola have markets, though larger grocery stores may require a taxi ride. If you shop carefully, this route can still save you money. Just be sure to allow yourself a few hours after arrival to get everything done.

PLANNING

For a crewed charter, your broker will send a preference sheet for both food and your wishes for the trip. Perhaps you'd like lazy days of sleeping late, sunning, and swimming. Or you might prefer active days of sailing with stops for snorkeling and exploring ashore. If there's a special spot you'd like to visit, list it so your captain can plan the itinerary accordingly.

PACKING TIPS

Pack light for any type of charter. Bring soft-sided luggage (preferably a duffle bag) since space is limited and storage spots are usually odd shapes. Shorts, T-shirts, and swimsuits are sufficient. Bring something a bit nicer if you plan to dine ashore. Shoes are seldom required except ashore, but you might want beach shoes to protect your feet in the water. Most boats provide snorkel equipment, but always ask. Bring sunscreen, but a type that will not stain cockpit cushions and decks.

WHAT YOU'LL SEE IN THE USBVI

Cruz Bay in St. John

MAIN CHARTER BASES

The U.S. and British Virgin Islands boast more than 100 stepping-stone islands and cays within a 50-nautical-mi radius. This means easy line-of-sight navigation and island-hopping in protected waters, and it's rare that you'll spend more than a few hours moving between islands.

Tortola, in the British Virgin Islands, is the crewed charter and bareboat mecca of the Caribbean. This fact is plainly apparent from the forest of masts rising out from any marina.

The U.S. Virgin Islands fleet is based in **St. Thomas.** Direct flights from the mainland, luxurious accommodations, and duty-free shopping are drawing cards for departures from the U.S. Virgin Islands, whereas the British Virgins are closer to the prime cruising grounds.

POPULAR ANCHORAGES

On a typical weeklong charter you could set sail from Red Hook, St. Thomas, then cross Pillsbury Sound to St. John, which offers popular north-shore anchorages in Honeymoon, Trunk, or Francis bays.

But the best sailing and snorkeling always includes the British Virgin Islands (which require a valid passport or passport card). After clearing customs in West End, Tortola, many yachts hop along a series of smaller islands that run along the south side of the Sir Francis Drake Channel. But some yachts will also visit Guana Island, Great Camanoe, or Marina Cay off Tortola's more isolated east end.

The islands south of Tortola include **Norman Island,** the rumored site of Robert Lewis Stevenson's *Treasure Island*. The next island over is **Peter Island,** famous for it's posh resort and a popular anchorage for yachters. Farther east, off Salt Island, is the wreck of the **RMS Rhone**—the most magnificent dive site in the eastern Caribbean. Giant boulders form caves and grottos called The Baths at the southern end of **Virgin Gorda.**

A downwind run along Tortola's north shore ends at **Jost Van Dyke,** where that famous guitar-strumming calypsonian Foxy Callwood sings personalized ditties that make for a memorable finale.

RECOMMENDED DIVE OPERATORS

Blue Waters Divers (✉ *Nanny Cay* ☎ *284/494–2847* ✉ *Soper's Hole, West End* ☎ *284/495–1200* ⊕ *www.bluewaterdiversbvi.com*) teaches resort, open-water, rescue, and advanced diving courses, and also makes daily dive trips. If you're chartering a sailboat, the company's boat will meet your boat at Peter, Salt, Norman, or Cooper Island for a rendezvous dive. Rates include all equipment as well as instruction. Reserve two days in advance.

FISHING

Most of the boats that take you deep-sea fishing for bluefish, wahoo, swordfish, and shark leave from nearby St. Thomas, but local anglers like to fish the shallower water for bonefish. A half day runs about $480, a full day around $850. Wading trips are $325.

Call **Caribbean Fly Fishing** (✉ *Nanny Cay* ☎ *284/494–4797* ⊕ *www. caribflyfishing.com*).

HIKING

Sage Mountain National Park attracts hikers who enjoy the quiet trails that crisscross the island's loftiest peak. There are some lovely views and the chance to see rare plant species that grow only at higher elevations.

SAILING

Fodor'sChoice
★
The BVI are among the world's most popular sailing destinations. They're clustered together and surrounded by calm waters, so it's fairly easy to sail from one anchorage to the next. Most of the Caribbean's biggest sailboat charter companies have operations in Tortola. If you know how to sail, you can charter a bareboat (perhaps for your entire vacation); if you're unschooled, you can hire a boat with a captain. Prices vary depending on the type and size of the boat you wish to charter. In season, a weekly charter runs from $1,500 to $35,000. Book early to make sure you get the boat that fits you best. Most of Tortola's marinas have hotels, which give you a convenient place to spend the nights before and after your charter.

If a day sail to some secluded anchorage is more your spot of tea, the BVI have numerous boats of various sizes and styles that leave from many points around Tortola. Prices start at around $80 per person for a full-day sail, including lunch and snorkeling equipment.

Aristocat Charters (✉ *West End* ☎ *284/499–1249* ⊕ *www.aristocatcharters. com*) sets sail daily to Jost Van Dyke, the Indians, and Peter Island aboard a 48-foot catamaran.

BVI Yacht Charters (✉ *Port Purcell, Road Town* ☎ *284/494–4289 or 888/615–4006* ⊕ *www.bviyachtcharters.com*) offers 31-foot to 52-foot sailboats for charter—with or without a captain and crew, whichever you prefer.

DID YOU KNOW?

The wreck of the RMS *Rhone*, which sank in 75 feet of water near Salt Island in 1867, is one of the most famous wreck dives in the Caribbean.

Catamaran Charters (⊠ *Village Cay Marina, Road Town* ☎ *284/494–6661 or 800/262–0308* ⊕ *www.catamarans.com*) charters catamarans with or without a captain.

The **Moorings** (⊠ *Wickham's Cay II, Road Town* ☎ *284/494–2332 or 800/535–7289* ⊕ *www.moorings.com*), considered one of the world's best bareboat operations, has a large fleet of well-maintained monohulls and catamarans. Hire a captain or sail the boat yourself.

If you prefer a powerboat, call **Regency Yacht Vacations** (⊠ *Wickham's Cay I, Road Town* ☎ *284/495–1970 or 800/524–7676* ⊕ *www.regencyvacations. com*) for both bareboat and captained sail and powerboat charters.

Sunsail (⊠ *Wickham's Cay II, Road Town* ☎ *284/495–4740 or 800/327–2276* ⊕ *www.sunsail.com*) offers a full fleet of boats to charter with or without a captain.

Voyage Charters (⊠ *Soper's Hole Marina, West End* ☎ *284/494–0740 or 888/869–2436* ⊕ *www.voyagecharters.com*) offers a variety of sailboats for charter with or without a captain and crew.

White Squall II (⊠ *Village Cay Marina, Road Town* ☎ *284/494–2564* ⊕ *www.whitesquall2.com*) takes you on regularly scheduled day sails to the Baths at Virgin Gorda, Cooper, the Indians, or the Caves at Norman Island on an 80-foot schooner.

SURFING

Surfing is big on Tortola's north shore, particularly when the winter swells come in to Josiah's and Apple bays. Rent surfboards starting at $65 for a full day.

HIHO (⊠ *Trellis Bay, Road Town* ☎ *284/494–7694* ⊕ *www.go-hiho. com*) has a good surfboard selection for sale or rent. The staff will give you advice on the best spots to put in your board.

WINDSURFING

Steady trade winds make windsurfing a breeze. Three of the best spots for sailboarding are Nanny Cay, Slaney Point, and Trellis Bay on Beef Island. Rates for sailboards start at about $25 an hour or $100 for a two-hour lesson.

Boardsailing BVI Watersports (⊠ *Trellis Bay, Beef Island* ☎ *284/495–2447* ⊕ *www.windsurfing.vi*) rents equipment and offers private and group lessons.

Virgin Gorda

WORD OF MOUTH

"[On our] first trip to [the] BVI, we stayed on Tortola and visted Virgin Gorda on a day trip and loved it. The next year we returned and stayed on Virgin Gorda. Virgin Gorda has better beaches; it's more quaint and quiet. We found it more peaceful."

—mnag

WELCOME TO VIRGIN GORDA

TOP REASONS TO GO

★ **Beautiful Beaches:** Virgin Gorda's stunning, white, sandy beaches are the number one reason to visit. The Baths are the most crowded, but other beaches are usually quiet.

★ **The Baths:** The ever-popular Baths, an area strewn with giant boulders—many are as big as houses—draw hordes of visitors. Go early or late to enjoy the solitude.

★ **Vacation Villas:** Virgin Gorda villas come in all sizes and price ranges. Some are so spectacular that they grace the pages of glossy magazines, but there are plenty of more modest choices.

★ **North Sound:** Even if you aren't a guest at one of North Sound's handful of resorts, you still should visit. Ferries depart frequently. Stay for lunch, or just enjoy an afternoon drink.

★ **Solitude:** You don't go to Virgin Gorda for the nightlife (although there is some here and there) or endless activities (but you might want to rent a kayak). This is a spot for relaxation.

Cockroach Island

George Dog

Coastal Islands ◆

West Dog

Great Dog

Sir Francis Drake Channel

Mango Bay

Mahoe Bay

Pond Bay

Little Dix Bay

Savannah Bay

Colison Pt.

2

St. Thomas Bay

Handsome Bay

← TO TORTOLA

Spanish Town

Fort Pt.

Virgin Gorda Airport

Little Fort National Park

The Valley

Copper Mine Bay

Spring Bay Beach

Devil's Bay

1

The Baths

Crook's Bay

Copper Mine Point

Stoney Bay

Fallen Jerusalem

Coastal Islands

1 The Valley. Virgin Gorda's main settlement has almost all the island's independent businesses and restaurants. There are several resorts in or around the main hub, with others near The Baths and Spring Bay to the southwest. The main ferry terminal is here as well.

2 Northwest Shore. Except for those resorts and villas in The Valley, most of the island's other resorts and prime villa rental areas are along the northwest shoreline.

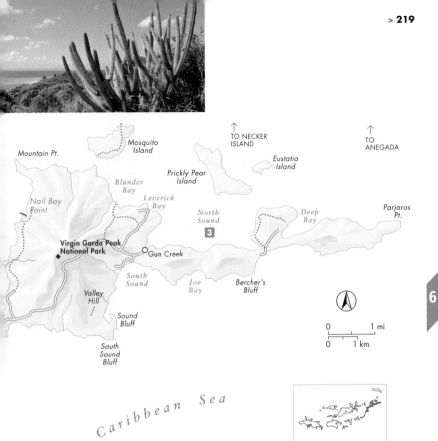

Mountain Pt.

Mosquito
Island

Blunder
Bay

Leverick
Bay

Nail Bay
Point

Virgin Gorda Peak
National Park

○Gun Creek

South
Sound

Valley
Hill

Sound
Bluff

South
Sound
Bluff

Prickly Pear
Island

North
Sound

3

Joe
Bay

Bercher's
Bluff

↑
TO NECKER
ISLAND

Eustatia
Island

Deep
Bay

Parjaros
Pt.

↑
TO
ANEGADA

0   1 mi
0   1 km

6

Caribbean Sea

GETTING ORIENTED

Beautiful beaches are scattered all over the island and are worth exploring. If you rent a car, you can easily hit all the sights in one day. The best plan is to explore the area near your hotel (either Spanish Town or North Sound) first, then take a day to drive to the other end. Stop to climb Gorda Peak, which is in the island's center.

3 North Sound. With no road access, this quiet and isolated part of the island is home to several resorts and frequent ferry service. The beautiful beaches and solitude keep visitors coming back. Be sure to spend at least one day here.

VIRGIN GORDA PLANNER

Do You Need a Car?

Virgin Gorda has a small road system, and a single, very steep road links the north and south ends of the island. You will probably need a car to get around for at least a few days of your stay unless you plan on staying put at your resort—unless your resort is reachable only by boat, in which case you should rent only for those days when you want to explore the island.

CAR RENTALS

None of the major companies have outlets on Virgin Gorda, but you can rent a car from several local companies.

Contacts L&S Jeep Rental (⌂ *South Valley, Virgin Gorda* ☎ *284/495–5297*). **Mahogany Rentals and Taxi Service** (⌂ *The Valley, Virgin Gorda* ☎ *284/495–5469* ⊕ *mahogany.nfshost.com*). **Speedy's Car Rentals** (⌂ *The Valley, Virgin Gorda* ☎ *284/495–5240* ⊕ *www.speedysbvi.com*).

Getting Here and Around

By Air: There's no nonstop service from the continental United States to Virgin Gorda. Air Sunshine flies between Virgin Gorda and St. Thomas and San Juan, Puerto Rico. If you have seven or more people in your party, it probably pays to hire a charter plane from St. Thomas or San Juan. Fly BVI is one of the local charter services. If you're traveling to North Sound from St. Thomas, Seaborne Airlines flies from the downtown Charlotte Amalie waterfront on Friday and weekends. If you're coming from Puerto Rico, Seaborne flies from Old San Juan with a connection in St. Thomas.

By Ferry: Ferries connect St. Thomas with Virgin Gorda; they leave from both Charlotte Amalie and Red Hook, but not daily. Ferries also link St. John and Tortola with Virgin Gorda. Ferries to Virgin Gorda land in Spanish Town. All ferries to Red Hook, St. Thomas, stop in St. John first to clear U.S. customs. Ferry schedules vary by day, and not all companies make daily trips. The BVI Tourist Board Web site has links to all the ferry companies, which are the best up-to-date sources of information for specific routes and schedules.

By Taxi: Taxi rates aren't set on Virgin Gorda and are by the trip, not per person, so you should firm up the fare with your driver before you start your trip. It's cheaper to travel in groups because there's a minimum fare to each destination, which is the same whether you have one, two, or three passengers. The taxi number is also the license plate number. Andy's Taxi & Jeep Rental offers service from one end of Virgin Gorda to the other. Mahogany Rentals & Taxi Service provides taxi service all over Virgin Gorda.

Contacts Andy's Taxi and Jeep Rental (⌂ *The Valley, Virgin Gorda* ☎ *284/495–5252*). **Mahogany Rentals and Taxi Service** (⌂ *The Valley, Virgin Gorda* ☎ *284/495–5469*).

Where to Stay

Virgin Gorda's charming hostelries appeal to a select, appreciative clientele; repeat business is extremely high. Those who prefer Sheratons, Marriotts, and the like may feel they get more for their money on other islands, but the peace and pampering offered on Virgin Gorda are priceless to the discriminating traveler. Villas are plentiful on the island and are widely distributed, but most of the resorts are concentrated in three places: The Valley (the island's main settlement), the Northwest Shore and the North Sound, which is reachable only by ferry.

Where to Eat

Restaurants range from simple to elegant. Hotels that are accessible only by boat will arrange transport in advance upon request from nonguests who wish to dine at their restaurants. Most other independent restaurants are in The Valley or the vicinity. It's wise to make dinner reservations almost everywhere except at really casual spots.

HOTEL AND RESTAURANT PRICES

Restaurant prices are for a main course at dinner and include any taxes or service charges. Hotel prices are per night for a double room in high season, excluding taxes, service charges, and meal plans (except at all-inclusives).

WHAT IT COSTS IN U.S. DOLLARS

	¢	$	$$	$$$	$$$$
Restaurants	under $8	$8–$12	$13–$20	$21–$30	over $30
Hotels	under $150	$150–$275	$276–$375	$376–$475	over $475

Essentials

Banks First Caribbean International is in Virgin Gorda Yacht Harbour. First Bank is across the street from Virgin Gorda Yacht Harbour.

Safety Although crime is rare, use common sense: don't leave your camera on the beach while you take a dip or your wallet on a hotel dresser when you go for a walk.

Tour Options Romney Associates/Travel Plan Tours (☎ 284/494–4000) can arrange island tours, boat tours, snorkeling and scuba-diving trips, dolphin swims, and yacht charters from its Virgin Gorda base.

Visitor Information Virgin Gorda BVI Tourist Board (✉ *Virgin Gorda Yacht Harbour, Spanish Town, Virgin Gorda* ☎ *284/495–5181* ⊕ *www.bvitourism.com*).

6

By Lynda Lohr

Progressing from laid-back to more laid-back, mountainous and arid Virgin Gorda fits right in. Its main road sticks to the center of the island, connecting its odd-shaped north and south appendages; sailing is the preferred mode of transportation. Spanish Town, the most noteworthy settlement, is on the southern wing, as are The Baths. Here smooth, giant boulders are scattered about the beach and form delightful sea grottoes just offshore.

Lovely Virgin Gorda sits at the end of the chain that stretches eastward from St. Thomas. Virgin Gorda, or "Fat Virgin," received its name from Christopher Columbus. The explorer envisioned the island as a reclining pregnant woman, with Virgin Gorda Peak being her belly and the boulders of The Baths her toes.

Virgin Gorda runs at a slow pace. Goats still wander across the roads in places like North Sound. But that's changing. Virgin Gorda Yacht Harbour, the center of commerce and activity in Spanish Town, is expanding. More hotels and condominium developments are in the works, and pricey villas are going up all over the island. That said, budget travelers can still find modest villas and guesthouses all over the island to while away a few days or more.

Virgin Gorda isn't all that easy to get to, but once you're here you can find enough diversions to make getting out of your chaise lounge worthwhile. You can drive from one end of the island to the other in about 20 minutes, but make sure to take time to visit Copper Mine Point to learn about the island's history or to hike up Virgin Gorda Peak to survey the surroundings. At numerous spots with stellar views, the local government has thoughtfully built viewing platforms with adjacent parking. It's worth a stop to snap some photos.

The scenery on the northeastern side of the island is the most dramatic, with a steep road ending at Leverick Bay and Gun Creek in North Sound. For lunch you can hop aboard a ferry to Biras Creek Resort, the Bitter End Yacht Club, or Saba Rock Resort. Head to the other end of the island for views of the huge boulders that spill over from the Baths into the southwest section of Virgin Gorda. You can find several restaurants dotted around this end of the island.

DRIVING IN VIRGIN GORDA

There are few roads, and most byways don't follow the scalloped shoreline. The main route sticks resolutely to the center of the island, linking The Baths on the southern tip with Gun Creek and Leverick Bay at North Sound. Signage is erratic, so come prepared with a map. Remember that driving is on the *left*.

In truth, though, it's the beaches that make Virgin Gorda special. Stretches of talcum-powder sand fringe aquamarine waters. Popular places like The Baths see hordes of people, but just a quick walk down the road brings you to quieter beaches like Spring Bay. On the other side of Spanish Town you may be the only person at such sandy spots as Savannah Bay.

If shopping's on your agenda, you can find stores in Virgin Gorda Yacht Harbour selling items perfect for rounding out your tropical wardrobe or tucking into your suitcase to enjoy when you get home.

Virgin Gorda has very little crime and hardly any frosty attitudes among its more than 3,100 permanent residents. In short, the island provides a welcome respite in a region that's changing rapidly.

EXPLORING VIRGIN GORDA

Virgin Gorda's most popular attractions are those provided by Mother Nature. Beautiful beaches, crystal clear water, and stellar views are around nearly every bend in the road. That said, remember to get a taste of the island's past at Copper Mine Point.

THE VALLEY

The Baths. At Virgin Gorda's most celebrated sight, giant boulders are scattered about the beach and in the water. Some are almost as large as houses and form remarkable grottoes. Climb between these rocks to swim in the many placid pools. Early morning and late afternoon are the best times to visit if you want to avoid crowds. If it's privacy you crave, follow the shore northward to quieter bays—Spring Bay, the Crawl, Little Trunk, and Valley Trunk—or head south to Devil's Bay. ⊠ *Off Tower Rd., The Baths* ☎ *284/494–3904* 🖃 *$3* ⊙ *Daily dawn–dusk.*

Fodor's Choice ★

Copper Mine Point. Here stand a tall stone shaft silhouetted against the sky and a small stone structure that overlooks the sea. These are the ruins of a copper mine established 400 years ago and worked first by the Spanish, then by the English, until the early 20th century. The route is not well marked, so turn inland near LSL Restaurant and look for the hard-to-see sign pointing the way. ⊠ *Copper Mine Rd.* ☎ *No phone* 🖃 *Free.*

6

The Baths are filled with grottoes and hidden pools.

Spanish Town. Virgin Gorda's peaceful main settlement, on the island's southern wing, is so tiny that it barely qualifies as a town at all. Also known as the Valley, Spanish Town has a marina, some shops, and a couple of car-rental agencies. Just north of town is the ferry slip. At the Virgin Gorda Yacht Harbour you can stroll along the dock and do a little shopping.

Coastal Islands. You can easily reach the quaintly named Fallen Jerusalem Island and the Dog Islands by boat. You can rent boats in Tortola and Virgin Gorda. They're all part of the BVI National Parks Trust, and their seductive beaches and unparalleled snorkeling display the BVI at their beachcombing, hedonistic best. ☎ *No phone* ✉ *Free.*

★ **Virgin Gorda Peak National Park.** There are two trails at this 265-acre park, which contains the island's highest point, at 1,359 feet. Small signs on North Sound Road mark both entrances; sometimes, however, the signs are missing, so keep your eyes open for a set of stairs that disappears into the trees. It's about a 15-minute hike from either entrance up to a small clearing, where you can climb a ladder to the platform of a wooden observation tower and a spectacular 360-degree view. ⊠ *North Sound Rd., Gorda Peak* ☎ *No phone* ✉ *Free.*

Spring Bay has boulders similar to those at The Baths.

BEACHES

Although some of the best beaches are reachable only by boat, don't worry if you're a landlubber, because you can find plenty of places to sun and swim. Anybody going to Virgin Gorda must experience swimming or snorkeling among its unique boulder formations, which can be visited at several sites along Lee Road. The most popular is The Baths, but there are several other similar places nearby that are easily reached.

THE VALLEY

The Baths. A national park, The Baths features a stunning maze of huge granite boulders that extend into the sea, and is usually crowded midday with day-trippers. The snorkeling is good, and you're likely to see a wide variety of fish, but watch out for dinghies coming ashore from the numerous sailboats anchored offshore. Public bathrooms and a handful of bars and shops are close to the water and at the start of the path that leads to the beach. Lockers are available to keep belongings safe. ⊠ *About 1 mi [1½ km] west of Spanish Town ferry dock on Tower Rd., Spring Bay* ☎ *284/494–3904* ⌸ *$3* ☉ *Daily dawn–dusk.*

Spring Bay Beach. Just off Tower Road, Spring Bay is a national-park beach that gets much less traffic than the nearby Baths, and has the similarly large, imposing boulders that create interesting grottoes for swimming. It also has no admission fee, unlike the more popular Baths. The snorkeling is excellent, and the grounds include swings and picnic tables. ⊠ *Off Tower Rd., 1 mi [1½ km] west of Spanish Town ferry dock, Spring Bay* ☎ *284/494–3904* ⌸ *Free* ☉ *Daily dawn–dusk.*

NORTHWEST SHORE

Nail Bay. At the island's north tip, Nail Bay will reward you with a trio of beaches within the Nail Bay Resort complex that are ideal for snorkeling. Mountain Trunk Bay is perfect for beginners, and Nail Bay and Long Bay beaches have coral caverns just offshore. The resort has a restaurant, which is an uphill walk but perfect for beach breaks. ⊠ *Nail Bay Resort, off Plum Tree Bay Rd., Nail Bay* ☎ *No phone* 🖅 *Free* ☉ *Daily dawn–dusk.*

★ **Savannah Bay.** This is a wonderfully private beach close to Spanish Town. It may not always be completely deserted, but you can find a spot to yourself on this long stretch of soft, white sand. Bring your own mask, fins, and snorkel, as there are no facilities. The view from above is a photographer's delight. ⊠ *Off N. Sound Rd., ¾ mi [1¼ km] east of Spanish Town ferry dock, Savannah Bay* ☎ *No phone* 🖅 *Free* ☉ *Daily dawn–dusk.*

WHERE TO EAT

Dining out on Virgin Gorda is a mixed bag, with everything from hamburgers to lobster available. Most folks opt to have dinner at or near their hotel to avoid driving on Virgin Gorda's twisting roads at night. The Valley does have a fair number of restaurants if you're sleeping close to town.

THE VALLEY

$$
AMERICAN
✕ **Bath and Turtle.** You can sit back and relax at this informal tavern with a friendly staff—although the noise from the television can sometimes be a bit much. Well-stuffed sandwiches, homemade pizzas, pasta dishes, and daily specials such as conch soup round out the casual menu. Local musicians perform Wednesday and Sunday nights. ⊠ *Virgin Gorda Yacht Harbour, Spanish Town* ☎ *284/495–5239* ⊕ *www.bathandturtle.com.*

$$$
CARIBBEAN
✕ **Chez Bamboo.** This pleasant little hideaway isn't difficult to find; look for the building with the purple-and-green latticework. Candles in the dining room and on the patio help make this a mellow place where you can enjoy a bowl of conch gumbo, something from the tapas menu, or one of the specialties such as lobster curry. For dessert, try the chocolate cake or crème brûlée. Stop by Friday night for live music. ⊠ *Across from and a little north of Virgin Gorda Yacht Harbour, Spanish Town* ☎ *284/495–5752* ⊕ *www.chezbamboo.com* ☉ *No lunch.*

$$$
AMERICAN
✕ **Fischer's Cove Restaurant.** Dine seaside at this alfresco restaurant that is open to the breezes. If pumpkin soup is on the menu, give it a try for a true taste of the Caribbean. Although you can get burgers and salads at lunch, local fish (whatever is available) and a cornmeal-based fungi is a tasty alternative. For dinner, try the Caribbean lobster or grilled mahimahi with lemon and garlic. ⊠ *Lee Rd., The Valley* ☎ *284/495–5252.*

$$$$
CONTINENTAL
✕ **Little Dix Bay Pavilion.** For an elegant evening, you can't do better than this—the candlelight in the open-air pavilion is enchanting, the always-changing menu sophisticated, the service attentive. Superbly prepared seafood, meat, and vegetarian entrées draw locals and visitors alike. Favorites include a Cajun pork loin with mango salsa and scallion potatoes, and mahimahi with warm chorizo and chickpea salad served with a zucchini and tomato chutney. The Monday evening buffet shines.

⊠ *Little Dix Bay Resort, Spanish Town* ☎ *284/495–5555* ⌣ *Reservations essential.*

$$$ ✕ **LSL Restaurant.** An unpretentious place along the road to The Baths, this small restaurant with pedestrian decor still manages to be a local favorite. You can always find fresh fish on the menu, but folks with a taste for other dishes won't be disappointed. Try the veal with mushrooms and herbs in a white-wine sauce or the breast of chicken with rum cream and nuts. ⊠ *Tower Rd., The Valley* ☎ *284/495–5151.*

AMERICAN

FERRY ISSUES

The ferry service from the public dock in Spanish Town can be a tad erratic. Call ahead to confirm the schedule, get there early to be sure it hasn't changed, and ask at the dock whether you're getting on the right boat. The Thursday and Sunday service between Virgin Gorda and St. John is particularly prone to problems.

¢ ✕ **Mad Dog's.** Piña coladas are *the* thing at this breezy bar just outside the entrance to the Baths. The menu includes great triple-decker sandwiches and hot dogs. ⊠ *The Valley* ☎ *284/495–5830* ▭ *No credit cards* ⊙ *No dinner.*

AMERICAN
☯

$$$ ✕ **Mine Shaft Café.** Perched on a hilltop that offers a view of spectacular sunsets, this restaurant near Copper Mine Point serves simple yet well-prepared food, including grilled fish, steaks, and baby back ribs. Tuesday night features an all-you-can-eat Caribbean-style barbecue. The monthly full-moon parties draw a big local crowd. ⊠ *Copper Mine Point, The Valley* ☎ *284/495–5260.*

AMERICAN

$$$ ✕ **The Rock Café.** Surprisingly good Italian cuisine is served among the waterfalls and giant boulders that form the famous Baths. For dinner at this open-air eatery, feast on chicken and penne in a tomato-cream sauce, spaghetti with lobster sauce, or fresh red snapper in a butter-and-caper sauce. For dessert, don't miss the chocolate mousse. ⊠ *The Valley* ☎ *284/495–5482* ⊕ *www.bvidining.com* ⊙ *No lunch.*

ITALIAN

$$$ ✕ **Top of The Baths.** At the entrance to The Baths, this popular restaurant starts serving at 8 am. Tables are on an outdoor terrace or in an open-air pavilion; all have stunning views of the Sir Francis Drake Channel. Hamburgers, coconut chicken sandwiches, and fish-and-chips are among the offerings at lunch. For dessert, the key lime pie is excellent. The Sunday barbecue, served from noon until 3 pm, is an island event. ⊠ *The Valley* ☎ *284/495–5497* ⊕ *www.topofthebaths.com* ⊙ *No dinner.*

AMERICAN
☯

NORTHWEST SHORE

$$$$ ✕ **Sugarcane.** The conch fritters are the stars on the menu of this Nail Bay Resort restaurant, a popular gathering place for vacationers staying in nearby villas. They're light, fluffy, nicely seasoned, and stuffed with conch, just the way conch fritters should be. For lunch, try the Rasta burger, a grilled veggie burger served on a roll with lettuce, tomato, and onion. The best choices on the dinner menu tend to be the fresh local fish prepared in a variety of ways. ⊠ *Nail Bay Resort, Bay Rd., Nail Bay* ☎ *284/494–8000 Ext. 707.*

AMERICAN

6

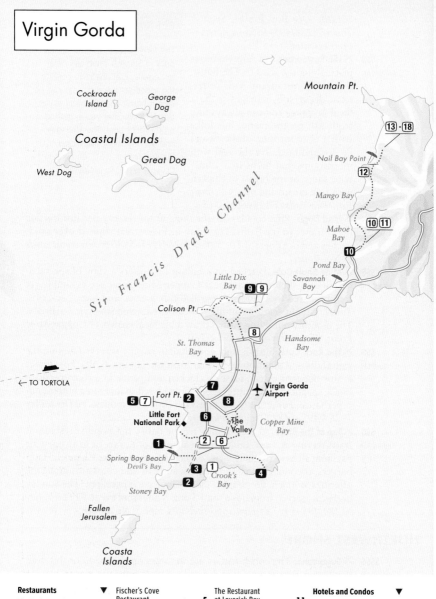

Virgin Gorda

Cockroach Island

George Dog

Coastal Islands

West Dog

Great Dog

Mountain Pt.

13 - 18

Nail Bay Point

12

Mango Bay

Mahoe Bay

10 11

10

Sir Francis Drake Channel

Little Dix Bay

9 9

Colison Pt.

Savannah Bay

Pond Bay

St. Thomas Bay

Handsome Bay

8

← TO TORTOLA

7

Virgin Gorda Airport

5 7

Fort Pt.

2

8

Little Fort National Park ◆

6

The Valley

Copper Mine Bay

2 - 6

1

Spring Bay Beach
Devil's Bay

3

1

Crook's Bay

4

Stoney Bay

2

Fallen Jerusalem

Coasta Islands

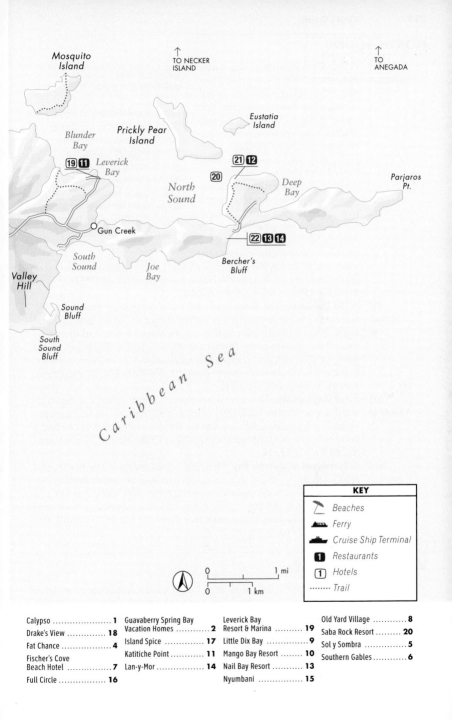

Mosquito
Island

↑
TO NECKER
ISLAND

↑
TO
ANEGADA

Eustatia
Island

Blunder
Bay

Prickly Pear
Island

19 **11** Leverick
Bay

21 **12**

20

Deep
Bay

Parjaros
Pt.

North
Sound

○ Gun Creek

22 **13** **14**

South
Sound

Joe
Bay

Bercher's
Bluff

Valley
Hill

Sound
Bluff

South
Sound
Bluff

Caribbean Sea

KEY	
☂	Beaches
🚋	Ferry
🚢	Cruise Ship Terminal
1	Restaurants
①	Hotels
·······	Trail

0 ——— 1 mi
0 ——— 1 km

NORTH SOUND

$$$$
CONTINENTAL

✕ **Biras Creek Restaurant.** This hilltop restaurant at the Biras Creek Hotel has eye-popping views of North Sound. The four-course prix-fixe menu changes daily and includes several choices per course. For starters, there may be an artichoke, green bean, and wild mushroom salad topped with balsamic vinaigrette, or cream of sweet potato soup accompanied by potato straws. Entrées may include pan-seared snapper over horseradish pearl pasta. The desserts, including a lemon ricotta cheesecake with a spicy passion-fruit sauce, are to die for. Dinner ends with Biras Creek's signature offering of cheese and port. ✉ *Biras Creek Hotel, North Sound* ☎ *284/494–3555 or 800/223–1108* ⌂ *Reservations essential.*

> ### EASTER ON VIRGIN GORDA
>
> Easter is also Carnival on Virgin Gorda. The celebration is smaller than those you'll find on more heavily touristed islands, but people visiting family and friends do come from around the Caribbean. If you're heading to Virgin Gorda during the three-day annual event, make sure you've booked your room well in advance.

$$$
SEAFOOD
★

✕ **The Clubhouse.** The Bitter End Yacht Club's open-air waterfront restaurant is a favorite rendezvous for the sailing set, so it's busy day and night. You can find lavish buffets for breakfast, lunch, and dinner, as well as an à la carte menu. Dinner selections include grilled mahimahi or tuna, local lobster, and porterhouse steak, as well as vegetarian dishes. ✉ *Bitter End Yacht Club, North Sound* ☎ *284/494–2745* ⊕ *www.beyc. com* ⌂ *Reservations essential.*

$$$
AMERICAN
☾

✕ **Fat Virgin's Café.** This casual beachfront eatery offers a straightforward menu of baby back ribs, chicken roti, vegetable pasta, grouper sandwiches, and fresh fish specials for lunch and dinner. You can find a good selection of Caribbean beer. ✉ *Biras Creek Resort, North Sound* ☎ *284/495–7052.*

$$$$
AMERICAN

✕ **Restaurant at Leverick Bay.** Offering casual meals at the beach, this restaurant draws cruise ship passengers on tour as well as hotel guests and locals. The menu includes burgers, pizza, roti, chili, and fish and chips for lunch. At dinner, the menu includes everything from wild salmon to Kobe beef. ✉ *Leverick Bay Resort & Marina, Leverick Bay* ☎ *284/495–7154.*

WHERE TO STAY

While villas are scattered all over Virgin Gorda, hotels are centered in and around the Valley, Nail Bay, and in the North Sound area. Except for Leverick Bay Resort, which is around the point from North Sound, all hotels in North Sound are reached only by ferry.

PRIVATE VILLAS

Visitors craving seclusion would do well at a villa. Most have full kitchens and maid service. Prices per week in winter run from around $2,000 for a one- or two-bedroom villa up to $10,000 for a five-room beachfront villa. Rates in summer are substantially less. On Virgin Gorda a villa in the North Sound area means you can pretty much stay put at night unless you want to make the drive on narrow roads. If you opt for a spot near the Baths, it's an easier drive to town.

BOOKING AGENCIES

The St. Thomas–based **McLaughlin-Anderson Luxury Villas** (⊠ *1000 Blackbeard's Hill, Suite 3, Charlotte Amalie, U.S. Virgin Islands* ☎ *340/776–0635 or 800/537–6246* ⊕ *www.mclaughlinanderson.com*) represents about 18 properties all over Virgin Gorda. Villas range in size from two bedrooms to six bedrooms, and come with many amenities, including full kitchens, pools, and stellar views. The company can hire a chef and stock your kitchen with groceries. A seven-night minimum is required during the winter season.

Tropical Care Services (⊠ *Box 1039, The Valley VG1150* ☎ *284/495–6493* ⊕ *www.tropicalcareservices.com*) manages about a dozen properties stretching from The Baths to the Nail Bay area. Several budget properties are included among the pricier offerings. Most houses have private pools, and a few are right on the beach. A sister company at the same number, Tropical Nannies, provides babysitting services.

Virgin Gorda Villa Rentals (⊠ *Box 63, The Valley VG1150* ☎ *284/495–7421 or 800/848–7081* ⊕ *www.virgingordabvi.com*) manages more than 40 properties near Leverick Bay Resort and Mahoe Bay, so it's perfect for those who want to be close to activities. Many of the accommodations—from studios to six or more bedrooms—have private swimming pools and air-conditioning, at least in the bedrooms. All have full kitchens, are well maintained, and have spectacular views.

For approximate costs, see the dining and lodging price chart at the beginning of this chapter. The following hotel reviews have been condensed for this book. Please go to Fodors.com for expanded reviews of each property.

VIRGIN GORDA GROCERIES

Virgin Gorda's grocery stores barely equal convenience stores elsewhere. The selection is small and the prices high. Many Virgin Gorda residents head to Tortola or even to St. Thomas to do their shopping. If you're coming here from another island, you might want to bring along one or two items you know you'll need.

THE VALLEY

$$$$
RENTAL
A Bigger Splash. A large villa with separate cottage nearby, A Bigger Splash is a good bet for families and groups of friends traveling together. **Pros:** beaches nearby; spacious rooms; good views. **Cons:** need car to get around; no air-conditioning; lots of stairs. ⊠ *Off Tower Rd., The Baths,* ⊕ *www.tropicalcareservices.com* ⇄ *4 bedrooms, 4½ bathrooms* ⚏ *In-room: no a/c, Internet, Wi-Fi. In-hotel: pool, laundry facilities* ⏹ *No meals.*

$$$$
RENTAL
Calypso. A five-minute walk puts you at a rock and sand beach, but many guests prefer to lounge about the spacious pool or relax on the extensive decks at this stunning villa. **Pros:** gorgeous decor; lots of space. **Cons:** need a car to get around. ⊠ *Off Tower Road, Crook's Bay* ⊕ *www.tropicalcareservices.com* ⇄ *3 bedrooms, 3½ bathrooms* ⚏ *In-room: a/c (some), Wi-Fi. In-hotel: pool, laundry facilities* ⏹ *No meals.*

$–$$
RENTAL

Fat Chance. A comfy cottage, Fat Chance is the kind of place budget vacationers adore. **Pros:** affordable price; good location for kids; walk to beach. **Cons:** no view; no air-conditioning; need car to get around. ⊠ *Off Tower Rd., The Baths* ⊕ *www.tropicalcareservices.com* ⟿ *2 bedrooms, 2 bathrooms* ⚹ *In-room: no a/c* ⟳ *5-night minimum* ⦿ *No meals.*

$–$$
HOTEL

Fischer's Cove Beach Hotel. The rooms are modest, the furniture is discount-store-style, and the walls are thin, but you can't beat the location right on the beach and within walking distance of Spanish Town's shops and restaurants. **Pros:** beachfront location; budget price; good restaurant. **Cons:** very basic units; thin walls; no a/c in some rooms. ⊠ *Lee Road* ⌂ *Box 60, The Valley VG1150* ☎ *284/495–5252* ⊕ *www.fischerscove. com* ⟿ *12 rooms, 8 cottages* ⚹ *In-room: a/c (some), no safe, kitchen (some), no TV (some), Wi-Fi. In-hotel: restaurant, beach* ⦿ *No meals.*

$–$$
RENTAL
★

Guavaberry Spring Bay Vacation Homes. Rambling back from the beach, these hexagonal one- and two-bedroom villas give you all the comforts of home with the striking boulder-fringed beach just minutes away. **Pros:** short walk to The Baths; easy drive to town; great beaches nearby. **Cons:** few amenities; older property; basic decor. ⊠ *Tower Road* ⌂ *Box 20, The Valley* ☎ *284/495–5227* ⊕ *www.guavaberryspringbay. com* ⟿ *12 1-bedroom units, 6 2-bedroom units, 1 3-bedroom unit, 16 villas* ⚹ *In-room: a/c (some), no safe, kitchen, no TV (some). In-hotel: beach, business center* ▭ *No credit cards* ⦿ *No meals.*

$$$$
RESORT
★

Rosewood Little Dix Bay. This laid-back luxury resort offers a gorgeous crescent of sand, plenty of activities, and good restaurants. **Pros:** convenient location; lovely grounds; near many dining options. **Cons:** expensive rates; very spread out; insular though not isolated. ⌂ *Box 70, Little Dix Bay off North Sound Rd. VG1150* ☎ *284/495–5555* ⊕ *www. littledixbay.com* ⟿ *73 rooms, 20 suites, 7 villas* ⚹ *In-room: a/c, no TV, Wi-Fi (some). In-hotel: restaurants, bars, tennis courts, pool, gym, spa, beach, water sports, children's programs, business center* ⦿ *No meals.*

$$$$
RENTAL
Fodor's Choice
★

Sol y Sombra. Tucked among giant boulders and sitting just off Little Trunk Bay Beach, this villa provides a lovely place to settle in for a Virgin Gorda vacation. **Pros:** lovely decor; beachfront location; tennis court. **Cons:** high price; need a car to get around. ⊠ *Off Tower Rd., Little Trunk Bay* ⊕ *www.smithsgore.com* ⟿ *5 bedrooms, 4½ bathrooms* ⚹ *In-room: a/c (some), Wi-Fi. In-hotel: tennis court, pool, gym, beach, laundry facilities* ▭ *No credit cards* ⟳ *5-night minimum* ⦿ *No meals.*

$$–$$$
RENTAL

Southern Gables. With lovely beaches just a short walk away, this villa is a good bet for families. An older property without a pool, it's short on flash but long on comfort. **Pros:** good views; good location; nice yard. **Cons:** no air-conditioning; bland decor; need car to get around. ⊠ *Off Tower Rd., Little Trunk Bay* ⊕ *www.tropicalcareservices.com* ⟿ *3 bedrooms, 2 bathrooms* ⚹ *In-room: no a/c, Internet* ⦿ *No meals.*

$–$$
RENTAL

Virgin Gorda Village. All the condos in this upscale complex a few minutes' drive from Spanish Town have at least partial ocean views. **Pros:** close to Spanish Town; lovely pool; recently built units. **Cons:** no beach; on a busy street; noisy roosters nearby. ⊠ *North Sound Rd.* ⌂ *Box 26, The Valley VG1150* ☎ *284/495–5544 or 800/653–9273* ⊕ *www. virgingordavillage.com* ⟿ *30 condos* ⚹ *In-room: a/c, no safe, kitchen, Wi-Fi. In-hotel: restaurant, bar, tennis courts, pool, gym, spa* ⦿ *No meals.*

NORTHWEST SHORE

$$$$
RENTAL
★
Baraka Point. With a main house that sits just above the water and smaller accommodations scattered about the 2-acre property, Baraka Point is a comfortable retreat for weddings or other large groups of people. **Pros:** stunning views; full staff; lovely decor. **Cons:** need a car to get around. ✉ *Baraka Point, Nail Bay* ⊕ *www.barakapoint.com* ➟ *9 bedrooms, 6 bathrooms* 🛏 *In-room: a/c (some), Wi-Fi. In-hotel: pool, gym, laundry facilities* ▭ *No credit cards* ☞ *7-night minimum* ⦿ *No meals.*

$$$–$$$$
RENTAL
Drake's View. The upstairs of this spacious villa has two bedrooms and the downstairs, a studio apartment, making it a good bet for groups that want to vacation together but need some space. **Pros:** good for groups; beach nearby. **Cons:** need a car to get around. ✉ *Off road to Nail Bay Resort, Nail Bay* ⊕ *www.nailbay.com* ➟ *3 bedrooms, 3 bathrooms* 🛏 *In-room a/c, Wi-Fi. In-hotel: pool* ☞ *7-night minimum* ⦿ *No meals.*

$$$$
RENTAL
Full Circle. Full Circle sits right at the edge of the sea on a lovely white-sand beach that is perfect for strolling, though sadly not for swimming. **Pros:** lovely beach; plenty of privacy; room to stretch out. **Cons:** can't swim at beach; expensive rates; need a car. ✉ *Off road to Nail Bay Resort, Nail Bay* ⊕ *www.nailbay.com* ➟ *3 bedrooms, 3 bathrooms* 🛏 *In-room: a/c (some). In-hotel: pool, beach* ☞ *7-night minimum* ⦿ *No meals.*

$$–$$$
RENTAL
Island Spice. With 180-degree sea views and a spacious deck with comfortable chaises and a hammock, Island Spice is a great villa for relaxing. **Pros:** spacious; lovely views. **Cons:** need a car. ✉ *Off road to Nail Bay Resort, Nail Bay* ⊕ *www.nailbay.com* ➟ *3 bedrooms, 3 bathrooms* 🛏 *In-room: a/c, Wi-Fi. In-hotel: pool* ☞ *7-night minimum* ⦿ *No meals.*

$$$$
RENTAL
★
Katitiche Point. Sitting on the point of the same name, this villa has stunning views of the sea from almost every vantage point. **Pros:** gorgeous views; full staff; lovely decor; rates include breakfast and lunch, wine, and bar. **Cons:** expensive; drive to restaurants; drive to beach. ✉ *Plum Bay Rd., Mahoe Bay* ⊕ *www.katitchepoint.com* ➟ *5 bedrooms, 6 bathrooms* 🛏 *In-room: a/c (some), Wi-Fi. In-hotel: pool, laundry facilities* ☞ *3-night minimum* ⦿ *Some meals.*

$$$
RENTAL
★
Lan-Y-Mor. In lush landscape complete with a waterfall, this villa is a wonderful honeymoon hideaway. **Pros:** lovely landscaping; good views; fully air-conditioned. **Cons:** need a car to get around; no railing on deck. ✉ *Nail Bay* ⊕ *www.tropicalcareservices.com* ➟ *1 bedroom, 2 bathrooms* 🛏 *In-room: a/c, Wi-Fi. In-hotel: laundry facilities, some age restrictions* ☞ *5-night minimum* ⦿ *No meals.*

$$–$$$$
RENTAL
Mango Bay Resort. Sitting seaside on Virgin Gorda's north coast, this collection of contemporary condos and villas will make you feel right at home. **Pros:** nice beach; lively location; good restaurant; small grocery store. **Cons:** construction in area; drab decor; some units have lackluster views. ✉ *Off Nail Bay Road* ✉ *Box 1062, Mahoe Bay VG1150* ☎ *284/ 495–5672* ⊕ *www.mangobayresort.com* ➟ *17 condos, 5 villas* 🛏 *In-room: a/c, no safe, kitchen, Wi-Fi (some). In-hotel: beach* ⦿ *No meals.*

$$–$$$
RESORT
★
Nail Bay Resort. Rambling up the hill above the coast, this beachfront resort offers a wide selection of rooms and suites to fit every need. **Pros:** full kitchens; lovely beach; close to town. **Cons:** busy neighborhood; bit of a drive from main road; uphill walk from beach. ✉ *Off Nail*

6

Bay Road ⌂ *Box 69, Nail Bay VG1150* ☎ *284/494–8000 or 800/871–3551* ⊕ *www.nailbay.com* ⇱ *4 rooms, 4 suites, 9 villas* ⌂ *In-room: a/c, kitchen (some). In-hotel: restaurant, bar, tennis court, pool, spa, beach, water sports, business center* ⏐◎⏐ *No meals.*

$$$–$$$$
RENTAL

▦ **Nyumbani.** With Nail Bay Resort's beaches just a short drive away, families and couples like to settle in to this villa for a casual vacation. Two bedrooms are at either end of the upper level, with another on the pool deck below. The living room opens onto a spacious covered deck where you can while away the afternoon with a good book. There are stellar views of the peninsula and the sea beyond. Furnishings are casual, with tile floors, wood and wicker furniture, and a spacious kitchen. **Pros:** good views; nice decor; resort amenities. **Cons:** need car to get around; on a badly paved road; stairs to climb. ⊠ *Off road to Nail Bay Resort, Nail Bay* ⊕ *www.nailbay.com* ⇱ *3 bedrooms, 3 bathrooms* ⌂ *In-room: a/c. In-hotel: pool* ☞ *7-night minimum* ⏐◎⏐ *No meals.*

NORTH SOUND

$$$$
RESORT
★

▦ **Biras Creek Resort.** Although Biras Creek is tucked out of the way on the island's North Sound, the get-away-from-it-all feel is actually the major draw for its well-heeled clientele. **Pros:** luxurious rooms; professional staff; good dining options. **Cons:** expensive rates; isolated location; difficult for people with mobility problems. ⌂ *Box 54, North Sound VG1150* ☎ *284/494–3555 or 877/883–0756* ⊕ *www.biras.com* ⇱ *31 suites* ⌂ *In-room: a/c, no TV (some), Wi-Fi. In-hotel: restaurants, bar, tennis courts, pool, spa, beach, water sports, business center* ⏐◎⏐ *All meals.*

$$$$
ALL-INCLUSIVE
☾
Fodor's Choice
★

▦ **Bitter End Yacht Club.** Sailing's the thing at this busy hotel and marina in the nautically inclined North Sound, and the use of everything from small sailboats to kayaks to windsurfers is included in the price. **Pros:** lots of water sports; good diving opportunities; friendly guests. **Cons:** expensive rates; isolated location; lots of stairs. ⌂ *Box 46, Beef Island, Tortola VG1150* ☎ *284/494–2746 or 800/872–2392* ⊕ *www.beyc.com* ⇱ *85 rooms* ⌂ *In-room: a/c (some), no safe, no TV. In-hotel: restaurants, bar, pool, beach, water sports, children's programs, business center* ⏐◎⏐ *All-inclusive.*

¢
RESORT

▦ **Leverick Bay Resort and Marina.** With its colorful buildings and bustling marina, Leverick Bay is a good choice for visitors who want easy access to water-sports activities. **Pros:** lively location; good restaurant; small grocery store. **Cons:** small beach; no laundry in units; 15-minute drive to town. ⊠ *Off Leverick Bay Road* ⌂ *Box 63, Leverick Bay VG1150* ☎ *284/495–7421 or 800/848–7081* ⊕ *www.leverickbay.com* ⇱ *13 rooms, 4 apartments* ⌂ *In-room: a/c, kitchen (some), Wi-Fi. In-hotel: restaurants, bar, tennis court, pool, spa, beach, laundry facilities, business center* ⏐◎⏐ *No meals.*

$
RESORT

▦ **Saba Rock Resort.** Reachable only by a free ferry or by private yacht, this resort on its own tiny cay is perfect for folks who want to mix and mingle with the sailors who drop anchor for the night. **Pros:** party atmosphere; convenient transportation; good diving nearby. **Cons:** tiny beach; isolated location; on a very small island. ⌂ *Box 67, North Sound VG1150* ☎ *284/495–7711 or 284/495–9966* ⊕ *www.sabarock.com* ⇱ *7*

Bitter End Yacht Club, on Virgin Gorda's east end.

1-bedroom suites, 1 2-bedroom suites ⚿ In-room: a/c, no safe, kitchen (some), Wi-Fi. In-hotel: restaurant, bar, beach, water sports ⧫ Breakfast.

NIGHTLIFE

Pick up a free copy of the *Limin' Times*—available at most resorts and restaurants—for the most current local entertainment schedule.

THE VALLEY

Bath and Turtle. During high season, the Bath and Turtle is one of the liveliest spots on Virgin Gorda, hosting island bands Wednesday from 8 pm until midnight. ⊠ *Virgin Gorda Yacht Harbour, Spanish Town* ☎ 284/495–5239.

Chez Bamboo. This is the place for calypso and reggae on Friday night. ⊠ *Across from Virgin Gorda Yacht Harbour, Spanish Town* ☎ 284/495–5752.

Mine Shaft Café. The café has music on Tuesday and Friday. ⊠ *Copper Mine Point, The Valley* ☎ 284/495–5260.

Rock Café. Rock Café has live bands nearly every night during the winter season. ⊠ *The Valley* ☎ 284/495–5177.

Leverick Bay Resort and Marina.

NORTHWEST SHORE

Little Dix Bay. The bar at Little Dix Bay presents elegant live entertainment several nights a week in season. ⊠ *Little Dix Bay* ☎ *284/495–5555.*

NORTH SOUND

Bitter End Yacht Club. Local bands play several nights a week at the Bitter End Yacht Club during the winter season. ⊠ *North Sound* ☎ *284/494–2746.*

Restaurant at Leverick Bay. This resort's main restaurant hosts live music on Tuesday and Friday in season. ⊠ *Leverick Bay Resort & Marina, Leverick Bay* ☎ *284/495–7154.*

SHOPPING

Most boutiques are within hotel complexes or at Virgin Gorda Yacht Harbour. Two of the best are at Biras Creek and Little Dix Bay. Other properties—the Bitter End and Leverick Bay—have small but equally select boutiques.

THE VALLEY

CLOTHING

Blue Banana. Blue Banana carries a large selection of gifts, clothing, and accessories. ⊠ *Virgin Gorda Yacht Harbour, Spanish Town* ☎ *284/495–5957.*

Dive BVI. You can find books about the islands here, as well as snorkeling equipment, sportswear, sunglasses, and beach bags. ⊠ *Virgin Gorda Yacht Harbour, Spanish Town* ☎ *284/495–5513.*

FOOD

Buck's Food Market. Buck's is the closest to a full-service supermarket the island offers, and has everything from an in-store bakery and deli to fresh fish and produce departments. There are two branches. ⊠ *Virgin Gorda Yacht Harbour, Spanish Town* ☎ *284/495–5423.*

Wine Cellar and Bakery. This bakery and liquor store sells bread, rolls, muffins, cookies, sandwiches, and sodas to go. ⊠ *Virgin Gorda Yacht Harbour, Spanish Town* ☎ *284/495–5250.*

GIFTS

Tropical Gift Collection. Tucked among the T-shirts and souvenir mugs are adorable kids' clothes, locally-made straw-embroidered bags, whimsical lamps with shades shaped like sails, and mahogany boxes carved to look like turtles. ⊠ *Tower Rd., The Baths* ☎ *284/495–5380.*

JEWELRY

Margo's Boutique. This is the place to buy handmade silver, pearl, and shell jewelry. (⊠ *Virgin Gorda Yacht Harbour, Spanish Town* ☎ *284/495–5237.*

NORTHWEST SHORE

GIFTS

Pavilion Gift Shop. This shop at Little Dix Bay has the latest in resort wear for men and women, as well as jewelry, books, housewares, and expensive T-shirts. ⊠ *Little Dix Bay Resort, Little Dix Bay* ☎ *284/495–5555.*

NORTH SOUND

CLOTHING

Fat Virgin's Treasure. Fat Virgin's sells cool island-style clothing in tropical prints, a large selection of straw sun hats, and unusual gift items like island-made hot sauces, artistic cards, and locally fired pottery. ⊠ *Biras Creek Hotel, North Sound* ☎ *284/495–7054.*

Pusser's Company Store. Pusser's has a trademark line of sportswear, rum products, and gift items. ⊠ *Leverick Bay* ☎ *284/495–7371.*

FOOD

Bitter End Emporium. This store at the Bitter End is the place for such edible treats as local fruits, cheeses, baked goods, and gourmet prepared food to take out. ⊠ *Bitter End Yacht Harbor, North Sound* ☎ *284/494–2746.*

Buck's Food Market. Buck's is the closest to a full-service supermarket the island offers, and has everything from an in-store bakery and deli to fresh fish and produce departments. There are two branches. ⊠ *Gun Creek, North Sound* ☎ *284/495–7368.*

Chef's Pantry. This store has the fixings for an impromptu party in your villa or on your boat—fresh seafood, specialty meats, imported cheeses, daily baked breads and pastries, and an impressive wine and spirit selection. ⊠ *Leverick Bay* ☎ *284/495–7677.*

GIFTS

Reeftique. This store carries island crafts and jewelry, clothing, and nautical odds and ends with the Bitter End logo. ⊠ *Bitter End Yacht Harbor, North Sound* ☎ *284/494–2746.*

Thee Nautical Gallery. This boutique sells attractive handcrafted jewelry, paintings, and one-of-a-kind gift items, as well as books about the Caribbean. ⊠ *Leverick Bay* ☎ *284/495–7479.*

SPORTS AND THE OUTDOORS

DIVING AND SNORKELING

Where you go snorkeling and what company you pick depends on where you're staying. Many hotels have on-site dive outfitters, but if yours doesn't, one won't be far away. If your hotel does have a dive operation, just stroll down to the dock and hop aboard—no need to drive anywhere. The dive companies are all certified by PADI. Costs vary, but count on paying about $75 for a one-tank dive and $110 for a two-tank dive. All dive operators offer introductory courses as well as certification and advanced courses. Should you get an attack of the bends, which can happen when you ascend too rapidly, the nearest decompression chamber is at Roy L. Schneider Regional Medical Center in St. Thomas.

There are some terrific snorkel and dive sites off Virgin Gorda, including areas around The Baths, the North Sound, and the Dogs. The Chimney at Great Dog Island has a coral archway and canyon covered with a wide variety of sponges. At Joe's Cave, an underwater cavern on West Dog Island, huge groupers, eagle rays, and other colorful fish accompany divers as they swim. At some sites you can see 100 feet down, but divers who don't want to go that deep and snorkelers will find plenty to look at just below the surface.

The **Bitter End Yacht Club** (⊠ *North Sound* ☎ *284/494–2746* ⊕ *www.beyc. com*) offers two snorkeling trips a day.

Dive BVI (⊠ *Virgin Gorda Yacht Harbour, Spanish Town* ☎ *284/495–5513 or 800/848–7078* ⊠ *Leverick Bay Resort and Marina, Leverick Bay* ☎ *284/495–7328* ⊕ *www.divebvi.com*) offers expert instruction, certification, and day trips.

Sunchaser Scuba (⊠ *Bitter End Yacht Club, North Sound* ☎ *284/495–9638 or 800/932–4286* ⊕ *www.sunchaserscuba.com*) offers resort, advanced, and rescue courses.

MINIATURE GOLF

The 9-hole mini-golf course **Golf Virgin Gorda** (⊠ *Copper Mine Point, The Valley* ☎ *284/495–5260*) is next to the Mine Shaft Café, delightfully nestled between huge granite boulders.

DID YOU KNOW?

The Baths, on Virgin Gorda's west end, is one of the best snorkeling spots on the island, but you can also arrange a snorkeling trip by boat from your resort.

You can learn to sail at Bitter End Yacht Club.

SAILING AND BOATING

The BVI waters are calm, and terrific places to learn to sail. You can also rent sea kayaks, waterskiing equipment, dinghies, and powerboats, or take a parasailing trip.

☾ **Bitter End Sailing and Kiteboarding School** (⊠ *Bitter End Yacht Club, North Sound* ☎ *284/494–2746* ⊕ *www.beyc.com*) offers classroom, dockside, and on-the-water lessons for sailors of all levels. Private lessons are $75 per hour.

If you just want to sit back, relax, and let the captain take the helm, choose a sailing or power yacht from **Double "D" Charters** (⊠ *Virgin Gorda Yacht Harbour, Spanish Town* ☎ *284/499–2479* ⊕ *www. doubledbvi.com*). Rates are $65 for a half-day trip and $110 for a full-day island-hopping excursion. Private full-day cruises or sails for up to eight people run $950.

If you'd rather rent a Sunfish or Hobie Wave, check out **Leverick Bay Watersports** (⊠ *Leverick Bay, North Sound* ☎ *284/495–7376* ⊕ *www. watersportsbvi.com*).

Other British Virgin Islands

JOST VAN DYKE, ANEGADA & THE SMALLER ISLANDS

WORD OF MOUTH

"If you explore the unknown spots of Anegada, you will be rewarded with unexpected gifts—such as a little altar of bleached conch, coral, and driftwood posed by the sea at the end of a spur off the road."

—seasweetie

WELCOME TO OTHER BRITISH VIRGIN ISLANDS

TOP REASONS TO GO

★ **Snorkeling in Anegada:** The wrecks and reefs draw snorkelers from all over the world to this beautiful, beach-fringed island.

★ **Bar-hopping in Jost Van Dyke:** The BVI's night-life capital is the place to go, especially for the special Halloween and New Year's parties. The Soggy Dollar and Foxy's Tamarind are favorites.

★ **Lying on the beach in Peter Island:** Palm-fringed Dead Man's Bay is particularly conducive to a romantic picnic.

★ **Turning Back the Clock at Cooper Island:** Nothing ever changes at this modest resort, and that's exactly how guests want it. Experience the Caribbean the way it used to be.

★ **Sailing the BVI:** Pick up a charter yacht in Tortola and enjoy a variety of experiences throughout the 50-some islands that make up the BVI.

1 Jost Van Dyke. With only 200-some inhabitants, the number of day-trippers easily outnumbers the permanent islanders.

2 Guana Island. This private island hosts both a wildlife refuge and a luxe resort.

3 Marina Cay. A tiny island of only 8 acres is in Trellis Bay, just off Beef Island.

4 Anegada. The only coral island in the BVI chain is surrounded by inviting (or dangerous) reefs, depending on whether you're a snorkeler or sailor.

5 Peter Island. A private island retreat, it is also popular with charter yachts.

West End Pt.
Bones Bight
Loblolly Bay
Red Pond
Table Bay

4

The Settlement
Budrock Pond

Flamingo Pond
Lower Bay
White Bay

Anegada
(15 miles north of Necker Is.)

Horse Shoe Reef

7 Necker Island

Prickly Pear Island

Eustatia Island

Mosquito Island

North Sound

Cockroach Island
George Dog

Great Camanoe

Long Pt.
Towing Pt.
North Bay
North Bay
West Dog
Long Bay

Guana Island 2

Kitto Ghut
Great Dog

Virgin Gorda Peak

South Sound

Berchers Bay

Little Camanoe

Monkey Pt.
Scrub Island

Pond Bay

VIRGIN GORDA

Trunk Bay
Josiah's Bay

Marina Cay 3

Handsome Bay

East End
Beef Island International Airport

Spanish Town
Virgin Gorda Airport

ROAD TOWN

Fort Shirley

Fat Hogs Bay
Beef Island

Copper Mine Pt.

Buck Island

Fallen Jerusalem

Road Harbour

Sir Francis Drake Channel

Broken Jerusalem

Anegada Passage

TORTOLA

Quart-a-Nancy Pt.

Round Rock

Manchioneel Bay

South Bay
Ginger Island

Salt Island

Great Harbour

Dead Chest

Cooper Island 6

Rock Hole

Salt Island Bluff
Markoe Pt.

Big Reef Bay

7

Pelican Island

White Bay

Peter Island 5

Privateer Bay

Peter Island Bluff

0 ————— 3 miles

0 ————— 5 km

Money Bay

Norman Island

6 Cooper Island. This hilly island is home to one of the more modest private-island resorts in the BVI, and it's also a popular anchorage for yachts.

7 Necker Island. Sir Richard Branson's private island is usually available to rent to large groups but is available for couples a few weeks out of the year—at an astounding price.

GETTING ORIENTED

More than 50 individual islands make up the British Virgin Islands. Jost Van Dyke, a sparsely populated island northwest of Tortola, has a disproportionate number of surprisingly lively bars and is a favorite for yachters. Flat Anegada, some 20 mi northeast of Virgin Gorda, is the only coral island in the BVI chain, and its extensive reef systems attract snorkelers and divers. Several other islands have private resorts, though many are uninhabited.

OTHER BRITISH VIRGIN ISLANDS PLANNER

Do You Need a Car?

You can rent a car or jeep on either Anegada or Jost Van Dyke. This may make sense in Anegada, where you might want to explore a variety of different beaches to maximize your snorkeling opportunities. However, in Jost Van Dyke, it's often just as easy to take a taxi or walk. In either island, both car/jeep rentals and gas are expensive, so be sure to make room for the costs in your vacation budget.

Banks and ATMS

Be sure to take cash if you travel to the smaller islands in the BVI. None has an ATM or a bank, though most resorts take credit cards.

CAR RENTALS

Abe and Eunicy Rentals (⊠ Little Harbour, Jost Van Dyke ☎ 284/495–9329). **Anegada Reef Hotel** (⊠ Setting Point, Anegada ☎ 284/495–8002). **D.W. Jeep Rentals** (⊠ The Settlement, Anegada ☎ 284/495–9677). **Lil' Bit Rentals** (⊠ Setting Point, Anegada ☎ 284/495–9932). **Paradise Jeep Rentals** (⊠ Great Harbour, Jost Van Dyke ☎ 284/495–9477).

Getting There and Around

You can fly to Anegada on a charter flight (affordable if you are traveling with a group), but all the other islands are reachable only by boat (or perhaps helicopter if you are visiting Necker Island). Anegada has ferry service from Tortola (via Virgin Gorda) three days a week, while Jost Van Dyke has regularly scheduled ferry service from Tortola, St. John, and St. Thomas, but not all these services run daily. You can rent a jeep on Anegada, and many people do, especially if they are staying for several days. It's possible to rent a car or jeep in Jost Van Dyke, but it's not really necessary.

Where to Stay and Eat

Both Anegada and Jost Van Dyke offer a choice of resorts and independent restaurants and bars; however, true luxury is in short supply. Most of the other smaller islands in the BVI are private and have a single resort, including the luxe choices Necker, Peter, and Guana islands, as well as the more modest Cooper Island and Marina Cay.

HOTEL AND RESTAURANT PRICES

Restaurant prices are for a main course at dinner and include any taxes or service charges. Hotel prices are per night for a double room in high season, excluding taxes, service charges, and meal plans (except at all-inclusives).

WHAT IT COSTS IN U.S. DOLLARS

	¢	$	$$	$$$	$$$$
Restaurants	under $8	$8–$12	$13–$20	$21–$30	over $30
Hotels	under $150	$150–$275	$276–$375	$376–$475	over $475

By Lynda Lohr and Susanna Henighan Potter

Tortola and Virgin Gorda are the largest—and most visited—of the British Virgin Islands, but the country is made up of 50-some islands and cays, many of them small and uninhabited. Of these outlying islands, Jost Van Dyke and Anegada get the lion's share of visitors, but several other smaller islands have notable resorts.

Anegada is most popular with snorkelers, sailors, and those looking to escape the modest crowds of the BVI, while Jost Van Dyke attracts partiers to its lively beach bars, along with a smaller contingent who spend a few days. Among the other islands, Guana, Necker, and Peter islands are luxe private-island resorts, while Cooper Island and Marina Cay are a bit more down-to-earth in terms of price. Norman Island is uninhabited, but it does have a floating restaurant on a ship moored off its coast. Billionaire entrepreneur Sir Richard Branson, owner of Necker Island, is building an ecoresort on Mosquito Island that is expected to open in 2014 with five three-bedroom villas.

Most of these islands are linked to Tortola by ferry. Some can be day-trip destinations (Peter Island, Jost Van Dyke, Marina Cay, Anegada, and Norman Island are all popular with day-trippers, and Cooper Island attracts many charter boats that moor for the night. Guana has no regular ferry service other than that offered to guests); Necker remains completely private.

JOST VAN DYKE

Named after an early Dutch settler, Jost Van Dyke is a small island northwest of Tortola and is *truly* a place to get away from it all. Mountainous and lush, the 4-mi-long (6½-km-long) island—with fewer than 200 full-time residents—has one tiny resort, some rental cottages and villas, a campground, a couple dozen cars, and a single road. There are no banks or ATMs on the island, and many restaurants and shops accept only cash. Life definitely rolls along on "island time," especially during the off-season from August to November, when finding

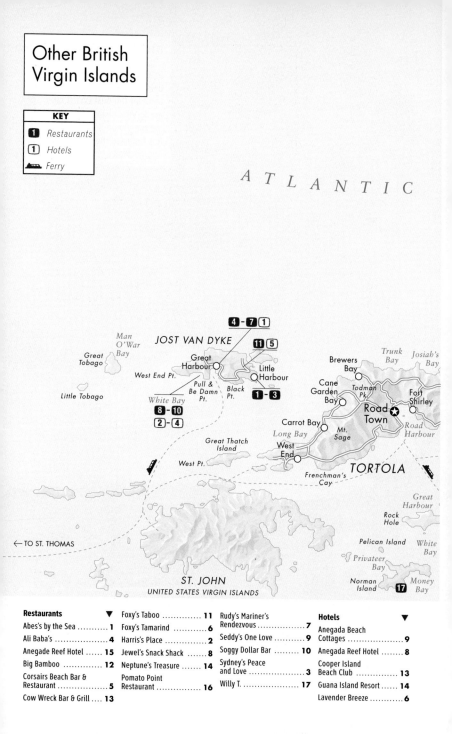

Other British Virgin Islands

KEY

1 *Restaurants*
1 *Hotels*
🚢 *Ferry*

ATLANTIC

Man O'War Bay

JOST VAN DYKE

Great Tobago

Great Harbour

West End Pt.

Pull & Be Damn Pt.

Little Tobago

White Bay

Black Pt.

Little Harbour

4 - **7** **1**

11 **5**

1 - **3**

8 - **10**

2 - **4**

Great Thatch Island

West Pt.

Brewers Bay

Cane Garden Bay

Todman Pk.

Trunk Bay

Josiah's Bay

Fort Shirley

Road Town

Road Harbour

Carrot Bay

Long Bay

Mt. Sage

West End

Frenchman's Cay

TORTOLA

Great Harbour

Rock Hole

← TO ST. THOMAS

Pelican Island

White Bay

Privateer Bay

Norman Island

Money Bay

17

ST. JOHN
UNITED STATES VIRGIN ISLANDS

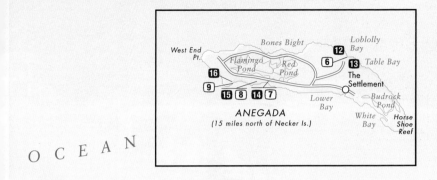

ANEGADA
(15 miles north of Necker Is.)

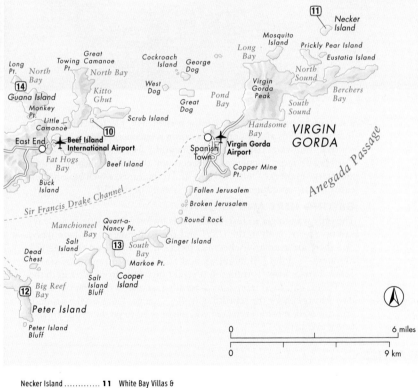

Boaters docking at Jost Van Dyke.

a restaurant open for dinner can be a challenge. Electricity arrived to Jost in the 1990s and water conservation is encouraged, as the primary source is rainwater collected in basementlike cisterns. Jost is one of the Caribbean's most popular anchorages, and there are a disproportionately large number of informal bars and restaurants, which have helped earn Jost its reputation as the "party island" of the BVI.

GETTING HERE AND AROUND

The only way to get to Jost Van Dyke is by ferry or private boat. Daysail operators, both in the USVI and the BVI, take guests here daily, and there are regularly scheduled ferries from West End, Tortola (25 minutes), St. John (30 minutes), and St. Thomas (60 minutes, via St. John). Ferries from Tortola run several times daily from West End; the St. Thomas/St. John ferry runs generally just once a day and not every day. Always check the schedules as they change. Once on the ground, you can walk most everywhere you might need to go, but you can also hire a taxi driver.

BEACHES

Sandy Cay. Just offshore, the little islet known as Sandy Cay is a gleaming scimitar of white sand, with marvelous snorkeling and an inland nature trail.

White Bay. On the south shore, west of Great Harbour, this long stretch of picturesque white sand is especially popular with boaters who come ashore for a libation at one of the beach bars.

WHERE TO EAT

Restaurants on Jost Van Dyke are informal (some serve meals family-style at long tables) but charming. The island is a favorite charter-boat stop, and you're bound to hear people exchanging stories about the previous night's anchoring adventures. Some restaurants don't take reservations (but for those that do, they are usually a requirement), and in all cases dress is casual. Most of the restaurants are also known for their nightlife, particularly during the week.

$$$ ✕ **Abe's by the Sea.** Many sailors who cruise into this quiet bay come so
ECLECTIC they can dock right at this open-air eatery to enjoy the seafood, conch, lobster, and other fresh catches. Chicken, ribs, and a Wednesday night pig roast (in season) round out the menu, and affable owners Abe Coakley and his wife, Eunicy, add a pinch and dash of hospitality that make a meal into a memorable evening. Casual lunches are also served, and an adjoining market sells ice, canned goods, and other necessities. Dinner reservations are required by 5 pm. ⊠ *Little Harbour* ☎ *284/495–9329* ⌂ *Reservations essential.*

$$$ ✕ **Ali Baba's.** Lobster is the main attraction at this beach bar with a sandy
SEAFOOD floor, which is just some 20 feet from the sea. Grilled local fish, including
🕐 swordfish, kingfish, and wahoo, are specialties and caught fresh daily.
★ There's also a pig roast here on Monday night in season and Friday night is roti night. Beware: Ali Baba's special rum punch is delicious but potent. Dinner reservations are required by 5 pm. ⊠ *Great Harbour* ☎ *284/495–9280* ⌂ *Reservations essential* ▭ *AE, MC, V.*

¢ ✕ **Christine's Bakery.** Fresh homemade breads, cakes, and other treats are
CAFE served at this modest bakery a few steps from the island's police station.
🕐 In the morning come for a breakfast of eggs, bacon, and toasted coconut bread. Christine's is also open at lunch, when she serves straightforward sandwiches. ⊠ *Great Harbour* ☎ *284/495–9281* ▭ *No credit cards* ✕ *No dinner.*

$$$ ✕ **Corsairs Beach Bar and Restaurant.** On an island known for seafood,
ECLECTIC it's the pizza that draws raves at this friendly beach bar considered by
🕐 some to be the "Cheers" of Jost. If pizza doesn't appeal, then choose from the reliably good, eclectic menu featuring Italian, Tex-Mex, Caribbean, and English specialties plus the island's only Thai-style lobster. Bring an appetite to breakfast, when the choices include hearty omelets and breakfast burritos. The bar is easily recognized by its signature pirate paraphernalia and a restored U.S. Army Jeep parked next to the steps-from-the-sea dining room. Live music, potent libations, and the only Jagermeister machine in the territory (it chills your shots to 28°F) keep things moving from happy hour into the night. Even if you're not hungry, this is a great hangout. ⊠ *Great Harbour* ☎ *284/495–9294* ⊕ *www.corsairsbvi.com.*

$$$$ ✕ **Foxy's Taboo.** It's well worth the winding hilly drive or sometimes-
ECLECTIC rough sail to get to Taboo, an eatery with a sophisticated menu and a
🕐 welcoming attitude. Located on Jost's mostly undeveloped East End, Taboo is less of a party bar than Foxy's in Great Harbour. At dinner you'll find specialties like wild boar, mango-tamarind chicken, and pizzas topped with everything from jalapeño peppers to prosciutto and kalamata olives. There are a dozen or more wines available by the

The Laid-Back Lifestyle at its Best

It's the laid-back attitude of Jost Van Dyke, which boasts a beach as its main street and has had electricity only since the 1990s, that makes the famous feel comfortable and everyday folk feel glorious. At no locale is this more true than at Foxy's Tamarind. Foxy Callwood, a seventh-generation Jost Van Dyker and calypsonian extraordinaire, is the star here, strumming and singing rib-tickling ditties full of lewd and laughable lyrics that attract a bevy of boaters and even celebrities like Tom Cruise, Kelsey Grammer, and Steven Spielberg.

What began in 1968 as a lemonade-stand-size bar, albeit with "modern" fixtures like a galvanized roof and plywood walls, has evolved into a bona fide beach bar with sand floor, wattle walls, and thatched roof that defines the eastern end of the beach at Great Harbour. Without the glitz of St. Thomas, glamour of St. John, or grace of Tortola, islanders like Foxy knew they needed to carve out their own unique niche—and have done so by appearing to have done nothing at all. Unhurried friendliness and a slice of quintessential Caribbean culture flow freely here.

Foxy, who fished for a living before he started singing for his supper, has traveled the world and had the world come to him for endless parties for Halloween, Labor Day weekend, and the New Year. The *New York Times* named Foxy's one of its three top picks for ringing in the millennium, and even Queen Elizabeth chose to honor Foxy, making him a Member of the Order of the British Empire (MBE) in 2009. A local newspaper headline from the occasion read: "Is Foxy Wearing Shoes?"

So what makes Foxy and his bar so popular, some 40 years on? He sums it up himself: "It's the quantity of people and the quality of the party. You can dance on the tables and sleep on the beach. No one is going to bother you."

bottle or glass, and don't miss the tiramisu for dessert. At lunchtime, even the burgers are a step up from average, and the salads are the best on the island. Coupled with a walk to the nearby Bubbly Pool (ask for a map at the bar), a visit to Taboo is a good way to while away a few hours. Dinner reservations are required by 4 pm. ⊠ *East End* ☎ *284/495–0218* ⊕ *www.foxysbar.com* ⚑ *Reservations essential* ⊗ *Closed Mon. No dinner Sun.*

$$$
ECLECTIC
🕒
★

✕**Foxy's Tamarind Bar and Restaurant.** The big draw here is the owner, Foxy Callwood, a calypsonian of fame who will serenade you with lewd and laughable lyrics as you fork into burgers, grilled chicken, barbecue ribs, and lobster. Check out the pennants, postcards and weathered T-shirts that adorn every inch of the walls and ceiling of this large, two-story beach shack; they've been left by previous visitors. On Friday and Saturday nights in season Foxy hosts an all-you-can-eat Caribbean-style barbeque with grilled fresh fish, chicken and ribs, peas and rice, salad and more, followed by live music. Other nights choose from steak, fresh lobster, pork, or pasta; at lunch Foxy serves sandwiches and salads. Whether because of the sheer volume of diners or the experience of the management, Foxy's is one of the most reliable eating establishments on Jost. And, for those who care, it is also home to the only espresso on the island. You're unlikely to find Foxy performing at night, but he takes the mic many afternoons, making this a popular happy hour pit stop. ⊠ *Great Harbour* ☎ *284/495–9258* ⊕ *www.foxysbar.com.*

$$
ECLECTIC
☺
★

✕ **Harris' Place.** All-you-can-eat lobster in a garlic butter sauce on Monday; freshly caught seafood on Thursday; pork, chicken, and ribs on Saturday: three good reasons to make your reservations early in the day at this quaint restaurant with the distinctive red roof and picnic tables underneath. Owner Cynthia Harris is as famous for her friendliness as she is for her food. Homemade key lime pie and expertly blended bushwackers are "to live for," as Cynthia would say, but diners also praise the fresh fish and lobster. Live music on Monday and Saturday evenings turns dinner into a party. Breakfast and lunch are served, too. ⊠ *Little Harbour* ☎ *284/495–9302.*

$
AMERICAN
☺

✕ **Jewel's Snack Shack.** This little wooden shack sells the best—and only—hot dogs on the island. You will also find burgers, fries, and ice-cream novelties on the simple menu. ⊠ *White Bay* ☎ *284/495–9286* ▭ *No credit cards* ☾ *No dinner.*

$$
ECLECTIC
☺
★

✕ **One Love Bar and Grill.** It's a toss-up whether Seddy Callwood's magic tricks or the finger-lickin' ribs and johnnycakes he serves are a greater draw. The Food Network's Alton Brown sought out this beachfront eatery and featured its stewed conch on a 2008 flavor-finding trip. Try that, or one of the signature lobster quesadillas or fresh garden salads. Seddy, Foxy Callwood's son, built his bar himself and decorated it with the flotsam and jetsam he has collected over years as a fisherman. Children's toys in the corner and outside mark this as a family-friendly place. There's live music on Thursday through Sunday afternoons in season, and Rueben Chinnery plays guitar on Saturday nights. ⊠ *White Bay* ☎ *284/495–9829* ⊕ *www.onelovebar.com.*

$$$$
ECLECTIC

✕ **Soggy Dollar Bar.** Candles illuminate this tiny beachfront, palm-lined dining room during the evening meal, making it one of the most romantic settings on the island. Each night the chef prepares a meat, chicken, and fish entrée with a choice of side dishes, appetizers, and desserts for a fixed price. The cuisine is familiar yet sophisticated—including choices like sweet and sour glazed pork, pan-fried snapper, and coq au vin. Don't miss the Painkiller ice cream, inspired by the Painkiller cocktail created here. Recently management has relaxed its reservations-only policy for dinner, but it is still wise to call ahead. For lunch, if you can find your way through the throngs ordering Painkillers at the bar, choose from flying-fish sandwiches, hamburgers, chicken roti, and conch fritters at the Soggy Dollar. ⊠ *Sandcastle, White Bay* ☎ *284/495–9888* ⊕ *www.soggydollar.com.*

$
AMERICAN

✕ **Sugar and Spice Snack Bar.** A handy choice for breakfast, this casual snack bar next to the ferry dock also serves burgers and sandwiches throughout the day. Proprietor Joan Chinnery brews an expert pot of local herbal tea, called bush tea, in the morning. It's open 7 days. ⊠ *Great Harbour* ☎ *284/543–9016* ▭ *No credit cards.*

7

CAMPING ON JOST VAN DYKE

Ivan's White Bay Campground. This bar, restaurant, and campground is a popular destination on Jost Van Dyke for those who don't mind roughing it. You can pitch your tent 6 feet from the sea or farther back under the sea-grape trees where there's an electric hookup and lamp. Or opt for a primitive cabin, where you can find just a bed, fan, light, and bucket of water to wash the sand off your feet. There's an outhouse, sun showers (basically a plastic sack hung from a tree branch), and a communal kitchen stocked with pots and pans. Expect to pay $20 for a bare site, $40 for an equipped site, or $65–$75 for a cabin. Camping reservations are essential. ⊠ *White Bay* ☎ *284/495-9358* ⊕ *www.ivanscampground.com.*

$$$ ✕ **Sydney's Peace and Love.** Here you can find great local lobster and
ECLECTIC fish, as well as barbecue chicken and ribs with all the fixings, including peas and rice, corn, coleslaw, and potato salad. All are served on an open-air terrace or in an air-conditioned dining room at the water's edge. The find here is a sensational (by BVI standards) jukebox. The cognoscenti sail here for dinner, since there's no beach—meaning no irksome sand fleas. Breakfast and lunch are served, too. Sadly, Sydney Hendrick died in 2010, but his wife and children are carrying on. ⊠ *Little Harbour* ☎ *284/495-9271.*

WHERE TO STAY

For expanded hotel reviews, visit Fodors.com.

$ ⛭ **Ivan's Stress Free Guest House.** Ivan's will give you a quintessential
RENTAL Caribbean experience and allow you to have some comfort doing it.
★ Ivan opened this "guest house" in 2007 a short walk up the hillside overlooking his campground. **Pros:** steps away from the best beach on the island; you can meet new friends at Ivan's convivial bar. **Cons:** basic furnishings; not within walking distance to other restaurants and nightlife (except Ivan's). ⊠ *White Bay* ☎ *284/495-9358* ⊕ *www.ivanscampground.com* ⊟ *No credit cards* ⌂ *In-room: a/c, no safe, kitchen, Internet. In-hotel: restaurant, bar, beach.*

$–$$ ⛭ **Sandcastle.** Sleep steps from beautiful White Bay beach at this tiny
HOTEL beachfront hideaway, an island favorite for more than 40 years. **Pros:** beachfront rooms; near restaurants and bars; comfy hammocks. **Cons:** some rooms lack air-conditioning; beach sometimes clogged with day-trippers; no children allowed. ⊠ *White Bay* ☎ *284/495-9888* ⊕ *www.soggydollar.com* ⌦ *2 rooms, 4 1-bedroom cottages* ⌂ *In-room: a/c (some), no safe, no TV. In-hotel: restaurant, bar, beach, some age restrictions* ⦿ *No meals.*

$$ ⛭ **Sandy Ground Estates.** Each of these seven privately owned one- and
RENTAL two-bedroom villas is distinct in decor, with interiors ranging from spartan to stylish. **Pros:** a place to get away from it all; secluded feel; each villa is unique. **Cons:** only reachable by boat; not accessible for people with disabilities, and best for people in good physical shape. ⊠ *Sandy*

Ground Estates ⓓ Box 594, West End, Tortola VG1130 ☎ 284/494–3391 ⊕ www.sandyground.com ⤳ 7 houses ☖ In-room: no a/c, no safe, kitchen, no TV. In-hotel: beach ⑩ No meals.

¢ ▦ **Sea Crest Inn.** Sea Crest offers the cheapest lodging on Jost Van Dyke,
RENTAL save for camping, and the location is smack-dab in the hub of Great Harbour. **Pros:** hospitable host; affordable rates; walking distance to restaurants and ferry. **Cons:** noise from nearby bar; basic furnishings. ⊠ *Great Harbour* ☎ 284/495–9024 ⊕ *www.bviwelcome.com/seacrestinn/seacrestinn.html* ⤳ *4 1-bedroom apartments* ☖ *In-room: a/c, no safe, kitchen. In-hotel: beach* ⑩ *No meals.*

$–$$ ▦ **White Bay Villas and Seaside Cottages.** Beautiful views and friendly
RENTAL staff keep guests coming back to these hilltop one- to three-bedroom
☖ air-conditioned villas and cottages. **Pros:** incredible views; full kitch-
★ ens; friendly staff. **Cons:** 10–15 minute walk to White Bay and Great Harbour's restaurants and beaches; rental cars recommended. ⊠ *White Bay* ⓓ *Box 3368, Annapolis, MD 21403* ☎ 410/571–6692 *or* 800/778–8066 ⊕ *www.jostvandyke.com* ⤳ *7 villas, 3 cottages* ☖ *In-room: a/c, no safe, kitchen, Wi-Fi. In-hotel: beach (some).*

NIGHTLIFE

★ Jost Van Dyke is the most happening place to go barhopping in the BVI, so much so that it is an all-day enterprise for some. In fact, yachties will sail over just to have a few drinks. All the spots are easy to find, clustered in three general locations: Great Harbour, White Bay, and Little Harbour (⤳ *see Where to Eat, above*). On the Great Harbour side you can find Foxy's, Corsairs, and Ali Baba's; on the White Bay side are the One Love Bar and Grill and the Soggy Dollar Bar, where legend has it the famous Painkiller was first concocted; and in Little Harbour are Harris' Place, Sydney's Peace and Love, and Abe's By The Sea. If you can't make it to Jost Van Dyke, you can have a Painkiller at almost any bar in the BVI.

SPORTS AND THE OUTDOORS

Abe and Eunicy Rentals (⊠ *Little Harbour* ☎ 284/495–9329) offers three types of vehicles—two-door Suzukis ($65 a day), four-door automatic Jeeps ($75 a day), and four-door automatic Monteros ($85 a day)—that will allow you to explore by land, or a fiberglass dinghy with a 15-horsepower engine ($60 a day) or inflatable dinghy with a 25-horsepower engine, radio, and CD player ($100 a day) for traveling around by sea. There's pickup and drop-off service from anywhere on the island.

JVD Scuba and BVI Eco-Tours (⊠ *Great Harbour* ☎ 284/495–0271 ⊕ *www.bvi-ecotours.com*) lets you see the undersea world around the island with dive master Colin Aldridge. One of the most impressive dives in the area is off the north coast of Little Jost Van Dyke. Here you can find the Twin Towers: a pair of rock formations rising an impressive 90 feet. A one-tank dive costs $70, two-tank dive $110, and four-hour beginner course $120. Colin also offers day-trips to

Sandy Cay and Sandy Spit, excursions to the Baths on Virgin Gorda, and also custom outings.

Paradise Jeep Rentals (✉ *Great Harbour* ☎ *284/495–9477*) offers the ideal vehicles to tackle Jost Van Dyke's steep, winding roads. Even though Jost is a relatively small island, you really need to be in shape to walk from one bay to the next. This outfit rents four-door Suzukis for $65 per day and Grand Vitaras for $80. It's located next to the Fire Station in Great Harbour. Reservations are a must.

ANEGADA

Fodor's Choice
★

Anegada lies low on the horizon about 14 mi (22½ km) north of Virgin Gorda. Unlike the hilly volcanic islands in the chain, this is a flat coral-and-limestone atoll. Nine miles (14 km) long and 2 mi (3 km) wide, the island rises no more than 28 feet above sea level. In fact, by the time you're able to see it, you may have run your boat onto a reef. (More than 300 captains unfamiliar with the waters have done so since exploration days; note that bareboat charters don't allow their vessels to head here without a trained skipper.) Although the reefs are a sailor's nightmare, they are a primary attraction for many visitors. Snorkeling, especially in the waters around Loblolly Bay on the north shore, is a transcendent experience. You can float in shallow, calm water just a few feet from shore and see one coral formation after another, each shimmering with a rainbow of colorful fish. Many local captains are happy to take visitors out bonefishing or sportfishing. Such watery pleasures are complemented by ever-so-fine, ever-so-white sand (the northern and western shores have long stretches of the stuff) and the occasional beach bar (stop in for burgers, local lobster, or a frosty beer). The island's population of about 180 lives primarily in a small south-side village called the Settlement, which has a handful of grocery stores, a bakery, and a general store. In 2009, Anegada got its first bank, but it is only open one day a week (and there is no ATM). Many restaurants and shops take only cash. Mosquitoes and sand flies can be murderous around dusk and dawn on Anegada; never come here without bug repellant and long-sleeved clothing.

GETTING HERE AND AROUND

You can get to Anegada from Tortola by ferry on Monday, Wednesday, and Friday; the trip takes about 90 minutes from Tortola with an interim stop in Virgin Gorda. There are morning and afternoon departures, making it possible to visit the island for the day. It's also possible to fly on a charter from Beef Island or St. Thomas; the flight from Beef Island takes only 10 minutes, and can be reasonably priced per person if you are traveling with a small group.

Anegada has miles of beautiful, white-sand beaches.

BEACHES

Cow Wreck Beach. Named for the cow bones that once washed ashore, this stretch of sand on the island's northwest cost has snorkeling, beach-combing, soft white sand and a casual beach bar and restaurant.

Loblolly Bay. A curve of shore on Anegada's northern coast, this bay is home to the best snorkeling on the island. The two beach bars at Lob-lolly East are often closed and this is the place for solitude; Loblolly West has a popular beachfront reastaurant, showers, a gift shop and snorkel gear rentals.

Pomato Point. A powder white-sand beach on Anegada's western shore, Pomato Point has the best sunset views. There is no easily accessible reef, but the water is calm and the views of Tortola and Jost Van Dyke are beautiful.

WHERE TO EAT

There are between six and 10 restaurants open at any one time, depending on the season and on whim. Check when you're on the island. Fresh fish and lobster are the specialties of the island. The going rate for a lobster dinner is $50, and it's almost always the most expensive thing on any restaurant menu.

$$$$
SEAFOOD
✕ **Anegada Reef Hotel Restaurant.** Seasoned yachters gather here nightly to share tales of the high seas; the open-air bar is the most lively on the island. Dinner is by candlelight under the stars and always includes famous Anegada lobster, steaks, and succulent baby back ribs—all prepared on the large grill by the little open-air bar. The ferry dock

is right next door, so expect a crowd shortly after it arrives. Dinner reservations are required by 4 pm. Breakfast favorites include lobster omelets and rum-soaked French toast; at lunch the Reef serves salads and sandwiches. ⊠ *Anegada Reef Hotel, Setting Point* ☎ *284/495–8002* ⌂ *Reservations essential.*

$$$
AMERICAN
★

✕ **Big Bamboo.** This beachfront bar and restaurant tucked among sea grape trees at famous Loblolly Bay is the island's most popular destination for lunch. After you've polished off a plate of succulent Anegada lobster, barbeque chicken or fresh fish, you can spend the afternoon on the beach, where the snorkeling is excellent and the view near perfection. Fruity drinks from the cabana bar and ice cream from the freezer will round out your day. Dinner is by request only. If your heart is set on lobster, it's a good idea to call in the morning or day before to put in your request. ⊠ *Loblolly Bay West* ☎ *284/495–2019* ⌂ *Reservations essential.*

$$$$
SEAFOOD

✕ **Cow Wreck Bar and Grill.** Named for the cow bones that once washed up on shore, this wiggle-your-toes-in-the-sand beachside eatery on the north shore is a fun place to watch the antics of surfers and kite-boarders skidding across the bay. Tuck into conch ceviche or the popular hot wings for lunch. The homemade coconut pie is a winner. Pack your snorkel gear and explore the pristine reef just a few strokes from the shore before you eat. Dinner is served by request; reservations required by 4 pm. ⊠ *Loblolly Bay East* ☎ *284/495–8047* ⊕ *www.cowwreckbeach.com* ⌂ *Reservations essential.*

$$$$
SEAFOOD
☾

✕ **Neptune's Treasure.** The owners, the Soares family, have lived on the island for more than half a century, and the Soares men catch, cook, and serve the seafood at this homey bar and restaurant a short distance from Setting Point. The fresh lobster, swordfish, tuna and mahimahi are all delicious. Homemade bread, a symphony of sides, and made-from-scratch desserts (including key lime pie and chocolate brownies), round out your meal. Dinner is by candlelight at the water's edge, often with classic jazz playing softly in the background. If you've tired of seafood, Neptune's has a nice variety of alternatives including vegetarian pasta, pork loin, and orange chicken. The view is spectacular at sunset. Breakfast is also served. Dinner reservations are essential by 4 pm. ⊠ *Benders Bay* ☎ *284/495–9439* ⊕ *www.neptunestreasure.com* ⌂ *Reservations essential* ☾ *No lunch.*

$$$$
SEAFOOD

✕ **Pomato Point Restaurant.** This relaxed restaurant and bar sits on one of the best beaches on the island and enjoys Anegada's most dramatic sunset views. Entrées include lobster, stewed conch, and freshly caught seafood. It's open for lunch daily; call by 4 pm for dinner reservations. Be sure to take a look at owner Wilfred Creque's displays of island artifacts, including shards of Arawak pottery and 17th-century coins, cannonballs, and bottles. These are housed in a little one-room museum adjacent to the dining room. ⊠ *Pomato Point* ☎ *284/495–8038* ⌂ *Reservations essential* ☾ *Closed Sept.*

WHERE TO STAY

For expanded hotel reviews, visit Fodors.com.

$$
HOTEL ⊞ **Anegada Reef Hotel.** Head here if you want to bunk in comfortable lodging near Anegada's most popular anchorage. **Pros:** everything you need is nearby; nice sunsets. **Cons:** basic rooms; no beach; often a party atmosphere at the bar. ⊠ *Setting Point* ☎ *284/495–8002* ⊕ *www. anegadareef.com* ⇨ *20 rooms* ⚿ *In-room: a/c, no safe, no TV. In-hotel: restaurant, bar, beach* ⏐◎⏐ *No meals.*

$$–$$$
RENTAL **Big Bamboo.** Location is this property's finest attribute: the four circular villas are just steps from beautiful Loblolly Bay. **Pros:** beachfront location; near restaurant and snorkeling. **Cons:** some may feel isolated; beach popular during the day. *Loblolly Bay West* ☎ *284/495–2019* ⇨ *4 villas* ⚿ *In-room: no a/c, no safe, no TV. In-hotel: restaurant, bar, beach* ⏐◎⏐ *No meals.*

$–$$
RENTAL ⊞ **Keel Point Cottages.** Picture yourself nearly alone in a tropical paradise; if that's your dream, then this may be your place. **Pros:** right on the water; new, well-kept property; rental car included. **Cons:** No on-site dining options (except your kitchen) and far from restaurants. ⊠ *Keel Point* ☎ *284/495–8019* ⊕ *www.keelpointcottages. com* ⇨ *4 cottages* ⚿ *In-room: a/c, no safe, kitchen, no TV. In-hotel: beach* ⏐◎⏐ *No meals.*

$$$$
RENTAL ⊞ **Lavender Breeze.** Cool trade winds whistle through this three-bedroom villa and its wood-and-wicker living and dining rooms that sit right on Loblolly Bay. **Pros:** gorgeous sea views; walk to restaurants. **Cons:** some find location too isolated. ⊠ *Loblolly Bay* ☎ *284/495–8045 or 888/868–0199* ⊕ *bvivillaconnection.com* ⇨ *1 villa* ⚿ *In-room: a/c, no safe, kitchen. In-hotel: beach* ▭ *No credit cards* ⏐◎⏐ *No meals.*

¢
B&B/INN ⊞ **Neptune's Treasure.** Basic waterfront rooms with simple but squeaky-clean furnishings and lovely views of the ocean are the hallmark of this family-owned guesthouse. **Pros:** waterfront property; run by a family full of tales of the island; nice sunset views. **Cons:** simple rooms; no kitchens; no beach. ⊠ *Between Pomato and Setting points* ☎ *284/495–9439* ⊕ *www.neptunestreasure.com* ⇨ *9 rooms, 2 cottages* ⚿ *In-room: a/c, no safe, no TV. In-hotel: restaurant* ⏐◎⏐ *No meals.*

SHOPPING

Sue's Purple Turtle. This shop is hard to miss: look for the purple building just past the ferry dock at Setting Point. Sue's is the best all-around gift shop on the island and offers resort wear, T-shirts, locally made jewelry, books, and a handful of essentials such as toiletries, drinks, and picnic items. ⊠ *Setting Point* ☎ *284/495–8062.*

Dotsy's Bakery. At Dotsy's, you can find a tempting array of fresh-baked breads, sandwiches, pizza, cookies, and desserts. ⊠ *The Settlement* 🕾 *284/495–9667.*

Faulkner's Country Store. Stop here for a taste of old-time Anegada or just to buy groceries or other necessities. ⊠ *The Settlement* 🕾 *No phone.*

SPORTS AND THE OUTDOORS

Anegada Reef Hotel. Call the Anegada Reef to arrange bonefishing and sportfishing outings with seasoned local guides. 🕾 *284/495–8002* ⊕ *www.anegadareef.com.*

Danny Vanterpool. Danny offers half-, three-quarter-, and full-day bonefishing excursions around Anegada. Cost ranges from $300 to $500. 🕾 *284/441–6334* ⊕ *dannysbonefishing.com.*

OTHER BRITISH VIRGIN ISLANDS

Of the 50-odd islands in the British Virgin Islands chain only 15 are inhabited, and several of those are privately owned, having been turned into private-island resorts. Some of these—most notably Necker Island, which is owned by Sir Richard Branson, and Peter Island, an upscale private-island retreat often visited by the rich and famous—are well-known among the jet-set crowd; others are not as well known but equally beautiful.

COOPER ISLAND

This small, hilly island on the south side of the Sir Francis Drake Channel, about 8 mi (13 km) from Road Town, Tortola, is popular with the charter-boat crowd. There are no paved roads (which doesn't really matter, as there aren't any cars), but you can find a beach restaurant, a casual hotel, a few houses (some are available for rent), and great snorkeling at the south end of Manchioneel Bay.

GETTING HERE AND AROUND

Unless you have your own sailboat, the only way to reach Cooper Island is on a private ferry from Road Harbour Marina. The 35-minute ride is included in the cost of your vacation at Cooper Island Beach Club.

WHERE TO STAY

$ 🏨 **Cooper Island Beach Club.** Diving is a focus at this small resort, but
RESORT   folks who want to simply swim, snorkel, or relax can also feel right at
Fodor's Choice   home. **Pros:** lots of quiet; the Caribbean as it used to be. **Cons:** small
★   rooms; modest furnishings; island accessible only by ferry. ⊠ *Manchioneel Bay, Cooper Island* 🕮 *Box 859, Road Town, Tortola VG1110* 🕾 *284/495–9084 or 800/542–4624* ⊕ *www.cooper-island.com* 🛏 *12 rooms* ⵣ *In-room: no a/c, no safe, no TV. In-hotel: restaurant, bar, beach, water sports* 🍽 *No meals, all meals.*

GUANA ISLAND

Guana Island sits off Tortola's northeast coast. Sailors often drop anchor at one of the island's bays for a day of snorkeling and sunning. The island is a designated wildlife sanctuary, and scientists often come here to study its flora and fauna. It's home to a back-to-nature resort that offers few activities other than relaxation. Unless you're a hotel guest or a sailor, there's no easy way to get here.

GETTING HERE AND AROUND

Unless you have your own sailboat, the only way to reach Guana Island is by the resort's private ferry, which will pick you up at Beef Island, Tortola.

WHERE TO STAY

$$$$
RESORT
Fodor's Choice
★

Guana Island Resort. Guana Island is a nature lover's paradise, and it's a good resort if you want to stroll the hillsides, snorkel around the reefs, swim at its seven beaches, and still enjoy some degree of comfort. **Pros:** secluded feel; lovely grounds. **Cons:** very expensive; need boat to get here. ⊠ *Guana Island* 🖃 *67 Irving Place, 12th fl., New York, NY 10003* ☎ *284/494–2354 or 800/544–8262* ⊕ *www.guana.com* 🛏 *15 rooms, 1 1-bedroom villa, 1 2-bedroom villa, 1 3-bedroom villa* ⚭ *In-room: a/c (some), no safe, no TV (some). In-hotel: restaurant, beach, water sports, business center* ⦿*All meals.*

MARINA CAY

☾ Beautiful little Marina Cay is in Trellis Bay, not far from Beef Island. Sometimes you can see it and its large J-shape coral reefs—a most dramatic sight—from the air soon after takeoff from the airport on Beef Island. Covering 8 acres, this islet is considered small even by BVI standards. On it there's a restaurant, a Pusser's Store, and a six-unit hotel. Ferry service is free from the dock on Beef Island.

GETTING HERE AND AROUND

There's a regularly scheduled ferry from Beef Island, Tortola, direct to Marina Cay. It's a short, 15-minute trip.

WHERE TO STAY

$$–$$$
HOTEL

Pusser's Marina Cay Hotel and Restaurant. If getting away from it all is your priority, this may be the place for you, because there's nothing to do on this beach-rimmed island other than swim, snorkel, and soak up the sun—there's not even a TV to distract you. **Pros:** lots of character; beautiful beaches; interesting guests. **Cons:** older property; ferry needed to get here. ⊠ *West side of Marina Cay* 🖃 *Box 76, Road Town, Tortola VG1110* ☎ *284/494–2174* ⊕ *www.pussers.com/t-marina-cay.aspx* 🛏 *4 rooms, 2 two-bedroom villas* ⚭ *In-room: no a/c, no safe, no TV. In-hotel: restaurant, bar, beach* ⦿*Breakfast.*

7

NECKER ISLAND

Necker Island sits off Virgin Gorda's northeast coast, reachable only by private ferry or helicopter. A mere speck in the British Virgin Islands, it's home to Sir Richard Branson's private estate. When he's not in residence, you and your friends are welcome to enjoy its gorgeous beaches and myriad amenities.

GETTING HERE AND AROUND

Guests (and only guests) of Necker Island will be whisked away from Beef Island on a private boat or helicopter.

WHERE TO STAY

$$$$
ALL-INCLUSIVE

Necker Island. You probably won't run into British magnate Sir Richard Branson, but you can live in his luxurious style when you rent his estate on Necker Island. **Pros:** gorgeous setting; an island for you and a few dozen friends. **Cons:** very expensive; need boat to get here. ⊠ *Necker Island* ⌂ *Box 1091, The Valley, Virgin Gorda VG1150* ☎ *212/994–3070 or 877/577–8777* ⊕ *www.neckerisland.virgin.com* ⤶ *10 rooms, 4 houses* ⌂ *In-room: a/c, no safe, no TV, Wi-Fi. In-hotel: tennis courts, pools, beach, water sports* ⏆ *All-inclusive.*

NORMAN ISLAND

This uninhabited island is the supposed setting for Robert Louis Stevenson's *Treasure Island.* The famed caves at Treasure Point are popular with day sailors and powerboaters. If you land ashore at the island's main anchorage in the Bight, you can find a small beach bar and behind it a trail that winds up the hillside and reaches a peak with a fantastic view of the Sir Francis Drake Channel to the north.

GETTING HERE AND AROUND

The only way to reach this island is by private boat or on a regularly scheduled trip that puts you aboard the *Willy T.* for a meal and drinks.

WHERE TO EAT

$$
SEAFOOD

⨯ **Willy T.** The ship, a former Baltic trader and today a floating bar and restaurant anchored to the north of the Bight, serves lunch and dinner in a party-hearty atmosphere. Try the conch fritters for starters. For lunch and dinner, British-style fish-and-chips, West Indian roti sandwiches, and the teriyaki chicken are winners. ⊠ *The Bight* ☎ *284/496–8603* ⊕ *www.williamthornton.com* ⌂ *Reservations essential.*

PETER ISLAND

Although Peter Island is home to the resort of the same name, it's also a popular destination for charter boaters and Tortola vacationers. The island is lush, with forested hillsides and white sandy beaches. There are no roads other than those at the resort. You're welcome to dine at the resort's restaurants.

DID YOU KNOW?

Necker Island is owned by Sir Richard Branson, and there are only a few weeks of the year when it is open to individual guests, starting at $25,000 per couple per week.

Peter Island, a private-island resort and popular anchorage for yachters.

GETTING HERE AND AROUND
The only way to reach Peter Island is by private boat or private ferry. Guests are brought over for free (only the first trip). The scheduled ferry trip from Peter Island's shoreside base outside Road Town runs $15 round-trip for nonguests.

WHERE TO STAY

$$$$
RESORT

Peter Island Resort. Total pampering and the prices to match are the ticket at this luxury resort. **Pros:** lovely rooms; nice beach. **Cons:** need ferry to get here; pricey rates. ⊠ *Peter Island* ✆ *Box 211, Road Town, Tortola VG1110* ☎ *284/495–2000 or 800/346–4451* ⊕ *www.peterisland.com* ⇄ *52 rooms, 3 villas* ⌂ *In-room: a/c, no TV. In-hotel: restaurants, bar, pool, gym, spa, beach, water sports, business center* ⏺ *No meals, all meals.*

Travel Smart

GETTING HERE AND AROUND

While St. Croix has a four-lane highway and St. Thomas has multiple lanes running along the Charlotte Amalie waterfront, the other islands in the region have only paved two-lane main roads that twist and turn up and down the hillsides. Potholes are common. Once you get into neighborhoods, most roads are paved, but particularly on St. John and in the British Virgin Islands you may find some that are still dirt or gravel. Planes connect the larger islands, but travel to St. John and the smaller BVI is only by ferry. Ferries also connect the larger islands with the smaller ones and with each other.

■TIP→ Ask the local tourist board about hotel and local transportation packages that include tickets to special events.

■ AIR TRAVEL

The nonstop flight from New York to St. Thomas or San Juan takes about four hours; from Miami to St. Thomas or San Juan it's about three hours.

Reconfirming your flights on interisland carriers is still a good idea, particularly when you're traveling to the smallest islands. You may be subjected to a carrier's whims: if no other passengers are booked on your flight, you may be asked to take another flight later in the day, or your plane may make unscheduled stops to pick up more passengers or cargo. It's all part of the excitement—and unpredictability—of travel in the Caribbean. In addition, regional carriers use small aircraft with limited baggage space, and they often impose weight restrictions; travel light, or you could be subject to outrageous surcharges or delays in getting very large or heavy luggage, which may have to follow on another flight.

AIRPORTS

The major airports are Terrance B. Lettsome International Airport on Beef Island, Tortola; Cyril E. King Airport on St.

AIRLINE TIP

If you have an afternoon flight, check your bags in early in the morning (keep a change of clothes in a carry-on), then go back to the beach for one last lunch, returning to the airport two hours before your flight departs. It makes for much easier traveling, saves time, and you get your last beach fix.

Thomas; and Henry Rohlsen Airport on St. Croix. There's a small airport (so small that it doesn't have a phone number) on Virgin Gorda.

Airport Information Terrance B. Lettsome International Airport (☎ 284/468–6494). **Cyril E. King Airport** (☎ 340/774–5100). **Henry Rohlsen Airport** (☎ 340/778–1012).

GROUND TRANSPORTATION

Ground transportation options are covered in the Essentials sections in individual island chapters.

FLIGHTS

There are nonstop and connecting flights, usually through San Juan, Puerto Rico, from the U.S. mainland to St. Thomas and St. Croix, with connecting ferry service from St. Thomas to St. John. There are no nonstop flights to the BVI from the United States; you must connect in San Juan or St. Thomas for the short hop over to Tortola or Virgin Gorda.

American Airlines and its subsidiary American Eagle are the biggest carriers to the Virgin Islands, with several nonstop flights a day from New York and Miami to St. Thomas and several connecting flights through San Juan. American also flies nonstop to St. Croix from Miami. The frequency of flights is seasonal.

Continental flies nonstop daily to St. Thomas from Newark, and US Airways has nonstop flights from Philadelphia and Charlotte, North Carolina. Spirit Airlines flies nonstop every day from Fort Lauderdale. Delta flies nonstop from Atlanta and in high season has a Saturday flight from Detroit. United also flies nonstop from Chicago and Washington, D.C.

Although connecting through San Juan is your best bet for getting to Tortola or Virgin Gorda, you can also fly from St. Thomas and St. Croix to Tortola and Virgin Gorda on Air Sunshine.

Some islands in the British Virgin Islands are accessible only by small planes operated by local or regional carriers. International carriers will sometimes book those flights for you as part of your overall travel arrangements, or you can book directly with the local carrier.

Airline Contacts American Airlines/American Eagle (☎ 800/433–7300, 340/776–2560 in St. Thomas, 340/778–2000 in St. Croix, 284/495–2559 in Tortola ⊕ www.aa.com). **Continental Airlines** (☎ 800/231–0856 ⊕ www.continental.com). **Delta Airlines** (☎ 800/221–1212, 340/777–4177 in St. Thomas ⊕ www.delta.com). **JetBlue** (☎ 800/538–2583 ⊕ www.jetblue.com). **Spirit Airlines** (☎ 800/772–7117 ⊕ www.spiritair. com). **United Airlines** (☎ 800/864–8331, 340/774–9190 in St. Thomas ⊕ www.united. com). **US Airways** (☎ 800/622–1015 ⊕ www. usairways.com).

Interisland Carriers Air Sunshine (☎ 800/327–8900, 800/435–8900 in Florida, 888/879–8900 in the USVI, 495–8900 in BVI ⊕ www.airsunshine.com). **Cape Air** (☎ 800/352–0714, 284/495–1440 in Tortola ⊕ www.flycapeair.com). **Fly BVI** (☎ 284/495–1747 in Tortola ⊕ www.bviaircharters.com). **LIAT** (☎ 888/844–5428, 866/549–5428 in USVI, 284/495–2577 in Tortola ⊕ www.liat. com). **Seaborne** (☎ 340/773–6442 ⊕ www. seaborneairlines.com).

▮ BOAT AND FERRY TRAVEL

Ferries travel between St. Thomas and St. John. You can also travel by ferry from both St. Thomas and St. John to the British Virgin Islands, and between the British Virgin Islands themselves. The companies run regularly scheduled trips, departing from Charlotte Amalie or Red Hook on St. Thomas; Cruz Bay, St. John; Gallows Bay, St. Croix; West End, Road Town, or Beef Island on Tortola; the Valley or North Sound on Virgin Gorda; and Jost Van Dyke. There's also regularly scheduled service between Tortola, Virgin Gorda, and Anegada a few times a week. Schedules change, so check with your hotel or villa manager to find out the latest. The ferry companies are all regulated by the U.S. Coast Guard, and prices are about the same, so there's no point in trying to organize your schedule to take one company's ferries rather than another's. Just show up at the dock to buy your ticket on the next ferry departing for your destination. If it all seems confusing—and it can be very confusing for travel to or around the BVI—just ask a local who's also buying a ticket. They know the ropes.

Although you might save a few dollars flying into St. Thomas if you're headed to the BVI, it's much easier to connect through San Juan for a flight to Tortola or Virgin Gorda. If you're headed to St. John or to points like North Sound, Virgin Gorda, or Jost Van Dyke, you'll have to hop a ferry regardless. If you're splitting your vacation between the U.S. and British Virgin Islands, ferries are the perfect way to get from one to another. You'll also get a bonus—views of the many small islands that dot the ferry route.

Dohm's Water Taxi runs from St. Thomas to St. John and any point in the BVI. You'll avoid the often crowded ferries, the crew will handle your luggage, navigate customs in the BVI, and you'll arrive at your destination feeling relaxed; however, you'll pay significantly more for the convenience.

There's frequent daily service from both Red Hook (15 to 20 minutes, $6 each way plus $2 for each piece of luggage) and Charlotte Amalie (45 minutes, $12 each way plus $2 for each piece of luggage) to Cruz Bay. The more frequent ferry from Red Hook to St. John leaves at 6:30 am and hourly starting at 8 am, the last at midnight; from St. John back to Red Hook, the first ferry leaves at 6 am, the last at 11 pm. About every hour there's a car ferry, which costs $42 to $50 (plus $3 port charges) round-trip; you should arrive at least 25 minutes before departure. From Charlotte Amalie the first ferry to St. John leaves at 10 am, the last at 5:30 pm; from St. John to Charlotte Amalie, the first ferry leaves at 8:45 am, the last at 3:45. The ferry between Charlotte Amalie and St. John is prone to cancellations, particularly in the slower fall months.

Reefer is the name given to both of the brightly colored 26-passenger skiffs that run between the Charlotte Amalie waterfront and Marriott Frenchman's Reef hotel every day on the half hour from 8 to 5. It's a good way to beat the traffic (and is about the same price as a taxi) to Morning Star Beach. The one-way fare is $6 per person, and the trip takes about 15 minutes.

A ferry run by V.I. Sea Trans connects Charlotte Amalie, St. Thomas, and Gallow's Bay, St. Croix Friday through Monday. Departure times depend on the day of the week, with the earliest ferry leaving St. Thomas at 7:45 am on Friday and the latest at 4:15 pm on Friday and Saturday. From St. Croix, the earliest ferry departs at 10 am Friday and the latest at 6:15 pm Friday and Saturday. This ferry is often cancelled in the slow fall months. The ferry costs $90 round-trip or $50 one-way.

There's daily service between Charlotte Amalie or Red Hook, on St. Thomas, and West End or Road Town, Tortola, BVI, by either Smith's Ferry or Native Son, and to Virgin Gorda, BVI, by Smith's Ferry. The fare is $45–$55 round-trip, and the trip from Charlotte Amalie takes 45 minutes to an hour to West End, up to 90 minutes to Road Town; from Red Hook the trip is only a half hour.

There's also frequent service from Cruz Bay to Tortola aboard an Inter-Island Boat Service ferry. The half-hour trip costs $45 round-trip; bring your passport if you plan to go to BVI (it's now required for all travel there).

The 2¼-hour trip from Charlotte Amalie to Virgin Gorda costs $40 one-way and $70 round-trip. From Red Hook and Cruz Bay, Inter-Island offers service on Thursday and Sunday; Speedy's offers service on Tuesday, Thursday, and Saturday.

On Friday, Saturday, and Sunday a ferry operates between Red Hook, Cruz Bay, and Jost Van Dyke; the trip takes 45 minutes and costs $60 per person round-trip.

Transportation Services STT operates a ferry between St. Thomas and Fajardo in Puerto Rico. The two-hour trip is generally done weekly and costs $125 round-trip; however, schedules change every month.

Ferry Contacts Dohm's Water Taxi (☎ 340/775–6501 in St. Thomas ⊕ www.watertaxi-vi.com). **Inter-Island Boat Service** (☎ 340/776–6597 in St. John, 284/495–4166 in Tortola). **Native Son** (☎ 340/774–8685 in St. Thomas, 284/495–4617 in Tortola ⊕ www.nativesonferry.com). **New Horizon Ferry Service** (☎ 284/495–9278 in Tortola). **North Sound Express** (☎ 284/495–2138 in Tortola). **Peter Island Ferry** (☎ 284/495–2000 in Tortola ⊕ www.peterisland.com). **Reefer** (☎ 340/776–8500 Ext. 6814 in St. Thomas ⊕ www.marriottfrenchmansreef.com). **Smith's Ferry** (☎ 340/775–7292 in St. Thomas, 284/494–4454 in Tortola ⊕ www.smithsferry.com). **Speedy's Ferries** (☎ 284/494–6154 in Tortola ⊕ www.speedysbvi.com). **Tortola Fast Ferry** (☎ 284/494–2323 in Tortola ⊕ www.tortolafastferry.com). **Transportation Services** (☎ 340/776–6282 in St. John). **V.I. SeaTrans** (☎ 340/776–5494 in St. Thomas ⊕ www.goviseatrans.com). **Varlack Ventures** (☎ 340/776–6412 in St. John ⊕ www.varlack-ventures.com).

▌ CAR TRAVEL

A car gives you mobility. You'll be able to spend an hour browsing at that cozy out-of-the-way shop instead of the 10 minutes allotted by your tour guide. You can beach-hop without searching for a ride, and you can sample that restaurant you've heard so much about that's half an hour (and an expensive taxi ride) away. On parts of some of the islands, you may need to rent a four-wheel-drive vehicle to really get out and about. Paved roads are generally good, but you may encounter a pothole or two (or three). Except for one divided highway on St. Croix, roads are narrow, and in hilly locations twist and turn with the hill's contours. The roads on the north side of Tortola are particularly serpentine, with scary drop-offs that will send you plummeting down the hillside if you miss the turn. Drive slowly. Many villas in St. John and the BVI are on unpaved roads. Four-wheel drive could be a necessity if it rains. A higher-clearance vehicle will help get safely over the rocks that may litter the road.

GASOLINE

Except in St. Croix, gas is up to $1 to $2 more per gallon than in the United States. USVI stations sell gas by the gallon; BVI stations sell it by the liter or the gallon, depending on the station. Most stations accept major credit cards, but don't count on that. Some stations have a pump-it-yourself policy, but it's still easy to find one with attendants, except on St. John. There's no need to tip unless they change a tire or do some other quick mechanical chore. You'll have to ask for a handwritten receipt if you're not paying by credit card. On smaller islands stations may be closed on Sunday.

PARKING

Parking can be tight in towns across the USBVI. Workers grab up the street parking, sometimes arriving several hours early to get prime spaces. It's particularly difficult to find parking in Cruz Bay, St. John. There are free public lots scattered around town, but they're usually filled by folks taking the ferry to St. Thomas. Instead, your rental-car company probably will allow you to park in its lot. Charlotte Amalie, St. Thomas, has a paid parking lot next to Fort Christian. A machine takes your money—$1 for the first hour and $5 for all day. In Christiansted, St. Croix, you'll find a public parking lot on Strand Street. Since the booth isn't staffed, there's no charge. There's also a public lot near Fort Christianvaern, but that lot is locked at 4:30 pm. It costs $1 for the first hour, and $6 for all day. Tortola has several free parking lots near the waterfront. On Virgin Gorda there's a free lot at Virgin Gorda Yacht Harbor. There are no parking meters anywhere in the USBVI. Even if you're desperate for a parking space in the USVI, don't park in a handicapped space without a sticker—unless you want to pay a $1,000 fine.

RENTAL CARS

Unless you plan to spend all your days at a resort or plan to take taxis everywhere, you'll need a rental car at least for a few days. While driving is on the left, you'll drive an American-style car with the steering wheel on the left. Traffic doesn't move all that fast in most USBVI locations, so driving on the left is not that difficult to master.

If you're staying on St. Thomas or St. Croix and don't plan to venture far off the main roads, you won't need a four-wheel-drive vehicle. On St. John and in the BVI, a four-wheel-drive vehicle is useful to get up steep roads when it rains. Many rental homes in St. John and the BVI are on unpaved roads, so a four-wheel-drive vehicle with high clearance may be a necessity if you rent a villa. While rental agencies don't usually prohibit access to certain roads, use common sense. If the road looks too bad, turn around.

Most car-rental agencies won't rent to anyone under age 25 or over age 75.

Some car-rental agencies offer infant car seats for about $5 a day, but check and check again right before you leave for your trip to make sure one will be available. Their use isn't compulsory in the USBVI, but they're always a good idea if you have small children. You might consider bringing your own car seat from home.

Book your rental car well in advance during the winter season. Vehicles are particularly scarce around the busy President's Day holiday. If you don't reserve, you might find yourself without wheels. Prices will be higher during the winter season.

You usually won't find any long lines when picking up your car or dropping it off. If your rental agency is away from the airport or ferry terminal, you'll have to allot extra time to get to there. Ask when you pick up your car how much time you should allot for returning it.

Rates range from $50 a day ($300 a week) for an economy car with air-conditioning, automatic transmission, and unlimited mileage to as much as $80 a day ($400 a week) for a four-wheel-drive vehicle. Both the USVI and the BVI have major companies (with airport locations) as well as numerous local companies (near the airports, in hotels, and in the main towns), which are sometimes cheaper. Most provide pick-up service; some ask that you take a taxi to their headquarters.

A driver's license from the United States or other countries is fine in the USVI and the BVI.

Major Agencies Alamo (🕾 800/462–5266 ⊕ www.alamo.com). **Avis** (🕾 800/331–1084 ⊕ www.avis.com). **Budget** (🕾 800/472–3325 ⊕ www.budget.com). **Hertz** (🕾 800/654–3001 ⊕ www.hertz.com). **National Car Rental** (🕾 800/227–7368 ⊕ www.nationalcar.com).

Local Agencies Dependable Car Rental (✉ St. Thomas, U.S. Virgin Islands 🕾 340/774–2253 or 800/522–3076 ⊕ www.dependablecar. com). **Itgo Car Rental** (✉ Tortola, British Virgin Islands 🕾 284/494–2639 ⊕ www.itgobvi.com). **Judi of Croix** (✉ St. Croix, U.S. Virgin Islands 🕾 340/773–2123 or 877/903–2123 ⊕ www. judiofcroix.com). **L&S Jeep Rental** (✉ Virgin Gorda, British Virgin Islands 🕾 284/495–5297).

St. John Car Rental (✉ St. John, U.S. Virgin Islands 🕾 340/776–6103 ⊕ www.stjohncarrental.com).

RENTAL CAR INSURANCE

Everyone who rents a car wonders whether the insurance that the rental companies offer is worth the expense. No one—including us—has a simple answer. If you own a car, your personal auto insurance may cover a rental to some degree, though not all policies protect you abroad; always read your policy's fine print. If you don't have auto insurance, then seriously consider buying the collision- or loss-damage waiver (CDW or LDW) from the car-rental company, which eliminates your liability for damage to the car. Some credit cards offer CDW coverage, but it's usually supplemental to your own insurance and rarely covers SUVs, minivans, luxury models, and the like. If your coverage is secondary, you may still be liable for loss-of-use costs from the car-rental company. But no credit-card insurance is valid unless you use that card for *all* transactions, from reserving to paying the final bill. All companies exclude car rental in some countries, so be sure to find out about the destination to which you are traveling. It's sometimes cheaper to buy insurance as part of your general travel insurance policy.

ROADSIDE EMERGENCIES

To reach police, fire, or ambulance, dial 911 in the USVI and 999 in the BVI. There are no emergency-service companies such as AAA in the USBVI. Before driving off into the countryside, check your rental car for tire-changing equipment, including a spare tire in good condition.

ROAD CONDITIONS

Island roads are often narrow, winding, and hilly. Those in mountainous regions that experience heavy tropical rains are also potholed and poorly maintained. Streets in towns are narrow, a legacy of the days when islanders used horse-drawn carts. Drive with extreme caution, especially if you venture out at night. You won't see guardrails on every curve, although the drops can be frighteningly steep. And pedestrians and livestock often share the roadway with vehicles.

You'll face rush-hour traffic on St. Thomas (especially in Charlotte Amalie); on St. Croix (especially in Christiansted and on Centerline Road); and on Tortola (especially around Road Town). All the larger towns have one-way streets. Although they're marked, the signs may be obscured by overhanging branches and other obstacles.

Drivers are prone to stopping in the road to chat with a passerby, to let a passenger out, or to buy a newspaper from a vendor. Pay attention when entering curves, because you might find a stopped car on the other side.

RULES OF THE ROAD

Driving in the Virgin Islands can be tricky. Traffic moves on the left in *both* the USVI and BVI. Almost all cars are American, which means the driver sits on the side of the car next to the road's edge, a position that makes some people nervous.

Buckle up before you turn the key. Police in the USVI are notorious for giving $25 tickets to unbelted drivers and front-seat passengers. The police are a bit lax about driving under the influence, but why risk it? Take a taxi or appoint a designated driver when you're out on the town.

Traffic moves at about 10 mph in town; on major highways you can fly along at 50 mph. On other roads, the speed limit may be less. Main roads in the USVI carry route numbers, but they're not always marked, and locals may not know them. (Be prepared for such directions as, "Turn left at the big tree.") Few USVI secondary roads have signs; BVI roads aren't very well marked either.

▌ TAXI TRAVEL

Taxis run the gamut from sedans to huge, open, multipassenger safari-vans. Rates are set by the government, but that doesn't mean that the occasional taxi driver won't try to gouge you. In the USBVI you'll also pay extra for your bags. Fares vary by destination and the number of people in the taxi, but count on paying $15 per person from Cyril E. King Airport on St. Thomas to Charlotte Amalie; $9 per person from Henry Rohlsen Airport on St. Croix to Christiansted; and $27 per person from Terrance E. Lettsome Airport on Beef Island, Tortola, to Road Town. Tip taxi drivers 15%. It's pointless to argue if you think the taxi driver has overcharged you. You won't win, and you might be delayed further should the driver call the police. Instead, forego the tip. Taxis are found at airports and ferry docks, at most hotels, and in tourist locations such as popular beaches and main towns. If you're staying at a smaller hotel, ask the front desk to call one for you. Villa vacationers should line up a taxi in advance, but be aware that many taxi drivers are reluctant to drive on unpaved roads.

Taxi options are covered in the Essentials sections in individual island chapters.

ESSENTIALS

▐ ACCOMMODATIONS

Decide whether you want to pay the extra price for a room overlooking the ocean or the pool. At less expensive properties location may mean a difference in price of only $10 to $20 per night; at luxury resorts, however, it could amount to as much as $100 per night. Also find out how close the property is to a beach. At some hotels you can walk barefoot from your room onto the sand; others are across a road or a 10-minute drive away.

Nighttime entertainment is often alfresco in the USBVI, so if you go to bed early or are a light sleeper, ask for a room away from the dance floor. Air-conditioning isn't a necessity on all islands, many of which are cooled by trade winds, but it can be a plus if you enjoy an afternoon snooze or are bothered by humidity. Breezes are best on upper floors, particularly corner rooms. If you like to sleep without air-conditioning, make sure that windows can be opened and have screens; also make sure there are no security issues with leaving your windows open. If you're staying away from the water, make sure the room has a ceiling fan and that it works. Even in the most luxurious resorts, there are times when things simply *don't* work; it's a fact of Caribbean life. No matter how diligent the upkeep, humidity and salt air quickly take their toll, and cracked tiles, rusty screens, and chipped paint are common everywhere.

The lodgings we list are the cream of the crop in each price category. We always list the facilities that are available, but we don't specify whether they cost extra; when pricing accommodations, always ask what's included and what costs extra. Properties are assigned price categories based on the range between their least and most expensive standard double rooms at high season (excluding holidays).

FODORS.COM CONNECTION

Before your trip, be sure to check out what other travelers are saying in Talk on www.fodors.com.

For lodging price categories, consult the price charts found near the beginning of each chapter.

APARTMENT AND VILLA RENTALS

Villas—whether luxurious or modest—are popular lodging options on all the Virgin Islands.

Renting a villa lets you settle in. You can have room to spread out, you can cook any or all of your meals, and you can have all the privacy you desire. Since most villas are in residential neighborhoods, your neighbors probably won't appreciate late-night parties or your children playing too loudly in the swimming pool. And you may be disturbed by your neighbor's weekend yard maintenance. That said, there's no better way to experience life in the USBVI.

Many villas are set up specifically for the rental market with bedrooms at opposite ends of the house. This makes them perfect for two couples who want to share an accommodation but still prefer some privacy. Others with more bedrooms are sized right for families. Ask about the villa layout to make sure young children won't have to sleep too far away from their parents. Villas with separate bedroom buildings are probably not a good idea unless your children are in their teens.

Most villas are owned by people who live somewhere else but hire a local management company to attend to the details. Depending on the island and the rental, the manager will either meet you at the ferry or airport or will give you directions to your villa. Most of the companies offer the same services with the similar degrees of efficiency.

You can book your villa through the numerous agencies that show up on the Internet, but they're usually not based on the island you want to visit. Booking through an island-based manager means that you can talk to a person who knows the villa and can let you know whether it meets your specifications. Your villa manager can also arrange for a maid, a chef, and other staffers to take care of myriad other details that make your vacation go smoothly. They're only a phone call away when something goes wrong or you have a question.

Catered To Vacation Homes focuses on St. John. Vacation St. Croix is based on St. Croix. McLaughlin Anderson has rentals across the USBVI.

Villa Management Companies

Catered To Vacation Homes (✉ *Marketplace Suite 206, 5206 Enighed, Cruz Bay, St. John, VI* ☎ *340/776–6641 or 800/424–6641* 📠 *340/693–8191* ⊕ *www.cateredto.com*).
McLaughlin Anderson (📠 *1000 Blackbeard's Hill, Suite 3, Charlotte Amalie, St. Thomas, VI 00802-6739* ☎ *340/776-0635 or 800/537–6246* ⊕ *www.mclaughlinanderson.com*).
Vacation St. Croix (📠 *4000 La Grande Princess, Christiansted, St. Croix, VI 00820* ☎ *340/718–0361 or 877/788–0361* ⊕ *www.vacationstcroix.com*).

HOTELS

Hotels range from luxury beachfront resorts, where the staff caters to your every whim and where you'll find plenty of activities to keep you busy, to small, locally owned hillside hotels with great views that cater to more independent-minded visitors. They're priced accordingly. At the smaller inland properties you'll probably want to rent a car to get out to the island's best beaches and interesting restaurants.

The USBVI are quite Americanized thanks to television and the influx of U.S. visitors, but some traditional Caribbean customs still apply. Common courtesy is particularly important in the islands, so always say hello when you enter a store and make some small talk before getting down to

business. Also, watch out for cars that stop suddenly in the middle of the road for chats with passersby and be aware that nothing, and we mean nothing, ever starts on time.

▮ COMMUNICATIONS

INTERNET

Many hotels now offer high-speed or dial-up Internet service. In most cases, Internet service is complimentary, but some resorts do charge a fee. Some provide computers in their lobbies if you've left your computer at home. You'll also find a few restaurants, bars, and businesses that offer Internet service for a fee. Specific coverage of Internet cafés can be found in the individual destination chapters.

On St. Thomas, Beans, Bytes & Websites is an Internet café in Charlotte Amalie. East End Secretarial Services offers long-distance dialing, copying, and fax services. Near Havensight Mall, go to the Cyber Zone at Port of $ale, where there are 16 computers. Rates for Internet access range from $5 to $8 for 30 minutes to $10 to $15 per hour.

St. Thomas Beans, Bytes & Websites (✉ *Royal Dane Mall, behind Tavern on Waterfront, Charlotte Amalie* ☎ *340/776–1265* ⊕ *www.usvi.net/cybercafe*). **Cyber Zone** (✉ *Port of $ale, Charlotte Amalie* ☎ *340/714–7743*). **East End Secretarial Services** (✉ *Upstairs at Red Hook Plaza, Red Hook* ☎ *340/775–5262*).

St. Croix A Better Copy (✉ *52A Company St., Christiansted, St. Croix* ☎ *340/692–5303*).

St. John Keep Me Posted (⊠ *Cocoloba Shopping Center, Coral Bay* ☎ *340/775–1727* ⊕ *www.keepmepostedstjohn.com*).

Tortola Trellis Bay Cybercafé (⊠ *Trellis Bay, Tortola* ☎ *284/495–2447*).

PHONES

Phone service to and from the Virgin Islands is up-to-date and efficient. Phone cards are used throughout the islands for long-distance and international calling; you can buy them (in several denominations) at many retail shops and convenience stores. They must be used in special card phones, which are also widely available.

CALLING WITHIN THE USBVI

Local calls from USBVI pay phones run 25¢, although some privately owned phones are now charging 35¢. Calls from the USVI to the BVI and vice versa are charged as international toll calls. In the USVI and BVI you dial just as if you were anywhere else in the United States.

The area code for the USVI is 340; for the BVI, 284.

In the USVI, dial 913 to reach the operator. In the BVI, dial 119. In both locations, dial 0 for advice on how to place your call.

CALLING OUTSIDE THE USBVI

The country code for the United States is 1.

Calling the United States and Canada from the USBVI is just like making a long-distance call within those countries: dial 1, plus the area code. To reach Europe, Australia, and New Zealand, dial 011 followed by the country code and the number.

If you're using a U.S.-based calling card, the U.S. access number should be on the back of the card. If you're using a local calling card, the access number will be on the back of your calling card.

CALLING CARDS

The cheapest way to phone home is by using a phone card to dial direct. You can buy phone cards at all grocery stores across the USBVI. Try Plaza Extra stores on St. Thomas and St. Croix, Starfish Market on St. John, Riteway supermarkets on Tortola, and Road Town Wholesale on Virgin Gorda.

MOBILE PHONES

If you have a multiband phone (some countries use different frequencies than what's standard in the United States) and your service provider uses the world-standard GSM network (as do T-Mobile, AT&T, and Verizon), you can probably use your phone abroad. Roaming fees can be steep, however: 99¢ a minute is considered reasonable. And overseas you normally pay the toll charges for incoming calls. Internationally, it's almost always cheaper to send a text message than to make a call, since text messages have a very low set fee (often less than 5¢).

There are no cell-phone rental companies in the USBVI. There are a few places that sell cell phones, but the price is much higher than in the United States. Cell phones from most U.S. companies work in most parts of the USVI if you have a roaming feature. If you're on St. John's north coast you may have some difficulties; you may find yourself connected to BoatPhone, a Tortola service. If you're on the south side of Tortola and at hilltop locations or near the ferry dock in Spanish Town on Virgin Gorda, you may be able to connect to AT&T and Sprint, but other locations in the BVI have sporadic service.

Contacts AT&T (☎ *340/777–7777 on St. Thomas and St. John, 340/690–1000 on St. Croix* ⊕ *www.att.com*). **Lime Wireless** (☎ *284/494–4444 in the BVI* ⊕ *www. cwcaribbean.com*). **Mobal** (☎ *888/888–9162* ⊕ *www.mobal.com*) rents mobiles and sells GSM phones (starting at $49) that will operate in 140 countries. Per-call rates vary throughout the world. **Planet Fone** (☎ *888/988–4777* ⊕ *www.planetfone.com*) rents cell phones, but the per-minute rates are expensive. **Sprint** (☎ *340/776–0770 on St. Thomas and St. John, 340/713–0055 on St. Croix* ⊕ *www.sprint.com*).

■ CUSTOMS AND DUTIES

You're always allowed to bring goods of a certain value back home without having to pay any duty or import tax. But there's a limit on the amount of tobacco and liquor you can bring back duty-free, and some countries have separate limits for perfumes; for exact figures, check with your customs department. The values of so-called "duty-free" goods are included in these amounts. When you shop abroad, save all your receipts, as customs inspectors may ask to see them as well as the items you purchased. If the total value of your goods is more than the duty-free limit, you'll have to pay a tax (most often a flat percentage) on the value of everything beyond that limit.

As long as you're not bringing in meat, passing through BVI customs is usually a breeze. If you want to bring that special cut of steak from home, you'll need a $25 agriculture permit, but it's not worth the effort since you can buy meat all over the BVI. You don't clear customs entering the USVI if you're coming from the United States. You can't take fruits and vegetables out of either the USVI or BVI, so eat up that apple on the way to the airport. You may travel with your pets to the USVI without any special shots or paperwork, but you need an import permit from the BVI Agriculture Department to bring in your pet.

U.S. Information U.S. Customs and Border Protection (⊕ *www.cbp.gov*).

■ EATING OUT

Everything from fast food to fine cuisine in elegant settings is available in the USBVI, and prices run about the same as what you'd pay in New York or any other major city. You'll find kid favorites McDonald's, Pizza Hut, KFC, and more on St. Thomas and St. Croix, but families will also find plenty of nonchain restaurants with kid-friendly menus. Resorts that cater to families always have a casual restaurant, but there are delis and other restaurants across the USBVI

that offer something for everyone on their menus. Most chefs at top-of-the-line restaurants and even some small spots went to a major culinary school, which means innovative and interesting cuisine. Don't be afraid to sample local dishes at the roadside restaurants on all the islands. More and more restaurants have vegetarian offerings on their menus, though true vegetarian restaurants are hard to find. Throughout the book, the restaurants we list are the cream of the crop in each price category. *For information on food-related health issues, see Health below.*

Unless otherwise noted, the restaurants listed in this guide are open daily for lunch and dinner.

PAYING

Most USBVI restaurants accept Master-Card and Visa, and some take American Express. A rare few accept Discover. Only large hotels and their restaurants take Diners Club. You will find the occasional restaurant that doesn't accept credit cards.

For dining price categories, consult the price charts found near the beginning of each chapter. For guidelines on tipping see Tipping, below.

RESERVATIONS AND DRESS

Regardless of where you are, it's a good idea to make a reservation if you can. In many places in the Caribbean it's expected, particularly at nicer restaurants. We only mention them specifically when reservations are essential (there's no other way you'll ever get a table) or when they're not accepted. For popular restaurants, book as far ahead as you can (often a month or more), and reconfirm as soon as you arrive. Large parties should always call ahead to check the reservations policy. We mention dress only when men are required to wear a jacket or a jacket and tie. Beach attire is universally frowned upon in restaurants throughout the Caribbean.

WINES, BEER, AND SPIRITS

Top-notch restaurants offer good selections of fine wines. Beer and spirits are available on all islands at all kinds of restaurants and roadside stands, but you may not find the brand you prefer. Cruzan Rum, manufactured in St. Croix, is available across the USBVI. Alcoholic beverages are available from the smallest corner rum shop to the fanciest resort at all hours of the day and night. The only prohibition comes during the day on Good Friday, when no one can sell drinks.

▮ ELECTRICITY

The USBVI use the same current as the U.S. mainland—110 volts. European appliances will require adaptors. Since power fluctuations occasionally occur, bring a heavy-duty surge protector (available at hardware stores) if you plan to use your computer.

▮ EMERGENCIES

Emergency personnel across the USBVI are well equipped to handle basic medical issues, but you'll find a bigger selection of doctors and dentists on St. Croix, St. Thomas, and Tortola. If you need one, ask your hotel or villa manager for a recommendation. There are hospitals on St. Thomas, St. Croix, and Tortola, and doctors and emergency facilities on the other islands. If you need hospital care on one of the smaller islands you'll face a boat ride to the closest hospital. St. John has an ambulance boat that whisks patients to Red Hook, St. Thomas, for an ambulance ride to Roy L. Schneider Hospital, but the emergency staff will accompany you on the public ferry to Peebles Hospital on

Tortola from the BVI outer islands. Air ambulances to the mainland are available from St. Croix, St. Thomas, and Tortola. The emergency number in the USVI is ☎ *911*. In the BVI, dial ☎ *999*.

ST. THOMAS

Coast Guard Marine Safety Detachment (☎ *340/776–3497 in St. Thomas*). **Rescue Coordination Center** (☎ *787/289–2041 in San Juan, PR*).

Hospitals Roy L. Schneider Hospital & Community Health Center (✉ *Sugar Estate, St. Thomas ✛ 1 mi [1½ km] east of Charlotte Amalie* ☎ *340/776–8311*).

Pharmacies Doctor's Choice Pharmacy (✉ *Wheatley Shopping Center, across from Roy L. Schneider Hospital, Sugar Estate* ☎ *340/777–1400* ✉ *Medical Arts Complex, off Rte. 30, 1½ mi [2½ km] east of Cyril E. King Airport* ☎ *340/774–8988*). **Kmart Pharmacy** (✉ *Tutu Park Mall, Estate Tutu* ☎ *340/777–3854*). **Medicine Shoppe** (✉ *Havensight Mall, Charlotte Amalie* ☎ *340/776–1235*).

Scuba-Diving Emergencies Roy L. Schneider Hospital & Community Health Center (✉ *Sugar Estate ✛ 1 mi [1½ km] east of Charlotte Amalie* ☎ *340/776–8311*).

ST. JOHN

Hospital Myrah Keating Smith Community Health Center (✉ *Rte. 10, east of Cruz Bay, Susannaberg* ☎ *340/693–8900*).

Pharmacy Chelsea Drug Store (✉ *The Marketplace, Rte. 104, Cruz Bay* ☎ *340/776–4888*).

ST. CROIX

Hospitals Gov. Juan F. Luis Hospital and Health Center (✉ *6 Diamond Ruby, north of Sunny Isle Shopping Center on Rte. 79, Christiansted* ☎ *340/778–6311*).

Pharmacy Kmart Pharmacy (✉ *Sunshine Mall, Cane Estate* ☎ *340/692–2622*).

TORTOLA

Hospitals and Clinics Peebles Hospital (✉ *Road Town, Tortola* ☎ *284/494–3497*).

Pharmacies J. R. O'Neal Drug Store (✉ *Road Town, Tortola* ☎ *284/494–2292*).

Medicure Pharmacy (⊠ *Road Town, Tortola* ☎ *284/494–6189*).

VIRGIN GORDA
Hospitals and Clinics Virgin Gorda Government Health Clinic (⊠ *The Valley, Virgin Gorda* ☎ *284/495–5337*).

Marine Emergencies VISAR (☎ *767 from phone or Marine Radio Channel 16*).

Pharmacies Medicure Pharmacy (⊠ *Spanish Town, Virgin Gorda* ☎ *284/495–5479*). **O'Neal's Drug Store** (⊠ *Spanish Town, Virgin Gorda* ☎ *284/495–5449*).

▌ HEALTH

Water in the USBVI is generally safe to drink. Mosquitoes can be a problem here, particularly after a spate of showers. Insect repellent is readily available, but you may want to bring something from home, because it's more expensive in the Virgin Islands. Dengue fever is a particular concern in the Virgin Islands.

Less dangerous, but certainly a nuisance, are the little pests from the sand-flea family known as no-see-ums. You don't realize you're being had for dinner until it's too late, and these bites itch, and itch, and itch. No-see-ums start getting hungry around 3 pm and are out in force by sunset. They're always more numerous in shady and wooded areas (such as the campgrounds on St. John). Take a towel along for sitting on the beach, and keep reapplying insect repellent.

Beware of the manchineel tree, which grows near the beach and has green apple-like fruit that is poisonous and bark and leaves that burn the skin.

Even if you've never been sunburned in your life, believe the warnings and use sunscreen in the USBVI. If you're dark-skinned, start with at least an SPF of 15 and keep it on. If you're fair-skinned, use a sunscreen with a higher SPF and stay out of the sun during midday. Rays are most intense between 11 and 2, so move under a sea-grape tree (although you

can still burn here) or, better yet, take a shady lunch break. You can also burn in this part of the world when it's cloudy, so putting sunscreen on every day no matter what the weather is the best strategy.

OVER-THE-COUNTER REMEDIES
Over-the-counter-medications like aspirin, Tylenol, and Mylanta are readily available in the USBVI. Kmart on St. Thomas and St. Croix have cheaper prices, but you can find a big selection of these products at grocery and drug stores across the USBVI. You can find a smaller selection (and considerably higher prices) on the smaller islands.

SHOTS AND MEDICATIONS
Health Warnings National Centers for Disease Control & Prevention (*CDC* ☎ *800/232–4636 international travelers' health line* ⊕ *www.cdc.gov/travel*). **World Health Organization** (*WHO* ⊕ *www.who.int*).

▌ HOURS OF OPERATION

Bank hours are generally Monday through Thursday 9 to 3 and Friday 9 to 5; a handful open Saturday (9 to noon). Walk-up windows open at 8:30 on weekdays. Hours may vary slightly from branch to branch and island to island.

Shops, especially those in the heavily touristed areas, are open Monday to Saturday 9 to 5. Those near the cruise ship piers may also be open on Sunday, but usually only if there is a ship in port.

HOLIDAYS
In addition to the U.S. federal holidays, locals in the USVI celebrate Three Kings Day (Jan. 6); Transfer Day (commemorates Denmark's 1917 sale of the territory to the United States, Mar. 31); Holy Thursday and Good Friday; Emancipation Day (when slavery was abolished in the Danish West Indies in 1848, July 3); Columbus Day and USVI–Puerto Rico Friendship Day (always on Columbus Day weekend); and Liberty Day (honoring David Hamilton Jackson, who secured freedom of the press and assembly from King Christian X of Denmark, Nov. 1).

Although the government closes down for nearly 20 days a year, most of these holidays have no effect on shopping hours. Unless there's a cruise-ship arrival, expect most stores to close for Christmas and a few other holidays in the slower summer months.

The following public holidays are celebrated in the BVI: New Year's Day, Commonwealth Day (Mar. 14), Good Friday (Fri. before Easter), Easter Sunday (usually Mar. or Apr.), Easter Monday (day after Easter), Whit Monday (1st Mon. in May), Sovereign's Birthday (June 16), Territory Day (July 1), BVI August Festival Days (usually first two weeks in Aug.), St. Ursula's Day (Oct. 21), Christmas, and Boxing Day (day after Christmas).

▌ MAIL

Airmail between the USBVI and cities in the United States or Canada takes seven to 14 days; surface mail can take four to six weeks. *For island-specific information on post-office locations, postal rates, and opening hours, see Mail and Shipping in the Essentials sections of individual island chapters.*

SHIPPING PACKAGES

Courier services (such as Airborne, DHL, Federal Express, UPS, and others) operate in the USBVI, although not every company serves each island. "Overnight" service is more likely to take two or more days, because of the limited number of flights on which packages can be shipped. Service to St. John and the smaller of the British Virgin Islands can take even longer.

Contacts FedEx (☎ *800/463–3339 in the USVI).* **Rush It** (☎ *284/494–4421 in the BVI)* takes your packages to the USVI for quicker delivery to the mainland.

▌ MONEY

Prices quoted in this chapter are in U.S. dollars, which is the official currency in all the islands. Major credit cards and traveler's checks are accepted at many establishments.

Prices throughout this guide are given for adults. Reduced fees are almost always available for children.

ATMS AND BANKS

You can find ATMs at most banks in the USBVI. The ATMs at FirstBank and Scotia Bank, the only two in St. John, sometimes run out of cash on long holiday weekends.

CREDIT CARDS

It's a good idea to inform your credit-card company before you travel, even if you're going to the USBVI. Otherwise, the company might put a hold on your card owing to unusual activity—not a good thing halfway through your trip. Record all your credit-card numbers—as well as the phone numbers to call if your cards are lost or stolen—in a safe place, so you're prepared should something go wrong. Both Master-Card and Visa have general numbers you can call (collect if you're abroad) if your card is lost, but you're better off calling the number of your issuing bank, since MasterCard and Visa usually just transfer you to your bank; your bank's number is usually printed on your card.

If you plan to use your credit card for cash advances, you'll need to apply for a PIN at least two weeks before your trip. It's usually cheaper (and safer) to use a credit card in the USBVI for major purchases (so you can cancel payments or dispute the charge if there's a problem).

Reporting Lost Cards American Express (☎ *800/528–4800 in U.S., 336/393–1111 collect from abroad ⊕ www.americanexpress. com).* **MasterCard** (☎ *800/627–8372 in U.S., 636/722–7111 collect from abroad ⊕ www.mastercard.com).* **Visa** (☎ *800/847–2911 in U.S., 410/581–9994 collect from abroad ⊕ www.visa.com).*

PACKING

A pocket LED flashlight to deal with the occasional power outage, bug repellent for mosquitoes, sunglasses, a hat, and sunscreen are essentials for any USBVI vacation. If you forget something, those items are available at stores across the USBVI, but are usually more expensive than what you would pay at home. Pharmacies can fill prescriptions with a call to your home drug store, but this may be the week the drug shipment didn't arrive. It's always safer to bring everything you need. Dress is casual even at the most expensive resorts, but men are usually required to wear a collared shirt in dining rooms. For dinner out women typically wear what the locals call "island fancy" (a flowy skirt and nice top will do). Bring your bathing suit, a cover-up, sandals, sturdy walking shoes if you're a hiker, beach shoes if you plan on strolling those luscious strands of sand, and a sweater or fleece if you're visiting in the winter when the nights are cool. In these days of packing light, rent snorkel gear on the island rather than bringing it unless you have a prescription mask. Shorts and T-shirts will do everywhere during the day. Don't forget a good book for whiling away those afternoons in the beach chair and your camera for bringing home those USBVI memories.

PASSPORTS AND VISAS

For U.S. citizens, a passport is *not* required to visit the U.S. Virgin Islands, though you must still provide proof of citizenship by showing an original birth certificate with a raised seal as well as a government-issued photo ID. There are no immigration procedures upon arriving in St. Thomas or St. Croix for anyone arriving on planes from the U.S. mainland or Puerto Rico, but on your return you will clear immigration and customs before boarding your flight.

If you visit the BVI by ferry from the USVI, you must go through customs and immigration procedures and prove your citizenship. U.S. citizens must have a passport to enter the BVI by ferry.

If you fly into the BVI, you must go through customs and immigration upon arrival and have a valid passport. Aside from paying the departure tax, there are no special departure procedures.

RESTROOMS

Restrooms across the USBVI are usually clean, neat, and free. You won't often find attendants, even at swanky resorts. Most gas stations do have restrooms, and they'll do in a pinch, but using the restroom in a restaurant, attraction, or shopping area is probably a better bet.

SAFETY

In the USVI ask hotel staff members about the wisdom of venturing off the beaten path. Although it may seem like a nice night for a stroll back to your hotel from that downtown restaurant, it's better to take a taxi than face an incident. Although local police go to great lengths to stop it, crime does occur. The BVI has seen less crime than its neighbors to the west, but again, better safe than sorry.

Follow the same precautions that you would anywhere. Look around before using the ATM. Keep tabs on your pocketbook; put it on your lap—not the back of your chair—in restaurants. Stow valuable jewelry or other items in the hotel safe when you leave your room; hotel and villa burglaries do occur infrequently. Deserted beaches on St. John and the BVI are usually safe, but think twice about stopping at that luscious strand of lonely sand on St. Croix and St. Thomas. Hotel or public beaches are your best bets. Never leave your belongings unattended at the beach or on the seats of your rental car. Be sure to lock the doors on your rental villa or hotel room. Break-ins can happen across the USBVI, so it's better to be safe than sorry.

■TIP➜ If you're wondering what to do with your cash and credit cards at the beach, consider buying a waterproof container to wear on a cord around your neck while you're in the water.

Contact **Transportation Security Administration** (*TSA;* ⊕ *www.tsa.gov*).

▊ TAXES

There's no sales tax in the USVI, but there's an 8% hotel-room tax; most hotels also add a 10% service charge to the bill. The St. John Accommodations Council members ask that hotel and villa guests voluntarily pay a $1 per day surcharge to help fund school and community projects and other good works. Many hotels add additional energy surcharges and the like, so ask about any additional charges, but these are not government-imposed taxes.

In the BVI the departure tax is $5 per person by boat and $20 per person by plane. There are separate booths at the airport and at ferry terminals to collect this tax, which must be paid in cash in U.S. currency. Most hotels in the BVI add a service charge ranging from 5% to 18% to the bill. A few restaurants and some shops tack on an additional 10% charge if you use a credit card. There's no sales tax in the BVI. However, there's a 7% government tax on hotel rooms.

▊ TIME

The USBVI are in the Atlantic Standard Time zone, which is one hour later than Eastern Standard or four hours earlier than GMT. During daylight saving time, between March and November, Atlantic Standard is the same time as Eastern Daylight Time since Daylight Saving Time is not observed.

▊ TIPPING

Many hotels in the USVI add a 10% to 15% service charge to cover the services of your maid and other staff. However, some hotels use part of that money to fund their operations, passing only a portion of it on to the staff. Check with your maid or bellhop to determine the hotel's policy. If you discover you need to tip, give bellhops and porters 50¢ to $1 per bag and maids $1 or $2 per day. Special errands or requests of hotel staff always require an additional tip. At restaurants bartenders and waiters expect a 10%– 15% tip, but always check your tab to see whether service is included. Taxi drivers in the USVI get a 15% tip.

In the BVI tip porters and bellhops $1 per bag. Sometimes a service charge of 10% is included on restaurant bills; it's customary to leave another 5% if you liked the service. If no charge is added, 15% is the norm. Cabbies normally aren't tipped because most own their cabs; add 10% to 15% if they exceed their duties.

▊ TRIP INSURANCE

Comprehensive travel policies typically cover trip-cancellation and interruption, letting you cancel or cut your trip short because of a personal emergency, illness, or, in some cases, acts of terrorism in your destination. Such policies also cover evacuation and medical care. Some also cover you for trip delays because of bad weather or mechanical problems as well as for lost or delayed baggage. Another type of coverage to look for is financial default—that is, when your trip is disrupted because a tour operator, airline, or cruise line goes out of business. Generally you must buy this when you book your trip or shortly thereafter, and it's only available to you if your operator isn't on a list of excluded companies.

At the very least, consider buying medical-only coverage. Neither Medicare nor some private insurers cover medical expenses anywhere outside of the

United States (including time aboard a cruise ship, even if it leaves from a U.S. port). Medical-only policies typically reimburse you for medical care (excluding that related to preexisting conditions) and hospitalization abroad, and provide for evacuation. You still have to pay the bills and await reimbursement from the insurer, though.

Another option is to sign up with a medical-evacuation assistance company. A membership in one of these companies gets you doctor referrals, emergency evacuation or repatriation, 24-hour hotlines for medical consultation, and other assistance. International SOS Assistance Emergency and AirMed International provide evacuation services and medical referrals. MedjetAssist offers medical evacuation.

Expect comprehensive travel insurance policies to cost about 4% to 7% or 8% of the total price of your trip (it's more like 8%–12% if you're over age 70). A medical-only policy may or may not be cheaper than a comprehensive policy. Always read the fine print of your policy to make sure that you are covered for the risks that are of most concern to you. Compare several policies to make sure you're getting the best price and range of coverage available.

■TIP➜ OK. You know you can save a bundle on trips to warm-weather destinations by traveling in rainy season. But there's also a chance that a severe storm will disrupt your plans. The solution? Look for hotels and resorts that offer storm/hurricane guarantees. Although they rarely allow refunds, most guarantees do let you rebook later if a storm strikes.

Insurance Comparison Sites Insure My Trip.com (☎ 800/487–4722 or 401/773–9300 ⊕ www.insuremytrip.com). **SquareMouth.com** (☎ 800/240–0369 or 727/564–9203 ⊕ www.squaremouth.com).

Medical Assistance Companies AirMed International Medical Group (☎ 800/356–2161 ⊕ www.airmed.com). **International SOS** (⊕ www.internationalsos.com). **MedjetAssist** (☎ 800/527–7478 ⊕ www.medjetassist.com).

Medical-Only Insurers International Medical Group (☎ 800/628–4664 ⊕ www.imglobal.com). **Wallach & Company** (☎ 800/237–6615 or 540/687–3166 ⊕ www.wallach.com).

Comprehensive Travel Insurers Access America (☎ 800/284–8300 ⊕ www.accessamerica.com). **CSA Travel Protection** (☎ 800/873–9855 ⊕ www.csatravelprotection.com). **HTH Worldwide** (☎ 610/254–8700 ⊕ www.hthworldwide.com). **Travelex Insurance** (☎ 800/228–9792 ⊕ www.travelex-insurance.com). **Travel Guard** (☎ 800/826–4919 ⊕ www.travelguard.com). **Travel Insured International** (☎ 800/243–3174 ⊕ www.travelinsured.com).

■ VISITOR INFORMATION

Stop by the tourism department's local offices for brochures on things to do and places to see. The offices are open only weekdays from 8 to 5, so if you need information on the weekend or on one of the territory's many holidays, you're out of luck. *(For locations, see* ⇨ *Visitor Information in the Essentials section of each chapter.)*

British Virgin Islands Tourist Board BVI Tourist Board (☎ 212/563–3117, 800/835–8530 in New York ⊕ www.bvitourism.com).

United States Virgin Islands Department of Tourism USVI Government Tourist Office (☎ 340/774–8784 or 800/372–8784 ⊕ www.visitusvi.com).

INDEX

PHOTO CREDITS

1, SuperStock/age fotostock. 2-3, Walter Bibikow/age fotostock. 5, Carlos Villoch - Magic-Sea.com/Alamy. **Chapter 1: Experience the U.S. & British Virgin Islands:** 8-9, Ellen Rooney/age fotostock. 10 (top), Jo Ann Snover/iStockphoto. 10 (bottom), Susanna Pershern/iStockphoto. 11, BVI Tourist Board. 13, George Burba/iStockphoto. 15, Sarah Holmstrom/iStockphoto. 16 (left), Ellen Barone/Alamy. 16 (top center), Guido Alberto Rossi/Tips Italia/photolibrary.com. 16 (bottom center), Carlos Villoch - MagicSea.com/Alamy. 16 (top right), U.S. Virgin Islands Department of Tourism. 16 (bottom right), Juneisy Q. Hawkins/Shutterstock. 17 (top left), Honky275/Flickr. 17 (bottom left), Nik Wheeler/Alamy. 17 (top center), Sunpix Travel/Alamy. 17 (bottom center), SuperStock/age fotostock. 17 (right), Ilja Hulinsky/Alamy. 18, BVI Tourism. 19, Charles Krallman/Surfsong Villa Resort. 20, Gary Blakeley/iStockphoto. 21, U.S. Virgin Islands Department of Tourism. 24, BVI Tourist Board. 25, Renesis/wikipedia.org. 26, Kborer/wikipedia. **Chapter 2: St. Thomas:** 27, Oscar Williams/Alamy. 28, Coral World Ocean Park, St. Thomas. 29 (top), Erik Miles/iStockphoto. 29 (bottom), U.S. Virgin Islands Department of Tourism. 32, Jeff Greenberg/age fotostock. 33 (top), Olga Lyubkina/Shutterstock. 33 (bottom), Atlantide S.N.C./age fotostock. 34, Juneisy Q. Hawkins/Shutterstock. 36-37, Walter Bibikow/age fotostock. 41, SuperStock/age fotostock. 46, Coral World Ocean Park, St. Thomas. 51, Bill Bachmann/Alamy. 62 (top), The Ritz-Carlton, St. Thomas. 62 (bottom), Shannon McCarthy/Villa Santana. 67, World Pictures/Alamy. 68, Louis Ible, Jr. Reichhold Center for the Arts. 70, Michael DeFreitas/age fotostock. 82, Alvaro Leiva/age fotostock. **Chapter 3: St. John:** 87, U.S. Virgin Islands Department of Tourism. 88, Jo Ann Snover/iStockphoto. 89. C. Kurt Holter/Shutterstock. 90 and 92, U.S. Virgin Islands Department of Tourism. 94-95, Ken Brown/iStockphoto. 97, Walter Bibikow/ age fotostock. 112 (top), Michael Grimm Photography/Caneel Bay/ Rosewood Hotels & Resorts. 112 (bottom), Maho Bay Camps & Estate Concordia Preserve. 115, Carlos Villoch - MagicSea.com/Alamy. 117, Kendra Nielsam/Shutterstock. 119, divemasterking2000/Flickr. 120 (top), Shirley Vanderbilt/age fotostock. 120 (center), Julie de Leseleuc/iStockphoto. 120 (bottom), Marjorie McBride/Alamy. 121, divemasterking2000/Flickr. 122 (top), David Coleman/iStockphoto. 122 (bottom), Steve Simonsen. 129, Gavin Hellier/age fotostock. 131, Nik Wheeler/Alamy. **Chapter 4: St. Croix:** 133, Bill Bachmann/Alamy. 134, Kelvin Chiu/iStockphoto. 135 (top), U.S. Virgin Islands Dept of Tourism. 135 (bottom), Steve Simonsen. 138, U.S. Virgin Islands Department of Tourism. 140-41, Bill Ross/Flirt Collection/photolibrary.com. 143, Walter Bibikow/age fotostock. 145, Marc Muench/Alamy. 163 (top and bottom), Villa Greenleaf. 169, Danita Delimont/Alamy. 170, Stephen Frink Collection/Alamy. 171, SuperStock/age fotostock. 173, U.S. Virgin Islands Department of Tourism. **Chapter 5: Tortola:** 175, Alvaro Leiva/age fotostock. 176 (top), BVI Tourist Board. 176 (bottom), lidian neeleman/iStockphoto. 177, Aliaksandr Nikitsin/iStockphoto. 180, Ramunas Bruzas/Shutterstock. 182-83, Christian Heeb/age fotostock. 185, Walter Bibikow/age fotostock. 191, World Pictures/age fotostock. 193, Walter Bibikow/age fotostock. 204, Alvaro Leiva/age fotostock. 207, Eric Sanford/age fotostock. 208 (top), Randy Lincks/Alamy. 208 (bottom), Steve Dangers/iStockphoto. 209 (top), Doug Scott/age fotostock. 209 (bottom), Slavoljub Pantelic/iStockphoto. 210, Doug Scott/age fotostock. 212, Giovanni Rinaldi/iStockphoto.213, Walter Bibikow/age fotostock. 215, Fotograferen.net/Alamy. **Chapter 6: Virgin Gorda:** 217, BVI Tourist Board. 218 and 219 (top), Joel Blit/iStockphoto. 219 (bottom), BVI Tourist Board. 221, Jeff Leach/iStockphoto. 222, Stefan Radtke/iStockphoto. 224-25, FB-Fischer FB-Fischer/imagebroker.net/photolibrary.com. 226, BVI Tourist Board. 227, Ellen Rooney/age fotostock. 237, Bitter End Yacht Club International, LLC. 238, parasola.net/Alamy. 241, Carlos Villoch - MagicSea.com/Alamy. 242, Bitter End Yacht Club International, LLC. **Chapter 7: Other British Virgin Islands:** 243 and 245 (top), BVI Tourism. 245 (bottom), Paul Zizka/Shutterstock. 247, Joel Blit/iStockphoto. 248-49, Kreder Katja/age fotostock. 252, Andre Jenny/Alamy. 259, Paul Zizka/Shutterstock. 265, fabio braibanti/age fotostock. 266, S. Murphy-Larronde/age fotostock.

ABOUT OUR WRITERS

Carol M. Bareuther, who lives in St. Thomas, works part-time for the government of the U.S. Virgin Islands. In her other life as a writer, she contributes to local, regional, and international publications on the topics of food, travel, and water sports. She's the author of two books, *Sports Fishing in the Virgin Islands* and *Virgin Islands Cooking*. She is the mother of Nikki and Rian, as well as the longtime partner of photographer Dean Barnes. She covered St. Thomas, Anegada, and Jost Van Dyke for this edition, and she contributed the spotlight on island cuisine and the yacht charter feature.

Long-time St. John resident **Lynda Lohr** lives above Coral Bay with her significant other and two chubby cats. She moved to St. John in 1984 for a bit of adventure; she's still there and still enjoying the adventure. The editor of *Island News,* a newsletter for people with a serious interest in the Virgin Islands, she also writes for numerous national, regional, and local publications as well as travel Web sites. On her rare days off, she swims at Great Maho Bay and hikes the island's numerous trails. For this edition, she covered St. John, St. Croix, Tortola, Virgin Gorda, and many of the smaller islands. She was also responsible for Travel Smart and contributed to the diving and snorkeling feature.